The History
of
Salt River Association
Missouri

Wiley J. Patrick

HERITAGE BOOKS
2011

HERITAGE BOOKS
AN IMPRINT OF HERITAGE BOOKS, INC.

Books, CDs, and more—Worldwide

For our listing of thousands of titles see our website
at
www.HeritageBooks.com

A Facsimile Reprint
Published 2011 by
HERITAGE BOOKS, INC.
Publishing Division
100 Railroad Ave. #104
Westminster, Maryland 21157

Copyright © 1909

Copyright © 2001 Heritage Books, Inc.

— Publisher's Notice —
In reprints such as this, it is often not possible to remove blemishes from the original. We feel the contents of this book warrant its reissue despite these blemishes and hope you will agree and read it with pleasure.

International Standard Book Numbers
Paperbound: 978-0-7884-1846-4
Clothbound: 978-0-7884-8830-6

YOUR BROTHER, WILEY J. PATRICK.

INTRODUCTION

History deals with facts that exist or have existed, and any account, however interesting, if not true, does not constitute history. From the viewpoint of history it is of vital importance to know that an account is really historical. It is a calamity that families and communities and churches and denominations and associations do not have some systematic method of recording and preserving their histories. This sad defect was clearly observed in my efforts to assist in gathering data for the History of Salt River Association. Statements and accounts handed down from one generation to another may or may not be history. Incomplete and imperfect minutes tell but a part of the events. Private papers and letters are too inaccessible to depend upon for public use. If the Baptist denomination would illuminate by its history and stimulate by its achievements, means must be devised to accurately record and securely preserve its history.

J. N. BASKETT.

Hannibal, Mo., July 10, 1909.

PREFACE

I have had the double task of *collecting the materials* and *writing*. Many have helped me. To them I acknowledge my indebtedness. I especially acknowledge obligation to the brief history prepared by Dalton Biggs, Esq., for the seventy-fifth anniversary of of the Association. It is worthy to be given permanent form. Professor Rider has by his connection with the Missouri Baptist Historical Society been able to give help which was indispensable; he freely gave his time and painstaking work. I am grateful to him.

The collection of facts as to men and events is incomplete, but I am grateful that we have been able to snatch this much from the ravages of time. Baptists have made a great deal of history; they have not been careful to preserve a written account of the history they have made. If each Salt River Baptist will become his own historian and glean wherever information may be found and preserve with this book, his collection will become priceless. Dr. Henry E. Vedder, of Crozer, says, "What study more fascinating, more instructive, more inspiring than the study of history?"

I feel, more deeply than another can, the imperfections of this work.   W. J. P.

Bowling Green, Mo., June 23, 1909.

TABLE OF CONTENTS

Chapter
- I. The Beginnings 11
- II. Organization 19
- III. Growth and elimination 54
- IV. The regions beyond 107
- V. Lengthening the cords 146
- VI. Separating for service 171
- VII. Strengthening the stakes 198
- VIII. Tried by fire 226
- IX. Enlargement and training 263
- X. Helping the weak 315
- XI. Baptist honor 351
- XII. Strengthening the things that remain 370
- XIII. Conclusion 379

CHAPTER I.

THE BEGINNINGS, 1796-1823.

One hundred years ago the seed of the Kingdom was here present. The children of the King appeared about this time on the territory which afterwards came within the limits of Salt River Association.

The first record of Baptists entering the ground of what became the Missouri Commonwealth gives the date as 1796, when they came to Cape Girardeau county. Speaking of the coming of the Reverend Thomas Johnson to that county in 1799, Duncan's History says: "During his stay, Mrs. Ballou, the wife of one of the oldest settlers, was converted under his preaching, and was baptised by him in Randol's Creek. This was undoubtedly the first baptism ever administered in Missouri." Sister Bettie A. Reid, the wife of our own James Reid of sacred memory, is descended from this sister Ballou.

This same History quotes the historian, John M. Peck, who says: "The first Baptist Church, called Tywappity, was organized in 1805 of some eight or ten members. This was the first religious congregation, other than Roman Catholics, that was gathered west of the 'Great River.' The next year (1806) the second, called Bethel, was gathered in the vicinity of the present site of Jackson."

During the closing years of the eighteenth century gracious revivals were given to the churches in the Carolinas, Virginia, Pennsylvania, Kentucky, Tennessee and Georgia. It seems to have been from the providential overflow from these revivals that Missouri received her first American settlers. The Baptists had shared largely in those revivals. Elder John Taylor in his History of the Ten Churches with which he held his membership in Virginia and Kentucky, gives the narrative, beautiful in its simplicity, of the revivals in northern Kentucky. Spencer's History of Kentucky Baptists says: "By the close of the year 1800, the revival had spread to all parts of the State. Immense numbers were added to the churches." An all-conquering revival is most effective in advancing the reign of Jesus Christ the Lord. Such a work enlarges the purposes and plans of men in their individual movements, and it brings together men and directs their counsels for the furtherance of the gospel, and it leads them to think and live upon a higher plane. It encourages the study of the Holy Scriptures and sweeps away the tons of pernicious literature that wicked men are throwing into families who are unsuspecting or unstable. Revivals multiply the power of ministers to preach and to reach the people in personal service. They make and cement peace between neighbors, purify the currents of conversation and correspondence. Sanitariums, orphans' homes, Christian schools and organized missionary efforts have come from the revival fervor in the hearts of the redeemed.

The American Republic had been a constitutional government only seven years when the first Baptists came to Missouri and General Washington, the first President, was in office. The western line of the country that had gained independence from England came only to the Mississippi river. Missouri was to them a foreign country with a foreign language, foreign laws, foreign customs and the Roman Catholic form of religion. New thoughts and things would stir them. The country west of the Mississippi was under the government of Spain and the secret Spanish Inquisition was then in force. These Baptists must have heard of imprisonment for preaching, for some of the first preachers who came to Kentucky and other westerly states had been imprisoned in Virginia for preaching. And when General Washington became President, the government of the United States had not established constitutional freedom in religion. Baptists had very much to do in securing an amendment which secured this freedom which opened the way for religious happiness in the trans-Mississippi territory. When the United Baptists of Virginia were in session August 8, 1789, they adopted an address to the President of the United States on the subject of religious liberty. The following is a quotation from that address: "When the Constitution first made its appearance in Virginia, we, as a society, had unusual struggling of mind, fearing that the liberty of conscience (dearer to us than property and life) was not sufficiently secured; perhaps our jealousies were heightened on account of the usage we received in Virginia under the British Government when mobs, bonds, fines and prisons were our frequent repast.

"Convinced on the one hand that without an effective national government the States would fall into disunion and all the consequent evils; on the other hand it was feared we might be accessory to some religious oppression, should any one society in the Union predominate all the rest. . . . According to our wishes the unanimous voice of the Union has called you, sir, from your beloved retreat to launch forth again into the faithless seas of human affairs, to guide the helm of the States. Should the horrid evils that have been so pestiferous in Asia and Europe—faction, ambition, war, perfidy, fraud and persecutions for conscience sake—ever approach the borders of our happy nation, may the name and administration of our beloved President, like the radiant source of day, scatter all those dark clouds from the American hemisphere.

"Samuel Harriss,
"Reuben Ford, "President.
"Clerk."

The following reply to this address was received:

"*To the General Committee representing the United Baptist Churches in Virginia*:

"Gentlemen:—I request that you will accept my best acknowledgments for your congratulation on my appointment to the first office in the Nation. The kind manner in which you mention my past conduct equally claims expression of my gratitude. After we had, by the smiles of Divine Providence on our exertions, obtained the object for which we contended, I retired at the conclusion of the war with the idea that my country could have no further occasion for my services, and with the intention of never entering again into public life; but when the exigencies of my country seemed to require me once more to engage in public affairs, an honest conviction of duty superseded my former resolution and became my apology for deviating from the happy plan which I had adopted.

"If I could have entertained the slightest apprehension that the Constitution framed in the Convention where I had the honor to preside might possibly endanger the religious rights of any ecclesiastical society, certainly I would never have placed my signature to it; and if I could now conceive that the General Government might ever be so administered as to render the liberty of conscience insecure, I beg you will be persuaded that no one would be more zealous than myself to establish effectual barriers against the horrors of spiritual tyranny and every species of religious persecution.

"For you doubtless remember I have often expressed my sentiments that every man conducting himself as a good citizen, and being accountable to God alone for his religious opinions, ought to be protected in worshiping the Deity according to the dictates of his own conscience.

"While I recollect with satisfaction that the religious society of which you are members have been throughout America, uniformly and almost unanimously, the firm friends to civil liberty, and the persevering promoters of our glorious revolution, I cannot hesitate to believe that they will be faithful supporters of a free, yet efficient, General Government. Under this pleasing expectation I rejoice to assure them that they may rely upon my best wishes and endeavor to advance their prosperity.

"In the meantime be assured, gentlemen, that I entertain a proper sense of your fervent supplication to God for my temporal and eternal happiness.

"I am, gentlemen, your most obedient servant,
"GEORGE WASHINGTON."

Only a few weeks after this correspondence James Madison, who had from his entrance into public life been an advocate of religious liberty, introduced in Congress a Bill to so amend the Constitution as to give free and equal rights and protection to all in matters of religion. He had the support of President Washington.

December 15, 1791, this amendment was ratified. It reads: "Congress shall make no law respecting an establishment of religion, or prohibiting the free exercise thereof." This was the first amendment to the Constitution of the new Republic and the friends of the amendment fondly hoped that it would put an end to tyranny on this vital question. But this hope did not become a realization. At the time of the formation of Salt River Association and for ten years afterwards some of our brethren were subjected to discriminating laws and ecclesiastical oppression. Referring to the ratification of the first amendment to the Constitution of the United States, Dr. Thomas Armitage of New York City, in his "History of the Baptists" says: "But this august event did not end the strife for religious freedom on American soil; the battle must be still pressed on the soil of New England. . . . Massachusetts had formed a State Constitution in 1780 and in that Convention the Baptists contended with pertinacity for their religious rights. Rev. Noah Alden, a lineal descendant of the Plymouth family, was a member of this Convention, and at that time pastor of the Baptist Church at Bellingham. He was also a member of the Convention which framed the Constitution of the United States." Mr. Alden and his supporters succeeded in so modifying the Bill of Rights as to make the ecclesiastical oppressions less rigorous. The fight was kept up. "The Warren Association kept a vigilant committee in existence." The courts enforced the laws, though in cases they were overlooked. "Petitions were circulated everywhere and sent to the Legislature, praying for a revision of the religious laws." There was at the time of these events, living in Cheshire, the Rev. John Leland, a native of Massachusetts and who had spent fifteen years of his ministry in Virginia, where he and other Baptists had known the iron hand of a religious establishment. He was a man of strong personality and of eloquence almost irresistible. One biographer says of him: "We doubt if his equal will ever be seen again." Dr. Armitage says: "The people of Cheshire elected Elder Leland to the Legislature for the purpose of pleading their cause," and he gives a quotation from one of his picturesque and burning speeches in that body on the subject of soul liberty. The decision referred to was rendered in 1811. He said:

"Mr. Speaker, according to a late decision of the bench, in the county of Cumberland, which, it is presumed, is to be a precedent for future decisions, these non-incorporated societies are nobody, can do nothing, and are never to be known except in shearing time, when their money is wanted to support teachers that they never hear. And all this must be done for the good of the State. One hundred and seventeen years ago wearing long hair was considered the crying sin of the land. A convention was called March 18, 1694, in Boston, to prevent it; after a long expostulation the Convention closes thus: 'If any man will now presume to wear long hair, let him know that God and man witness against him.' Our pious ancestors were for bobbing the hair for the good of the colony; but now, sir, not the hair but the purses must be bobbed for the good of the State. The petitioners pray for the right of going to heaven in that way which they believe is the most direct, and shall this be denied them? Must they be obliged to pay legal toll for walking the King's highway, which has been made free for all? . . . Since the Revolution, all the old States, except two or three in New England, have established religious liberty upon its true bottom, and yet they are not sunk with earthquakes or destroyed with fire and brimstone. Should this commonwealth, Mr. Speaker, proceed so far as to distribute all settlements and meeting houses which were procured by public taxes among all the inhabitants, without regard to denomination, it is probable that the outcry of sacrilege, profanity and infidelity would be echoed around; and yet, sir, all this has been done in a State which has given birth and education to a Henry, a Washington, a Jefferson and a Madison, each of whom contributed their aid to effect the grand event. . . . These petitioners, sir, pay the civil list, and arm to defend their country as readily as others, and only ask for the liberty of forming their societies and paying their preachers in the only way that the Christians did for the first three centuries after Christ. Any gentleman upon this floor is invited to produce an instance that Christian societies were ever formed, Christian Sabbaths ever enjoined, Christian salaries ever levied, or Christian worship ever enforced by law before the reign of Constantine. Yet, Christianity did stand and flourish, not only without the aid of the law and the schools, but in opposition to both. We hope, therefore, Mr. Speaker, that the prayers of thirty thousand, on this occasion, will be heard, and that they will obtain the exemption for which they pray."

But it was not until 1833 that the Bill of Rights was so amended as to completely separate church and State in the Commonwealth of Massachusetts. Then all the States had conformed to the Constitution of the General Government. Our Association was then ten years of age.

These States along the Mississippi were settled mostly from the river out and usually first on the lands adjacent to the river. So we find another settlement of Baptists in the vicinity of St. Louis. Here Fee Fee Church was organized in 1807. John Snethan, Sr., a native of New Jersey, and Miss Prudence Box, a native of South Carolina, became Baptists in 1801; in 1802 they were married in Kentucky. In 1808 they moved to Missouri and settled near Loutre Island, in what is now Montgomery county.

Baptists came into Lincoln county and settled on the waters of Bryant's Creek in what came to be known as Stont's Settlement. Immigration came into Pike county. Some settled on the waters of Ramsey's Creek, some on the waters of Calumet Creek. It was near the same time that pioneers came onto Peno Creek in the vicinity of what is now known as the old Paris Road.

Most of our early settlers came from the South. Boats did not come even as far north on the Mississippi River as St. Louis until 1817, so that the early citizens had to come by wagons or on horseback. This caused them to shorten their journey by settling on the first satisfactory land they reached. Ralls and Marion counties, therefore, received the incoming population about the same time, or a little later.

Some Baptists found homes in the vicinity of New London, Ralls county. Still others found their homes on the waters of Bear Creek, a few miles west of Hannibal.

CHAPTER II.

ORGANIZATION, 1823-1824.

The Churches that first constituted Salt River Association formed an irregular line on the west side of the Mississippi River and were situated from four to ten miles from that river. This embraces a strip of land about sixty miles in length with beautiful streams of water of various sizes, fertile valleys and table lands, gentle hills, abrupt bluffs and some elevations that in a country of a high general altitude would be called mountains. Some things that were said and done by those noble men and women who subdued the wild features of the land and began the work of the kingdom are lost beyond our recovery. "But the mountains keep the inimitable outline: The liquid stars shine with the same light and move on the same pathway: and between the mountains and the stars, two other changeless things, frail and imperishable, the flowers that flood every springtide, and the human heart whose hopes and longings and affections and desires blossom immortally."

Stretching along the uplands, parallel with the valley of the Jordan but some distance from it, were the ancient, sacred cities of Palestine; coming down from the north and in the order of their situation Shechem, Shiloh, Bethel, Jerusalem, Bethlehem, Hebron and Bersheba. Bear Creek, New London, Peno, Bethlehem, Ramsey Creek and Union Churches that formed Salt River Association are related in situation very much the same way to the Mississippi River.

And it gives life and confirmation to our faith to know that He who was the God of Abraham was the God of our fathers in this new land and that he is our God. "The mercy of the Lord is from everlasting to everlasting upon them that fear Him, and his righteousness unto children's children."

The first of these six churches to come into existence was Ramsey Creek. I will give the story of this Church in the language I used on the occasion of her seventy-fifth anniversary.

The first records of the Church were lost, but there was in 1891 personal and circumstantial evidence to sustain the belief that the organization occurred in 1816. The country was so sparsely settled that all advancement had to be made in the most elementary way. Prof. M. S. Goodman, in an article written for the History of Pike County, gave some account of the early days of Ramsey Creek Church. He said: "This is the oldest religious organization within the limits of Pike county. It was planted in the almost unbroken forests of Calumet, and through the lapse of years that have succeeded, it has been vocal with the praises of the Christian's God. Among the earliest members, as shown by the old records as belonging to the Baptist Church at Ramsey may be mentioned Edmond Mountjoy, Michael Tilletson, Thomas Buchanan, Mary Mountjoy, Nancy Carter, —— Plunket, Ann Buchanan, Nancy Leach, Gibson Jackson, Robert Burns, Matthew Sapp, Elizabeth Boxley, Richard Sanders, Jeptha Jeans, Daniel Moss and others." John McCune was one of the early members. Prof. Goodman gives Stephen Ruddell as the minister who organized the church and who was the Pastor from the time of organization until 1823. There are still preserved records of the church meetings held during the early period of her history. One meeting, July 13, 1821, when two persons were received into fellowship. There was a report of a committee "appointed to examine into the qualifications of a brother, whether he should be tolerated and admitted as a preacher of the Gospel." The record mentions that Brother Ruddell was absent on a trip to Kentucky. On the 4th day of August, 1821, a meeting was held when a sister "gave in her experience and was received for baptism," as did a brother the same day. The next day they were baptized. In these meetings John Morris was clerk. There is a list before us which gives additions to the church as early as February 21, 1818. John McCune and his wife Polly McCune were dismissed November 5, 1819, to go into the constitution of Peno Church.

The church has had five houses of worship. The first one was located a little east of north of the present house. It was built of logs; the size was that of a single square; the logs were unhewn. It seems to have been built about 1813. The citizens united in the work. It was used for school, worship and other neighborhood gatherings.

About 1817 a log house was built the size of a double square, the logs hewn, the floor puncheon. This second house stood a little west of north of the present house, some fifty feet from this foundation. Each man brought a log or logs. This house continued to be used until the first brick house was built; steps towards which were taken in March, 1830. These houses were used freely by worshipers of all denominations. The ground on which they stood belonged to an individual member of the church, Edmond Mountjoy. June 5, 1830, "the deed for the lot of ground where the meeting house stands was delivered by Bro. Mountjoy to the church, in order to be entered on record."

The life of the church during the first seven years of her existence seems to have been one of peace and prosperity. The immigration from other States and other communities of this State, strengthened every interest. Progress was made towards subduing the forests and building homes. But in the spring of 1823, troubles and divisions were brought to the house of the Lord. We again quote from Prof. Goodman's article: "The land upon which the first church . . . was built, was deeded by Edmond Mountjoy to the Baptists and it is claimed by many of the oldest citizens that it remained as one church (Baptist) until May, 1823, when Hughes and Rodgers, known as 'New Lights,' came from Kentucky, and a protracted effort was held at Ramsey, and several having applied for membership, a dispute arose as to who should administer the ordinance of baptism, the Baptist Pastor or the 'New Light' preacher, and Mr. Rodgers having officiated, Rev. Ruddell surrendered his charge of the church and a split at once ensued. . . . Certain it is as shown by the records that the Baptists reorganized formally on the 26th of April, 1823, and that about the same time Dr. H. Hughes was sent by his father from Kentucky to look after the spiritual wants of those, who differing from the Baptists teachings, now organized under the name of 'Reformers'"

"Mr. Ruddell was taken prisoner by the Indians on their attack on Ruddell's Station in Kentucky; he was carried away to the northwest and adopted into the tribe. . . . He married a daughter of the chief and adopted their customs. After the lapse of many years he heard of his relations in Kentucky, and with his Indian wife found his way back to his native State. His wife soon died, and he professed religion, learned his native language (which he had about forgotten while among the Indians) and began preaching. When Elder Peck visited Ramsey's Creek Church in 1818, Elder Ruddell was then pastor."

Of the early history of the church, Perry Wells, who came to St. Louis county in 1815, and to Ramsey's Creek settlement in 1817, stated, "I am of the opinion that the Baptist church was organized and in operation some time previous to 1818, and it was the current belief that the Baptist church was the first and oldest church organization in the vicinity. In the year 1820, I went to school in this meeting house."

George Fielder, who came to St. Louis county in 1821, and to Ramsey's Creek settlement in February, 1822, states that "At that time there was a log house near the location of the present house and known as Ramsey's Creek Baptist Church. The pastor was Stephen Ruddell the first time I attended church. That Edmond Mountjoy was clerk at that time."

Organization.

Mrs. Polly Sutton, a daughter of Thomas Buchanan, states that, "I remember the baptism of my father and mother at Ramsey Creek Church, which occurred April 24, 1820. Stephen Ruddell was the Baptist preacher. I am of the opinion that my father was a Deacon of the church, elected, perhaps, soon after he joined the church."

Geo. Fielder said of Ruddell: "He was a square, heavy-set man, about 5 feet 9 or 10 inches high, weight about 180 pounds, straight, slow of motion, slow of speech, matured his speech before he uttered it, hardly ever spoke a sentence unless it meant something; spoke good English, showed the Indian habits in his manner and dress. He continued to hunt and fish with special friends among the Indians. He was active in quieting troubles between the whites and Indians. He had hazel gray eyes, auburn hair, worn long, dark complexion, coarse features, big nose, high cheek bones, broad face, big mouth, solemn look; talked but little, but to the purpose, a good, strong voice, with pleasant tone. In the pulpit he spoke calmly, solemnly and to the point, never saw him shed tears when preaching. In 1822 he seemed to be the rise of fifty years. He kept smooth shaven. He lived about two miles east of Ramsey Creek church on the farm known as the Beauchamp farm, John Beauchamp bought it of Ruddell. While living here he had a wife and two children, a son and a daughter. The son, Paul, was drowned in the Mississippi while attempting to rescue a woman from a sinking boat. The daughter, Sally, was married to Noah Beasley, who then lived on the Judge Newton McDannold farm. Stephen Ruddell was a truthful, honest, good disposed man in his daily life. Never meddled or concerned himself about other people's business unless called upon."

FROM 1824 TO 1834.

The church book contains the following record:

"Ramsey Creek, Pike county, Missouri. April 26, 1823. We, whose names are under written, being conscious that our present condition is an unhappy one, and such as we wish to try to alter, . . . finding ourselves as sheep without a shepherd and exposed to the wolf until enfolded or embodied, do therefore wish to show ourselves on the Lord's side." To this record there are subscribed the names of ten brethren and sisters. The record continues with the same date: "Agreeable to appointment the brethren and sisters . . . met at meeting house and were legally constituted as a church of Christ by our brother, Davis Biggs, and gave each other the right hand of fellowship."

Davis Biggs became Pastor and continued in office until 1833. Edmond Mountjoy was made clerk of the church. At this first meeting the church appointed the clerk to write a letter to Cuivre Association, which was to meet in June following. The ensuing July, Thomas Buchanan was chosen Deacon, and also treasurer.

During Mr. Biggs' pastorate there were sixty-seven additions to the church, fifty-three of these by experience and baptism.

During this time the *discipline* of the church was decided, impartial, wholesome. It was enforced against such as had been guilty of intoxication, riotous conduct, fraud, adultery, profane swearing, heresy, or wounding a brother's feelings. That it was exercised to restore those overtaken in faults is evident from the fact that effort was made to restore them and that when evidence of repentance was shown they were restored. But when the sinful persisted in their sins, then they were cut off, that the church might be saved.

The *commemoration of the Lord's death* was observed regularly and scripturally, or as they expressed it in their record, "uniformally." In this period loose communion gave the church some trouble. Now and then, a member, disregarding the teachings of the New Testament, and disregarding the fact that Christ gave the supper to his churches, not to sects teaching doctrines contradictory to each other, and to His word, some of which sects have sprung up with the suddenness and unstableness of mushrooms, in the nineteenth century, preferred the use of the bread and wine as a social feast, to the use of them in faithfulness to Christ. But the church held firmly the truth of God and practiced His precepts and God blessed the church.

In the time in question the church had two Deacons. In July, 1823, Thomas Buchanan was chosen to the office of Deacon. In February, 1830, the church decided to have "another Deacon, and Bro. James Janes was chosen to act with Bro. Thomas Buchanan as Deacon."

In December, 1830, Mr. Buchanan resigned as treasurer. "Bro. Janes was appointed in his stead." In June, 1832, Bro. John Beauchamp was chosen treasurer. The clerks for the church were: Edmond Mountjoy, who served informally from April, 1823, the time of the reorganization, until September, 1824, when he was made permanent clerk. At the July meeting, 1828, Bro. Mountjoy resigned the clerkship, and Bro. Gibson Jenkins was elected to fill the vacancy. Bro. Jenkins resigned at the September meeting, 1832, and John Beauchamp was elected to the position.

At the meeting, March 6, 1830, "It was proposed that four commissioners should be appointed to superintend *the building of a brick meeting house* for the church, and they were appointed accordingly. Their names are E. Mountjoy, A. Buford, Mr. Givens, and John Beauchamp."

There must have been a time when the church had no house in a condition for use, as they met on various occasions in private houses for the transaction of business. This would be after the log house was in a condition for use and before the first brick was finished.

FROM JANUARY, 1834, TO MAY, 1838.

This period embraces the pastoral labors of two brethren. February, 1834, Elder John H. Sturgeon was called to the pastorate. Bro. Sturgeon came from Long Run church, in Kentucky. Prosperity and peace marked his labors. Under his labors six were baptized into the fellowship of the church and nine were received by letter. A wholesome discipline was maintained. The church, which for several years had sought for ministerial gifts in her membership, licensed Brother Lewis Ford. This occurred in March, 1835. He came to Ramsey Creek church from Grassy Lick church, Montgomery county, Ky. His death occurred on his homestead in 1841. He is remembered as a man of good mind, upright life and useful in the spiritual as well as the temporal work of the church.

After the discontinuance of Elder Sturgeon's pastoral relation with the church, Elder Ephraim Davis was called to the pastorate. He entered upon his duties immediately and continued as Pastor until the close of the period under consideration. Four were received in this time by experience and baptism and twelve by letter. One was dismissed by letter. The church watched over her membership with strict attention to their consistency and godliness. One brother voluntarily makes acknowledgment "for getting angry," the clerk is appointed to correspond with a sister living in another State as to non-attendance. The query is raised, "Is it good order or consistent with the religion of Jesus Christ for professors of religion to attend barbacues where there is fiddling and dancing?" The grosser sins were duly treated. In June, 1836, steps were taken to have the "meeting house repaired, so as to make it comfortable."

The first mention of a stated salary for the sexton was November, 1835, and the salary was made $5. The first mention of *Pastor's salary* was September, 1836. The amount raised was $23, "and agreed that the subscription should stand open till the meeting in course." In February, 1836, Newton McDonnold was chosen to fill the deaconship, an office to which he had been set apart in Kentucky.

A distinguishing feature of this period was the mold and impulse that was given to the business of the church. Such men as Thomas Buchanan, Edmond Mountjoy, John Beauchamp and Ruben McDonnold would give character and force to any body of men. They were Christian gentlemen of piety, spirit and purpose. Mountjoy had died August 28, 1832. McDonnold united with the church December, 1835. He had been a Deacon in Kentucky, where he gave his best manhood to the Lord's service. He is remembered as a generous contributor, a wise counselor and a Christian of large views. All his powers found full scope in his labors for the Lord, whose kingdom needs men who will lay for its growth and aggressiveness broad and deep plans.

The usefulness of men of business in their relation to Christ has been felt from Joseph of Arimathea to this day. No amount of oratory, music, or scholarship can take the place of business capacity. Each must fill his own place. Even one such man as these early burden-bearers of Ramsey Creek insures, by the blessing of God, the order and prosperity of the business department of church work.

In this period the church had mothers in Israel whose fragrant memories abide. Of these may be mentioned Sisters Buchanan, Sallie Givens, Crysena Jacoby, Nancy Buford and Susan Ford.

Elder John Hume Sturgeon was born in Jefferson county, Kentucky, October 8, 1791. He was the son of Thomas Sturgeon, who, according to Spencer's History of Kentucky Baptists, was remarkable for his piety and zeal. That history says, "John H. Sturgeon professed religion and was baptized into the fellowship of Long Run church about the sixteenth year of his age. He soon began to pray in public, and, afterwards to exhort sinners to repent and seek the Lord. He was licensed to preach about 1812 . . . His life was one of eminent purity and devoted piety." Bro.

Sturgeon was ordained December 4, 1829, by George Waller, Francis Davis, Zacheus Carpenter, John B. Curl and John Dale, "to the sacred office of the ministry," "having by sufficient testimonials, fully certified of his moral character, real piety and sacred knowledge in divine things, as well as ministerial gifts and abilities." While in Kentucky he was Pastor of Long Run church. In the autumn of 1833 he came to Pike county, Missouri, and soon became pastor of Ramsey Creek church. The wife of Brother Sturgeon was Miss Margaret Northerton, daughter of John and Winfred Northerton. The marriage was January 26, 1815. They were blessed with nine children, three of whom still live. The eldest of these, Wm. K., says, "My father was a loving, devoted man to his family, loved by all who knew him, especially for his devotedness to the cause of God. In sickness he was untiring and faithful. He was a good nurse. No disease kept him from going to minister to their spiritual as well to their temporal wants. In the cholera he was untiring in his ministrations. It took nearly all of some families." His death occurred September 16, 1834, on his homestead. His body rests on that farm while many of his offspring love to honor the memory of this man of God. His works follow him.

Elder Ephraim Davis was born in Franklin county, Kentucky, but was reared in Shelby county, in that State. Duncan's History says of him: "In May, 1835, he became pastor of Union (now New Hope) Baptist church, and continued such until his death. He was strongly Calvinistic in his doctrines, a good man, and much beloved by the church. His preaching was better calculated to feed the flock than to call sinners to repentance. . . . He died in 1851."

FROM MAY, 1838, TO APRIL, 1850.

"This church unanimously agrees to call Bro. A. D. Landrum to the care of this church to preach to us the first Saturday and Sunday and Sunday after the third Saturday in each month." This call for Elder Landrum's labors for two Sundays

Organization.

in each month indicated the rising strength of the church. They soon began to reap the fruits of their increased efforts in planting and watering. The period of Mr. Landrum's pastorate embraced twelve years. In this time there were one hundred and five additions by experience and baptism, by letter forty-nine. During this period the church sent out her first colony to organize another church. They were given letters of dismission December, 1849, and went into the organization of Buffalo Knob church. The whole number dismissed by letter during the period of Bro. Landrum's ministry was fifty-five. The discipline of the church was unrelaxed. And besides their strictness in holding the immoral and heretical members to due account, they were called on to deal with some excellent persons, who for a time were self-willed and disregardful of the actions of the church. The whole number excluded in this period was thirty-five. The honor of the church and the purity of the membership were held as superior to personal or family considerations. There were twenty-one deaths. The church clerks were Lewis Ford, James Anderson, Alexander McDonnold and William K. Sturgeon. In May, 1849, Brother Matthew Givens was chosen Deacon. The following month he was ordained by Elders Landrum and A. G. Mitchell.

From the organization of the church the colored people had received careful religious consideration. They had had a place in the house of worship, they were given time to attend preaching, they were received into the fellowship of the church and dismissed just as other members, and the same standard of Christian life was required of them. The result was that by the grace of God a very large part of the additions to the church were colored people. In August, 1843, definite seating capacity was provided and reserved for them. Two of the colored brethren were in September, 1845, licensed to preach the gospel. One of these, Brother David, is remembered as an orderly walking Christian, noted for his piety, and his preaching did good among his own race. The white people, too, respected him for his piety.

In February, 1846, Bro. A. G. Mitchell, who had in Virginia, been licensed to preach, united with our church by letter. His ordination occurred November, 1848. Brethren Landrum and T. T. Johnson being the ordaining Presbytery. The church encouraged Bro. Mitchell to go forth into the field preaching.

Ramsey Creek Church was conservative in spirit and positive in practice on the mission question, which was now agitating the churches and associations. In August, 1841, the church "agreed to take up the proposition in respect to employing a preacher to labor in the bounds of the Association." And in September of the same year, after speaking of a contribution for the support of the ministry, they say, "This was the usage of the United Baptists in the peaceful and happy seasons that were enjoyed in days and years that are past and gone." In May, 1847, the church voted to "leave our members as individuals free to do as they please," about giving to missions. The Pastor and Deacons being prudent, pious and faithful men, the church kept united by the tender mercies of our Heavenly Father in the fellowship of the gospel and the labor of the Lord. Individual freedom is a strong bond of union, when that freedom is the freedom of Christ's freemen. Personal godliness cements organized oneness. And these precious truths of divine revelation and christian experience have been verified in the history of our beloved church.

While Elder A. D. Landrum was our Pastor he planted and watered, and God gave the increase. This man of God was abundant and fruitful in labors. He left his impress on our church. And others received the benefits of his able ministrations.

In personal appearance he was a cultivated gentleman, with auburn hair, sandy beard, open countenance, gentle in his motion, easy in gesture, tasteful in dress. In the pulpit he stood erect, spoke deliberately,

Organization.

except in exhortation, when he would become animated. His voice was pleasing, being mellow and resonant. In size he was above medium. He used good language, and the subject-matter of his sermons was prepared. Bro. Landrum received the favorable regard of all who knew him. His residence was three miles south of the church. The ability of this honored brother was felt in other fields than the pastoral office. For eleven years he was moderator of Salt River Association. Windsor, Henry county, was our brother's home in the closing days of his earthly pilgrimage. There he fell asleep in Jesus, September 1, 1861, aged 55 years, 9 months and 12 days. When Bro. Landrum became our pastor he was thirty-two years of age. His native home was Clark county, Kentucky.

The standard-bearers of this time in the church were Ruben McDonnold, Terisha Turner, Newton McDonnold, James Anderson, Alexander McDonnold and Phillip Thurmond.

Brother Turner was paralyzed during services in our church. He served the Lord in suffering to the end. Bro. Anderson served the church in the capacity of clerk as did also Brother Alexander McDonnold. Newton McDonnold was noted for his pacific counsel and careful management of the financial interests.

FROM 1850 TO 1883.

This period embraces the time of the pastoral services of Elder A. G. Mitchell. The time is thirty-three years, or, speaking with exactness, it was thirty-two years and nine months from the beginning of his services to the beginning of the services of his successor. As the human family is counted, the generation that was born in 1850 passed from earth in 1883. Men die, but institutions may survive generations. The Church of Jesus Christ above other of all institutions. "The gates of hell shall not prevail against it." The church-life during this pastorate was characterized by some things instructive and helpful.

The church maintained her integrity through the fires and thunders of the Civil War. Not a doctrine was surrendered, nor was discipline relaxed.

In the summer of 1872 the church added over two acres to the churchyard. This gives to the place of worship a homelike appearance and accommodations that lend additional pleasure to the house of the Lord. In the nature of things worshipers can best worship when their surroundings correspond to those they enjoy in their own houses. No one ought to be willing to give to the Lord that which is less excellent than what he uses for himself. David said, "See, now, I dwell in an house of cedar, but the Ark of God dwelleth within curtains."

In March, 1856, the church laid plans for building a new house of worship. In June following a building committee was appointed consisting of N. McDonnold, Phillip Thurmond, W. S. Ellis and J. E. Dougherty. The house seems to have been completed towards the close of 1867, as in December of that year the building committee were instructed to get stoves for the house. This house which was brick and which stood where the present one stands, was 40x60, ceiling fifteen feet high and was from time to time supplied with necessary furniture and comforts.

At the September meeting, 1850, arrangements were made to reverently bury the dead and to carefully care for their graves. And this interest was repeatedly shown at subsequent meetings. Such men as T. Buchanan, N. McDonnold and Geo. Fielder were appointed to carry out the will of the church. The result is we have a cemetery where our beloved dead may rest in peace, not to be exposed or ploughed over as is likely to be done sooner or later with family cemeteries. The account of Abraham's burial of Sarah is sweetly solemn, tinged with a touch of immortality. "And Sarah died in Kirjatharba. . . . And Abraham stood up from before his dead and spake unto the sons of Heth, saying, I am a stranger and a sojourner with you; give me a possession of a buryingplace with you, that

I may bury my dead out of my sight. . . . And the field of Ephron, which was in Machpelah, which was before Mamre, the field, and the cave which was therein, and all the trees that were in the field, that were in all the borders round about, were made sure unto Abraham for a possession in the presence of the children of Heth, before all that went in at the gate of his city. And after this Abraham buried Sarah his wife in the cave of the fields of Machpelah before Mamre; the same is Hebron in the Land of Canaan. And the field and the cave that is therein, were made sure unto Abraham for a possession of a buryingplace by the sons of Heth." Every place where we bury our dead ought to be "made sure."

At the January meeting, 1868, William D. Major was elected treasurer. In May, 1872, Thos. J. McDonnold was elected to this position, as was J. R. Smith in June, 1882.

February, 1851, A. McDonnold was elected clerk. He served until June, 1854, when J. G. Barnes was chosen as his successor. January, 1857, William S. Ellis was elected clerk, and served until June, 1878, when A. L. McDonnold was chosen as his successor. At the November meeting, 1882, B. H. Watts was elected clerk, which position he has filled to the present time.

Two Deacons were elected July, 1866. They were William D. Major, and Thomas J. McDonnold. These brethren were ordained the following month, Elder J. F. Smith assisting the Pastor. Two others were elected to the office of Deacon, July, 1878. They were A. M. Tinsley and Wm. Bibb. Their ordination occurred at the regular meeting the following month, Elder W. H. Burnham helping the Pastor.

At the March meeting, 1882, J. R. Smith was elected to the deaconship. At the April meeting following the Pastor and Elder W. M. Tipton ordained him. During this period the church was one of the leaders in extending the gospel into new territory and in strengthening the weak churches.

The church entered a new field of usefulness by helping in the general effort of the denomination to give educations to young men called of God to preach the gospel. They had enjoyed the ministry of able preachers and they knew there was a difference between the messenger thoroughly furnished and the one poorly furnished. The message is judged by the messenger. If we would have the truth readily received by the people we must send them preachers whose presence, piety, words and wisdom incline those who hear to receive that truth. To have such men the churches must provide for their education.

In December, 1851, the church ordained to the gospel ministry W. W. Mitchell, Brethren J. F. Smith and A. D. Landrum together with the Pastor acting as the ordaining Presbytery.

At the July meeting "Daniel, a servant of Dr. Meriwether, is granted the privilege to exhort and expound the Scriptures to his color."

In August, 1880, Brethren William A. Bibb and Charles A. Mitchell were granted license to preach. April 30, 1882, they were ordained to the full work of the ministry, Elder W. M. Tipton, aiding the Pastor. The church in this period made a forward movement in Sunday School work by taking the election of the officers and the support of the school into their own hands as a part of their church business and responsibility.

The church was repeatedly blessed with refreshings from the presence of the Lord. Some of these may be especially mentioned. At times the church seemed to go on without ministerial help to aid the Pastor. In August, 1858, twenty-four were added to their number.

A like blessing was bestowed on the church in September, 1866. In this revival Elder T. N. Sanderson was the ministerial help. In February, 1869, a revival began, the power of which continued until towards the close of 1870.

Organization.

A revival of great power was enjoyed by the church in November, 1877. Elder Joshua Hickman preached the gospel that was signally owned and honored. In this revival twenty-seven were added to the church. In March, 1880, the grace of God brought salvation to sinners and the church was revived. The good work went on into April, the Pastor being aided by Elder J. D. Biggs.

Eld. A. G. Mitchell, the Pastor, labored with this church during the best years of his life. He began his pastorate at Ramsey at the age of thirty-seven years.

Ramsey Creek Church dismissed members to go into the organization of Dover, Prairieville, Ebenezar and Clarksville churches, besides the members who went into Peno and Buffalo Knob previously mentioned.

Besides the ministers previously mentioned as having preached at Ramsey Creek on one occasion or another should be mentioned Elders J. T. Williams, James Reid, B. F. Hixson and James Lillard. These men of God were used of God for the furtherance of the gospel.

FROM 1883 TO 1891.

This period embraces the pastorates of Elders J. D. Biggs, J. D. Hacker and nearly three years of the present pastorate.

Bro. Biggs became pastor in March, 1883, and continued for three years and ten months. Under his ministry seven were received into the church by experience and baptism and eleven by letter. Elder J. D. Harker helped the pastor in a revival. The church grew and prospered.

Bro. Hacker became pastor in March, 1887, and continued one year.

In October, 1888, W. J. Patrick began the pastoral care of the church. At the February meeting, 1886, the church elected Edgar McDonnold and W. M. Waters to the Deaconship.

In May, 1890, Jas. C. Mackey and Wm. S. Ellis were chosen to the deaconship. Their ordination occurred at night of the 29th of that month. In this service the Pastor was assisted by Elders W. A. Bibb, J. D. Biggs, E. J. Sanderson and M. S. Whiteside.

Each year the church has been blessed with a season of revival. In January, 1889, Dr. G. L. Black, of Liberty, assisted in one of these delightful services. In November of that year we had Elder A. N. Bird, of the same place, and in November, 1890, we had Elder Wm. A. Bibb, of Bowling Green.

The church, which through all her history, had led in financial carefulness and liberality came during this period to a promptness and method in support of the Pastor that deserves special commendation. The method of monthly payments was adopted and has been maintained with integrity. This helps to solve the important question of a Pastor's finances, a stumbling-block over which good men have been known to stumble. It is difficult for a minister of the gospel to tell a groceryman of his sins when his own grocery account due the man is overdue, and his soul does not spontaneously generate exuberance of ecstacies to woo the world to religion while he is bending beneath the big bulk of borrowed burdens. Next to downright immoralities there is, perhaps, no greater hindrance to a Pastor than debt. The church should promptly pay the Pastor and then the Pastor should pay as he goes, —or not go.

Another feature of the finances of the church deserves mention. When the church was in the midst of the effort to build a house she appointed committees to raise money for District, State, Home and Foreign Missions. However great our home duties, we may show a sympathizing interest and cooperative spirit in our fellow-men who have not the gospel. However straightened we may be at home the habit and grace of helping others should be maintained. The Christian should feel himself linked to the whole line

Organization. 37

of gospel churches which girdle the earth and on some of which the sun shines every hour in the twenty-four.

In July, 1887, the north gable of the house of worship fell in and over a third of the adjoining ceiling fell down. This catastrophe caused a called meeting of the church to be held. They met July 30, with Wm. A. Bibb in the chair. They appointed a building committee, consisting of J. M. Givens, William R. McDonnold, and R. D. Ellis. At the August meeting a soliciting committee was appointed consisting of W. M. Waters, J. W. Treadway, T. J. McDonnold, B. H. Watts and Sisters Lou Markey, Carrie Renean, Ada Carver, Emma Givens and Marmie McDonnold. It was decided to build a brick house 32x46 with ceiling, eighteen feet high, the house to have a recess in the northern end, three windows on each side of the house and one window on each side of the recess, one double front door, surmounted by transoms, two front windows and two flues to be supplied by two stoves, and the house to be covered with tin. The house was finished accordingly and nicely furnished. The cost of the house and furniture was $2,038.38. The opening service was held the first Sunday in May, 1888, Dr. W. Pope Yeaman preached the sermon on the occasion.

In the service of song the church has been considerate, conservative and scriptural. The hymns are selected with respect to the gospel of the grace of God, which they express, and the music for the holy impress with which it carries this gospel to the senses and affections of the worshipers. We would with voice and instrument speak forth the praises of our God and Saviour. The recent great revival among the Telugus may remind us of the power of sacred song. There have been, we are told by a correspondent of the *Central Baptist,* "Over eleven thousand believers baptized in three revivals." "In 1853 the Missionary Union almost concluded to withdraw its aid; . . . but for the inspiring hope awakened by Dr. S. F. Smith's stirring verses, written during the evening, after the

discussion and distributed among the audience next morning. I refer to the lines beginning:
"Shine on, Lone Star! thy radiance bright
    Shall yet illume the western skies."

Prof. R. P. Rider says in the *Baptist Quarterly Review*, "When the churches realize the power of music as a spiritualizing medium, and awake to the importance of purging the service of the sanctuary from all triviality or effeminateness and speak *among themselves* in psalms and hymns and spiritual songs, singing and making melody in their hearts to the Lord, we shall see a new Reformation, and Zion will arise and put on her beautiful garments."

God is to be honored with the first fruits and the best fruits that land and sea produce. The highest use to which the purest water can be put is for baptizing one who has been saved by the Grace of God through Jesus Christ; the highest use to which bread and wine can be put is the commemoration of the Lord's death till He come. And gold and silver when purest and brightest are no more than worthy to bear the emblems of Christ's body and blood. But since they are the best the earth affords let us use them with thanksgiving. While the church was in business session in August, 1889, there was presented to the church a silver communion set, the gift of Mrs. N. Virginia Ayres, for which kindness the church expressed an appreciation in a vote of thanks to the kindly giver.

It is beautiful to see the heart of the church enlarged as the years come and go. No work of the Lord has ever knocked at our door to be turned empty away. The last great interest to which the church laid its hand was the Baptist Sanitarium, St. Louis. A former Pastor, Elder J. D. Biggs, was the first agent for the institution, the church contributed freely towards founding it, and her members have given it a liberal cooperation. It is Christian to care for the body and thereby we may reach the soul of the one who knows not our Lord. Under the economy of our holy Christianity, relieving the sick and preaching the gospel are fellow helpers.

In this last period we have had men and women who rejoiced as the sheep of the great Shepherd to eat food in His green pastures to follow Him by the still waters and who know His voice. And as laborers they have borne the burden and hot winds of the day in which they lived.

Elder James Duvall Biggs is a distinct character among men. He has a combination of strong and opposing qualities which seem to blend and lose themselves in each other rather than abide side by side in the man. He has mildness and amiableness that blend with strong decision and fire that foes cannot quench. In scholarship he is thorough, accurate and comprehensive. In childhood he enjoyed what was equivalent to the best academic advantages, the instructions of a master in learning. When we look along the whole line of an education, as a man looks along a gun barrel, it is seen to embrace the primary, academic, collegiate and university advantages. All these Brother Biggs had and he improved them. If he had turned his attention to the work of educating, he could have become eminent in languages or mathematics; had he turned this attention to song, fame and fortune were open to him; had he turned his attention to money making, he might have gained fame and fortune.

But God called him to preach. He obeyed. Languages, mathematics, fame, fortune and money when compared to the gospel are as the sunflower compared to the sun. J. D. Biggs[1] is a great-grandson of Davis Biggs. The church, at the business meeting in March, 1889, voted to observe her seventy-fifth anniversary. A leading motive was to preserve the history which must be rescued soon or never. History is nothing if not accurate. It is due to our Heavenly Father, who has saved us and kept us, to make a public acknowledgment of his goodness. And we would transmit the

---

[1] Elder James D. Biggs fell asleep in his Lord, Wednesday, July 28, 1909, in Odessa, Missouri.

record of God's goodness to us to our children through the coming generations in the loving hope that our God will be their God and our people their people. Salt River Association has produced men of historical tastes and attainments. Among these men were Judge Horatio N. Baskett, of New Hope, and Judge Alexander P. Miller, of Mt. Pisgah church. The historical spirit ought to be caught by our younger people and the knowledge of history acquired. A part of the wealth of Baptists is in their history. Our God has been to us a pillar of cloud by day and a pillar of fire by night for almost nineteen hundred years, and this is an assurance of what He will do as the centuries come and go.

On the 27th and 28th of May, 1891, Ramsey Creek Church had this seventy-fifth anniversary. A history was read, Elder J. D. Biggs preached on the 27th, and Dr. W. Pope Yeaman on the 28th. The subject of an address by Elder James Reid was "The Relation of the Older Churches to New Fields."

Elders S. F. Thompson and T. N. Sanderson spoke on "Preservation of Baptist History." Elders E. J. Sanderson and James Reid spoke on "Holding the Ground Already Gained." Dr. J. T. Williams spoke on "What Shall the Second Seventy-five Years Witness?" Dr. Yeaman and Brother J. N. B. Hepler spoke on "Not the Years Gone by, but the Service Rendered the True Standard of Worth."

Deacon James C. Markey and wife led the song service, except the song, "Come Thou Fount," which was led by Deacon T. R. Mitchell, of Mill Creek Church in an old tune. Prof. M. S. Goodman said editorially in *The Sentinel*, Clarksville:

"Never have we witnessed a celebration in which there was a profounder interest manifested or where better efforts were put forth to make it a positive and unqualified success. As early as 9 o'clock the crowd commenced to gather, coming in buggy and barouche, in sulky and surrey, in cart and carriage, in landau and lumber wagon, on horseback and in herdic and in every other imaginable and conceivable manner; a few, perhaps, even bobbing up serenely upon buckboard or bicycle. The people came as to a coronation, and the dignity of their bearing, the elegance of their attire and the character of their equipages stamped them an assemblage of right royal men and women convening to do honor to one greater than earthly prince or potentate and whose gentle reign is destined to continue long after monarchs shall have been forgotten and kingdoms and empires shall have crumbled into dust. Just before 10 o'clock the peal of organ and burst of sacred song called to worship, and within a few minutes the spacious church was filled to overflowing. The handsome house was beautifully decorated. On the walls hung pictures of many of the sainted dead, about pulpit and altar were flowers rare and exotic, while above the alcove in letters of living green stood out in bold relief the single word, 'welcome.' To the left of this and wrought out of the same material were the figures 1816, signalizing the date when the first religious temple planted in these western wilds, now known as Northeast Missouri, with all its culture and refinement, was dedicated to the Christian's God by those pious pioneers who had come with strong arms and an abiding faith to carve for themselves and loved ones homes from the almost impenetrable forests. On the right of this same word was the date 1891."

PENO CHURCH.

Rising in the fertile upland prairie of the west central part of Pike county, Peno Creek, with clear water, gravel bed and bordered by varying bluffs and lowland banks and gently rising hills, runs with a general course towards the northeast. From where the old Louisiana and Paris road crosses it, the creek opens out into a belt of productive farming land. At a point some two miles north of this road, the belt is broken into some symmetrical swells, cut by rivulets from the highlands. Here William Biggs settled and reared a large family, prospered and became active in moulding our first laws and civilization. He had a large part in the upbuilding of Peno Church.

Peno Church was organized December 25, 1819, in the house of Mr. John McCune. In the constitution were the Rev. Leroy Jackson, Polly Jackson, Joseph Trotter, John McCune, Polly McCune, Thomas Hedges, William Biggs, Betsey Biggs, Betsey Shannon, Susan Doyle, William McCoy, John Carr. Mr. Jackson rendered the ministerial service on the occasion. They did not build a house of worship but used a schoolhouse or private homes. The church grew and multiplied. Some of the Baptists who have done valiantly for the Lord were saved and baptized at Peno. The Pastors were A. D. Landrum, Walter McQuie, L. C. Musick and J. M. Johnson. Bro. Landrum was Pastor some fourteen years.

STOUT'S SETTLEMENT CHURCH.

Judge Horatio N. Baskett, who was for many years clerk of the church, gives, in Duncan's History, definite information of the organization of this church. He says: "Stout's Settlement Baptist Church, Lincoln county, was organized June 16, 1821, by Elders Bethuel Riggs and Jesse Sitton, the latter of whom is supposed to have been the Pastor until 1828, when he was dismissed by letter and left the State." Later the church changed her name to Union.

The church built a house in an early day but I have not been able to get the date. I have from E. D. Frazier, Elsberry, Missouri, this interesting account of the house:

"My father and mother were both members of that church from '37 or '38 till they both died—father in 1844 and mother in 1857. The house was an old-fashioned hewed log house standing north and south, fronting east, with a little pen built in the center of the wall on each side, one for the pulpit and the other for the front door, with one window on either side of

Organization. 43

the pulpit, small windows and one good sized window on each side of the front door. The house, I think, was about twenty by forty feet and had a door in each end, house heated by stoves. It stood on a nice little elevation slanting gradually east till it reached about seventy-five yards from the house and came to a small drain out of the opposite bank of which there came a fine spring of good everlasting water, which was known as the 'Union Spring.' The water of the spring ran off down a branch northeast about one-fourth of a mile and emptied into one branch of Bryant's Creek.

A schoolhouse stood about fifty or sixty yards from the church, where I went to school to a Baptist preacher."

BEAR CREEK CHURCH.

The valley of Bear Creek, Marion county, is rich in soil and must have been inviting to early settlers. The Baptists began work there before Marion county was organized. Bear Creek Church was given organic form August 5, 1821, in the home of George Turner. The business meeting was set for the first Saturday in each month.

Her constituent members were George Turner and wife, Anna Turner, Chas. L. Turner and wife, Phoebe Turner, John Rush and wife, Margaret Rush, Samuel Conway, Susan Gregory, Francis McRea and Fannie Wassen. Brethren Davis Biggs and Frank Worson aided in the constitution of the church.

The Articles of Faith adopted were:

"*Art.* 1. We believe in one only true and living God, the Father, Son and Holy Ghost.

"*Art.* 2. We believe that the Scriptures of the Old and New Testaments are of divine authority, and the only rule of faith and practice.

"*Art.* 3. We believe in the doctrine of original sin and that all of Adam's posterity are sinners by nature, and that they have neither will nor power to deliver themselves from their condemned and sinful state.

"*Art.* 4. We believe in the doctrine of election by grace, and that God chose his people in Christ before the foundation of the world.

"*Art.* 5. We believe that sinners are justified before God only by the imputed righteousness of Christ.

"*Art.* 6. We believe that God's elect are regenerated by the Holy Spirit, and that good works are an evidence of a gracious state and not a cause of it.

"*Art.* 7. We believe that the saints shall persevere in grace and never finally fall away.

"*Art.* 8. We believe that Baptism and the Lord's Supper are ordinances of Jesus Christ and that true believers are the only proper subjects for baptism; that baptized believers are the only fit subjects for the Lord's Supper, and that immersion is the only Scriptural mode of baptism.

"*Art.* 9. We believe that joys of the righteous and the punishment of the wicked will be eternal.

"*Art.* 10. We believe in the resurrection of the dead, both of the just and the unjust.

"*Art.* 11. We believe that no minister has a right to administer the ordinances of the gospel only such as have been regularly baptized, called and come under the imposition of hands of a Presbytery by the authority of the Church of Christ."

The meetings were at first held in George Turner's residence. John Rush was moderator and Charles L. Turner clerk. In November following the two brethren were licensed to preach. The church had no regular Pastor for about two years and did not have a house of worship for ten or twelve years. During that time they held their services in residences and in an old cooper-shop about five miles from Hannibal, near where the brick house now stands, which is not far from Bear Creek Station. February the second, 1822, Samuel Conway was elected Deacon. C. L. Turner was elected clerk March the third, 1822. The first Pastor was the Elder Leroy Jackson, elected in 1823. March the third, 1822, messengers were appointed to join with the messengers of other churches in the organization of an Association, which was organized and called Salt River.

BETHLEHEM CHURCH.

There is some reason to believe that Baptists settled on the waters of Calumet Creek as early as 1811, perhaps earlier. They were citizens who had enjoyed educational and business advantages in the homes from which they came. They showed discriminating judgment in finding homes in this fine district of valley and table lands. I have no account of preliminary meetings or the steps which led up to the organization of the church. It is a pleasure to write of men who recorded their religious business definitely, and safely preserved the record. Here is the account of the proceedings in the formation of the church, taken from their own church-book:

"May the 10, 1823. The following professors of the Baptist Church and order met at Joel Griffith's on the day and date above, and, after sermon being preached by Elder Davis Biggs, came forward and professed themselves to be in peace, and produced letters of dismission and gave themselves to the Lord and to one another by the will of God and agreed to watch over one another and maintain the order and government necessary for the well-being of said church members.

"In the constitution were Silas Wilson and Elizabeth Wilson, Joel Griffith and Peggy Griffith, Vincent Kelly and Susanna Kelly, Ann Barnett, John and Sarah Allen. . . .

"The church then appointed brethren Allen and Kelly Deacons.

"Brother Biggs was appointed to draw up some Articles of Faith and a plan of decorum."

In July following the act of organizing, these Articles of Faith were adopted:

"*First.* We believe in one only true and living God, and that he is made known unto us in the office and under the character of Father, Son and Spirit.

"*Secondly.* We believe in election by grace and the saint's final perseverance.

"We believe that believers in Christ are the only subjects and that immersion is the apostolic mode of baptism and the door to communion.

"We take the Old and New Testaments for our general rule of faith and practice, believing it to be a safe guide, and that every church has a right to hold her own keys and govern herself."

The clerk speaks of the church as "The Church of Jesus Christ on the waters of Buffalo and Calumet."

At the December meeting, 1823, by an act of the church the name Bethlehem was adopted. Bro. Biggs had served them as Pastor up to this date.

"The Church at Bethlehem then called Bro. Davis Biggs to take the care of them another year, which he agreed to do." They did not build a house for several years after they became a church. They worshiped in the houses of the membership. They set May and September as the times for communion seasons.

NEW LONDON CHURCH.

In 1823 the Baptists of New London organized themselves into a church. The data is meager as to particulars, but the fact is well established. The written minutes of the first session of Salt River Association give; "New London Church: Messengers, Dabney Jones, William Forman, William Carson. The membership was fourteen." I take this from the minutes in this connection to establish the fact of an early New London Church inasmuch as there is no existing record of the church and as there is no one living who remembers that there was a Baptist Church in New London in those early days.

SALT RIVER ASSOCIATION.

The six churches, Ramsey Creek, Stout's Settlement, New London, Bethlehem, Bear Creek and Peno, having agreed to meet by messengers at Peno Church, Saturday, August 23, 1823, to confer as to the wisdom

Organization.

of organizing an Association, met agreeable to appointment. "The introductory sermon was preached," says the record, "by Brother Jeremiah Taylor from "Chronicles, twelfth chapter, thirty-second verse; And of the children of Isaachar, which were men that had understanding of the times, to know what Israel ought to do; the heads of them were two hundred; and all their brethren were at their commandments."

The enrollment showed the following list of messengers:

Ramsey Creek: Thomas Buchanan.

Stout's Settlement: Joseph Sitton, Jesse Sitton, William Sitton.

New London: Dabney Jones, William Forman, William Carson.

Bethlehem: Joel Griffith, Vincent Kelly, Silas Wilson.

Bear Creek: George Turner, Charles L. Turner, John Rush, Bannester Gregory.

Peno: Davis Biggs, William Biggs, Leroy Jackson.

Elder Davis Biggs was elected moderator. William Carson was elected clerk. A committee of one from each church was appointed to prepare a Constitution and Rules of Decorum and make report on Monday. Adjourned till 9 o'clock Monday. On Sunday, the twenty-fourth, Brother Jesse Sitton preached from II Corinthians, 8:9: "For ye know the grace of our Lord Jesus Christ, that though he was rich, yet for your sakes he became poor, that ye through his poverty might become rich."

Brother Davis Biggs followed from Ephesians, 4:5: "One Lord, one faith, one baptism;" Brother Jeremiah Taylor from the Gospel by John, 14:1, 2: "Let not your heart be troubled: ye believe in God, believe also in me. In my Father's house are many mansions: if it were not so, I would have told you. I go to prepare a place for you;" Brother Leroy Jackson from the Prophet Isaiah, 25:10: "For in this mountain shall the hand of the Lord rest, and Moab shall be trodden down under him, even as straw is trodden for the dunghill." Saturday they closed with prayer by the moderator. Monday, the 25th, they opened with prayer by Bro. Taylor.

The Committee on Constitution and Rules, which consisted of Jesse Sitton, William Carson, Silas Wilson, Charles L. Turner and William Biggs, reported. The report was discussed, amended and adopted.

"Agreed that this Association be called the Salt River Association in the State of Missouri. Bro. Leroy Jackson was appointed to preach the next introductory sermon and in case of failure Davis Biggs." The Association adjourned to be held at Bear Creek Church, Ralls county, to begin on the first Saturday in October, 1824. The limits of Bear Creek Church were within what was then Ralls county.

The entire membership of the new Association was ninety-five, as follows: Ramsey Creek, 18; Stout's Settlement, 9; New London, 14; Bethlehem, 11; Bear Creek, 18; Peno, 25. The resident ministers were Leroy Jackson, Davis Biggs and Jesse Sitton. Bro. Jeremiah Taylor seems to have been a visitor.

So far as I can learn there was no church owning a house of worship at the time Salt River Association was formed.

The place of meeting was on Peno Creek, the house being situated on a hill rising in a column of hills from the first bottom on the east bank of the stream. Walnut, white oak, hickory and cherry trees densely covered the ground which lay open for stock-range and convenient travel. The wild rose, the goldenrod and a profusion of other flowers adorned the undulating stretches of woodland. Coming down from the untamed prairie which lay five or six miles to the southwest was Middle Creek, a small stream, which entered Peno less than a half-mile across and south from Peno Church. The house was built of hewn logs and fronted south. It was some twenty by twenty-five feet in size, the long way east and west, the pulpit in the north side opposite the front door. A door was on the west, a window was on the north over the pulpit, and the

ELDER JEREMIAH VARDEMAN.

HON. WM. CARSON.

house being used for school purposes, a long window was in the east and another window was in front. A stove was towards the northeast corner. The house was situated some one hundred yards off the Palmyra and St. Louis road, which was a main thoroughfare for the transportation of goods and for driving live stock to market. The stage carrying the United States mail and four-horse and six-horse wagons were constantly on the road.

The lateness of the time in summer when the organization occurred would find these early citizens with a few days they could snatch from the imperious duties of their newly opened farms. With the reap-hook the husbandman had harvested his wheat crop, which he would later tramp out on his threshing-floor, his corn was well grown and only needed to be protected from the ravages of squirrels, coons, turkeys and deer. Their cattle and young horses were running on the range and were growing into money without expense for pasture.

They had chosen a geographically central place for the meeting and they would come to it on horseback. A ride of one day would bring the remotest of them to Peno. These Missouri pioneers were representative men. They were gentlemen of education, culture and large business capability. They had brought with them to their new homes personal characters and material possessions. They desired to set forth before their fellow-citizens Jesus the Christ crucified for them. They came to the meeting as they lived at home, dressed in the clothes produced by the industries of home life, shoes, pants, shirts and coats made at home. Imported goods from the cities were rare, but gentle manners and devout hearts were many.

Articles of Faith of Salt River Association, adopted August the 25th, 1823:

"1. We believe in one only true and living God, and that there are three offices in the godhead, the Father, the Son and the Holy Spirit, and these three are one.

"2. The Scriptures of the Old and New Testaments are the word of God, and the only rule of faith and practice.

"3. That by nature we are fallen and depraved creatures.

"4. That salvation, regeneration, justification and sanctification are only by the life, death, resurrection and ascension of the Lord Jesus Christ and the operation of the Holy Ghost.

"5. That all the saints will finally persevere through grace to glory.

"6. That believer's baptism is only by immersion and is necessary to the receiving the Lord's Supper.

"7. That the salvation of the righteous and the punishment of the wicked will be eternal.

"8. That no minister has a right to administer the ordinances until he legally comes under the imposition of hands.

"9. That it is our duty to be tender one towards another and study generally the happiness of God's people at large and endeavor to promote the honor and glory of God.

"10. We believe in election by grace.

"11. It is our duty to commune with all orderly Baptists only.

"12. That each church has a right to keep up its own government as to it may seem best."

Elder Davis Biggs.

Spencer in his history of "Kentucky Baptists," Semple, in his Virginia History, and Cathcart, in his "Baptist Encyclopedia," all got the name wrong.

It is not David but Davis Biggs. Duncan in his history of "Missouri Baptists" says Davis Biggs was born in Camden county, North Carolina, March 8, 1763. "His father, John Biggs, who emigrated from England many years before the Revolutionary War, was of Welsh extraction. He was a soldier of the war of 1766. On account of which and during his ab-

Organization. 51

sence the British and Tories stripped him of almost everything he could call his own, save his lands." He seems to have enjoyed the best advantage, educationally, within easy reach of his home. Duncan's history further says "When Davis Biggs was but a boy his father died, not a great while after which he determined to try a seafaring life, to commence which he embarked on the Black Ship which was going out to the West Indies after a cargo of salt. In these days the seas were infested with pirates who captured many a merchant vessel and filled their coffers with the rich treasures on board. The Black Ship was a medium sized vessel of sixty-two guns. They had a pleasant sail out and with difficulty secured their cargo of salt and started home. On the way they had a desperate encounter with two privateers and after several hours battle succeeded in driving back the pirates and were no more molested. Once more at home our young seaman concluded he had enough of a sailor's life and determined to spend the remainder of his minority at the old homestead under the care and training of fond and loving mother.

He had three brothers, Robert, the eldest, and John and Imoriah, the last named became a Baptist preacher but was cut down in the prime of life in the State of North Carolina. He professed religion in early life. At the age of eighteen years he married Miss Anna Morris, daughter of Jesse Morris of Camden, North Carolina. He began preaching about the age of twenty years and in 1797 was called to the pastorate of the Baptist church of Portsmouth, Virginia. He seemed to have been an active Christian and an exhorter and teacher in the church before he was formally licensed to preach. He was licensed in 1791. We learn from Semple's history that Baptists at Portsmouth church under the labors of Eld. Davis Biggs moved on in a tranquil manner. We also quote from that history as follows: "Eld. Biggs is a sound and ingenious preacher and esteemed by his acquaintances as an exemplary man."

Spencer's "History of Kentucky Baptists" says of him: "He came to Kentucky about the year 1804 and was at different times a member of Indian Creek church in Harrison county, and Silas church in Bourbon. In 1811 he preached the introductory sermon before Elk Horn Association. He labored in Kentucky at least sixteen years and here as in Virginia maintained a good character and was a useful preacher." He came to Missouri in 1820 and settled in Pike county, living a short time on Peno Creek and then moving to Grassy Creek, five miles northwest of Louisiana, where he died. The following account of him is interesting as coming from his grandson, ex-Senator George K. Biggs. He says of him: "He was a very pious man in his family, having family worship every night and morning regularly as the day came. Once or twice a week at such times he would sing, "The day is past and gone," and in the morning would sing, "And when we early rise to view the unwearied sun," and at other times he would sing, "Saw ye my Savior." He was extremely pleasant if they all did as he said. If not he would say, "Order must be had in my family." I never heard him give my grandmother a short word. He was all kindness if we did right. I sometimes thought he was a little hard, but I found he was not.

"I was raised to believe my grandfather Biggs could do no wrong, but afterwards saw that I was mistaken. I stayed with him and grandmother six months in the fall and winter of 1831 and 1832, going to school. Then I learned to know him. He was a very hard student then, although about seventy-nine years of age. He was rather a dignified man and would have no idlers around him. He always had something for idle hands to do, either spiritual or temporal work at home or abroad. In preaching his voice was smooth and pathetic, never on a loud key. He would commence in an ordinary tone and raise his voice as he proceeded. He always quoted scripture to sustain his points. He was a very strong Baptist and made no compromises. I remember many of his sermons and was raised under his preaching. His sentences were well rounded and he spoke very distinctly but not very fast. He did not have much of a sing-song and I thought him lacking in this respect, for that was the fashion in those days. A favorite subject with him was Paul shipwrecked. I almost fancy I hear my dear old grandfather and see him standing still with his hands uplifted and his eyes running over the congregation with Brother Paul and his shipload of anxious souls which he got every one to land and not one lost. And then I have seen them weeping in the congregation. He would then sit down and commence singing, 'Saw ye my Savior and God,' in his pleasant voice, and I thought it the finest music I ever heard. He often used similes in his preaching; he loved the parables and Christ's Sermon on the Mount. I have heard the brethren say, if you want doctrine, get Bro. Biggs; want revival, get Bro. Suggett or Gentry; or later, Bro. Vardeman. He was a strong reasoner. His height was about five feet six or seven inches; weight from one hundred and seventy-five to two hundred pounds, shoulders rather round and stood a little stooped. He was a very stout man and enjoyed good health. His head was round and large and his forehead tolerably prominent.

Cathcart's Encyclopedia says of Elder Davis Biggs: "He labored with marked success for fifty years and the prosperity of the denomination in northeast Missouri is largely due to his ministry." He was the first moderator of Salt River Baptist Association, which place he held for six years. He died August 6, 1845. His wife, Anna Biggs, died ten days later. Both deaths occurred on the old homestead on Grassy Creek and the honored patriarch and his faithful wife lie side by side in the neighboring cemetery.

CHAPTER III.

GROWTH AND ELIMINATION, 1824-1834.

At Peno the Association adjourned to meet in 1824 with Bear Creek Church, but there is no record of a meeting in that year. There is a blank in the record book where the record ought to be, indicating that there was an expectation that it would be inserted. I have asked, "Was there a meeting in 1824?" but I have no answer.

In 1825 the Association met with Ramsey Creek Church. The introductory sermon was preached by Elder Davis Biggs from the text, "And they stoned Stephen, calling upon God, and saying, Lord Jesus, receive my spirit."

Elder Davis Biggs was elected moderator and William Sitton clerk. The visiting brethren were Darius Bainbridge and Bethuel Riggs. "Letters from seven churches were received," from which I conclude that the seventh, Providence, came into the Association in 1824. The membership had grown from 95 to 175. There was preaching by Elders Riggs, Bainbridge and Sitton. Two additional churches are given in the list this year, Siloam and Bethel. The messengers from Siloam were Wm. Williams, Thomas Brashere and Stafford McGee; James Laythem was the messenger from Bethel.

In 1826, Siloam Church, Pike county, was the place of meeting. The introductory sermon was preached by Elder Jabus Ham from the text: "So he drove out the man." The visiting brethren were Thomas R. Musick and Jabus Ham. South River Church was received into the Association; the messengers were Hawkins Smith and Benjamin Thomas.

In 1827 the Association met with Bethel Church, Marion county. The introductory sermon was preached by Elder Davis Biggs from the text: The forty-seventh chapter of Ezekiel. It seems to have been an expository sermon, abundant riches for which is found in this chapter. Jeremiah Taylor was chosen moderator and Wm. Carson clerk. Salt River Church, Ralls county, and Quincy, Ill., churches were received into the Association. The messengers from Salt River were Bethuel Riggs, Isaac Ely and William Forman; from Quincy, William Roberds and James G. Wooton. The visitors were James Suggett, John Greenhalgh, Edward Turner, Joseph Littrel, Joseph Bragg and Thomas R. Musick. There was preaching by Elder James Suggett, John Greenhalgh, E. Turner and Thomas R. Musick. Union meetings were appointed for Ramsey Creek, New London and Bear Creek Churches.

Peno Church entertained the Association in 1828. Elder Vivian Ridgeway preached the sermon from the scripture: "Who was delivered for our offences, and was raised again for our justification." Davis Biggs was chosen moderator and Wm. Carson clerk. The membership had increased to 281. The visitors were Edward Turner, J. Ratcliff, James Littrel, David Hubbard, David Clark, James Suggett, Vivian Ridgeway and James Barnes. In the early days of the Association the matter of correspondence and corresponding messengers had a large place in the advancement of the kingdom of Jesus Christ. It was the principal means of mutual information and coöperation. These visiting messengers carried in their own persons most of the spirit and purpose of evangelism which has since taken form in the organization of boards and societies, which are usually represented by agents. A letter was granted to the church in Stout's Settlement to unite with Cuivre Association. There was preaching by Elders Ridgeway, Barnes, Ratcliff, Hubbard, Turner and Suggett.

Ramsey Creek entertained the body in 1829. Elder Leroy Jackson preached. His text was: "So thou, O son of man, I have set thee a watchman unto the house of Israel; therefore thou shalt hear the word of my mouth, and warn them from me." Davis Biggs was chosen moderator and William Biggs clerk; the father moderator, the son clerk. Atlas Church, Illinois, was received into fellowship, bringing a membership of five. Ozeas Hale was the messenger. The membership of the Association now is 271. The visiting brethren were J. Ratcliff, Joseph Oliver, David Hubbard, —— Stendrow, —— Gilliland, John Lee, James Suggett and Anderson Woods. There was preaching by Elders Suggett, Ratcliff, Woods and Lee.

"South River Meeting House," Marion county, was the place where the session of 1830 was held. The sermon was preached by Elder Davis Biggs from the text: "The throne had six steps, and the top of the throne was round behind: and there were stays on either side of the place of the seat, and two lions stood beside the stays. And twelve lions stood there on the one side and on the other upon the six steps." William Fuqua was chosen moderator and William Carson clerk. Spencer Creek Church was received into the Association; William Desine and Elijah Williams were the messengers. The membership was 13. The whole number in the churches now was 343. The visiting brethren were Edward Turner, Thomas Turner, James Suggett. The church in Quincy having ceased to send messengers, a committee was sent to inquire into her condition. They reported at this meeting that "they had visited said church and ascertained she had *desolved* her constitution." There was preaching by Thomas Turner, E. Turner, James Suggett and William Fuqua.

Siloam Church entertained the body in 1831. Elder William Fuqua preached the introductory sermon from the scripture: "Again he sent forth other servants, saying, tell them which are bidden, behold, I have prepared my dinner: my oxen and my fatlings are killed, and all things are ready: come unto the marriage." Wm. Biggs was chosen moderator and Wm. Carson clerk. Bethlehem Church, Monroe county, was received into fellowship; her membership was 20. Edward Turner and John Looney were the messengers. The visiting brethren were Allen McGuire, James Barnes, David Hubbard, Darius Bainbridge, George W. Zimmerman, John M. Faulconer and John Lee. "By request, the church at Atlas is dismissed from this Association with a view of joining a new Association." Elders Christy Gentry, Bainbridge, Hubbard, Turner, McElfresh and McGuire preached on the occasion.

"October, May, June and August were the times chosen to hold the union meetings of the Association. These were for revival, not business meetings. Great interest was taken in the spiritual advancement and the Biblical instruction of the church members. This is shown in the records in many ways. Over and over a day was set apart for fasting and prayer; sometimes a church would send the request and the acceptance would be general and cheerful. This service is one calling for heart-tone and voluntary devotion. The urgency comes not from without but from within, not from thunder-riven Sinai or even from the cry on the great day of the feast, but our Holy Lord gently approaches us with words of grace falling like honey from the rock and putting the key into our hands. He bids us withdraw from the maddening throng when we are hungering after righteousness, and join with those who are poor in spirit that we may give the body its true, lower place while the soul seeks its own supreme awakening at a throne of grace. The feet of these men must have sometimes touched the mount of transfiguration. "My soul shall be satisfied as with marrow and fatness; and my mouth shall praise thee with joyful lips," said David. Also, they appointed frequent meetings where churches were to cooperate in gospel service. Such meetings must have been theological seminaries, pentecostal seasons and evangelistic advancement all in one. One of these meetings was held at Bear Creek in 1830, "Elders Wm. Fuqua, J. Taylor and Mordecai Boulware to attend." At another time Elders Davis Biggs and Leroy Jackson were to attend. At another, "Brethren Vardeman, Hendren, Gentry, Turner, McQuie and Taylor agreed to attend it." In this way Bible doctrine and life, gospel rites and service, Christian experience and growth would be preached as having their source and roots in the love of God revealed in Jesus the Anointed One and by the personal operation of the Holy Spirit. It makes one's heart burn within him to think of such assemblies where the truth was firmly held, the whole message delivered, the worshipers were reverent and the songs were both prayer and praise.

New London Church appears in the minutes for the last time in 1831. The record is sorrowful. It runs: "New London, no letter. Church dissolved." In 1828 messengers came for the last time. They were Dabney Jones and James Turley. The membership was then sixteen, the day of business meeting the fourth Saturday. It is strengthening to the faith of the disciples to see that these men of God having done all, stood, notwithstanding in some places the ground seemed lost. At the same session at which New London is recorded as dissolved we have this beautiful record:

"On motion of Brother D. Biggs it is agreed that the messengers of this Association do request all the members of their respective churches to engage in solemn prayer to God for a revival of religion among us, between sunset and dark of each day." The eye of faith was on God and the incoming year placed the feet of the messengers who bring good tidings upon the mountain of God. "The word of God increased; and the number of the disciples multiplied."

Bear Creek Church, in territory now in Marion county, was the home of Salt River Association in 1832. Elder Edmond Turner preached the introductory sermon from the text: "For God, who commanded the light to shine out of darkness, hath shined in our hearts, to give the light of the knowledge of the glory of God in the face of Jesus Christ." Wm. Biggs was elected moderator and Wm. Carson clerk. Salem Church, Ralls county, was received into Associational fellowship; her numerical strength was 31. Elder Jeremiah Vardeman was her messenger. The visiting brethren were Thomas Fristoe, James Suggett, Theodoric Boulware, — McCutchen, — Bailey and David Hubbard. Sermons were preached by Elders Hubbard, Boulware, Suggett, Fristoe, Turner and Vardeman. The churches now have 419 members.

The Association was entertained in 1833 by a new church on the west fork of Peno, now called Mt. Pleasant. Elder Christy Gentry preached the annual sermon from the scripture: "For Christ is the end of the law for righteousness to every one that believeth." Wm. Biggs was chosen moderator and Wm. H. Holmes clerk. The Association received into her fellowship nine new churches. They were Palmyra with twenty-eight members; the messengers were Wm. McCree, Wm. Wright, Wm. Brice, George Mock; Mt. Pleasant of Pike county with eighty-eight members; Joseph Coldwell and Samuel Lewellen were the messengers; North Fork with twenty-five members; George Williams and David Hubbard Jessur, messengers; Union, with fifty-four members, the messengers, Waggoner Capps and Daniel Capps; Mount Pleasant, Marion county, (nothing more given); Noix Creek of Pike county, with thirty-three members, the messengers, Walter McQuie, Thos. B. Hedges; Gwinn's Creek of Lincoln county, with nineteen members, the messengers, John Palmer, Peter Moss and John Daniel; Little Union of Marion county, with thirty-two members, the messenger, Noah Flood; and Union of Pike county, with thirteen members, L. C. Musick, messenger. The visitors were Brethren Woods, Counts, and George W. Zimmerman. There was preaching by Elders Woods, Hubbard and Gentry. The membership of the churches had now reached 874.

The session of 1834 was one of great purport. Salt River Church, Ralls county, entertained the body, September 22d to 24th. Elder David Hubbard preached the introductory sermon from the text: "Therefore I said, Harken to me; I also will show mine opinion." Wm. Biggs was chosen moderator and Wm. Carson, clerk. Six new churches were received into the fellowship of the Association. These were Indian Creek, with fourteen members, the messengers were A. M. Leak, Joseph Carman, E. Peak; Mt. Moriah, with twenty-four members, the messengers, B. Parsons, R. Travis, W. Holloway; Elk Fork with thirteen members, messenger, Ezra Fox; Wyaconda, with nineteen members, messenger, Robert Senclair; Mount Pleasant, (no more is told); Gilead, with twenty-three members, messengers, J. M. Lillard, J. Thomas and S. Briscoe; Mt. Pisgah, Pike county, with twenty-two members, messengers, H. Hawkins, E. Bondurant and J. F. Hedges. The visiting brethren were: Anderson Woods, John M. Peck and Brother Zimmerman. There was preaching by Elders Peck, Woods, Patterson and Hubbard, and Brother Vardeman delivered an exhortation to a large congregation at the close of which several mourners came forward to be prayed for.

There had been constant and rapid growth. Steadily new churches had been added to the Association. Some had gone out, as I have narrated, and still in 1834, there were twenty-six churches, more than quadruple the number that were in the organization nine years previous. The Lord had dealt bountifully with Salt River Association. The membership of the churches was now 1,143.

The territory had now become large, reaching to the north indefinitely, for what is now the State of Iowa had not, in 1834, been organized into a Territorial Government. To meet the existing conditions steps were taken to constitute a new Association out of the Salt River membership. Those who wanted to go into the new body requested dismission for that purpose and the Association took this action:

"The following churches, in compliance with their request, were dismissed to form a new Association, viz: Bethel, Little Union, Palmyra, Bear Creek, Pleasant Hill, Salt River, Providence, South River, Wyaconda, Gilead, Indian Creek, North Fork, Paris and Elk Fork; the said churches to meet by messengers at Bethel, Marion county, Missouri, on the Friday before the 3rd Saturday in October, 1834, to organize; Brother C. Gentry to act as moderator, and William Carson as clerk until a moderator and clerk are elected." This movement took more than half of the churches into the new body. It is not within the scope of this volume to follow these men and churches in their new fields, but some account of the churches while they were with us and life-sketches of some of the men are in harmony with our intention.

The laymen in the first session of the body gave promise of substantial service by our business men. Thomas Buchanan, William Sitton, William Carson, Vincent Kelly, Banester Gregory, William Biggs and Dabney Jones were some of them. They were men of character and capability; that promise has been realized in our business men of each generation.

MT. PISGAH BAPTIST CHURCH.

By Judge A. P. Miller, Written 1883.

Mt. Pisgah was organized December 5, 1833, at the house of Harmon Hawkins, within three hundred yards of where the meeting-house now stands, it being the second Baptist church (Peno being the first) constituted in Cuivre township, Pike county, Missouri, five miles northwest of Bowling Green. It was principally a colony of the old Peno church, some four miles north, which is now extinct. This same Peno church was organized in December, 1819, it being in territorial times, or before the great commonwealth of Missouri was a State in our federal union. In the organization of Mt. Pisgah church, there were nineteen members, all of whom have passed over the river to their reward. There were three ministers in attendance to aid this little band in erecting the cross at Mt.

Pisgah, and the same was declared to be known and named as Mt. Pisgah church.

The following persons went into the organization at the time: Harmon Hawkins, Edward Bondurant, Benjamin B. Moore, Benjamin T. Hawkins, Thos. T. Johnson, Diggs Luck, William G. Hawkins, Geo. Hardin and Sisters Jincy Hawkins, Nancy Moore, Lavina Bentley, Elizabeth Tinker, Jemima Thomas, Lucy Luck, Marguerite M. Johnson, Rachel Moore, Jane and Milley, two colored women. They then proceeded to elect Harmon Hawkins and Thos. T. Johnson to the office of Deacons, and William G. Hawkins, church clerk.

The little band after organization at once began to look around for a house to worship God in. Deacon Harmon Hawkins agreed to take the job of erecting a huge log house 24x30 feet, one story high, with a shingle roof and a plank floor, with two plank doors and three windows to be filled with glass, and a plank box for a pulpit. All of this work was done by piecemeal or at odd times by the brethren and a few outside friends. Deacon Hawkins cut, scored and hued the logs, and he and his son, William G., built the chimney of stone; taken all together it was a pretty fine house for that age of the church and country. Very little money, not exceeding twenty dollars, was used in making this, the second house of worship in Cuivre township. In fact the members were poor financially, having very little money for any purpose. This house was sold for twenty or twenty-five dollars in 1852.

The first Saturday in February, 1834, the church called Deacon Thomas T. Johnson to become her pastor, after being set apart by ordination.

At the June meeting, 1834, a Presbytery consisting of Elders Davis, Biggs and Walter McQuie, met with the church and proceeded to set apart by ordination, Bro. Thomas T. Johnson, to the gospel ministry, who was then installed by the church as their pastor, which position he held continuously until 1844.

At the June meeting, 1835, Bro. Edward Bondurant was chosen Deacon. At the February meeting, 1837. appointed Bro. Benjamin Johnson, Deacon, Bro. Bondurant having removed from the county. At the February meeting, 1844, Deacons Hawkins and Johnson, being displeased with the action of the church in some case of discipline, asked for letters of dismission, which were granted—thus creating a vacancy in the office of deacon and at the same meeting Brothers Henry Sisson and Roland Gooch were chosen instead.

In February, 1844, Elder Walter McQuie, was chosen and installed as Pastor, Elder Johnson declining to serve longer. Elder McQuie continued to serve in the pastorate until January, 1846, a period of two years. The years of 1839 and 1840 the church was blessed with a glorious revival, between forty and fifty additions being made to the church.

At the February meeting, 1851, Elder James F. Smith became Pastor, there having some two months previous been a great revival with some fifty additions to the church, in which Elder Smith was the principal actor. In May following, 1851, Elder Smith and family became members of the church by letter.

In July, 1851, the church appointed a building committee with instructions to have completed at as early a day as possible, a new house of worship, to be 40x60 ft. of frame work, and the whole management, construction, etc., to be given to Brothers A. P. Miller, Henry Sisson and James M. Frier.

In September, 1851, she dismissed twenty-five members by letter to organize a new church on North Cuivre, afterwards called "Concord," and still later or in a few years the church "Concord" was dissolved, a part of the members returning to the mother church.

In February, 1852, Brother W. G. Hawkins tendered his resignation as clerk, and Brother A. P. Miller was elected thereto. In May, 1852, the church held its first meeting in their new house. In August, 1853, the building committee turned over the church, the new house completed, at the cost of about ten hundred and fifty dollars, exclusive of materials and labor furnished, such as hauling and burning lime kiln.

In April, 1854, Elder William Hurley agreed to preach one Sabbath in each month for one year. In June, 1854, fourteen members were dismissed to go to a new organization at Bowling Green, Mo.

In October, 1854, Elder Hurley was released from his engagement with us, he having received a call from Ashley. At the November meeting, 1855, Elder Smith tendered his resignation as Pastor, he having been invited to become the Pastor of two churches in Callaway county, he having served the church here nearly five years. In May, 1856, we called Elder William W. Mitchell to the pastorate, which he accepted.

In October, 1856, the church granted license to preach the gospel to Brothers A. P. Rodgers and Thomas H. Luck. In December, 1857, Elder W. W. Mitchell tendered his resignation as Pastor, which was accepted, having served one year and eight months.

In January, 1858, the church unanimously called Elder Jno. T. Williams. In March, 1858, he accepted and entered upon the duties. At the October meeting, 1858, a Presbytery consisting of Elder John T. Williams and W. W. Mitchell met with the church and proceeded in the usual way to set apart to the gospel ministry Brother A. P. Rodgers.

In March, 1859, Elder John T. Williams, on account of other engagements, tendered his resignation as Pastor, which was accepted, he having served one year. The church then called to the pastorate Elder Alex P. Rodgers, who accepted at the next May meeting, 1859. The church invited Elder Jno. M. Johnson to occupy one Sunday in each month, which he consented to do.

In September, 1861, the church declined to send messengers to the Association on account of political disturbances then existing. At the May meeting, 1862, Elder Rodgers tendered his resignation as Pastor; accepted—time of service, three years. Elder

Growth and Elimination. 65

Rodgers at the June meeting was recalled and at the following July meeting accepted, 1862.

At the April meeting in 1864, owing to a military order issued by Gen. Rosecrans, meetings for business were suspended till December following. The meetings were resumed.

During the time of the suspension, Elder Rodgers resigned again, having served the church this time about two years—in all five years. In November, 1864, the church called Elder M. M. Modisett to the care of the body, who accepted and entered upon the duties at once. Elder John T. Williams was invited to occupy our pulpit one Sunday in each month—agreed to.

In April, 1871, elected two Deacons, Benjamin H. McPike and M. R. K. Biggs, Deacons Roland Gooch having died within the last year, and Henry Sisson within the last month.

At the meeting October, 1872, Elder Modisett tendered his resignation, having served the church continuously for eight years. During his pastorate, with the assistance of Elder H. M. Boyd, of the C. P. Church in 1867-68, about thirty hopeful converts were baptized. At the October meeting, 1872, by a unanimous vote, Elder A. G. Mitchell was called to take the oversight of the church, who at the December meeting following accepted and immediately entered upon the duties. October meeting, 1875, granted letters of dismission to several members to form a church at Curryville. At the November meeting, 1876, Elder A. G. Mitchell resigned his charge as pastor, which was accepted, he having removed from this to St. Charles county. He served the church for a period of four years with his characteristic faithfulness.

At the December meeting, 1876, by a unanimous vote, Elder Wiley J. Patrick was invited to become their Pastor, who, in January, 1877, accepted, and at once entered upon the duties, and is now (1883) still serving the church with great acceptance.

At the August meeting, 1877, Bro. A. P. Miller offered his resignation as church clerk, which was accepted and Bro. William B. McPike was elected his successor.

A protracted meeting was held for seventeen days, at which some twenty souls were added to the church. In October, 1879, a series of meetings were held and eleven were added to the church by baptism. In October, 1883, ten more were added to the church by baptism. In December, 1884, twelve were added to the church.

At the June meeting in 1887 Elder W. J. Patrick declined to accept the call of the church, having served ten years continuously.

At the October meeting, 1887, Bro. W. A. Bibb became Pastor and served till January meeting in 1893. Quite a number were added to the church during his pastorate.

At the February meeting, 1894, Elder F. M. Birkhead was called and at once accepted the care of the church; served till February, 1901.

At the March meeting in 1901 Eld. E. J. Edwards was chosen Pastor and at the December meeting following gave up the care of the church.

Eld. A. P. Rodgers acted as supply till December, 1902, when J. W. Long accepted the call of the church. During his pastorate the present church building was erected, he taking a very active part in the work, and said building was dedicated to the cause of the Master August 2, 1903.

At the September meeting Brother Long offered his resignation, which was accepted with reluctance by the church.

At the November meeting, 1903, Eld. E. L. Barkley was chosen Pastor. During his pastorate he was assisted in a protracted meeting in February, 1904, by Bro. J. H. Briscoe, of Knox City, Mo., and thirty-six were added to the church. Brother Barkley served one year.

At the April meeting, 1905, Bro. J. H. Terrill was elected as Pastor and served the church for two years.

In January, 1908, Bro. Luke Kirtley accepted the call of the church and is pastor at present, 1909.

MT. PLEASANT CHURCH.

By T. J. Ayres.

This body was organized February 26, 1833, following a great revival, which seemed to have sprung up spontaneously in the neighborhood. The services were held in the homes of Judge George Mock, Wm. Brown, Wm. Hammers, Corben Benn and perhaps other homes. Eld. Jeremiah Vardeman was the minister in charge. The records do not show just the number or names of the constituent members. The writer learned the above facts, with some others, from Sister Clarinda Brashears, who was for some years a member of this church. She was a daughter of Wm. Brown, above referred to as one at whose house a part of these revival services were held. Since interviewing this sister she has passed away, at the advanced age of eighty-six years. She was about twelve years of age and remembered distinctly that the ice was cut and some fifteen or twenty were baptized on one occasion, including her father and mother. She also remembered that a daughter of Mrs. George Pearce, who was delicate, was included in the number, and that her mother was much concerned, lest her baptism might prove to be injurious. She also recalled that a certain citizen, while out hunting in the timber, came upon Mr. John Brown (father of the late George and James Brown) down on his knees praying in a loud voice. The records do not show who composed the organizing presbytery. Rev. J. Vardeman was Pastor from the organization. An unusual action of the church in October, 1835, was the calling of Eld. Christy Gentry "to superintend the pastoral care of the church jointly with" Elder Vardeman. In May,

1836, a resolution was adopted "taking up the subject of contributing to the support of the gospel," and a committee was appointed to receive contributions.

In June, 1836, Elders J. Vardeman and C. Gentry assumed pastoral care jointly. In August following the treasurer was ordered to pay each pastor $15.

In April, 1838, Timothy P. Rodgers was admitted to membership and in July of same year was licensed to preach. Eld. J. Vardeman continued as Pastor until his death, which occurred between the April and May meetings in 1842. Eld. J. M. Bailey succeeded to the pastorate up to September, 1844, and he was succeeded by Eld. Walter McQuie. A division on the question of missions occurred at the August meeting, 1843, and several members took letters.

At the May meeting, 1844, "a vigilance committee was appointed to see that no intrusions are practiced on the church by the Mormons, and to guard the rights and privileges of the church while exercising any of her religious functions." When Elder McQuie was called a committee was appointed to learn how much "in trade" would be required to secure his services. Elder McQuie accepted the call, but the amount "in trade" required was not recorded.

In 1845 the treasuryship was transferred from the treasurer to the Deacons, and a committee appointed to settle with the treasurer, revealed the fact that the church was in debt to the treasurer $2.74, whereupon two contributions reduced the deficit to $1.99 1-4. Eld. T. T. Johnson was called to the pastorate in January, 1846, and served one year, and Eld. Wm. H. Vardeman succeeded him in January, 1847. The first definite action looking to mission work in the Association was taken in July, 1847.

The first reference to Eld. Dudley V. Inlow, in the records, shows that he was appointed clerk pro tem at the May meeting in 1848; at the June meeting same year Bro. Wm. Brown was elected Deacon, and D. V. Inlow clerk. In July he was appointed to write the letter to the Association to meet at Bethel church in Ralls county the following September, and Eld. Wm. H. Vardeman prepared first letter to the General Association. Rev. J. M. Johnson was called in November, 1848, but did not begin his pastorate until April, 1849.

Rev. D. V. Inlow was licensed to preach October 26, 1850. At the July meeting, 1851, the church agreed to ordain him, which ordination occurred at the regular meeting in October following. The record does not show who took part in the ceremonies. In December following Brother Inlow (at his request) was released from the clerkship, and Bro. J. H. Ayres was elected clerk. The church built a brick house. The first service in the new building was the regular September meeting, 1857.

The November meeting, 1860, was protracted. The pastor was assisted by Revs. J. H. Keach and M. M. Modisett; church greatly revived and eighteen added to the membership.

Eld. J. M. Johnson served continuously as Pastor till March, 1862, and Eld. H. M. King was called in April and served till March, 1865. One remarkable thing was that the services at this church continued practically without a break throughout the war.

Will the reader pardon a digression just here, while the writer relates an incident, briefly, which occurred in 1864.

The author of this history (Dr. W. J. Patrick) had come from his home in Monroe county to perform his first marriage ceremony, uniting his friend and schoolmate, Dr. S. B. Ayres, and Miss Sue E. Woodson in marriage. A meeting being in progress at Mt. Pleasant, the writer, at his request, went with him to the meeting. After the service, and just as we left the church, a squad of armed men, under the leadership of a party claiming authority to conscript men for the southern army, came charging down from the west and intercepted us. After skillful manoeuvering and faithful promises, we were temporarily excused, attended the wedding, but in the midst of the ceremony a rap at the door was followed by the entrance of a squad of armed men, which frightened and to some extent scattered the crowd, some going without partaking of the wedding feast. Such is war.

The church employed various pastors from this date with varying successes and reverses, to-wit: Elders Wheeler, E. J. Sanderson, W. A. Bibb, S. S. Keith, E. Jennings and perhaps others, with reasonably regular services up to May, 1897, since which no regular services have been maintained, except that records show that Rev. J. W. Trower preached from March till October, 1899.

The records further show that Deacon Chris Liter called a meeting September 10, 1901, at which Brethren W. J. Patrick and J. D. Biggs each preached a sermon, and the church appointed two committees, one to look after the property and the other to revise the list of membership, but the records do not show that anything more has been done. Thus it seems that this, at one time one of the strongest churches composing the Association, has become almost extinct.

NOIX CREEK CHURCH.

By J. S. Martin, A. M. Edwards, C. S. Burks.

From the best information we can gather from the oldest members now living, the church was organized about the year 1831. We can not tell who was first Pastor. The church came into the Association in 1833. Messengers: Walter McQuie and Thomas B. Hedges, but the following ministers were occasionally at the church and preached between 1831 and 1840: Davis Biggs, Wm. Hurley, Jeremiah Vardeman, — Bowers, David Hubbard, W. D. Grant, T. T. Johnson, Walter McQuie, J. F. Hedges, J. M. Johnson. Services were first held in a log schoolhouse situated half-mile south of John E. Shannon's residence and fifty yards east of where the first church building was erected.

The following churches were offshoots of Noix Creek: Louisiana, Walnut Grove, Mt. Zion, Bethany, Grassy Creek, Sugar Creek. Bro. A. D. Landrum was Pastor from 1842 until about 1850, when he quit the ministry on account of failing health, and during all these years the church had a steady growth.

Rev. J. F. Smith held a protracted meeting with the church in November, 1850, which resulted in about seventy-five being added to the church, soon after which he was called to the pastorate of the church, in which capacity he served until 1856, holding a successful protracted meeting in November of each year.

Rev. M. M. Modisett was elected Pastor in 1856 and served the church several years and was succeeded by J. T. Williams. Then came H. M. King and others.

The following preachers were licensed by the church to preach: S. G. Givens, Ed. Jennings, G. B. Smith, W. W. Brown, E. J. Edwards, John Davenport, Byron Bibb.

When the Civil War came it did not seem to disturb the church but very little, but everything seemed to move on as if there was no conflict raging. It seemed that when we met to worship those of the Union and Confederate armies met around the same altar and rejoiced in the forgiveness of their sins.

The following are a few of the old members: Uncle Billie Shannon (father of J. E.), Thomas Hedges, J. F. Hedges, Geo. W. Peay, N. B. Edwards, O. C. Tinker, William Waddell, Morris Biggs, Dr. W. W. Wise, John Shepherd, James Brown, R. T. Martin; Sisters: Mrs. Champ Smith, Mrs. Diggs Luck, Mrs. Matilda Peay, Mrs. Jane Edwards, Susan Martin, Mrs. Shannon and many others. It was said those old brethren and sisters were so strong in the faith that they would receive what they asked for in prayer, that they always took their raincoats and umbrellas when they went to their church to pray for rain.

From 1861 to 1871 was the Civil War and Reconstruction period, but notwithstanding the turbulent times our church moved on in the enjoyment of peace and quiet and had several good revivals. Brethren H. M. King, M. M. Modisett and J. T. Williams were Pastors. J. D. Biggs was Pastor from '72 to '75, and the church did efficient work under his preaching. Next was James Reid, and J. D. Biggs again. W. A. Bibb served as pastor for several years, then followed W. S. Tucker. His labors were greatly blessed and his untimely death was a great loss to the church. Jas. L. Downing then served as Pastor for one year. Next came J. D. Hacker, Chas. E. King, J. P. Stewart, J. W. Long, J. H. Terrill and G. W. Sanderson. R. T. Campbell then served us. Eld. J. D. Watson then became Pastor.

The church has had three new church buildings since its organization. The first located near J. E. Shannon's, the second located about one mile east of this site on the Bowling Green and Louisiana gravel road, and the next move being its present site.

HISTORY OF THE FIRST BAPTIST CHURCH OF PALMYRA.

Compiled by the Clerk, Howard P. Smith, on the Occasion of the Seventy-fifth Anniversary.

The First Baptist Church, originally called the Old Baptist Church, of Palmyra, Marion county, Missouri, was constituted the second Saturday in February, 1833.

The constituent members numbered nineteen; five males and fourteen females. The names are as follows: Spencer Clack, Stacy Longmire, John Longmire, Anthony Pool, Michael Bower, Polly Brown, Susan Morton, Sally Lewis, Martha Samuel, Eveline Overton, Polly Eastin, Martha Moore, Lucy Thomas, Amy Pool, Mariah Bower, Sally Pritchard, Elizabeth Clack, Mary Ellis and Lucy Dudley, none of whom are living today.

Mary Rabe was the first person received by experience and baptism, the date being March 7, 1833.

Growth and Elimination.

The first meeting after the constitution of the church was held March 9, 1833, at which time Michael R. Bower was elected clerk, and a committee appointed to draft the Rules of Decorum, and the clerk authorized to purchase a blank book in which to record the proceedings of the church. At a subsequent meeting held Saturday, April 13, 1843, the committee reported the Rules of Decorum, which were adopted, and together with the Articles of Faith are recorded in the original record book still in possession of the church.

Regular monthly meetings were held on Saturday before the second Lord's day at 11 o'clock a. m., at which time members were received, sermons preached and the business of the church transacted.

At the meeting held Saturday, July 2, 1833, M. R. Bower tendered his resignation as clerk and Wm. Wright was elected to fill the vacancy. This brother occupied the position of clerk for about ten years and during his term of office failed to record the proceedings of the church from the year 1836 until November, 1842. At the meeting held on the above date, mention was made of the death of Brother Clack. Brother Clack was a Baptist minister, a member of the church at the time it was constituted. He moved to Palmyra sometime in 1832, and died of cholera in June, 1833. The following is recorded at this meeting, July 2, 1833:

On motion ordered that a committee be appointed to wait on Brethren Taylor, Vardeman, Hendren and Fuqua and request that they would consent to take charge of the church until some permanent arrangement can be made toward calling a Pastor. The church called no Pastor for two years although Rev. Robert Hendren seemed to have acted in that capacity, as on several occasions he was moderator of meetings.

We here quote from the history of the church, read by a former clerk, Prof. Hezekiah Ellis, on the occasion of the golden anniversary of the church, twenty-five years ago.

"At this time there was but one church in Palmyra, a Methodist church, situated in the western part of the town; here the Baptists and Presbyterians sometimes held their meetings. A schoolhouse stood on the block south of the Methodist church, in which the Baptists sometimes held meetings. After the court house was built the Baptists held meetings there until the Baptist church house was built.

At the meeting held Saturday, Aug. 10, 1833, Levin Brown and Wm. Wright were ordained to the deaconate and at the same meeting it was ordered that application be made to be attached to Salt River Association, to which body nearly all of the churches in northeast Missouri belonged. The church remained in Salt River Association until the organization of Bethel Association, which occurred October 17, 1834, at Bethel church, Marion county, Missouri.

The record shows that William Hurley was the first Pastor regularly called, action being first taken at a meeting held June 27, 1835, and the brother entered upon the work July 11, 1835."

When churches went into other Associations, as Palmyra did, I do not longer follow them.   W. J. P.

THE PARIS CHURCH.

At the house of Mr. Eli Bozarth, three miles south of Paris, Missouri, brethren and sisters met and were organized into a church May 7, 1831, by Elders Archibald Patterson and Edward Turner. The constituent members were John Luney, Mary Luney, Paul Herriford, Sarah Herriford, John H. Curry, Matilda Curry, Benjamin Luney, Mary Luney, Isaac Coppage. Edward Turner, Lucretia Turner, Nancy Donaldson, Mary Smith, C. C. Acuff, Peter N. Mahan, John C. Mahan, John Hocker, Fanny Pool and a black man, Peter. The name given to the church was Bethlehem. At the June meeting Eld. Edward Turner was chosen to supply the pulpit; John Luney and John Hocker were elected Deacons, and John H. Curry was elected clerk. At the meeting the following August the church agreed to enter the Salt River Association and she elected E. Turner, J. Luney and J. Hocker messengers to that body, to attend the approaching session of the Association, which met with Siloam Church, Pike county, the first day of October, 1831. The church was received into associational fellowship. At the April meeting, 1832, the name of the church was changed to that of Middle Fork. In 1833 William Armstrong succeeded J. H. Curry in the clerkship of the church. "During this year a church called Eanon was consolidated with this church. It was during this year that the old brick meeting-house that stood by the bridge was built." At the April meeting, 1833, Dr. Gustavus M. Bower was licensed to preach. The church appears in Salt River Association in 1834 with Paris as her name. The messengers this year are E. Turner, A. Patterson, W. Arnold, W. Saling, who served in the body when she met with the Salt River Church, Ralls county, on the 22nd day of August, 1834. The churches in the northern and western parts of the Association having come to an understanding to form a new Association, the Paris messengers at this session obtained a letter to go into the new body. John Davis was chosen to prepare a letter to the contemplated new organization. E. Turner, A. Patterson, W. Arnold and William Saling were chosen as messengers to help form the new body, which met with Bethel Church, Marion county, the 3rd Saturday in October, 1834. The organization was effected and this younger sister was called Bethel; the first moderator was Eld. Christy Gentry, the first clerk was Hon. William Carson.

The church at Paris came into Salt River Association with twenty members. She went out with seventy. Besides the place previously mentioned, her messengers served in the body at Bear Creek Church, Marion county, and at Mt. Pleasant, Pike county.

SALEM CHURCH.

For seventy-seven years Salem Church, Ralls county, has stood as a bulwark of strength, faithful in most everything except the preservation of their own history.

When Eld. Jeremiah Vardeman settled in central Ralls in 1830 there was not a Baptist church in the county. New London Church, the first plant our heavenly Father planted there, had died. Bear Creek on the north and Peno on the south were the nearest churches, either one ranging from fifteen to twenty miles distant. The church is situated on the border of a beautiful upland valley in which the timber land and the prairie irregularly encroached upon and yielded to each other.

True to his Kentucky ministry, Mr. Vardeman at once began the evangelization of the people. On the 5th day of May, 1832, he organized Salem Church. The number in the organization was eighteen. From the fact that when the Association was in session at Bear Creek Church, Marion county, 5th to 8th of October following, Mr. Vardeman was the messenger would show that he himself was a member of the new church. The record of the Association says: "A letter from a newly constituted church called 'Salem,' petitioning for admittance into the Association, was received and read and, after examination, the same was unanimously received." The church at this time numbered thirty-one.

The condition of Salem in the sixties shows that she had prospered during her thirty years of church life. At this time Eld. J. H. Keach was Pastor. In this time God gave them a great revival. Eld. H. M. King was the ministerial help. Under Brother Keach's ministry Bro. James D. Biggs was ordained a preacher. The presbytery was composed of Elders J. H. Keach, *Moderator,* J. F. Smith, M. M. Modisett and W. C. Busby. Brother Biggs was examined and the record says: "In answer to the interrogations he arose, spoke at some length, giving abundant evidence of a Christian, his call to the ministry and ability to teach." This was the third Saturday in June, 1869. At this service Judge Milton Biggs united with the church. The Sunday following Bro. J. D. Biggs was ordained to the gospel ministry and I have heard him say that on that same day he baptized his Uncle Milton.

Brother George T. McGrew was licensed to preach by Salem in 1900 and was ordained at Greenton, November 9, 1906. He died soon afterward. He was a choice young minister.

In 1872 Eld. W. C. Busby succeeded Elder Keach in the pastorate. Eld. B. F. Hixson became Pastor in 1874. Eld. James D. Biggs was chosen Pastor January, 1879, and served two years. Eld. Wiley J. Patrick was elected to the pastorate in December, 1881, and served ten years. Then Eld. H. B. Rice became Pastor. In May, 1893, Elder W. M. Tipton was called. He accepted. During his pastorate the house of worship, which had been an excellent one, was removed, and a neat, American-Gothic, frame house was built. In June, 1899, Elder J. W. McAtee accepted the pastorate. Later M. E. Broaddus was Pastor.

Elder Geo. T. Baker subsequently served the church some years as Pastor, then came Elder Oliver Reed.

Salem has had many gracious revivals. Some of the Lord's chosen servants have served in that goodly field. The church has always maintained active cooperation in the advancing column of the denomination.

Supplement by David Clark.

Some of the constituent members: James Ledford and wife, Nancy; Mrs. Elizabeth McGrew, Mrs. Nancy Conn, Thomas Conn and wife, Mildred A., John Jeffries, Dabney Jones, Henry Inlow and wife,

Solona, Thomas Ellis and wife, Elizabeth, Wm. Boyd and wife, Edna.

The Pastors: Jeremiah Vardaman, Walter McQuie, David Hubbard, Benjamin Stevens, William H. Vardaman, L. C. Musick, John H. Keach, W. C. Busby, B. F. Hixson, Jas. D. Biggs, W. J. Patrick, H. B. Rice, W. M. Tipton, J. W. McAtee, M. E. Broaddus, George T. Baker, Oliver Reed, present pastor.

Some of the Deacons: G. W. Ledford, Burgess Lake, William H. Clark, Samuel Guttery, G. A. Lake, W. B. Guttery, M. C. Biggs, J. W. Keach, James M. Keach, Wallace Swiggert.

The Clerks: Absolam Ellis, George W. Ledford, Joseph McGrew, A. J. Gordon, James C. McGrew, M. C. Biggs, W. B. Guttery, J. Guy Biggs, James Evans, Samuel Neely, present clerk.

Houses: There have been four houses of worship constructed at Salem. First, a log house; second, a brick house, built 1844, which cost about $1,000; third, a frame house, built 1855, which cost about $1,500; fourth, a frame house, built 1898, which cost about $2,500.

SALT RIVER CHURCH.

By S. P. Spalding.

The church known as the Salt River church, was organized in the year 1833. Its building was of hewn logs. The first and only regular pastor was Christy Gentry; Rev. Jerry Vardaman preached at times. Daniel Bowling, on whose farm the church building stood, was the custodian of the house and one of the first members. Other members were as follows:

Col. Martin and wife, Warren Finley and wife, Christy Gentry and wife, Chappel Carstarphen and wife, Joseph Hampton and wife, Daniel Summers, John Ray, William Greathouse, Adoniram Smith and others.

. The house was situated on section 28, township 56, range 6. The church ceased to exist in about 1848; its furniture was moved to Bethlehem.

JUDGE H. N. BASKETT AND WIFE.

By their Son, J. N. Baskett, M. D.

Horatio N. Baskett was born in Shelby county, Kentucky, January 6, 1809. He attended the neighberhood schools, and by close application in and out of the schools, laid a substantial foundation for an education, upon which he continued to build to the end of his days on earth. In his early manhood he was converted and united with the Baptist church in his native county.

At the age of twenty-nine he married Almeda Griffith, also of Shelby county, Kentucky. Four years later, in 1842, he, with his wife and one child, moved to Lincoln county, Missouri, and located on a farm near New Hope, where he spent most of his subsequent life.

He was a public-spirited man, and ever kind, just and generous. For a number of years he served his township as justice of the peace. Twice he was elected to the office of county judge and served in this capacity for two terms of six years each. His uncompromising integrity and naturally judicial mind, peculiarly fitted him for such a position, which he honored with his just and popular rulings. He penetrated into the realm of political matters with an unusual intelligence and was well versed in all current topics of his day. His rich store of general information, his keen intellect and his assiduous application to all public affairs entrusted to him enabled him to discharge these manifold duties with satisfaction to his constituents, and with honor and pride to his friends. But it was in his home and in his church life where his true worth was best known. Kind, sympathetic, loving and loved in his home, respected, honored and esteemed in his church relations.

He was generous to a fault, but uncompromising when truth or principle was involved. Shortly after locating in Lincoln county, he, with his wife, united with Union church, called later New Hope. He was devoted and loyal to his church and served as Deacon and church clerk for a number of years.

His heart and his purse were always open to the cause of Christianity, and his advice sought in many church councils. He honored his Lord and Master. His motto, as exemplified in his life, was: "Jesus first, others next, self last."

All but two of the eleven children were born on the farm near New Hope. They were taught by precept and example to honor God and love their neighbors. Seven of the eleven children survived their father, who died at his home in New Hope, March 29, 1889, at the mature age of eighty years.

Almeda Griffith was born January 19, 1817, in Shelby county, Kentucky. She attended the schools in the vicinity of her home, and in Maryland, where she went on horseback, at the age of fifteen to make her home with an uncle, her father having died.

At the age of twenty she returned to her native home and shortly afterward was married to Horatio N. Baskett, of the same county. In 1842 they, with their only child, came by steamboat to Lincoln county, Missouri, where they settled on a farm near New Hope. Here, together, they lived and toiled for nearly a half century. No one but an early settler of a new country can fully appreciate the deprivations and hardships which they had to undergo; through it all she manifested the courage and faith of a true wife and a Christian mother. Her home was always open to the needy and suffering. The weary minister of the gospel always found it a place of welcome. Hospitality to all who entered her home, devotion to her family, and faithfulness and loyalty to her church, were the crowning virtues of her noble character.

In early life she gave her heart to God through Jesus Christ, and united with the Baptist church in Shelby county, Kentucky. She removed a short time before her death to make her home with her daughter,

Mrs. G. W. Whiteside, when she united by letter with Mill Creek church.

Seven of the eleven children born to her were reared to maturity, and had stamped indelibly upon their hearts and consciences the impress of her godly nature and consecrated life. None of them ever left the parental roof unattended by her prayers and benedictions. With patience and resignation she awaited the summons to join her husband and other loved ones, on the golden shores of eternity. She died at the home of her son-in-law, George W. Whiteside, April 27, 1907, at the age of four score years and ten.

ELIZABETH MCCUNE BIGGS.

By her Grandson, James D. Biggs.

She was married to William Biggs in 1809 or '10. She was quite young when married. Their family, when completed, numbered twelve children, six boys and six girls. They all lived to be grown. "Aunt Betsey," as she was called by the people of the neighborhood, was a woman of more than ordinary character. She had a great stock of "gumption," commonly called common sense. She took a very practical view of business and religion too. She was diligent in business, fervent in spirit, serving the Lord. In her life and in the raising of her children there were two things constantly before her mind—industry and obedience to rightful authority. She was reared a Presbyterian, but when she saw the plain teachings of the word of God, she was swift to obey and soon was buried with her Lord in Baptism. Her religious duties were a pleasure to her. Her example and precept were in harmony with each other. She did what she taught others to do. She loved the word of God. She read it with her family and tried to follow its precepts. She loved the house of God, and was always in her place, unless prevented by sickness or some other Providential cause. She really meditated on the word of God.

She wanted its truths unfolded to her mind. She liked the character of preaching that made plain the meaning of the word. Her hymn-book was a constant companion with her Bible, and although she did not sing much, she loved to read the hymns. The hymns, she said, put things in easy form to remember. Many a precious truth was held in rhyme by her. She spent a few moments every morning by herself with the Bible, hymn-book, and often, The Pilgrim's Progress. A very busy woman had time to read the word of God and pray. Religion was to her a reality.

She never grew morose over trials, nor over-elated over the successes of life, but with a faith that laid hold of the promise of God, she kept the even tenor of her way. She had a great many mottoes, that were the embodiment of great truths. Like her Master, in many respects,

"Her wisdom was not far to seek, She was so human;
Whether high or low, far from her kind, she neither sank nor soared;
She was an equal guest at every board, and ever held herself at manhood's simple level."

In the raising of her children, which were left to her alone after her husband's death, she exercised more than usual wisdom. In answer to the question of a dear friend as to how she had raised so large a family so well, she said, "With prayer and hickory."

It was a remarkable fact that she had a good control of her family as long as she lived. They loved to obey the mother. In fact they all held her wisdom as being above their own.

Let me give one incident, which will illustrate the matter. She was at the reception of the writer at my father's house in 1871. The women who were there had let some of the cooking burn. As soon as father smelled the affair, he quickly arose and started for the kitchen, his mother, then seventy-six years of age, met him at the door and said, "Now, Johnnie, go right back and sit down." He said, "I don't see why they should let anything burn." She said, "Hush, and go back and sit down." He went back and sat down and after she had gone out he turned to me and said what he wanted to say to her, but was afraid. Or rather from force of habit, which through all the years he had been forming, he obeyed. The sons and daughters all recognized her love of the right and her adherence to it. It was not often that they presented for consideration any subject and asked her advice, and then failed to take it.

With all her good qualities, she was a very humble woman. When she was nearing the river, brother John H. Keach went to see her and talked with her about her hopes and prospects for the future. She realized that she had done so little for Him who had done so much for her. Brother Keach told her she had been a very useful woman. She had raised a large family of most respectable children, and not a black sheep among them. She answered, "Yes, not a black sheep, but some of them have some pretty black spots on them."

Flattery never seemed to strike in on her sincere soul. She knew herself too well to listen to anything that would magnify her goodness. She knew her own heart, and she knew the hearts of others quite well also. So often she would say, "It is by grace through faith and that not of ourself; it is the gift of God."

Her second eyesight came to her when she was about seventy years old, and she read the finest print without glasses. She read a great deal after this, and her eyes seemed as good and strong as they were in her youth. She retained her vigor up to the last few months of her life. Almost any neighbor could tell you some great story of her horseback riding. Her faithful old horse was named Mac. She would mount old Mac and gallop eight or nine miles with perfect ease to herself and apparently to old Mac, too. I think she kept this up till she was about eighty years old. Somewhere about this time, her son, William, took her on the train to Alexandria to see her son, George. He seemed to think that she would be frightened at the speed of the train; so, very patronizingly he said, "Mother, is this going fast enough for you?" She replied, "Yes, Will, but it is the first time in my life that I ever rode fast enough to suit me, but this is not too fast."

When I was a boy I thought she was a great woman. When I became a man I thought she was a greater woman. With her many excellencies she was well rounded. No one virtue seemed to far outshine any other. Like most good women her intuitions were of the most perfect nature. She could reason well, but she seemed to know so many things without having to reason about them. This really seems to be the highest form of knowledge. This, I think, is Godlike. Men have to reason a thing out and very often after they have reasoned well they still do not know the right, or they do not seem to be well assured of the truth, the certainty of the position. What is a syllogism anyway? Is it not a pair of crutches which a man puts forward and then throws his weight upon and swings himself a little in advance? Intuition is like God's knowledge, it knows without reasoning. With people, however, intuition is partial. With God it is perfect; it may be cultivated, I think, until it seems nearly perfect. It appeared to have reached a very high degree of efficiency in her case. Hence, her judgments were usually wise and just. Her friends would consult her on any subject that interested them and she was frank and faithful in her advice.

She passed peacefully away at a good old age, and they laid her away near the house of worship where she had so long and so usefully served the Master, near the site of the Old Peno Church.

Hon. William Biggs was a son of Elder Davis Biggs. His daughter, Peggy, who became Mrs. J. E. Shannon, professed conversion while her father was a member of the Legislature. He came home horse-

back to hear her experience and see her baptized.
When the Legislature was in session at St. Charles in
June, 1821, an Act was passed providing for the location of the permanent seat of government. The House
appointed a committee of three on this location. Mr.
Biggs was put on the committee. He had the reputation of being a man of sound judgment, large information, uprightness and ability before an audience.

DR. G. M. BOWER.

Dr. Bower began life while General Washington
was in his first term of the presidency of the new republic, and in the general vicinity of the President's
home. He received his medical education in Philadelphia and subsequently settled at Georgetown, Kentucky, for practice.

When twenty-two years of age he was commissioned by Governor Shelby an assistant surgeon in the
army and marched on foot to the Canada line. He
was in numerous fights with the Indians, including the
one on the river Raisin. He was captured by the
British and Indians and left in the hands of the Indians.

Dr. Bower was engaged in staunching the blood and
binding up the shattered limbs of the suffering soldiers
in a log hut, as the dying and dead lay heaped together
on a bed of straw, when an Indian warrior seized him,
and wresting the surgical instrument from his grasp,
tomahawked the wounded men, and carried the doctor
off a prisoner. He was stripped of his clothing and a
blanket given him and he was taken to the city of Malden. His rank became known and suitable clothing was
furnished him. But one day his uniform was taken
off, a blanket was thrown to him, a cotton handkerchief was tied around his head, and he was carried by
the Indians in a canoe over the river to Detroit. "After being marched around the town several times, to
draw the attention of the populace, Doctor Bower
was ordered to mount a store-box in the street and

was offered for sale to the highest bidder. Several bids were made, the last eighty dollars, which was by a merchant, and the doctor was knocked off to him." On returning to Kentucky he volunteered as a captain and raised a company of one hundred picked men. He marched straight back to Detroit, Governor Shelby commanding. Very soon they won the celebrated victory on the River Thames and regained the whole of Michigan, which had been lost early in the war.

The army immediately returned to Malden, Captain Bower commanding the whole line. He returned to Kentucky and practiced his profession.

"In view of his manly bearing and elegant accomplishments as a gentleman, Governor Dishea commissioned Dr. Bower a captain of the seventy-seventh Regiment Kentucky Light Dragoons in 1825, and mounted on milk-white horses, this magnificent company marched all the way to Fayette to meet, welcome and escort the Marquis De Lafayette to the City of Versailles."

In 1832 Dr. Bower came to Missouri and settled near Paris. He was elected from the second district to the house of representatives of the United States Congress the first Monday in August, 1842, and served two years. While in Congress he served on the Committee on the District of Columbia and on the Committee on Militia. He also served in the capacity of surgeon general and of paymaster general.

Two years after his arrival in Missouri he assisted in the organization of the General Association. He was of the company who seem to have collected in Monroe county. They traveled together. There were Dr. Bower, Wm. Armstrong and daughter, who is still with us, the excellent and devoted Mrs. Williams, Anderson Woods, Wm. Hurley, Noah Flood, Jeremiah Vardeman and his son, Jerry, and many others who journeyed some seventy-five miles together. The company numbered about thirty-five. J. M. Peck was with them.

Sister Williams says: "About noon each day we spread our luncheons out by the water, where our horses had been fed and watered. And on the grass we ate and rested. Brother Bower and my dear old mother made a pot of coffee, which Brother Hurley enjoyed with them. We rested about two hours, for the green headed flies were terrible. Gopher hills and buffalo trails obstructed the roads. There were no bridges."

Dr. Bower once gave me some account of his trip, warming with enthusiasm as he talked of Missouri and her mission work. At the third meeting of this body which he helped to form, he was elected clerk. This was at Bethlehem church, Boone county, in 1836.

When I first knew him, about 1855, he was living the life of a private citizen on his ample and imposing homestead, where his body now rests. What he said was quoted as the final word on any occasion; what he did was accepted as worthy of imitation.

Hon. Marion Biggs, of California, who was a member of the same church in earlier life, says of him: "Dr. Bower was, I may say, the pillar of the Baptist church in Paris. He was a soldier, statesman, and above all, a true Christian and a perfect gentleman."

In dress and personal bearing he was faultless. He was fond of horseback riding and was enthusiastic for the chase. He had as a favorite saying: "I would rather wear out than rust out," and in his life he exemplified the saying. His best energies were given to the service of his Lord. Politics, his profession, his farm, the chase, were all made tributary to Christian duty. Early in his professional life he united with the church in Georgetown, Kentucky, under the ministry of Doctor William C. Buck.

In church business he was prompt, incisive and courteous. He held firmly the great doctrines of grace and in early life he sometimes preached. He was a strong friend of his pastor, the Rev. Sylvester Allen Beauchamp. He said that the greatest orator he ever heard was President William Thompson, though he had been associated in public life with Clay, Calhoun and Webster.

The reforming, elevating influence of this American nobleman was beautiful. I do not remember to have seen any one act or speak rudely in his presence. Hardened must have been the one who could do so. Of him Colonel W. F. Switzler says: "He was a citizen of the highest character and an eminent physician," and his close personal friend, Col. Benjamin Davies, says: "Nature's mould has formed but few such men. The soul of honor, the perfection of moral and physical courage, the embodiment of purest friendship; the best of husbands; the kindest of fathers, the soundest of Democrats and beau ideal of the old Virginia gentleman."

Doctor Bower received his crown of glory November 17, 1864.

HON. WILLIAM CARSON.

Brother William Carson was born May 14, 1798, in the valley of Virginia, and died November 3, 1873, at Palmyra, Missouri.

His Grandfather Carson, came from near Armagh City, Ireland. One of the family was among the besieged in Dorry, when the Catholics persecuted the Presbyterians. His maternal Grandfather Williams was of Welsh descent, a native of Maryland.

Brother Carson joined the Baptist church at Winchester, Virginia. He was baptized by its Pastor first Sunday in August, 1819. He came to Missouri and settled at New London. In January, 1820, he united with Peno church (Rev. Davis Biggs, Pastor), fifteen miles from his residence, being the nearest church. In about three years, he, with others, organized a church at New London. In 1823 he aided in the organization of Salt River Association. He was present at the last meeting of that body, before his death, and expressed gladness at being with them, just fifty years after their organization. He was their first clerk. In 1824 he was appointed by President Monroe Register of the United States Land Office at Palmyra, to which place he removed in 1825. The same year he changed his membership to Salt River church, three miles south of Palmyra, also organized a Sunday School in the town of Palmyra, the first organized north of Salt River, and to the day of his death, he was an active and efficient Sunday School worker. In 1834 Bethel, Little Union, Palmyra, Bear Creek, Pleasant Hill, Salt River, Providence, South River, Wyaconda, Gilead, Indian Creek, North Fork, Paris and Elk Fork churches were dismissed from Salt River Association to form the Bethel Association. He was elected its first clerk, and served as clerk or moderator for more than twenty years. He was a constituent member of the Missouri Baptist General Association when organized in 1834, under the name of the Central Society, and was clerk of that body in 1837 and 1840, and moderator in 1855.

He was a member of the convention that met at Boonville in 1850, to locate William Jewell College, drew up its charter, and a petition to the Legislature for an act of incorporation. His walk was that of an earnest, faithful Christian. It was the same at home and abroad, whether around the fireside with friends, or alone with his family, or traveling on the highway, or engaged in public or private business; by his honesty, frankness and fidelity to his Master, he impressed all who knew him with his eminently social and Christian qualities, and the fragrance of his religion all along the wayside of life.—(Written by John J. Suter, Palmyra, Mo., for the historical meeting of the First Baptist Church, Palmyra, January 29, 1899.)

The following beautiful tribute is paid to Brother Carson by his daughter, Mrs. J. S. Green.

"Never shall we forget what we saw and heard at the last meeting of Salt River Association when with the gravity of an old patriarch he arose and said: 'I am glad, dear brethren, to be with you. Just fifty years ago I was present at the organization of your body, and had the honor of being its first clerk." On the second day of October, 1823, he married in the city of St. Louis, Alethea Seely, a native of St. Louis county, and settled on a farm six miles south of New London.

In 1830 he was elected to the State Legislature, and served fourteen years, four years in the Senate. For twenty-seven years he lived on his farm six miles northwest of Palmyra. His membership was with the Bethel church until 1862, then with the church in Palmyra. He was a constituent member of the General Association when organized in 1834, under the name of the Central Society. He was sunshine in the midst of his family. His house was the resting place of those who preached the gospel; here they always found a welcome and untiring attention from him and his devoted wife. From 1864 to the time of his death, November 3, 1873, he was retired from the more active duties of business life, but was no less faithful to the Master's cause. He delighted to mingle with the people of God, and attended church services three times the day before he died. No language will express the life work of this good man better than that of the Apostle; 'Diligent in business, fervent in spirit, serving the Lord.'"

MRS. ALETHEA CARSON.

Sister Alethea Carson, wife of Wm. Carson, was baptized in 1825 by Elder Fuqua, into the fellowship of Salt River church, lived and died an earnest Christian worker in the Master's vineyard.

We are encouraged to emulate her Christian character and example. Just before her death she repeated the following:

"Hail, sweetest, dearest tie that binds
Our glowing hearts in one,

> Hail, sacred hope, that tunes our minds
> To harmony divine
> It is the hope, the blissful hope,
> Which Jesus' grace has given,
> The hope when days are past,
> We all shall meet in Heaven."

REV. CHRISTY GENTRY.

(Read at the Unveiling of his Monument by the Author.)

His Ancestry, Birth and Early Life.

The years that clustered around 1790 made a period of stirring events. The Constitution of the United States was adopted 1789. The meeting at Kettering, England, which resulted in sending Wm. Carey to India was in 1792. Kentucky was admitted into the Union of States in 1792. While Kentucky was still a part of Virginia, October 14, 1790, Christy Gentry was born in Madison county. He was the fourth son of Richard and Jane Harris Gentry, who were married in Albermarle county, Virginia, April 1, 1784. Harris was his mother's maiden name. The father died Sunday, February 12, 1843, at 10 o'clock a. m. The mother had died September 18, 1821. They were natives of Virginia. As soon as the son's child perception was open to public events important movements, social, political, and religious, were occurring around him to stir him. Mr. Thomas Benton Gentry, at the Gentry family reunion at Crab Orchard Springs, Ky., in August, 1898, spoke of the father of our deceased Bethlehem Pastor as "the Richard Gentry who fought in the war for American independence, and who was present at the surrender of Lord Cornwallis at Yorktown, Va., 1781." He further says, speaking of the family ancestry, "We trace it back to the two British soldiers who came over from England to America about the year 1677."

I have been able to get nothing as to Brother Gentry's early life.

His marriage and removal to Missouri.

May 28, 1812, Mr. Gentry married Miss Lucy Christy, of Clark county, Kentucky. In 1830 he moved to Missouri and settled on the Rollins farm, two miles northwest of Sidney. This farm was owned by Dr. Rhodes Rollins, one of the founders of the Missouri State University. It is said that Dr. Rollins and Mr. Gentry were old friends in Kentucky. Mr. Gentry had inherited several negroes whom he brought with him. Towards them, he and Mrs. Gentry, were indulgent to the extent of rendering them unprofitable and even expensive.

God gave Mr. and Mrs. Gentry eleven children— Amanda F. was married to Mr. Elisha Moore; Richard Gentry married Caroline M. Whitaker; William Tandy Gentry married Hattie C. Morris; Christy Gentry married Evodia Redman; Rhodes Rollins Gentry never married; Joshua Henry Gentry married Mary Angeline Elliot; Overton Harris Gentry married Susan Elzea; Mary Jane, Richard Tandy, Joseph and Ruben died in childhood. Soon after settling in Ralls county, he with the neighbors for five or six miles around organized a private school and employed a Mr. Brent as teacher. After he had taught a month or two he was drafted as a soldier in the Black Hawk war. When the war was over Mr. Brent returned and continued his school.

In 1834 he bought of Clem Greene the farm that became his home until near the time of his death.

He was a close observer of persons and nature, he had definite ideas of distance and direction. He could go on a straight line through the untrodden woods, he was a great reader and had a supply of religious books. Mr. Gentry had a liking and a skill for hunting. Many are the incidents related of him with gun and in the chase. One Saturday on his way to church he shot a deer near B. A. Spaulding's; R. M. Spaulding, then a boy was with him. They caught the deer near the church.

Dr. J. J. Norton says, "He was pre-eminently a manly man in every respect. Physically he was much above the average, fully six feet high, slightly stooped in shoulders, angular, muscular with no surplus flesh, weighing about one hundred and eighty pounds, with prominent and distinctly defined features of face, expressing kindness, yet indicative of decided convictions and courage to maintain them when necessary. He was a helpful, cheerful, hopeful man, with strong hard sense, well fitted physically and morally to meet and overcome the many difficulties of frontier life and to leave an impress of his life on the community. The way in which the obligations and the duties growing out of the varied relations of life are discharged is a good standard with which to estimate character. I knew him and his family well. I never knew a husband and wife who enjoyed each other's company more or manifested more interest for each other than did Uncle Christy and Aunt Lucy. He loved his children and delighted in seeing them enjoy themselves. I have heard him say that he thought this was a good world and that it was created for the good and pleasure of man. The only criticism I ever heard regarding his family life was that possibly he was too indulgent with his young slaves. He and his wife enjoyed greatly informal visits for an afternoon or evening with a neighbor or entertaining a neighbor in their own home. Especially did they make it pleasant in their home for the friends of their children visiting them. I have frequently heard three men now eighty years old say there was no place they enjoyed visiting and spending an afternoon or night more than at Uncle Christy's. He deplored greatly any bickering and ill-feeling between neighbors, and he made it his business to restore harmony and he was successful. I was the family physician of all his neighbors for many years. It was but seldom if ever that I had a patient who was seriously sick for several days that I did not meet him there. He once said to me as we were riding under the high bluffs west of Cincinnati on Salt River, after calling my attention to the scenery, 'Jimmie, is it not wonderful that He who created this world would think in compassion of frail, weak, sinful man?' On a visit to one of their neighbors he and Aunt Lucy were invited by the hostess to look at her garden, where she presented him with a boquet of beautiful fragrant roses. With thanks he accepted it, but told her that for several years his sense of smell had been lost. She commiserated him for his misfortune. He replied, 'Yes, I miss many sweet odors, yet I am saved from many an offensive odor.' He was a close observer of nature, especially of animals."

J. Porter Bush says of him, "He had an eye like an eagle's. He was a merciful man. I do not believe that he would have stepped on an ant. Great and uniform kindness characterized the man. He had a distinct personality and a manly bearing that naturally drew to him those who desired benefit from one of strength and wisdom, and those who desired the sympathy of his tender heart, as well as those who desired his companionship. In those earlier days in Missouri it was a custom of Dr. Rollins to visit him once or twice a year and spend a few days with him hunting. He attracted young men and boys to a wonderful degree. He loved children and could read with them playing around him. Mr. Hiram Underhill says that Mr. Gentry settled a great many difficulties between men. He insisted that each one should have his rights and do right. He hewed to the line. Both parties would usually listen to him. It could be said of him, as it was said of Cornelius, 'a just man and one that feareth God.'" He acted alike to all. He practiced even-handed justice, was equitable, impartial. This is one of the highest attainments a man can make. To be liberal, learned or eloquent does not mark so great a greatness as to be just. One who is just pleases God and has power with men. This power Mr. Gentry had as is illustrated by the following incident concerning a minor matter related by Mr. Jas. W. Lear: "The Bethel Association met at Bethel church, Marion county. Among other matters someone proposed to suggest to the several churches of the Association the propriety of changing the rules by which the time of church meetings were governed by the Sundays instead of the Saturdays. The suggestion caused quite an animated discussion, friendly but with some earnestness. The thought of anything like excitement in a religious assembly usually so quiet and kind enlisted my serious attention. After several earnest speeches, pro and con, Uncle Christy arose quietly and calmly and said, 'Brother Moderator, the Baptists have been acting under the rule as it now stands for many years and I have long thought that under the blessings of our Heavenly Father they have been doing well enough and it seems to me that it is well enough to let well enough alone.' Perfect quiet prevailed and the suggestion was withdrawn. It made an impression on my mind at the time that I have loved to think of ever since, that so brief a statement, made so calmly and gently, should so fully still a seeming excitement. This is a case where the man was greater than the words spoken. The man! the man! the just man!

As a Christian and a Minister.

R. M. Spalding says, "About 1833, he, with Moses Hawkins, Daniel Bowling, Warren Finley, Col. Martin, James Buford, J. F. Hawkins, Wm. Greathouse, Isaac Ely, J. C. Dawson, and probably others, determined to organize a church and build a house of worship, which was done about that time. The house was built on the land of Daniel Bowling, two miles west of Spalding's Springs. The house was built by Ben Foreman. Soon after the organization of the church many were added to it. C. Carstarphen, H. Graves, Bob Henry, Nathan and Josh Snider, several Lansdales, A. Smith, J. M. Hampton, Dr. Williams, and many others.

Mr. S. H. Elzea says, "About Christmas of 1841-2, a protracted meeting was held in Hannibal by the Revs. Parks, Henderson, Broadus and Gentry. I was converted in that meeting. Mr. Gentry asked me 'Have you reason to believe that the Lord has pardoned your sins?' I answered him 'I know it.' He put the question of my reception to the church and they gave me the hand of fellowship. This was my first acquaintance with Mr. Gentry. In 1843 I united with Old Indian Creek Church, so he was now my Pastor and he continued to be for many years. Through life he gave his time and talents for the good of the Cause. He was faithful. He often said that he would be willing to spend his time if he thought he would save one soul. As a preacher, he made things plain. He was instructive, it was easy to listen to him, his voice was smooth and pleasant, he was earnest in warning sinners to repent. His voice would become sympathetic and he would speak in tears. I never in my life heard any one speak a hard word of Brother Gentry. He was beloved by everybody, by all denominations. In business he was honest and true." Sister Evotia Gentry says of the revered father of her husband: "He was fearless. He preached without taking the Test Oath. When his son, Christy, said, 'Papa, don't go, your life may be in danger,' the father said, 'Son, I do not believe that they will hurt me. The Lord has called me to preach.' During the Civil War he often met the soldiers. He would talk to them about their souls, and they would let him go on. His preaching was pathetic. Under it the people sometimes shed tears. His voice was not loud or boisterous, but persuasive, gentle and kind."

Bro. B. F. Hixson says, "My impressions from the few times that I heard him preach was that he had his subjects well in hand, and presented them in a concise, clear and pleasant manner. He was fond of a good joke, and he was companionable. I took charge of

RAMSEY CREEK HOUSE OF WORSHIP.
Ramsey was in the Organization of the Association.

SPENCER CREEK HOUSE OF WORSHIP.
The last house in which the Association met.

Bethlehem Church in the neighborhood of which he had lived a long time and of which he had been Pastor. He was held in the highest esteem as a Pastor, citizen and neighbor, being loved by everybody."

A great many young people showed their esteem for him by having him officiate at their marriages. He gave as the extremes of his marriage fees—the largest $50 and suit of clothes; the smallest a gourd of tar.

Bro. J. D. Biggs says, "I saw Bro. Gentry at the session of the Bethel Association at Palmyra. I remember him as a man of great earnestness. The people seemed to expect from him something unusually good. He impressed me as a man of wisdom and what he said had weight. As I looked at his face I thought I saw in him that controlling dignity that was seen in Dr. John A. Broadus. Some question, perhaps Missions, was before the body. There had been a good many talks, but when he spoke everything seemed to be concentrated on his views and the business moved off according to those views. His appearance, his speech, impressed me. I shall never forget the man. He was a leader."

The following letter to him, given in full, will help to illustrate his labor and fellowship in the gospel:

"HANNIBAL, Sept. 25, 1854.

"Dear Bro.:—You are always desirous of helping on the Cause whenever an opportunity presents itself. I thought I would write to you and say that we intend holding a protracted meeting at Providence Church commencing on the second Sabbath in October. I have written to Bro. Smith, and hope he will be there. Bro. Modisett has promised to attend. Cannot you give us the benefit of your presence? All seem cold and sinners are unconcerned. Come over and help us if possible. May the Lord prosper you abundantly in all things.

"Yours in Christ,
"J. T. WILLIAMS."

The minutes of Bethel Association held with Mt. Prairie Church in 1861, show that Mr. Gentry was Moderator. The minutes say "Sunday morning at 9 o'clock met for prayer. Eleven o'clock preaching at the house by Elder Smith Thomas, and in the afternoon preaching by Elder M. M. Modisett, preaching also in Col. Green's camp by Elders Cleveland, Gentry, Kaylor and Haines."

Mr. Gentry was Pastor of The Bethlehem Church from December 6th, 1856, to June, 1865, and he was moderator until his death. Bro. D. V. Inlow succeeded him.

Dr. Norton says, "I have known well but two or three others who had such perfect, confident faith in Christ as an all sufficient Saviour. Yet, I don't think I ever knew any one who had as much sympathy for frail human nature and as much charity for the weak and erring Christian. I do not think that he was a great reader except of the Bible. He was never at a loss to quote any passage he wanted. He never impressed me as an orator or as a logical debater, but more as an affectionate, honest, sincere man, profoundly impressed with the sacredness and the importance of the interest involved and the importance of accepting then and there the salvation provided in the Gospel of Christ. His manner in the pulpit, as elsewhere, was generally calm and deliberate, but at times he would become unusually earnest in his appeal to the unconverted. He would lean on the pulpit and plead with them not to neglect their immortal souls. He had a strong, musical voice, there was no difficulty in understanding what he said. He loved to preach of the wondrous love of God, especially as manifested in the gift of His Son as an all sufficient Savior of sinners.

Evening time.

Rev. W. R. Painter says: "I never heard him preach. All that I ever knew of him I learned by a few visits to his home. I regarded him as one of the purest, best men I ever knew, being in that particular the peer of Wilhoit and Fristoe. When I knew him he was old and infirm and not engaged in the work of the ministry, but he was keenly interested in the affairs of the Kingdom and he manifested the kindliest feeling towards the younger preachers who were to be the successors of the older brethren. He had the warmest welcome for the visiting brother, to whom he extended a simple but unbounded hospitality. He loved to spend the evening around the fireside recounting the trials and the triumphs of his ministry. Of each he had an abundance—his full share. He was wonderfully cheerful and fully reconciled to be shelved, seeming to bid godspeed to all who were taking up the work he was laying down.

One habit he and his good wife seemed to enjoy and which they kept up till the last, very deeply impressed me. It was this: every morning before rising they would join in singing a hymn of praise to God. Sometimes it was 'Awake My Soul in Joyful Lays.' I always felt better and happier after a visit to his cheerful home, after receiving his benediction at parting. My brief association with him gave me the ambition to be a good man and especially to win souls to Christ."

Some of Rev. Gentry's favorite hymns were: "The Morning Light is Breaking," "Broad is the Road that Leads to Death," "Show Pity, Lord, Oh, Lord, Forgive," "The Day is Past and Gone," "Alas, and Did My Savious Bleed," "O, When Shall I see Jesus," "I Would Not Live Alway," "How Tedious and Tasteless," "On Jordan's Stormy Banks," "How Happy Are They," "There is a Fountain," "From Greenland's Icy Mountains." He and his wife sang well.

He rests from his labors.

March 14, 1866, at the home of his son, Christy, Brother Gentry went to the rest that remains for the people of God. In his last hours there were present with him his wife, his sons, Tandy and Christy, and the wife of the last named, and some of the younger members of the family. His body was laid to rest at Bethlehem. Brother J. Frank Smith preached his memorial sermon. The church adopted resolutions in honor of him and some of the other members recently deceased. The ones mentioned are Rev. Christy Gentry, Christy Gentry, Jr., Trustee and Deacon, J. C. Dawson and wife and Deacon C. K. Moss, and J. M. Hampton, who was clerk of the church. The resolutions are: "While we sadly miss these familiar forms and deeply deplore the loss their labors, their fond admonitions, their good advice, example and rich experience, we will cheerfully submit to His will, who we know doeth all things well, realizing that what is our loss is their eternal gain. In gratitude for their many labors and services in our behalf and in love for their Christian character we will fondly cherish their memories in our hearts and in the divine assistance will try to imitate their virtues.

"We will pray that God, who is all powerful to will and to do, may raise up others who will cheerfully assume the labors they so faithfully performed, and fit and qualify them to discharge the same, in that way that His name may be honored and His cause promoted in our midst."

Dr. Norton says: "He died of valvular disease of the heart. He suffered greatly at times from asthma. Frequently during his last illness as he often did while in health he expressed his perfect confidence in Him in whom he had put his trust. Yet during his last illness and frequently before he expressed the dread of physical suffering and agony of dissolution and an apprehension that he might not be able to endure as a Christian man should."

His works follow him.

Though this Christian patriarch has gone from earth, he still speaks to us. There are living persons who today are living better lives than they otherwise would because they came under the example and ministry of this man of God. His great-grandson, Mr. Jas. E. Hampton, is preaching the same message that was his ancestor's joy. These words of Goldsmith are as true of him as if they had been written in his honor:

"At church with meek and unaffected grace,
His looks adorn'd the venerable face
Truth from his lips prevail with double sway,
And fools who came to scoff remain to pray.

The service past, around the pious man,
With steady zeal each honest rustic ran,
Even children followed with endearing wile
And plucked his gown to share the good man's smile.

His ready smile a parent's warmth expressed,
Their welfare pleased him and their care distressed;
To them his heart, his love, his grief were given,
But all his serious thought had rest in heaven."

Brother Gentry's mortal part is here. That which is immortal has entered into his inheritance. "They that be wise shall shine as the brightness of the firmament, and they that turn many to righteousness as the stars forever and ever."

HON. W. A. HARRIS.

Mr. Harris was born in Rappahannock county, Virginia, in the year 1805, and was a lineal descendant of the Reverend Samuel Harriss, a noted Baptist minister of Virginia, in the early history of that State, he having been ordained in 1759. His education was received in the city of Alexandria, Virginia, in which town he afterward studied law under the distinguished Judge Cleggett. Completing his law studies, he then went to Shenandoah county and commenced the practice of his profession, and was soon after elected to represent his county in the Legislature. During the session he was one of the prime movers in the division of Rappahannock county, cutting off that which formed Page county.

In 1841 he was elected a member of Congress. At the beginning of the twenty-seventh Congress, Harris was placed on Committee on District of Columbia; during the Congress he was also placed on the Committee on Indian Affairs to fill a vacancy. At the close of his term of office he took charge of the administration "organ," the *Constitution,* under President Tyler's administration.

After Mr. Polk's election, he assumed control of the administration paper called the *Spectator,* and by President Polk was appointed Minister Plenipotentiary to the Argentine Confederation, South America, holding this responsible position for a term of six years.

Returning to Washington, Mr. Harris, an original friend of Mr. Buchanan's declined a foreign appointment, preferring to edit the "organ" of the administration, the *Union,* which he continued to edit up to the election of Mr. Lincoln.

Mr. Harris, being a man of strong southern sentiment, his connection with the paper ceased with the close of Mr. Buchanan's term of office. He then established a paper known as the *Argus,* published in the English, French and Spanish languages, and continued to edit this paper until the close of the Civil War, when he was stricken with paralysis. Soon afterward he was brought to his home in Pike county, Missouri, where his family had remained throughout the war, and where he died in the year 1864.

In Virginia, Brother Harris belonged to the antimission Baptists. In Missouri, he did not identify himself with a church, but attended Mt. Pisgah church and gave her his support. He was a close friend of Col. W. G. Hawkins.

ELDER J. H. KEACH.

By Dalton Biggs, Esq.

Elder J. H. Keach was born in Virginia in 1807, and moved to Kentucky when eight years of age. He was converted there under the preaching of Rev. Edmond Waller in 1826; he was powerfully converted, which led Rev. Waller to predict that he would some day become a preacher. He came to Missouri in 1831, and located in Marion county, and later in Ralls county. He married Miss Mary Lake, who survived him. He was a Bible student and a born theologian; his sermons were of a doctrinal and experimental character. Being a Bible student from the time of his conversion, he was from the beginning a good preacher, and as he ripened in experience and learning, he soon took rank among our best preachers. Brother Keach was of that disposition and frame of heart and mind to make not alone an evangelist and debater, but good in all these, warm-hearted, strong minded and pure in his daily walk of life. He was suited to fill a long and useful pastorate. Such men we need and such men the denomination then needed, and he admirably and nobly filled the place. He was born, raised and trained for a Pastor, and the pastorates that he filled were always strengthened and built up. Would that we had more like Father Keach. He died in January, 1878, triumphant in the cross of Christ.

To this able tribute I may add: Brother Keach lived the life of a man of business, until he came to Missouri. Indeed, he lived largely from his agricultural industry after he entered the ministry. He moved to Missouri in 1831, and became a member of Bethel Church, Marion county. He was ordained to the ministry in 1842. Elder Jeremiah Taylor was the Pastor and one of the ordaining council. His yokefellows in the ministry were Jeremiah Taylor, P. N. Haycraft, James M. Lillard, James F. Smith, Christy Gentry, William Hurley, M. M. Modisett, Nathan

Ayres and H. M. King. He had the pastor-heart, he loved the church and every member received the shepherd's care.

He was a safe counselor. Those who were in trouble went to him for help and they always found in him a wise friend. He lived a man among men. As between man and man, he was self-reliant, free from sycophancy and whims, never seeking undue favors or making clandestine solicitations of benefactions. In business he bore himself as a man capable of standing on his own ground. This made him a leader of religious thought and life. A man who joined farms with him said, "I do not see how any man can live near J. H. Keach and not go to heaven."

In church life he believed in discipline, both educative and corrective. He preached the word of the Lord and he visited the wayward to win them to the right. He wanted to save the individual and he wanted to save the church.

In sickness Brother Keach was attentive, gentle and thoughtful, seeking to render to each one the service which would result in the greatest good.

His pastorates were blessed with large increases, sometimes under his own ministry of the word, sometimes when he had other ministers to help him. In 1848 he was blessed with a revival at Bethel church, Marion county, when among others he baptized his daughter, Sarah A., now Mrs. Wood. Bro. James F. Smith was his ministerial help.

In the winter of 1859 and 1860, the Lord gave to his Salem pastorate a gracious revival, with Bro. L. C. Musick as fellow-helper. In this revival Bro. James Duvall Biggs made a profession of faith in the Saviour.

Brother Keach was crowned with blessings on his ministry at Salem and Bethel in Ralls; the boundaries of the two churches interlap.

Bro. H. M. King assisted him and there was a great revival; some eighty persons united with the two churches.

Brother Keach received his crown January 11, 1878, in his seventy-first year.

MRS. NANCY M'DONALD.

This sister was a daughter of Mr. Thomas J. Buchanan, who came from Tennessee in the early years of the nineteenth century and who became one of the builders of Ramsey Creek Church.

On March the 10th, 1836, she was married to Mr. Hiram McDonald of Lincoln county. God gave them eight children. Sister McDonald was born December 16, 1818, and is still in the Lord's service at the age of nearly ninety-one. Her membership is at New Hope, where she was baptized. I was once her Pastor and she strengthened me. She is a mother in Israel, "a keeper at home," true to the Lord and His church.

She told me that her father while living here in young manhood became concerned for his salvation and rode horseback to Kentucky to hear Jeremiah Vardeman preach and to receive from him his spiritual instruction.

After Mr. Vardeman came here he preached in her father's neighborhood and she, then a child, heard him. "My father," said she, "was a man that took his children to church." It was a joy to listen to this ninety-year-old sister tell of the graces of the early Christians.

ELDER DANIEL MOSS.

September 29, 1827, Daniel Moss united with the Ramsey Creek Church by a letter from Poplar Run Church, Fleming county, Kentucky. In 1828 he was chosen a messenger to the Association from Ramsey Creek, but he was not present in the body. He was earnest in his public ministry and faithful in family worship at home.

Elder Moss was born in the year 1773. In 1796 he married Miss Sarepta Hathaway and he died November 6, 1829, and was buried in the Moss cemetery, some three miles northeast of Auburn. Eld. M. S. Whiteside, who has been worthily preaching the gospel for more than fifty years, is a grandson of Elder Moss, his father, Jacob Whiteside, having married a daughter of that pioneer minister. In 1827 Daniel Moss was a messenger from this Association to Cuivre Association. By the act of the Association in 1827, "Brother Jeremiah Taylor was appointed to preach the introductory sermon at the next Association; and in case of failure, Brother Daniel Moss." But when the body met in 1828 neither of them was present.

CHAPTER IV.

"TO PREACH THE GOSPEL IN THE REGIONS BEYOND," 1835-1843.

At this time Salt River Association is an equipped, seed-sowing body in the midst of the world-field.

The absorbing duties of the new country and the establishing and nourishing the young churches had largely occupied the efforts of the brotherhood up to this time. Now they will lift up their eyes and behold the fields gleaming with harvest whiteness and begin to lend a helping hand to those who are obeying the command: "Go ye, therefore, and teach all nations, baptizing them in the name of the Father, and of the Son, and of the Holy Ghost: teaching them to observe all things whatsoever I have said unto you; and, lo, I am with you always, even unto the end of the world." Great events were stirring the nations; an empire had been opened west of the Mississippi River; except Mexico, all of North America was open to the gospel or was opening.

Western commerce had penetrated the markets of the far east, providing transportation for the heralds of the cross going to distant lands, new interest was reviving in the publication of the Holy Scriptures and our Salt River fathers shared the general awakening to the larger possibilities for service that the God of the nations was giving. These things dawned upon them gradually and they walked in the light while they had the light. The question of having the Bible printed without perversions or misleading illustrations appealed to the Baptists, one of whose fundamental doctrines is that the Bible is the only rule of faith and practice. This raised the question of printing houses and, consequently, Bible Societies. The money-loving, self-seeking world must not be relied on for the bread of life, so this became a vital question in the churches. And the people of God came to a deeper consciousness of their duty to their children. The teachings of the Scriptures concerning the young showed them the pure milk that would nourish the young. This led to the Sunday teaching service which came to be called the Sunday school.

In 1834 Adoniram Judson completed the translation of the Bible into the Burman tongue. This translation greatly increased the interest in the circulation of the Scriptures among the nations in their own languages. Mr. Judson, being an American, his movements brought honor to his countrymen and the spirit of missions and stirred them to large endeavor. Salt River Association felt the impulse.

In 1835 the Association met with Noix Creek Church, September 18-21. Elder Davis Biggs preached the sermon from the text: "For the eyes of the Lord are over the righteous, and his ears are open unto their prayers; but the face of the Lord is against them that do evil." William Biggs was chosen moderator and Thos. T. Johnson clerk. There was preaching by Elders J. Bower, David Hubbard and William Hurley. "Appointed a committee of five brethren, viz., John Lewis, James Nichols, A. Martin, Thos. T. Johnson and Edward Bondurant, to visit the church at Mt. Moriah with a view to labor with and try to settle a matter of disorder." The first Saturday in December was set apart for fasting and prayer. The circular letter said: "In proportion as we love our Bibles, so will we aid, that others may possess this Bible too."

In 1836 the Association held her session at Mt. Pisgah Church, September 9-12. Brother Jeremiah Vardeman preached the introductory sermon; text: "Ye should earnestly contend for the faith." The afternoon session of the first day day was opened with prayer by Brother Ephraim Davis. Brother William Biggs was elected moderator and Brother Thomas T. Johnson clerk. Six Miles Church, Illinois, was received into the Association. W. Foreman, J. Sanson and F. Collard were the messengers. The newly organized Association, Bethel, sent as messengers, Brethren Wm. Carson and Christy Gentry. Salem sent Matthew Davis and Samuel McClure. On Sunday there was preaching by Hurley Fuqua and Jeremiah Vardeman.

In 1837 the Association met with Bethlehem Church and Brother Ephraim Davis preached the annual sermon from the Scripture: "But call to remembrance the former days, in which, after ye were illuminated, ye endured a great fight of afflictions." On Saturday there was preaching by Elds. Levi Kenman and David Hubbard; on Sunday by Elders E. Davis, Wm. Fuqua and David Hubbard. Brother L. Kenman was a visitor. But little business was transacted. The amount of money in the hands of the treasurer was $29.25. At this time Union Church, Pike county, was advised by the Association to dissolve and let the members go into neighboring churches. It seems that they did this. L. C. Musick and H. Hayden were members.

In 1838 the body met with Siloam Church. Brother T. T. Johnson preached the sermon from the text: "For what the law could not do, in that it was weak through the flesh, God sending his own son in the likeness of sinful flesh, and for sin, condemned sin in the flesh." "Elected by ballot to preach on Saturday, Brethren Gentry, Fuqua and Vardeman; to preach on Lord's day, Brethren Hurley, Ham and Landrum."

In 1839 the Association met with Ramsey Creek Church and Brother William Davis preached the opening sermon. The text was: "I am the door; by me if any man enter in, he shall be saved, and shall go in and out, and find pasture." William Biggs was re-elected moderator and William McLeod was elected clerk. "Agreed that the Association meet hereafter on Friday and arrange and continue till Monday following to finish the business." Lord's Day Brethren Vardeman, Elledge and Bowers preached. The visiting brethren were J. Elledge, Tyre Jennings, —— Fraile, Thomas T. Elton, William Sitton and A. S. Knapp.

In 1840 Spencer Creek Church was the place of meeting. Brother William Biggs was continued as moderator and Brother T. T. Johnson was again made clerk. No sermon. The visitors were Brethren Gilmore, Knapp, Crews, Bowers, Elledge, Inslem and Hendron.

Since the session of 1839 there had been unrest and even active discord in some of the churches. "The Baptist Central Convention of Missouri" had been organized in 1834. That body had adopted the following resolution:

"That in the opinion of this meeting, the call for the preaching of the gospel upon the frontiers and within the bounds of the Salt River, Salem, Mount Pleasant and Concord Associations is imperative." This is the body now known as "The Missouri Baptist General Association." There was strong opposition to the organization of this convention. Some who opposed it most strongly visited Salt River Association. The first moderator of the convention, Rev. Jeremiah Vardeman, was a member of Salt River Association and the clerk of the third session of the convention, Dr. G. M. Bower, was a member of a Salt River Association church. The opposition was against all activities outside of individual church and district association work. Sunday schools, Bible societies and missionary societies were especially obnoxious to the opposers. Some of our best churches and some of our most intelligent members were on each side of the question. The question of doctrine did not seem to be in the controversy, though later some doctrines were seriously strained from their historic interpretation as each side opposed the other. Such straining seems to be one of the evils of persistent controversy. Disruption was now threatened. Bethlehem had raised the question of *separation* of those who opposed missions from those who supported them. She sent a copy of a

The Regions Beyond.

communication, giving her grievances, to the churches of the Association and she received many replies, some favorable, some unfavorable to her position. The following two communications give the merit of the controversy:

PREAMBLE AND RESOLUTIONS FROM BETHLEHEM TO CHURCHES OF THE ASSOCIATION.

"The committee appointed by the Bethlehem church at their December meeting, 1839, to take into consideration the state of the church and to report to the next meeting, after due deliberation and prayerful investigation of the matter have concluded to present the following preamble and resolutions for their consideration, to-wit:

"Whereas, it is with deep regret and heartfelt sorrow we have witnessed the giant strides that are being made by the various religious denominations in the world to introduce into the church innovations which are calculated to alarm the true followers of the meek and lowly Jesus, inasmuch as they are not authorized by holy writ as a church appendage, they come to us in the shape of societies by the following names (to-wit): Temperance, Missionary tract, Sunday School, Abolition and various others, out of which we have no hesitation in believing will grow materials calculated in their nature to sap the foundations of our civil as well as religious liberty, for as money appears to be the prop by which they are all upheld, in proof of which we would refer you to the constant and repeated calls on the liberality of the people for money as though the arm of God had become impotent and that the great Jehovah had not the power to effect his purpose without the aid of poor mortal man and his filthy lucre. It is argued that the money is necessary for the purposes of aiding our Lord and Saviour in the spread of the gospel. Brethren, is there any enlightened Christian that has experienced the love and power of God that believes that Jesus Christ needs the assistance of mortal man in the way we believe that God's work is carried on and will be carried on by his own omnipotence and power, and we believe that those large drafts of money which are drawn from the people in many cases in a fraudulent manner are not actually used for the purposes which we are told that it is used for but that it is a great portion of it placed in a situation that eventually it will become the engine by which our religious liberties will be shaken from one end of Christendom to the other. Brethren, we had fondly hoped and prayed that our beloved Salt River Association would have shot the gulf and steered clear of the Baals of modern time, but, lo, we are sorry to say that they have crept in among us as we witnessed at the last Association, for at that meeting it was plain to be seen that a decided preference was given to the preachers who come from associations publicly declared by their minutes to have gone fully into all the societies and that without any hesitation the correspondence was freely continued, therefore

"*Resolved,* That we are in favor of and deem it our duty to contribute to the support of the gospel in any lawful and laudable way that is necessary and agreeable to the word of God, but that we do most solemnly protest against the introduction into the church of any of the above recited societies or Baals, believing that they are calculated to engender strife and confusion and that they ought not to be named in the church as a part of our discipline or government. Believing likewise that they are the inventions of men for filthy lucre's sake and that we have no fellowship with those things as an essential part of a Christian's duty, and further

"*Resolved,* That inasmuch as there has not been any public action in the Salt River Association on the subject above recited and therefore it is not known who is for and who is against it we would respectfully and in the bonds of love invite all our sister churches composing that body to take up the subject and examine it and if they feel to foster the seeds of discord and confusion we shall have to separate but we hope better things of our brethren and that they will come out from the Babel and join with us trying to put down the monster, and further

"*Resolved*, That any church in the Association or member of a church that wishes it shall be furnished with a copy of this preamble and resolution.

SAMUEL PEPPER,
GARRET GOODMAN,
JOEL GRIFFITH,
THOS. HUNTER,
JOHN JONES,
WM. MCLEOD,
Committee.

and further

"*Resolved*, That we send a copy of this preamble and resolutions to every church in the Salt River Association—when Brother James McLeod agreed to convey copies to Salem, Mt. Pleasant, Spencer and Peno, Brother Hunter to Noix Creek, Brother Goodman to Siloam, Brother Pepper to Ramsey Creek, Brother —— to Pisgah, Brother Wm. McLeod to Six Mile, Illinois.

"By order of the church at their January meeting, 1840.

"WM. DAVIS, Moderator.
"WM. MCLEOD, Clerk."

"THE BAPTIST CHURCH OF PENO, PIKE COUNTY, MO., TO THE BAPTIST CHURCH OF BETHLEHEM.

"Dear Brethren: Your letter was received at our March meeting, and a committee appointed to answer the same. You state in your communication that you have taken up the society questions. Are we to understand you brethren that you are opposed to any member joining a temperance society or a Bible society or a missionary society or the sending his children to a Sunday school when an opportunity may offer, or the giving of his money to any of these institutions? We have no rule in our church compelling any member to give to any society nor have we any to prohibit the giving if they wish so to do. We know of no church in the general Union that compels her members to give one cent to any of the societies of the day, and it would most assuredly be very hard to forbid a brother favoring sobriety and temperance, or the sending his children to a Sunday school, or the printing of the Scriptures in foreign languages, or the sacrificing of property, life and health to spread the gospel in heathen lands, but if your object is to prevent the churches from making those societies a test to fellowship in our churches, and that it shall become a part of church discipline to contribute to some one or all of those societies we should immediately dissent from such a rule, we are certainly for all of our members and churches to act freely and as to them may appear right in those matters, to give or withhold, and if we do not tolerate this course the time may soon come when the churches must be consulted as to the kind of religious newspapers and periodicals that must be read amongst her members. There is one other society which you have named—*Abolition,* and it appears to us as if this was brought in as a kind of driver to frighten the churches by naming a society which is odious to the community in general. It is our object to abide and stand by the general Union of Baptists and the doctrine that each church has the right to keep up her own rules of business. Brethren, we now ask you by the most solemn interrogative whether you know of any church in the general Union of Baptists that makes it a test of fellowship to be a member of any or all of the above recited societies or imposes a tax upon any of her members to aid in the building up of any of said societies? If this is the law we are ignorant of the place and church. We are of the opinion that those matters of having money is left to the free volition of the community. Dear brethren, if you cannot live with us on the terms of the general Union and allow our brethren to use their money as to them may seem right for the spread of the gospel at home or abroad, or the printing of the Scripture, either in our own language or foreign, without a breach of fellowship on your part, you will have to leave us. You intimate in your letter that the great Jehovah needs not mortal man nor filthy lucre to aid in effecting his work; then, brethren, does the great Jehovah need mortal man or lucre to put down error? Brethren, ponder well your course and if you cannot live with the general Union of Baptists, let us part in peace, not with bickerings and hard speeches, but separate if we must by consent and praying that God in his infinite goodness may overrule it all for his glory and the salvation of sinners. By order of the church second Saturday, April, 1840.

WM. M. BIGGS, Ck."

This communication from Bethlehem had secured the coöperation of some other churches and the Association took up the matter and the following proceedings were had: "Agreed to attend to the condition of the churches at Spencer Creek, Bethlehem and Union.

"*Resolved,* That we consider the secession of the above churches a palpable violation of their covenant engagement with the Salt River Association and we do affectionately advise and admonish those brethren to reconsider the course that they have taken and return again to the bosom of the Association." From this time these churches do not appear in the list of churches. It was an instance where good men differed.

Of Bethlehem church, Prof. M. S. Goodman, whose father was one of her members, says: "I would have written the history of that body but for the reason that I could not find in the minutes any statement of the time or place of its organization and nothing regarding its first members, which facts my physical condition prevents me from attempting to run down. It is possible that Mr. Thos. McIlroy, of Louisiana, may be able to give you some information upon these matters.

"This church separated from the Salt River Baptist Association in the early forties. They, the members, never were in touch with the doctrines of the Baptist Church as we have it to-day. From the beginning a great majority of them were Calvinists, not Arminians, and immersion was about the only doctrine in common with the two bodies. My father, a member of Bethlehem, was never in agreement with the majority after they withdrew from the Salt River Association but continued to worship with the body until his death in 1858. 'There was never a body of better men; of greater integrity or uprightness of character, or more decision and determination than those who planted their little church in the primeval forests of an unsettled country and whose unwavering faith in the promises of God made them strong and steadfast in the conviction that they were the children of a beneficent Father.'"

I knew some of the Spencer Creek men. They were Christians of character, piety and strength, deserving the affectionate consideration the Association at this session gave them. Doubtless good things could be said of members of Union Church. The one thing lacking was they did not *behold the fields white to the harvest* and respond to the need.

The agitation of the question of missions seems to have quickened the spirit of evangelism and the Association adopted the following: "*Resolved,* That we recommend to the churches composing this Association the propriety of obtaining and sending a preacher whose labors are approved by the churches to labor in the bounds of this Association in destitute places and report to the next Association."

This resolution shows a well-defined scriptural conception of evangelistic operations. Approval by the churches surpasses being accredited by any board or secretary. And "destitute places" are the places for evangelists if they would walk in God's light. A church that is able to choose and pay a minister for revival or any other service but relies on others to do these things for them needs to be fed on milk, not on meat, for they are not able to bear meat, or soon will be unable by reason of not being exercised. All honor to the Salt River Association men of 1840 who pointed to the "destitute places." There was preaching by Elders Gilmore, Hubbard, Hurley, Bowers, and Vardeman.

In 1841 the Association met with Salem Church. The sermon was preached by Brother W. McQuie from the text: "Neither pray I for these alone, but for them also which shall believe on me through their word; that they all may be one; as thou, Father, art in me, and I in thee, that they also may be one in us: that the world may believe that thou hast sent me." Brother Anderson Woods, of Bethel Association, accepted a seat in the body, also Brethren Bowers and Greenlief, of Illinois. Correspondence with Cuivre Association was discontinued. The churches that had opposed the position the Association had taken on missions were discontinued from membership in the Association. "Lords' Day, September 12. Preaching by Brethren Woods, Bowers and Landrum, at the close of which the Lord seemed graciously to bless the word spoken by his servants by the powerful and energetic influence of the Holy Spirit, for poor sinners were brought to bow before a throne of grace and supplicate for mercy." Sulpher Lick, of Lincoln county, and Bethel, of Ralls, were received into the fellowship of the Association at this session. Sulpher Lick had eighty members; her messengers were Lewis Duncan, S. Gilliland, J. C. Pace, George Clare. Bethel had thirty members; her messengers were J. Vardeman, J. M. Johnson, Robert Briggs, Sr., and S. Brashears.

Mount Pleasant Church was the place of meeting in

1842. Brother David Hubbard preached the sermon from the text: "O Lord, revive thy work." Adiel Church, Pike county, was received into associational fellowship with twenty-seven members. Her messengers were Peter Moss, Robert Sloss, John Woods and —— Hawkins. "Appointed a committee consisting of J. Wood, J. M. Johnson, Walter McQuie, J. Culbertson, W. Carson and B. Stevens to express the views and feelings of this Association relative to the character of their departed and much lamented brother, Elder Jeremiah Vardeman." This committee closes their report saying that they "rejoiced in knowing that he continued the unwavering advocate of our principles to the end, and that 'in his death he had hope,' having leaned his head upon the blessed Saviour and breathed his life out sweetly there." The corresponding brethren were Thomas Ford, Gentry, Stevins, Haycraft, Carson and Jacob Bowers.

In their annual corresponding letter they say of the churches "that some of them have enjoyed interesting revivals." There had been eighty-nine baptisms. Brethren Hurley, Bowers, Haycraft and Gentry were appointed to preach on Lord's Day. "Adopted the following, to-wit: *Resolved*, that this Association approve of the object and principles of operation of the General Association of Baptists in the State of Missouri."

In 1843 the Association held her session with Sulpher Lick Church. Elder Thomas T. Johnson preached the opening sermon from the text: "He that believeth on the Son of God hath the witness in himself." Four new churches were received into the fellowship of the Association: Saverton, Ralls county, with ten members; Joseph Jeffries and Charles W. Stewart the messengers; New Salem, Lincoln county, with thirty-four members; J. Ricks, G. Admire and W. W. Wise the messengers; Mt. Hope, St. Charles county, with twenty-seven members; James Carr and Reuben Harris the messengers; Camp Creek, Warren county, with ten members; George W. Owing and Philip Glover, the messengers. Elder James Suggett from Bonne Femme, and Elders A. Broadus and N. Parks, from Bethel Association, were received to seats in the body as corresponding members. There was preaching by Brethren Suggett, Broadus and Parks on Saturday, and by the same brethren on Lord's Day. This action was taken: *"Resolved,* That in consequence of the Bethel Association having set apart the first Saturday in November, 1843, for the purpose of prayer and thanksgiving, we the Salt River Association, recommend to the churches to set apart the same day for the same purpose."

BETHEL CHURCH, RALLS COUNTY.

By Mrs. Kate Brashears.

Bethel Baptist Church was organized the first Saturday in August, 1840, Elder Jeremiah Vardeman as moderator. The names of members in the constitution are as follows: Abraham Buford, Mary Buford, Mary Hill, Mary Shulse, Susanah Shulse, James Cox, Sarah Cox, Mary Cox, Robert Briggs, Rebecca Briggs, James Culbertson, Rebecca Culbertson, John Ralls, Lettitia Cox, John M. Johnson, Sally Johnson, Polly Jane Johnson, Dortha Spotswood, Rachel Norton, Eleanor Shulse, James Turley, Mary Cleaver, Solomon Brashears, Jamima Brashears, Jeremiah Vardeman, Lucinda Vardeman, Jeremiah Vardeman, Jr., William Vardeman, Anthony, colored, Queen, colored, Henry, colored.

At first they held services at the neighbors' houses and open air services in the woods. From 1840 to 1842 there is no record. In 1842 the church called Brother Benjamin Stevens as pastor, which place he faithfully filled until March, 1849, during which time there were many additions to the church. The second Saturday in January, 1844, Brother James Cox and James Culbertson were ordained as Deacons. Brother A. D. Landrum was pastor from March, 1849, until

July, 1850; Elder William H. Vardeman from 1850 to 1851; Brother William Hurley from 1851 to 1855.

The church undertook to build a large church on a corner of Brother Culbertson's farm and it was blown down before completed. They had to return to the old church. In 1868 they built the house that they have at present. They abandoned the site on Brother Culbertson's and built where the old church stood.

Elder John Keach served as pastor from 1855 to 1868; Elder B. F. Hixson from 1868 to 1884; Elder Bland Beauchamp, 1885 to 1886; Elder B. F. Hixson, 1886 to 1894; Elder S. S. Keith, 1894 to 1895; Elder E. S. Graham, 1895 to 1897; Elder W. A. Bibb from March, 1898, to October, 1898; Elder James Reid, 1900 to 1901; Elder G. W. Eleston, 1902, three months; Elder W. J. Patrick, 1902 to 1904; Elder M. E. Broaddus from August, 1905, to March, 1906; Elder G. T. Baker, 1906 to 1908. We have been without a pastor for several months. Elder R. T. Campbell fills our pulpit once a month in afternoon.

NEW SALEM CHURCH.

By W. A. Bibb.

New Salem Church of Lincoln county, Missouri, was organized in the year 1843 in the private home of Brother Thomas Shields by Eld. A. D. Landrum and moved to Brother William Overall's, and we worshipped there until a church was built in 1858, near where the present building stands, which they used for forty years. The constituent members were W. W. Wise, Malvina Wise, Cordelia Wise, Mrs. Nancy Crenshaw, William Overall, Elizabeth Overall, Patsy Shields, John M. Ricks, Lydia Tipton, David, Elizabeth and Lucinda Furgerson, George Admire, Rosaline Brisco, Elizabeth Parker, Thomas Shields. There have been seven clerks: George Admire, Dennis Swan, F. D. Hardesty, I. M. Magruder, C. F. Miller, E. M. Magruder. Fourteen Pastors have served this church: Lewis Duncan, W. D. Grant, W. W. Mitchell, C. A.

Mitchell, Wm. F. Luck, M. S. Whiteside, James Reid, W. M. Tipton, F. M. Birkhead, J. S. Eames, William Callaway, W. P. Bibb, W. N. Maupin and W. A. Bibb, the present Pastor. Many brethren have assisted these pastors in revivals, whose names are loved by this church. Winfield Church was organized out of New Salem membership and many of her children are scattered over the country, but there remains a strong body. Brother F. M. Birkhead was converted, licensed and ordained to preach here and he served as pastor for nine years. Now New Salem Church has 235 members still on her record; has preaching twice a month, has prayer meeting once a week, gave for missions $83.70 last year, will give over $100 this year. She has a number of Deacons, namely, Brothers John Overall, E. M. Magruder, Loyd Cockrel, Frank Elston and Robert Kelly. There are many of the first members' descendants now members of the church. The Magruders, Overalls, Crenshaws, Elstons, Sittons, Birkheads, Prices, Shields, Dixons, Argins, Harlows, Kelleys, Days, Houstons, Cannons, Bois, Terrells, Millers, Bacons and many others who have cast their lot with the church. The brethren are harmonious and hope for a great future. We look hopefully for greater things. While our dear Brother Reid was Pastor, in explaining inconsistent praying by way of illustration, he said men often prayed for that they did not want. A brother prayed, "Lord, draw in the wanderings of our minds from things on the earth and place them on things in Heaven." His boy had gone with hogs to market but something got wrong and he returned to the church where the brother was praying and he arose and said, "How far did you get the hogs?" He did not want most what he prayed for. He knows how to answer better than we ask. A great and good man has gone to the Shepherd of the fold.

Uncle Frank Hardesty was clerk for twenty-five years of Salem Church, missing only two meetings. Brother Luck was called as Pastor of the church for lifetime. Brother E. W. Dorsey was licensed to preach and ordained at New Salem. He has contributed much to the good of the cause and is now a Pastor of churches; also C. B. Tucker, another Pastor, holds his membership here. W. N. Maupin, a former Pastor, holds membership with New Salem.

The present building was built in 1898. Also Foley, Star Hope, Highland Prairie, Harmony Grove and Winfield Churches were all organized out of this church membership.

ELDER WILLIAM DAVIS.

For several years Elder Davis was an active member of Salt River Association. In 1839 he preached the introductory sermon and he offered the closing prayer of that session of the Association. He was a Pastor and efficient in his work. He was a cultivated gentleman and an able preacher. His family has kindly permitted me to make this quotation from his writing, giving his deep experience of grace. He wrote: "I felt the obligation I was under to repent, but repentance seemed to be far from me; I tried all manner of prayer; my burden left me and a hope sprung up in me that my sins were pardoned. I felt calm and easy, went to the church, told some of my exercises of mind, was received and the next day baptized by Elder McCoy."

The date of his conversion is not known, but I copy the record of his ordination and ministerial authority: "To all those to whom these presents may come; This is to certify that the bearer hereof, our beloved Brother William Davis, was on the 13th day of April, 1837, set apart by solemn ordination and fully invested with all the functions of the Gospel Ministry at the instance, and by order of the United Baptist Church of Jesus Christ at Buck Creek, Shelby county, Kentucky.

"Given under our hands this 21st day of April, 1837.
"GEORGE WALLER,
"PHILLIP BURRUS,
"R. GIDINGS,
"Presbytery."

Mr. Davis was a Kentuckian and came to Missouri in the first half of the nineteenth century. He lived and died in Pike county, where he was honored and revered. He left children and grandchildren who have honored his memory in worthy lives. In 1840 he went with the anti-mission Baptists.

COL. WM. G. HAWKINS.

By Dalton Biggs, Esq.

Of all those whose memory we cherish, perhaps none enjoyed a more enviable life or a longer term of usefulness than Col. W. G. Hawkins. Born in Kentucky in 1808, he came to this State and settled in Pike county in 1830 on the farm a few miles northwest of Bowling Green, where he resided to the day of his death, which occurred in 1889, in his eighty-second year. Deacon Hawkins was for many years prominent not only in the councils of the church, but in county and State affairs as well. He held many positions of honor and trust, being the first assessor of his county, filling the position of deputy sheriff two terms, serving two terms as sheriff, and four terms in the State Legislature. He was noted among his peers as a safe, conservative, prudent man, whom all could approach for advice with confidence, with assurance of wise counsel. Among his many sterling traits of character, perhaps his strongest fort consisted in his ability to avert a pending disturbance. One instance to illustrate this fortunate characteristic. At one time when there was a subject up for discussion and decision before Salt River Association, which had been under consideration from session to session, until perhaps every member had taken sides, the discussion having reached a point where an explosion seemed unavoidable, when brethren sat with bated breath, Colonel Hawkins, tall and commanding, yet feeble, arose from his seat near the center of the house, securing the attention of the moderator, said, "I move you, sir, that this whole matter be laid on the table, and left there for time and eternity to settle." It was a master stroke. Promptly the motion was seconded, and carried with such hearty unanimity as the writer has seldom seen. That matter still rests, where by his wisdom, it was placed, and there it doubtless will remain until settled in the day of final accounts.

ELDER LAFRENIERE CHAUVIN MUSICK.

Duncan's History says of Elder Thomas R. Musick: "He was doubtless the first Baptist minister that ever permanently settled in the State." He was a native of Virginia and his first visit to Missouri was in 1797, when he visited his older brother, Abraham, in St. Louis. He preached a great deal in the territory since embraced within the limits of Salt River Association. Under the Spanish Catholicism preaching the gospel was forbidden. "When forbidden to preach on the land, he would take a boat and push out in the stream and preach to the people on the shore." This quotation is from Misses N. and M. Musick, daughters of L. C. Musick. I further quote: "In 1819 Capt. Lewis Musick moved to Pike county. In 1822 our great-grandmother, Mary Nevel Musick and wife of Thomas R. Musick, died. After her death, when in North Missouri, Thomas R. Musick made his home with his son, Captain Lewis Musick. At one time he taught school in a room of his son's house. In 1837 Captain Lewis Musick moved to West Cuivre, Audrain county. It was at the house of Captain Lewis Musick that Thomas R. Musick preached his farewell sermon in North Missouri. He was going to St. Louis and he felt that he might not see his people again. He crossed Loutre

River when it was high, his faithful horse swam out with him, but he was so wet that he took cold, from which he died at the house of his nephew, —— Musick, December 2, 1842." He was buried at Fee Fee Church. He was born October 10, 1757. He attended the sessions of Salt River Association held October, 1827, with Bethel Church, Marion county.

Elder L. C. Musick was a grandson of Elder Thomas Roy Musick, a son of Captain Lewis Musick, and was born near Creve Coeur Lake, St. Louis county, Mo., July 29, 1815. In 1819 his father moved to Pike county and the son pursued his studies in the schools of his neighborhood and in Bowling Green. He made a public profession of faith in Jesus Christ and united with the church in March, 1833. He soon began to preach and was ordained in October 1835. He married Miss Jane D. Hayden. Brother Musick was in the pastorate some, served as missionary of Salt River Association and preached in Florida, Georgia, Kansas, Indian Territory, California and Illinois. He was in the ministry seventy-two years and five months. He died on his farm southeast of Vandalia at 11 o'clock a. m. January 14, 1908, aged ninety-two years, five months and fifteen days. He held firmly the teachings of the scriptures and preached them with fidelity. He raised a family of children and several of them and their mother left the earth in advance of him.

ELDER B. STEVENS.

By his son, Dr. B. Q. Stevens.

Benjamin Stevens was born in the county of Sussex, England, suburbs of London, October 22, 1801. His father's name was Benjamin Stevens, who moved to Chatham when Benjamin was quite a youth. He was very devoted to his mother, who died when he was twelve years old, and he composed the accompanying verses as he sat by her grave. He was a very devoted member of the Episcopal Church or Church of England and until 1825 he worked in that church, but his wife being a Baptist drew his attention more to the reading of the Bible and in 1825 he joined the Ebenezer Baptist Church in England with his wife. He married Sarah Foster at Chatham Church, England, September 24, 1823. To this union were born fourteen children, seven girls and seven boys, five of whom survive, three girls and two boys.

When arriving in New York City in 1831 he went to Rev. Dunbar's church, a Baptist Church in New York. He worked at the tinner's trade making wire shovels and holding meetings every Sabbath when opportunity offered. He went from New York to Pittsburg, Pa., where he taught school and he was constable one year. He came to Missouri in 1835 and was persuaded by Revs. Hurley and Hendron to take the field of Salt River Association as a missionary and he organized several churches, namely, the Ebenezer, Crooked Creek and Oakland. He died in Hannibal, Mo., April 19, 1896.

His wife, Sarah Foster Stevens, was born December 17, 1805, at Chatham, county of Kent, England. Died July 30, 1899.

He was an excellent father and ruled his home well. He received his education in the public schools in England. He taught school in Pittsburg and a writing school in Missouri. He educated his children at home as there were no good schools in that wild country that we could go to.

MOTHER'S GRAVE.

By B. Stevens.

How sweet is the mem'ry of her that I love—
The thought of my mother, whose spirit's above!
On the spot where she's buried the green grass does wave,
And she silently lies in the cold, dreary grave.

Grave, grave,—mother's grave;
I sigh and I weep o'er my dear mother's grave.

A mother!—sweet name! ever dear to my breast,
While I weep o'er thy tomb, thy spirit's at rest.
The Lord, He hath taken; 'tis right, for He gave,
Tho' I'm left an orphan, to weep o'er thy grave.
　　Grave, grave, etc.

I'm cast on this wide world of sorrow to roam;
I sigh when I think of my once happy home:
My joys are all fled—all the comfort I have
Is the hope I shall meet her beyond the cold grave.
　　Grave, grave,—mother's grave;
　　I know I shall meet her beyond the cold grave.

At the age of 90, he attended regularly the services of his church.

REV. JEREMIAH VARDEMAN.

By Rev. J. M. Peck, D. D.

[Taken from the Christian Repository.]

This distinguished minister was one of a class somewhat rare in the annals of the Church. He possessed the peculiar talent of bringing the leading truths of the gospel home to the consciences of his hearers. His illustrations were singularly vivid, his language strong, simple, and well suited to convey clear thoughts to every class, even the most illiterate; while the deep fountains of feeling gushed forth from his own heart, and poured like a shower of rain over the minds of his hearers. In deep emotions, vivid conceptions of gospel truth, and the power of exciting sympathy, he resembled Whitfield.

There were occasions, when, in an unpremeditated exhortation, he seemed to touch every chord of the soul, and by the outpourings of gospel admonitions, in a simple and affectionate style, would strike the consciences of all around him. There was not the least affectation in the style and manner of his preaching. He had never studied the arts of the rhetorician, and despised all tricks and artifice in moving the passions. In allusion to the practice among frontier people, of winnowing grain in a primitive fashion, he spoke of the labored efforts of some preachers in getting up excitements, as "making wind with a blanket."

In portraying the lost state of man as a sinner, and the way of recovery by Jesus Christ, he was a master workman.

Jeremiah Vardeman was the youngest of twelve children, and a descendant from Swedish ancestors on his father's side, and from Welsh by the maternal side. Traits of character peculiar to each nation were conspicuous in him. His birthplace was on New River, in what is now Wythe county, Virginia, July 8, 1775, about twelve miles above old Fort Chiswell. Both his father and grandfather were natives of Sweden. The latter, John Vardeman, senior, with his family emigrated to America and settled in South Carolina in the early part of the eighteenth century, and there died, as his descendants reported, at the extreme age of one hundred and twenty-five years. He was a member of the Lutheran Church in his native country, and united with the Protestant Episcopal Church in South Carolina, and was esteemed for his piety and moral worth.

His son, John Vardeman, Jr., was seven years old when his father came from Sweden, but recollected many incidents of his native country. While living in South Carolina he married Elizabeth Morgan, who was a native of Wales, and soon after removed and settled in Bedford county, Virginia, on the eastern slope of the Blue Ridge, and not far from the celebrated Peaks of Otter. While residents here, John Vardeman, Jr., and his wife, professed religion in a time of persecution, and became members of the Baptist Church, and ever after maintained a devout Christian profession to extreme old age.

About 1767, he removed with his young family to the settlements on New River, and in 1777, pushed still further into the southwestern corner of Virginia, on Clinch River. It was then a time of trouble with the southern and western Indians, and Mr. Vardeman, with his family, entered the neighboring fort at Shadrach White's residence, on the Maiden Spring Fork of Clinch River, in what is now known as Russell county. Among the families who forted at White's, were the Messrs. Skeggs, James, Henry and Richard, all noted hunters and explorers in the southwest at an early day.

In the autumn of 1779, Mr. Vardeman, with many other emigrants, moved to the wilds of Kentucky, and settled near Crab Orchard, in Lincoln county.

Jeremiah, the youngest son, was old enough to, and actually did, take part in the Indian wars before their close by Wayne's victory in 1794, and served repeatedly as a scout. Reared from early childhood in the wilderness of Kentucky, and during troublous times, his opportunities for education were limited indeed. And the very little he obtained was more from the family circle and his own natural desire to obtain knowledge, than from school exercises. The only acquisitions he made were in reading, writing, and the common principles of arithmetic. When he attained to manhood, and especially after he professed religion, he read just enough for profitable cogitation. He acquired the habit of deep and intense thought and reflection, while riding, walking, or even while laboring on the farm. His pious parents taught their children the lessons of Jesus Christ, and daily offered up prayers for their salvation.

It was about the year 1792, when Jeremiah Vardeman was about seventeen years of age, that a revival of religion was commenced in Cedar Creek Baptist Church. The ministers, who were co-laborers in that district of country, were John Bailey, Lewis Craig, William Bledsoe, William Marshall and Peyton Nowlen. The meetings were not continuous or protracted, as in modern times. The regular periods for preaching in each settlement were monthly, when on ordinary occasions the meetings would be held on Saturday and the Lord's day; in seasons of special revival more frequently, with two or three social prayer-meetings during each week, with occasional sermons by some visiting preacher. During this revival, Jeremiah Vardeman and his two elder brothers, Amasiah and Morgan, with many other persons in Lincoln county, professed to be converted. Cedar Creek is a branch of Dick's River. Elder William Marshall had gathered this little Church, but about the time of the revival, Elder William Bledsoe was elected Pastor; that is, monthly supply. He was a smart, rather than a pious preacher, and the church was under his care when young Vardeman and his brothers united with it. Subsequently Bailey became a Universalist, and was disowned as a minister by the regular Baptists, though for some time after he preached among the "Separates." Bledsoe also apostatized to Universalism, and then became indifferent to a religious life, and reckless in his conduct.

Mr. Vardeman always protested the preaching of these men had no effect in awakening his conscience. He was under conviction two or three months, during which the instructions and prayers of his father and mother, and the truths of the Bible which he read, were deeply impressed on his conscience.

When the hope of salvation dawned on his mind, and he enjoyed reconciliation with God through Jesus Christ, he felt strong and deep convictions that it was his duty to call sinners to repentance. He felt that he must preach the gospel at any sacrifice, but the ordinary objections arose in his mind—his youth—his inexperience—his deficiency in knowledge, and the fear he should disgrace the calling should he make the attempt. His education at school scarcely deserved the name, and he resisted the impressions as well as he could, until they measurably wore off. He remained in the church very comfortably for two or three years. He was a mere novice, and no one thought of calling him to speak or pray in public. During that period he was habitual in secret prayer, but made no effort to pray or exhort in the presence of others.

Some of his associates, about his own age, made frequent attempts to draw him into circles of frivolity and worldliness. They repeated to him the *words* of Scripture, without regard to the connection and meaning. "There is a time to dance." Young Vardeman's natural temperament induced in him fondness for social pleasures and hilarity, and by the inducements of his young friends he was drawn, first partially and then wholly, within the circle of their influence. The next downward step was in yielding to their entreaties, much against his conscience, to attend as a mere spectator, a dancing school some one had started in the settlement of Crab Orchard. It was only for once, and then he would be more strict and watchful, were his own cogitations. Persons of much respectability were there and treated the youthful professor with marked attention. Amidst the whirl of excitement, gayety, and hilarity, and against the monitions of his own conscience, he was over-persuaded and induced to sign his name to the list of pupils to the school.

Forty years after this fatal step towards the downward course in his Christian profession, we heard him narrate with pungent feelings of sorrow and abhorrence this fatal error of his youth. He frankly confessed, that while putting his name to the subscription, he felt like a criminal signing his own death warrant. By a desperate effort he braved it out, and went through a regular course of lessons in dancing. Before this fatal night he had never attended a dancing school, or a country frolic. Educated as he had been, under the constant supervision of religious parents, and habituated to the universally prevailing idea that balls, dancing and sports of all kinds, were a violation of the Christian profession and a forfeiture of Christian character, it is nothing strange he should regard his conduct as a violation of the profession he had made. His parents and two brothers were members of the same church, and were grievously affected at the conduct of Jeremiah, who now left the church without apology or explanation. He regarded himself as unworthy the Christian name, and offered no excuse for his folly and sin.

During this period of worldliness and hilarity, he became engaged to Miss Elizabeth James, daughter of Richard James, Esq. Her parents were both pious and devout members of Cedar Creek Church, and regarding young Vardeman as a vain, light-minded young man, who wasted his time in frivolity, they were opposed to the match. The result was a common one with thoughtless youth on the frontiers, an elopement and marriage.

His young wife, though religiously trained, had then made no profession of religion. Her parents, most excellent people, though sorely grieved, had the good sense to perceive that further hostility was useless, forgave the delinquents, and with young Vardeman, removed to Pulaski county, on the waters of Cumberland River. There young Vardeman became the leader of the young people in every species of mirth and amusement; none could sing and play on the violin so enchantingly; none so jovial and full of hilarity as Jeremiah Vardeman. He was the life and soul of every dance and country frolic, and his young wife, much to the grief of her father and mother, joined him in all these recreations. Thus nearly three years of his life passed away to no useful purpose. In a worldly sense he was not immoral. He never swore profanely; was temperate in drinks; kind-hearted, generous and honorable in all his dealings with his fellow-men. His duty to God was wholly neglected, and he lived after the course of this world; yet he was not a happy man. In the midst of his associates, in gayety, music and dancing, he was full of enjoyment, but conscience was then stifled. There were seasons of mental disquietude which none can realize, but those who have drank the wormwood and gall, after a season of backsliding. Conviction of his sin and folly often drove him back to sinful pleasures for temporary relief.

His religious friends, with a single exception, gave him up, under the impression he would go on, step by step, the downward course. That exception was his pious mother. She clung to him with a mother's love, strengthened by faith in the divine promises, and in the power and grace of the Lord Jesus Christ. She was a woman of persevering prayer, and the more thoughtless and worldly he became, the more fervently she prayed. It seemed to others presumptous, when she would say with the deepest emotions, "I know Jerry will be reclaimed; God is faithful, and I feel assured he is a prayer-hearing God."

There was a plain, unlettered Baptist preacher in Pulaski county, by the name of Thomas Hansford, a man of great zeal and fervent piety, who was instrumental in awakening the consciences of his hearers, and whose self-denying efforts in preaching the simple truths of the gospel God blessed abundanty. Vardeman was not so hardened but that he would attend meetings with his wife. On one of these occasions Mr. Hansford was led to preach from 2 Pet. 2:22— "But it happened unto them according to the true proverb—the dog is turned to his own vomit again, and the sow that was washed, to her wallowing in the mire." The preacher expounded the preceding verses and applied the text in a most pungent and feeling manner to the consciences of those who had professed religion and apostatized. There had been some previous indications of a revival of religion in the settlement, by unusual seriousness for some time. Vardeman was present, and suddenly and powerfully convicted of his backslidings. In giving the writer a narrative of this incident in his life in 1834, he remarked, while the big tears rolled down his cheeks, "If brother Hansford had poured coals of fire over my naked body, it would not have burned me worse than that sermon did." His wife was convicted of her sin and guilt at the same time. Both went home from the meeting under pungent distress. Vardeman could not labor, and for two or three days spent his time in the woods, sometimes on his knees, and then prostrate on the ground, deploring and confessing his sins, and pleading with God for mercy. He compared himself to Jonah, who fled from his duty to Tarshish, and was cast overboard in the storm. The impressions he had received to preach the gospel, when he made a profession of religion, now rolled on his mind with crushing force. He felt great distress for turning back from his Christian profession and engaging in the frivolity and amusements of the world; but his heaviest convictions, and those which filled his soul with the deepest anguish, and which he regarded as the cause of his turning back to wallowing in the mire, was his refusal to follow Christ in preaching the gospel, or calling sinners to repentance. This conviction now rolled on him with ten-fold force, until in his heart and with his voice he said, "Lord, what wilt thou have me to do? I will do anything the Lord requires, if it kills me." He obtained some relief while reading and meditating on Malachi, 4:-2—"But unto you that fear my name shall the sun of righteousness arise with healing in his wings, and ye shall go forth and grow up as calves of the stall." This comforted him, and he solemnly vowed to the Lord that he would forsake all worldly pleasure and vain amusements, and preach the gospel to his fellow creatures.

The people, at that time, in Pulaski county, and in most parts of Kentucky, lived in log cabins, scattered through the forests, with a clearing for corn and other grain for each family. These were some distance apart, with few wagon roads, and their intercourse with each other was by narrow trails for single horses, through the cane-brakes, brush-wood, and dense forests called "bridle-paths." A prayer meeting had been appointed at one of these cabins, which Mr. Vardeman and his wife attended the night after he had made the solemn resolution just recorded.

There was no minister present, but so much interest was felt that men, women, and children came from several miles distant. A rumor had been circulated that young Vardeman would preach, of which he had heard nothing. Some of the church members conducted these social meetings without much formality. They sung hymns, prayed, and talked, as they were inclined, or as impressions moved them. Before the close, one of Vardeman's neighbors, who knew the effect of the sermon, and his seriousness, invited him to speak. He arose, but in narrating the circumstance told the writer, he never could remember what he said, how long he spoke, or whether he said anything. The only recollection he retained was, the people of all classes were weeping and sobbing around him. Another social meeting was appointed the next Sabbath, which Mr. Vardeman, on request, promised to attend.

At this meeting he waited for older persons to take the lead, after which, with deep feelings and tears gushing from his eyes, he gave an exhortation, mingled with confessions of his own backslidings, and called on his young associates to forsake their sinful amusements and follow Christ, and they would enjoy what he then felt—peace of conscience and salvation through the blood and righteousness of Jesus Christ.

To his surprise and amazement, young and old were crowding forward to give him their hands, and with audible voices exclaiming, "O, Mr. Vardeman, pray for me!" Another exclaimed, "O, Mr. Vardeman, do pray for me, for I'm a heap bigger sinner than ever you was!" Probably there were twenty or more standing around, and in various phraseology confessing their sins, and begging him to pray for them.

There is nothing strange or unnatural in such a state of excitement, among plain, honest-hearted, frontier people, meeting in a social, though religious manner, in a log cabin. It is the spontaneous bursting out of the heart, unchecked by the conventionalities of a higher civilization. Mr. Vardeman, who had never attempted to pray in public, was taken by surprise; the call was unexpected; there was no time for reflection; he thought of his vow to the Lord when he obtained relief, and without hesitation fell upon his knees with the crowded assembly, weeping and sobbing, and calling on the Lord for mercy around him, he attempted to pray for the first time in the hearing of others. What he said, or whether there was any coherency in his language or thoughts, he was unable to recollect.

These social meetings were continued each successive Sabbath, and two or three times during the week with similar effects; only before he closed, he gave an invitation to all who felt their own sinfulness and guilt, and their need of the power and grace of Christ, and desired the special prayers of God's people, to come forward and give him their hands, and he would plead for them before the throne. This practice became very common and frequent, especially in seasons of revival, with most religious denominations throughout this valley. Large meetings were frequently held in the open air under the umbrageous forest, or in school-houses, dwelling-houses, and other shelters, in bad weather. We have not been able to trace the practice beyond the little social meeting, when the people spontaneously moved forward and entreated the speaker to pray for them. Connected, as it was with his first efforts to exhort unconverted sinners, he always followed the practice where he saw those signs of serious impression and anxiety, which he was quick to discern. He was opposed to all artifice, and all preternatural excitements, and cautiously guarded his congregations from mistaking their willingness to have the prayers of the people of God, for submission to Jesus Christ and his righteousness on the terms of the gospel.

It was not many days before a number of his former associates in worldly pleasures gave evidence of a saving conversion to Christ. His wife, whom he tenderly loved, was one of the first. News of the revival, and of the change in the course of Mr. Vardeman, and his preaching, as the people called it, reached Lincoln county; and his parents, brothers, and friends, urged him to visit them. His father and brothers were fearful he would make a failure in attempting to speak in their presence. Morgan Vardeman testified that his first discourse there was solemn and effective. He spoke with great freedom, and seemed to want neither words nor matter.

The church of which he had been a member restored him to fellowship, and gave him a license in the old Baptist form; a certificate merely stating that he had "a gift" of usefulness, and had liberty to use it wherever Providence opened the door. He now gave out appointments and preached several times in quick succession. All classes came out to hear him, and in a short time upwards of twenty of his former associates in Lincoln county, and members of the dancing-school that led him astray, became humble and obedient disciples of Christ.

We are deficient in materials for a full history of Mr. Vardeman's ministerial labors for several successive years. He was ordained probably in 1801, and the next year removed to Lincoln county, and lived on rented land. He sustained his family by labor on the farm, while he spent all the time he could command in reading and in preaching the gospel. He was a most impressive and popular preacher wherever he went. He purchased a small farm in 1804, four miles from Standford, the seat of justice, which, that year was cultivated by Isaac Goodnight, as a "cropper." Mr. Goodnight, who lived in Warren county, in 1842, furnished the writer some interesting facts of Elder Vardeman of that period. He was one of his associates in worldliness and folly during his backsliding state, and bore testimony to his thorough reformation, and his early preaching. Mr. Goodnight was not then a professor, but subsequently became a member of the Baptist Church.

At that period, Elder Vardeman had the charge of four churches, and the same season (1804) he made a preaching tour to Lexington, Limestone (Maysville) and several other places. From that period, we find him connected with the South District Association. The church he first joined belonged to the Tate's Creek Association, for it is found on the minutes of that body in 1801.

While connected with that branch of the South District Association that seceded from the old South Kentucky party, the name of Jeremiah Vardeman appears frequently on the Annual Minutes of the Elkhorn, Tate's Creek, North District, and other bodies of the United Baptists, as a corresponding visitor, and as one of the selected preachers for the Sabbath. Before the close of 1804, the family register contained the names of four children, and before the decease of his first wife, in 1818, ten living births had been recorded.

His ministerial labors were abundant for several successive years in Lincoln, Pulaski, Montgomery, Jessamine, and adjacent counties. Although he had an increasing family, and his salary and perquisites by no means adequate to their support, he contrived by good economy, great industry, and a judicious use of his time, to provide for their wants and continue his labors without ceasing in the gospel ministry. His mental powers were strong, vivid, and quick in action. Great numbers were converted and baptized under his ministrations, and for many years he preached more sermons, and to larger congregations, and baptized more converts, than any minister in the Mississippi Valley. He kept no journal or register of his labors, and did not appear to think he was doing anything extraordinary.

Early in 1810 he was called to the pastoral charge of the church of David's Fork, in Fayette county, about ten miles east of Lexington. He removed his family to that settlement, purchased a small farm and commenced regular pastoral labors and monthly preaching in April. This church had for its Pastor about two years a young and promising minister by the name of Hunt, who died, leaving a widow and family of small children. The church, pursuing a very common policy in those days in obtaining a preacher, had purchased Mr. Hunt a farm, which in two years after, became the property of his widow. Had they purchased a piece of land and improvements for a parsonage, and thus furnished their minister a comfortable residence for the time being, it would have been a wise and economical measure, and remained from generation to generation, to furnish a partial income towards the support of the Pastor. As it was, they were under necessity of aiding Mr. Vardeman in purchasing his farm, which appears to have been done with great cordiality and liberality.

He was also Pastor, monthly, of two other churches in Montgomery county, Lulbegrud, and Grassy Lick, which relation he sustained by annual appointments for several years, until he was obliged to decline in order to supply other places.

A secession from the old church of Bryant's Station called Mr. Vardeman as their monthly Pastor in 1811, and he sustained that relation, as he did the one at David's Fork, till 1830. Evil surmisings and unchristian jealousies at the time, with the influence of party spirit that had produced a division among the churches in the Elkhorn association, attributed the division in the church at Bryant's Station to Mr. Vardeman. We have evidence before us that he had no personal concern in the matter; that the causes of the division had been increasing for some years, and that the secession had been consummated before he took charge of the Elkhorn party.

A gracious and extensive revival followed his ministrations in David's Fork and the other churches in a few months after the commencement of his labors. In 1810, 185 were converted and baptized in David's Fork Church. In 1817, in another revival, about 125, and in 1827-28, 250, besides frequent additions in the intervening years. In three consecutive years, at Lulbegrud, the accessions by baptism were 165, and at Grassy Lick, 90.

In the winter of 1815-16 Mr. Vardeman made his first visit to Bardstown, in Nelson county, then the seat of Roman Catholic influence in Kentucky. We have the particulars of this and of subsequent visits to Bardstown, and the effect of his preaching, from the correspondence of the late Samuel McKay. Priest Baden was unwise enough to enter the lists against him, and lost several of his congregation. Vardeman disliked controversy, but in bringing the whole armament of gospel truth to bear with tremendous effect on error, no man could excel him. He visited that part of Kentucky three times and preached with his accustomed success.

In 1816, we find him in Lexington, holding a series of meetings, and the church he attended at Bryant's, held a church-meeting in that city, to examine and receive converts. Next year the First Baptist Church of Lexington appears on the minutes of the Elkhorn Association, with thirty-six members.

The same year, 1816, he commenced a series of meetings in Louisville. The late Hon. Judge Rowan, a distinguished jurist and statesman, was a warm, personal friend of Mr. Vardeman, and regarded him as one of the greatest pulpit orators he had ever heard. There were but few professors of religion in Louisville and but one house of worship, and that owned and occupied by the Methodists. This was obtained, and the influence of Judge Rowan brought out a class of persons not accustomed to attend worship on ordinary occasions. Colonel McKay, who was present, says: "His fame as a preacher brought out immense congregations of people for several successive days, to whom he preached with great effect; and from these meetings the city of Louisville is indebted, in the great measure, for its flourishing churches. Immediately after Mr. Vardeman's visit, a large Presbyterian church arose, then the first Baptist Church, and so on."

Early in 1818 Elder Vardeman met with the sore affliction of the death of his first wife, with an unconscious infant, in child-bed. He was devotedly attached to her, and the stroke was so sudden and severe as almost to crush him. His severe mental depression alarmed his friends, who wisely thought if he could journey and become engaged in revivals under his preaching this despondency would pass away. The churches he regularly served released him for eight months and provided a substitute in the late Elder William Spencer, and he made a long tour to the southern part of Kentucky and Tennessee. The preceding year, in company with other ministers, he had labored in raising up a church of seventy members, in Jessamine county, called Providence. Another series of meetings, which he attended in 1825, gave this church an addition of 125 members. He aided in establishing another church in Paris, the seat of justice of Bourbon county, and at different periods he attended the churches at Boone's Creek, Cane Run, and Silas.

Early in the spring of 1820, Mr. Vardeman made a visit to Nashville, the capital of Tennessee. There were but three Baptists living in the place, who belonged to Mill Creek, four miles distant. At first the meetings were held in the Methodist church-house; but when its further occupancy by the Baptists was not desired, they removed to the courthouse. He was accustomed in these protracted meetings, to have one or two brethren to aid him. On this occasion Rev. Isaac Hodgen, another very successful itinerant, was his coadjutor. He was obliged to leave, after a few days, to meet other engagements; but Mr. Vardeman continued for several weeks. We have an interesting sketch of these labors and of successive Baptisms from the late Col. Wm. Martin, of Smith county, Tennessee, whose business engagements kept him in the city that season. Another communication, from C. C. Trabue, Esq., casts light on this scene of his labors; but we have no room in this sketch for these documents. Converts were multiplied, a large number were baptized, and a Baptist church was organized, that by the first of October numbered one hundred and fifty members, and had commenced the erection of a spacious house of worship.

It was in the winter of 1828, or '29, he was invited to hold a series of meetings in Cincinnati, and where similar success followed; over nine hundred converts professed faith in Christ, and were baptized.

The family of Elder Vardeman had become large; his farm was too small, and in too dense a population for convenience; and his servants, which had originated from a single family, could fare better in a new country than in a closely settled neighborhood. He appeared to feel as anxious for their temporal and spiritual welfare as for his own. Young ministers, of promising talents and usefulness, had been raised up, and men sound in the faith, and large experience, came from other States and filled the chasm left by erratic reformers. The advance in the denomination, which a few years had produced, induced him to think his labors might be spared in Kentucky. Age was creeping over him; and young children, the fruits of a third marriage, were gathering around his board. Kentuckians by many hundreds, within a few years previous had gone out from that State to Illinois, Missouri, and other Western regions. So he sold his farm, then much too small for his large family and dependents, made a farewell excursion through Kentucky and Tennessee, and in October, 1830, he had pitched his habitation on the border of a beautiful and fertile prairie, near Salt River, in Ralls county, Missouri. Here, in a short time, he had comfortable houses for his own family and those of his dependents, and more than two hundred acres of rich, virgin soil, under cultivation.

Nor was he neglectful of the moral wilderness around him. Without waiting for some church to call him, and insure him a stipulated salary, he proceeded to collect together the scattered sheep of Christ's flock, and gather them into folds. His labors were abundant in the ministry, and gratuitously bestowed. Several churches grew up under his immediate labors. He soon had for a coadjutor, Rev. Spencer Clack, who removed from Bloomfield, Ky., and settled in Palmyra, the county seat of Marion. By their joint labors a church was built up in that town.

For some years Mr. Vardeman had been growing corpulent, and his usual weight was three hundred pounds; yet his muscular frame was well proportioned, and his personal appearance graceful and commanding. His voice was powerful, sonorous, and clear; his enunciation distinct, and he could be heard in the open air for a great distance. He took an active part in bringing the Baptist denomination in Missouri into active and harmonious co-operation in benevolent efforts.

In August, 1834, he presided in a convention to organize a system of domestic missions in that State, which has since grown into the General Association.

Still the infirmities of age were creeping over him, and his giant frame and vigorous constitution showed signs of decay. Yet he continued his ministerial labors without relaxation. For nearly two years before his death he became unable to stand while preaching, and sat in an armed chair while he addressed the people with deep pathos. Only two weeks before his final departure, in company with another minister, he visited the Sulphur Springs, at Elk Lick, which appeared to afford him benefit. Before they left they constituted a church; a measure not contemplated in the visit. There was a revival, and, notwithstanding his weakness, Elder Vardeman baptized five converts; the last service of that kind he ever performed. He had then baptized more Christian professors than any man in the United States. As he kept no registry of these and other labors, the accurate number can never be ascertained; probably not less than eight thousand converts. In the churches he regularly attended the converts under his ministry continued to maintain their christian standing in an equal proportion to those baptized under ordinary excitements or by settled Pastors.

On the Lord's day before his death he attended the appointment of another preacher in the church in his immediate neighborhood. He was free from pain, his appetite good, and his mind clear and calm in view of death. After the first sermon he spoke with the usual effect half an hour or more, from Heb. 2:3— "How shall we escape if we neglect so great salvation?" The following week he grew worse, though little alarm was felt by him or his family about speedy dissolution. But on Saturday morning, the 28th of May, 1842, he called his family around him, gave some directions, bade them farewell, and sank in death like a child falling asleep—all within fifteen minutes—in the sixty-seventh year of his age.

Rev. Vardeman was married three times. The marriage and death of his first wife have been noticed already. She was the mother of eleven children; one died with the mother at birth; one lived only two days; and the rest, four sons and five daughters, lived to grow up, profess religion, and give good evidence of the genuineness of their conversion. Of these, six died before their father. The eldest son died in 1817, at the age of seventeen years, in the enjoyment of the Christian hope. The second son and fourth child, by name Ambrose Dudley, was born October 25, 1804. He became a scholar, studied the medical profession, professed religion, and commenced preaching the gospel, giving promise of great usefulness. He was smitten with fever, and died after a few days illness, while his father was from home on a preaching excursion, June 25, 1829, in the twenty-fifth year of his age. Two sons by his first wife are living in Missouri; both professed religion in youth. William Henry is a preacher, and a Pastor of a church in St. Charles county.

He married for his second wife Miss Elizabeth Bryan, in 1821, who had one child, not a professor at the period of her father's death. Mrs. Vardeman, the second wife, died in 1822. His third wife was Miss Luly Bullock, daughter of the late Thomas Bullock, Esq., of Woodford county, to whom he was married in 1823. She still survives, and has charge of his farm and numerous dependents. She was the mother of four children, two of whom were baptized and joined

DEACON J. L. DAWSON.

ELDER J. F. SMITH.

DR. J. A. THOMAS.

ELDER WM. F. LUCK.

the church the autumn after the decease of their father.

We will only add, that Mr. Vardeman was a most affectionate husband, a prudent and kind father, a humane and considerate master, an upright and patriotic citizen; and his memory to this day is cherished and venerated by a large circle of surviving friends and Christian brethren.

CHAPTER V.

LENGTHENING THE CORDS, 1844-1854.

Larger things are to now be done and greater results must be expected. The Association had received freely, freely she must give. The door of opportunity was open. God's people must enter into the larger service. Salt River Association must take her place in the front line of Jehovah's battling army.

In 1844 the annual meeting was with the Noix Creek Church. Elder David Hubbard preached the sermon from the text: "And that repentance and remission of sins should be preached in his name among all nations, beginning at Jerusalem." New Hope and Troy churches, Lincoln county, were received into the fellowship of the Association. The body voted "that as a means of diffusing religious knowledge and offering an opportunity of circulating information in regard to the condition of the Baptist churches in Missouri, we recommend to the churches of our body to aid in the circulation of the *Missouri and Illinois Baptist.*" This act of the Association showed their judicious estimate of Christian journalism. This field of usefulness has been cultivated to the edification of the Lord's disciples and the furtherance of the truth. It has been sometimes sown in tares. A religious periodical that is edited in the light of holy scripture, in the love of the truth, with scrupulous sense of justice to all men and institutions, borne above self-seeking interests and sordid gain, may promote the prosperity of the churches and be the means of fellowship and an awakening to the brotherhood. It must be free from censoriousness, flattery or sinister policy. Such a paper deserves the literary, financial and spiritual support of the denomination. The Missouri editors of the paper approved by our brethren in 1844 were I. T. Hinton and R. S. Thomas; which was enough to give confidence.

The sustained spiritual interest in the Association is shown by this action at this meeting: "The Association recommends to the churches composing the same the fourth Saturday in October as a day of fasting and prayer in conjunction with the Mount Pleasant and General Associations." On Saturday Elders Hurley and Flood preached; on the Lord's Day Elders Bowers, Hurley and Haycraft.

In 1845 the place of meeting was Mt. Pisgah Church. Elder Walter McQuie preached the sermon from the text: "To the intent that now unto the principalities and powers in heavenly places might be known by the church the manifold wisdom of God."

Elder A. D. Landrum was elected moderator and Elder Thomas T. Johnson was elected clerk. Martinsburg Church, Illinois, Bethlehem and Zion and West Cuivre churches were received into the Associational fellowship. The Martinsburg messengers: David Hubbard, J. Hubbard; Zion: J. H. Dutton, J. Walker, G. Owens, P. Glover; Bethlehem: Jacob Capps, M. Spires, S. Marble; West Cuivre: W. S. Adams, J. N. Griffin, J. M. Fuqua. At this session information was given that the Camp Creek Church had dissolved and that the members had joined Zion Church, which had just been received into the Association.

The Association *"Resolved,* That in accordance with the request of Salem and Mt. Pleasant Churches that an executive committee of three be appointed by the Association to procure a minister or ministers to ride and preach in the bounds of the Association for such time as funds may be procured for that purpose." This is the first time the body had an executive committee and the fact that they did appoint one showed the desire to keep the missionary work alive all the year around. The brethren selected were W. Waddell, Hiram G. Edwards and George W. Peay. The Pastors were asked to lay the work before the churches and raise funds.

Since the previous meeting Elder Davis Biggs had received his crown of glory and by vote the Association put on record these memorial sentiments: "*Resolved,* That in the death of Elder Davis Biggs our Association has lost one of our ablest ministers, the cause of missions one of its warmest friends and the cause of God one of its most zealous and unflinching advocates.

"*Resolved,* That while we sympathize with the relatives of the deceased in their loss, we rejoice with them that he died as he had lived, full of faith and good works, preaching to, praying for and exhorting sinners up to the last hour of his life." The corresponding letter, written by Brother Samuel Lewellen, says: "Our Association continues to enlarge her borders, having received four new churches at our present session."

In 1846 Salt River Association met with Ramsey Creek Church. It is impressive and quickening to see the scriptures selected by the preachers of that day as texts for the opening sermons. They came right to the heart of the heavenly message of grace. On this occasion the sermon was preached by Elder David Hubbard from the text: "The gospel of the kingdom shall be preached in all the world for a witness unto all nations; and then shall the end come." The brethren had lifted up their eyes and were looking towards "all the world," the Americas, Europe, Asia, Africa and the islands of the sea. Towards large parts of the earth they could do little more at that time than look, for many nations were then closed against the gospel. The promises of God gave them grace to look and labor. Wiliam Biggs was elected moderator and T. T. Johnson was elected clerk. Elders Hurley, Hill and Stevens preached on Saturday. One of the pleasant, fraternal features of the sessions of the Association from the first was the presence in the body of visiting brethren. At this session Elders Suggett, Hill, Hurley, Stevens, Bower, Harris, Grant and Capps and George K. Biggs, J. Floyd and J. J. Worthington accepted seats in the body. The report of the executive committee was received and so well satisfied was the Association with the work done that the same men were reappointed and the same plan agreed upon for the incoming year. The year's work in District Missions was given in detail. The executive committee said they "procured the services of Elder A. D. Landrum at seventy-five cents a day with instructions to call in assistance if needed." Brother Landrum reported to the committee: "I have spent seventy-seven days, preached ninety-seven sermons, ridden seven hundred miles and received of the committee $33 and from brethren and friends $45.75. I succeeded in obtaining the services of Brother Hubbard to the amount of $23.30, including ferriage, leaving a balance in my hands of $7. . . . I have baptized eighteen hopeful converts and heard the experience of eleven during a protracted meeting, which were baptized by Brother McQuie in connection with Mt. Pisgah Church."

In the minutes for 1846 is given for the first time a connected list of the ministers belonging to the Association, namely: "A. D. Landrum, David Hubbard, Walter McQuie, Ira M. Bailey, Robert Gilmore, John Duncan, James Duncan, William H. Vardeman, William D. Grant, John C. Herndon, Jacob Capps, Thomas T. Johnson."

Zion Church was the place of meeting in 1847. Elder William H. Vardeman preached the introductory sermon from the scripture: "They which builded on the wall, and they that bare the burdens, with those that laded, every one with one of his hands wrought in the work, and with the other hand held a weapon. For the builders, every one had his sword girded by his side, and so builded. And he that sounded the trumpet was by me." A. D. Landrum was chosen moderator and Hiram G. Edwards clerk. Elders Hill, Renfro and Hurley preached on Saturday and Elders Landrum and Hurley on Sunday. On Sunday a collection was taken for the District Mission work. The mission plan was continued.

It was *"Resolved,* That the Association set apart the Friday before the second Sunday in December next as a day of fasting and prayer to Almighty God to renew his work of grace in our midst." When the spirit of revival was low those good men humbled themselves before God and sought the renewal of his blessing.

One of their great leaders, the Hon. William Biggs, had died since the previous meeting and they recorded this memorial testimony to his honor: *"Resolved,* That in the death of William Biggs, the former moderator of this Association, we have sustained an irreparable loss, and we deeply sympathize with the bereaved family for the loss they have sustained."

At this meeting a committee was appointed to collect some lost minutes and the clerk was ordered to enter them in the book of records, thus showing the interest felt by the men of this time in the preservation of our history. By a vote of the Association the ministers selected to labor were instructed to "labor mainly with the weak churches and destitute settlements."

The session of 1848 was held with Bethel Church. Elder A. D. Landrum preached the sermon from the scripture: "Of these things put them in remembrance, charging them before the Lord that they strive not about words to no profit, but to the subverting of the hearers. Study to show thyself approved unto God, a workman that needeth not to be ashamed, rightly dividing the word of truth." Brethren P. N. Haycraft, John H. Keach, C. Gentry, James F. Smith, Winder C. Dingle, William Carson, Warren Finley, Robert C. Hill, William G. Sweeney, —— Griffin and Thomas Sweeney were received from corresponding Associations. The executive committee reported that Elder John M. Johnson had been employed and that he labored one hundred and seven days at seventy-five cents per day. The same plan of mission work was continued. A collection of $92.75 was taken. Fifteen dollars per month was voted for missionaries the incoming year. The Association recommended to the churches to sustain the *Western Watchman*, St. Louis. Since the previous meeting Elder John C. Herndon had finished his course on earth. The body adopted the following memorial in his honor:

"*Resolved,* That in the death of Elder John C. Herndon the Association has lost one of her ablest ministers, the cause of missions one of its warmest friends and the cause of God one of its most zealous advocates.

"*Resolved,* That while we sympathize with the relatives of the deceased, we rejoice that he died as he had lived, full of faith and good works and with the brightest hope of a glorious immortality beyond the grave." The circular says: "We trust that throughout our denomination increased interest will be taken in the family altar, and in personal devotion to the cause of Christ."

Elder R. S. Thomas, who was the clerk of the General Association, was present. The Association invited him to deliver an address in behalf of that body and that a collection be taken for the mission work of the same. The collection was $24.15. The interest in the larger mission work was growing.

The Association met in 1849 with Noix Creek Church. Elder David Hubbard preached the introductory sermon from the word of the Lord: "Glory to God in the highest, and on earth peace, good will toward men." Eighteen dollars per month were voted to pay the ministers employed by the Association. Elders A. G. Mitchell and T. T. Johnson were employed. There was preaching on Sunday: forenoon by Elder Hubbard, afternoon by Elders Hurley and Suggett. On Saturday the preaching was by Elders Hurley, Hill and Suggett. A collection was taken on Sunday for the General Association.

In 1850 the session was held with Mt. Pleasant Church. The sermon was preached by Elder A. D. Landrum. His text was: "And he that winneth souls is wise." A. D. Landrum was chosen moderator and A. P. Miller clerk. Two new churches were received, namely: Camp Creek, Ralls county, and Buffalo Knob, Pike county. Camp Creek messenger, John M. Johnson; Buffalo Knob messengers, A. G. Mitchell, L. A. Edwards, J. Anderson, E. C. Bright. Brethren J. F. Smith, N. Ayres, J. J. Bradley, N. Flood, R. C. Hill and T. Hubbard accepted seats as corresponding members. Elders B. B. Carpenter and Griffin and Brother H. Carmer accepted seats as visiting brethren. There was preaching by Elders Carpenter, Flood, Hill and Hurley. The ministers were by a resolution requested to preach on the proper observance of the Christian Sabbath to each congregation within Salt River bounds.

The report of the executive committee gave good results. There had been three missionaries in the field and spiritual blessings crowned their labors. They paid the missionaries in full and sent out an encouraging and joyful circular letter. They asked that collections be taken "at an early period to sustain preaching in the bounds of our Association."

In 1851 the session was held with Ramsey Creek Church. The introductory sermon was delivered by Elder John M. Johnson from the words: "Then had the churches rest throughout all Judea and Galilee and Samaria, and were edified; and walking in the fear of the Lord, and in the comfort of the Holy Ghost, were multiplied."

North Cuivre, Pike county, and Mill Creek, Lincoln county, were received into the Association. The messengers of North Cuivre were J. J. Mitchell, R. H. Johnston, T. Stanford, J. O'Banion; Mill Creek, A. G. Mitchell, J. Whiteside, D. Ellis, R. D. Ellis. Elders Hurley and Modisett accepted seats. There was preaching by Elders Smith, Vardeman, Hurley, Modisett and Hill. The missionaries reported one hundred and thirty-seven additions to the churches besides one church of ten members organized. T. T. Johnson and James F. Smith were elected missionaries for the en-

Lengthening the Cords. 153

suing year at $1 per day. The corresponding letter expresses these joyful words: "Since our last correspondence with you many of our churches have been wonderfully blessed with an outpouring of the spirit of God, and large additions of useful members to their numbers." The ministers in 1851 were L. C. Musick, A. D. Landrum, T. T. Johnson, W. McQuie, J. F. Smith, E. T. Lamb, Lewis Duncan, John Duncan, Malen Spyres, A. C. Davenport, W. H. Vardeman, John T. Johnson, J. N. Griffin, John M. Johnson, A. G. Mitchell, W. D. Grant, David Hubbard.

Licensed: W. W. Mitchell, D. V. Inlow, John F. Hedges.

The Association met in 1852 with Salem Church. Elder James F. Smith preached the sermon in course. His text was: "For we are his workmanship, created in Christ Jesus unto good works, which God hath before ordained that we should walk in them." The Association received into her fellowship four newly organized churches: Sugar Creek, Providence and Indian Creek, Pike county, and Middletown, Montgomery county. The messengers from Sugar Creek: W. Penix, W. W. Waddell, E. Ferrell, E. Hostetter; Providence: D. V. Inlow, Thomas Burks; Middletown: Samuel Crutcher; Indian Creek: J. Motley, Levi Moore. Elders William M. Jesse, Hurley, Gentry, Ayres, Tilford, Modisett and Brethren Hatcher, Bradley, Utterback, Leachman and Armstrong accepted seats in the body. The Association "instructed the moderator to appoint a special committee, consisting of one messenger from each church together with the missionaries of the last year to act in connection with the executive committee, in devising a plan for associational preaching and to make out a report for the present session, setting forth their views as to the most efficient and harmonious plan for its future operations." The committee was: N. McDannold, A. Ellis, W. Brown, W. W. Wise, A. P. Miller, A. Cates, J. Culbertson, E. Hayden, J. M. Ricks, J. H. Thomas, R. S. Duncan, D. Hubbard, J. H. Dutton, M. Spyres, W. S.

Adams, J. M. Johnson, S. A. Edwards, J. J. Mitchell, D. Ellis, W. Penix, D. V. Inlow, S. Crutcher, Levi Moore. The report of this committee was:

"*Resolved,* That we now proceed to appoint a missionary or missionaries, whose duty it shall be to labor *generally* with the weak churches and destitute settlements so long as funds may be procured for that purpose, and that the executive committee procure funds and fill vacancies and confer with the missionary or missionaries upon all suitable occasions, and that the missionaries, in their annual reports, state their fields of operation." Thomas T. Johnson and William W. Mitchell were elected missionaries for the ensuing year. The missionaries for the preceding year reported thirty-one baptisms and other good results from their labors. The executive committee for the incoming year were: George W. Peay, William W. Waddell and Henry Sisson. By appointment, Elder J. H. Keach took a collection of $41.20 for the General Association. The Association approved the objects of the American and Foreign Bible Society, which was represented by Eld. John Teasdale. There was preaching by T. T. Johnson, M. M. Modisett, D. Hubbard, A. G. Mitchell, N. Ayres, William Hurley and James F. Smith.

The session of 1853 was with Mt. Pisgah Church, September 9 and 10. The sermon was preached by Eld. Wm. Hurley from the text: "The secret things belong unto the Lord our God: but those things which are revealed belong unto us and to our children forever, that we may do all the words of this law." Three new churches were received, Louisiana, Pike county; Cottonwood; Lincoln county; and Mount Pleasant, Montgomery county. The messengers were: From Louisiana, A. D. Landrum, G. W. Peay, J. Haynes and C. Bacon; from Cottonwood, W. Brunk, E. Owen and J. H. Bain; from Mt. Pleasant, J. H. Talbot and Robert Badger. The visiting brethren were Brethren Modisett, Wilkinson, Leachman, Bradley, Ellege, Ingmire, Hobbs and Williams. Elders W. W. Mitchell and T. T. Johnson had been employed by the board. *The*

Western Watchman was commended. The wish for the organization of a new Association came from Indian Creek Church. To this the Association replied: "We recommend the churches wishing to enter into a separate organization to hold a convention with the Mt. Zion Church in Montgomery county on Friday before the third Sunday in May next and then apply by letter and messengers to our next annual Association for letters of dismission." The ministers at this time were A. D. Landrum, T. T. Johnson, W. McGuire, James F. Smith, Lewis Duncan, John Duncan, J. Nicholls, A. C. Davenport, W. H. Vardeman, John H. Keach, J. M. Johnson, W. D. Grant, D. V. Inlow, J. N. Griffin, L. C. Musick. The board was the same as in the previous year.

The year 1854 is unreported. I have been able to find no minutes, written or printed. The place of meeting was Mill Creek. Brethren J. R. Gipson and J. R. Powell were present, and others I have seen and can trust. Elder John M. Johnson preached the introductory sermon. A. D. Landrum was moderator and A. P. Miller clerk. Mt. Hope, St. Charles county; Sulpher Lick, Lincoln county; Zion, Montgomery county; Bethlehem, Lincoln county; Union Hill, Ralls county; North Cuivre, Pike county; Middletown, Montgomery county; Indian Creek, Pike county; Cottonwood, Lincoln county, and Mt. Pleasant, Montgomery county, disappear from the subsequent records and doubtless they had gone into the new Association proposed in 1853, being dismissed from Salt River in 1854. Two churches were received: Bowling Green and Union. The messengers from Bowling Green in 1855, the year following, were V. Henley, L. C. Musick, A. McDannold, W. W. Wise; those from Union were, in 1855, I. T. Nelson, J. McDaniel, J. Thompson, H. N. Baskett. Elders John Gipson and John F. Hedges were there in 1854. Elder Modisett preached on Sunday a strongly controversial sermon. The attendance was large. Elder James E. Welch was there and spoke repeatedly on the destitute fields.

BUFFALO KNOB CHURCH.

By S. F. Jett for Committee on History.

The Buffalo Knob Baptist Church was organized on the fourth Saturday in November, 1849, by Brother Albert G. Mitchell and Brother Lamb. The following are the names of those who constituted the organization: Simpson Edwards, Thomas Page, John W. Turpin, Albany Turpin, Addison Tinsley, Casandra Tinsley, Eliza Edwards, Ann Edwards, Eliza Page, Mary Spears, Sarah A. Jacobs. They elected as officers, Simpson Edwards and Thomas Page, Deacons, the same being ordained by the foregoing ministers, and Addison Tinsley was elected clerk. A. G. Mitchell was called to the pastorate of the church for one year and he was continued as pastor until the fourth Saturday in November, 1876, when he offered his resignation, which was accepted. Brother James Reid was called as pastor and the call was accepted. He continued as pastor two years and eight months. Brother Reid resigned, and on the fourth Saturday in May, 1880, Rev. A. G. Mitchell was again called and served the church two years and two months. On the fourth Saturday in October, 1881, Brother W. M. Tipton was called. He served the church continuously until the third Sunday in March, 1890. On the third Saturday in April, 1890, Brother W. J. Patrick was called to the care of the church and served the church four years. On the fourth Saturday in September, 1894, Brother J. D. Biggs was called. He served the church two years. On the fourth Saturday in April, 1897, the church again called Brother W. M. Tipton, who accepted and served two years and nine months. On the first Saturday in March, 1900, the church called Brother W. A. Bibb, who served six years and nine months. On the first Saturday in January, 1907, the church called Brother J. H. Terrel as a supply. He served the church eight months. The following named men served as Deacons and clerks from the organization until the present time:

Deacons: Simpson Edwards, Thomas Page, S. P. Dawson, Pike Lindsey, Jack Powell, S. F. Jett.

Clerks: Addison Tinsley, James Anderson, W. W. Mosby, W. R. Edwards, John Hogue, W. H. Edwards, J. P. Jett, D. C. Edwards.

The present pastor is George W. Wright. Brother S. P. Dawson, Sr., was ordained to the ministry in Buffalo Knob Church. The church was organized in a log schoolhouse and subsequently built a house of worship. They moved to Edgewood in 1881, built a house and took the name of the town. The church has had many precious revivals.

LOUISIANA CHURCH.

By Mrs. Sue E. Ayres.

The First Baptist Church was organized March 26, 1853—D. V. Inlow moderator and G. W. Peay clerk—with thirty-six members. Brother A. D. Landrum preached the sermon. Josiah Haynes and Robert W. Peay were elected Deacons and Robert W. Peary clerk. They worshiped in Wood's schoolhouse until the church was built on the corner of Seventh and Georgia streets.

The following ministers have served as pastors: James F. Smith, 1853; M. M. Modisett, 1854; A. D. Landrum, 1856; J. T. Williams, 1857; H. M. King, 1860; J. B. Fuller, 1862; A. F. Randall, 1865; —— Keith, ——; W. H. Steadman, 1868; Robert Gibson, 1868; James D. Biggs, 1872; W. M. Tipton, 1880; J. F. Kemper, ——; W. P. Throgmorton, 1890; W. A. Gibony, 1892; J. M. McManaway, 1894; B. W. M. Simms, 1897; C. F. J. Tate, 1899; A. F. Hauser, and Wm. P. Pearce. Brethren Williams and Steadman each was Pastor a second time. The church has been blessed with some gracious revivals. She has sent several men out into the ministry. We have had choice spirits in our membership, a number of whom have gone to rest. Brother Angus Reed superintends our Sunday school, which has an enrollment of 253 with fourteen officers and teachers. We have a Baptist Young People's Union.

The present house of worship was built in 1891 and is valued at $16,250. It was dedicated November 15, 1891. The present membership is 471. The church has a residence for the minister. Dr. C. G. Skillman is now filling the pulpit.

MILL CREEK CHURCH.

By Elder R. T. Campbell.

On July 12, 1851, a meeting was held in the schoolhouse near the home of Brother D. Ellis for the purpose of organizing a church. Religious services were conducted by Brother T. T. Johnson acting as moderator and J. J. Gibson as church clerk.

The Church Covenant and Articles of Faith were then read and adopted and the church was organized with the following constituent members: Albert G. Mitchell, James A. Mitchell, Reason D. Ellis, Thomas G. Ellis, Sarah Ann Ellis, Hannah Ellis, Jacob Whiteside, Lydia V. Whiteside, Duncan Ellis, Nancy Ellis. The church then elected Brother A. G. Mitchell as Pastor and Duncan Ellis clerk. Brother A. G. Mitchell was Pastor until the year 1872, a period of fifteen years. Brother W. W. Mitchell was pastor from the year 1872 to the year 1874. Saturday, January 16, 1875, the church called Rev. M. M. Modisett as Pastor. He held that position for one year. Rev. Wiley J. Patrick was called as Pastor of the church January 15, 1876. He resigned in 1890, having been the Pastor for fourteen years and six months. Rev. E. J. Sanderson was called on November 22, 1890. He resigned February 23, 1895, after serving as Pastor almost five years. Rev. W. M. Tipton was called to the church March 9, 1895, and remained in charge for three years and one month. Brother W. H. Stone was called as Pastor on May 25, 1898, and remained one year and six months, resigning November 25, 1900. E. J. Sanderson was called for the second time June 26, 1901, and resigned on February 22, 1902. In May, 1902, Brother James Reid was called as Pastor, but did not accept. December 27, 1902, Rev. E. Anderson was called. He resigned November 22, 1904. Rev. J. D. Watson was called December 24, 1904. He was Pastor for two years. R. T. Campbell was called January 26, 1907, and is the Pastor at present.

Elders M. S. Whiteside, W. S. Tucker and Russell B. Whiteside entered the ministry in Mill Creek Church.

SUGAR CREEK CHURCH.

By J. J. Penix.

The first day of May, 1852, the following persons met at Sugar Creek schoolhouse for the purpose of being organized into a Baptist Church: Wm. W. Waddell, Lois Waddell, Wm. Penix, George R. Waddell, Mildred Waddell, James P. Waddell, Hannah G. Johnson, Patsey Caldwell. The ministers in the service were Elders A. D. Landrum, John M. Johnson and Thornton T. Johnson. The church was duly organized. William W. Waddell and William Penix were elected Deacons and Wm. Penix clerk. Elder John M. Johnson was chosen Pastor. At the June meeting there were three additions. At the July meeting Wm. W. Waddell, Enoch Hostetter and Wm. Penix were appointed a building committee. The church became a member of the Association that same year, sending Wm. W. Waddell, Ezekiel Ferrill, Enoch Hostetter and Wm. Penix as messengers. In February, 1853, Geo. R. Waddell, James W. Johnson, James P. Waddell and Ezekiel Ferrill were added to the building committee. The house was built from the native forest and it now stands, a monument to the faithful services of the committee. God had people who were willing to sacrifice for the blessed Master. The first service in this house was held the second Sunday in July, 1853. Up to this time they had received sixteen white and seven colored members. In a revival in 1854, the Pastor was assisted by Elder Jesse Gibson in a revival over Salt River,

Salt River Association.

which resulted in eighteen additions to Sugar Creek Church. They afterwards organized into Salt River Church on the first Saturday in January, 1855. Brother W. W. Waddell was treasurer of Sugar Creek as long as he lived. In 1856 Elders M. M. Modisett and A. D. Landrum helped the Pastor in a revival that brought into the church twelve members. The church in 1857 paid her Pastor $75 for the pastoral year. The Pastor and Elder L. C. Musick preached in a revival that was blessed with five additions. In December, 1860, the Pastor was helped in revival services by Elder H. M. King and God gave them forty additions. May, 1863, the Pastor resigned. October, 1863, Elder J. W. Place preached in a revival that brought eight into the church and he was called the following month and preached one year. December, 1864, Elder W. W. Mitchell was called and served two months. In March, 1865, Elder J. M. Johnson was again called and continued in the pastorate the rest of his days. Elder M. M. Modisett became Pastor in May, 1866. He held a revival in February, 1868, with fourteen additions. Elder T. N. Sanderson preached in a revival in February, 1870, with four additions. In 1870 Haw Creek Church was organized out of members from Sugar Creek. March, 1871, Elders M. M. Modisett and Robert Gibson held services resulting in six additions. The following month Elder Modisett resigned. In June following Elder G. W. Foster became Pastor and in August he was assisted in revival services by Elder A. F. Randall; twelve were added. February, 1874, the Pastor and Elder J. T. Williams held revival services in which God gave them twenty-four souls. February, 1875, Elder J. D. Biggs became Pastor and served until the following October. February, 1878, Elder —— Bush preached in a series of meetings and fourteen were added. Elder J. F. Cook became Pastor in November, 1878. H. F. Unsell and J. J. Penix were ordained to the deaconship in February, 1879. Elder Isaac H. Denton protracted the services and two were added. Deacon Wm. Penix, who had served the church as clerk since her organization, resigned. On motion of Brother G. R. Waddell a vote of thanks was given him. His son, J. J. Penix, was made his successor. Elder J. D. Biggs was Pastor during 1881 and he was succeeded by Elder W. M. Tipton for a period of five years. In this time a revival is mentioned with eighteen additions and one with six. April, 1887, Elder W. A. Bibb became Pastor and continued until July, 1891. In November, 1891, Elder S. P. Smith became Pastor and served eleven months. Elder C. W. Davis became Pastor in March, 1893. He was helped in special services by Elder J. D. Hacker with eighteen additions as a result. March, 1896, Elder C. E. King became Pastor. Elder B. M. S. Simms helped in a revival with thirteen additions. Then Elder W. A. Bibb again served the church for a brief period. November, 1902, J. J. Penix resigned the clerkship and Sister Pearl Gordon was elected to succeed him. In November, 1902, W. H. Doyle became Deacon. Elders W. P. Bibb and J. W. Long served the church for brief periods. December, 1903, Elder E. W. Chewing became Pastor and served for some time. Lee Unsell and James Lee Reading were ordained to the deaconship in July, 1907.

HON. DABNEY JONES.

By Geo. E. Mayhall.

I regret that I have not made much progress in the matter of obtaining information concerning the late Dabney Jones. This much I have gathered that is definite. He came to Missouri Territory from Virginia in the year 1817 and was quite a celebrity in a local way in the early days. He united with the Baptist Church in New London, in fact it is claimed that he and James Turley were instrumental in organizing the New London church. No records of the early church here are in existence now so far as known. Dabney Jones is said to have transferred his church membership from New London to Salem, when Salem

Church was organized, and was a liberal contributor to the erection of the old brick structure which was used as a church by Salem congregation in its early days. He represented Ralls county in the Legislature, was sheriff and collector of the county in its primitive history, and while he had his faults as all humans have, was a useful and highly respected citizen. He died at his home on Spencer Creek, Ralls county, in the year 1852. His funeral was preached by Rev. Wm. H. Vardeman, then a citizen of Ralls county. I was a boy then, but I was present at the funeral of Mr. Jones.

ELDER DUDLEY VARDEMAN INLOW.

The subject of this sketch was the son of Henry and Salome (Poston) Inlow. He was born in Bourbon county, Kentucky, on November 24, 1825. In his early childhood his parents moved to Pike county, Missouri, where Dudley grew to manhood, having given his heart to the Lord while yet a child. Early in his life he felt impressed that it was his duty to preach the Gospel, to which impression he yielded some years later. Finally he decided to give himself fully to the work of the ministry, and was ordained in 1850. Elder J. M. Johnson, who baptized him at Mt. Pleasant, and others ordained him. One of the first churches that he preached for was Providence, north of Curryville. He constituted this church and preached for them into the fifties. His first sermon was in Mt. Pleasant, his home church.

In the year 1856 he married Elizabeth Dowell, the eldest daughter of James and Lucy Dowell, a prominent Baptist family of Monroe county, Missouri. To this union were born four daughters and two sons.

His ministry was chiefly devoted to the churches in Pike, Ralls, Monroe, Marion, Shelby and Knox counties. He was sound in the faith and persuasive in his preaching. Many churches were organized under his ministry, while others grew from weak mission points to strong, self-supporting churches. Going as he did, on horseback from home to home, and from church to church, he became a well-known character in northeast Missouri. Being Pastor of many of the churches throughout this section of the State, at one time or another, he had hosts of friends and followers who literally owed their spiritual life to the Gospel as he preached it. He, with a few others, did much of the pioneer work in what is now a strong Baptist section of our State.

In a letter of filial affection Elder R. M. Inlow wrote:

"In regard to my father's library, I would say that he was a great admirer and constant reader of Andrew Fuller, Charles H. Spurgeon and Christmas Evans. He had many books on the Doctrines; Bunyan and Baxter, and a fair collection on history and other subjects relating to his work. His method of selecting and developing his text grew out of a study of the Word itself. In reading the scriptures a passage would fasten itself upon his mind and, as he proceeded with his daily work, he developed it according to the best of his ability."

A Tribute by Judge R. N. Sharp.

"Brother Inlow was my Pastor for a number of years at Ebenezer Church in Bethel Association. He was a man of a very logical mind and could reach the hearts of the people.

"He had a fine memory. I have heard him divide his sermons into six parts and follow them all six without notes (he never used notes). If he had had the advantages of a college education he would have been a power indeed. He was a good Pastor and much loved by the people of his churches. He did a great deal of mission work, preaching at schoolhouses in the community, and was a power with the people, especially among the rural people.

"His preaching was evangelistic and led many to accept the Savior. He was a witty man; seemed ready at all times to meet criticism.

"There were two D. D's, one a Presbyterian, the other a Baptist, who had a discussion. Both lost their temper and had some sharp words. A friend of Brother Inlow, who was a Presbyterian, said to him, 'I hear that your Baptist preacher was about to whip my Presbyterian brother.' Brother Inlow answered, 'We Baptist preachers claim to be doing every good work, and I think your preacher needed a whipping.'

"I was with him in the city of Hannibal in company with a brother, Tom Caldwell. We were walking, with Brother Inlow in front of us. Brother Inlow was a very spare, tall man. Brother Caldwell said to me, 'I reckon you brethren at Ebenezer would not want Brother Inlow any longer?' I told him, 'No, we think he is long enough.' He stepped up beside Brother Inlow and said, 'Brother Sharp said the brethren at Ebenezer don't want you any longer.' Brother Inlow stopped and asked, 'What is the matter?' and seemed very much confused. I told him we thought he 'was long enough.' We had a good laugh and walked on. I was with him when he died at his home at Philadelphia, Mo. The last word he said to me was 'Brother Sharp, we will soon be separated for a little while.'

"He had no fears of the future and died rejoicing in his Savior."

In 1867, Brother Inlow bought a farm out from Palmyra, where his children were reared and became honorable men and women, all of whom have come to occupy active positions in Baptist churches. Yielding to the persuasion of his family, he gave up the more active work of the ministry as feeble health and old age bore down upon him. The last decade of his life was quietly spent with his devoted wife in their home in Philadelphia, Missouri, where, surrounded by multitudes of Baptists and others who loved him with devotion—men and women and children who had come to love the Savior under his preaching—he spent his last days. In a sense, he was regarded as the father of them all and, at the same time, the deserving recipient of their many kindnesses and expressions of unchangeable fellowship and devotion.

In 1897, he suffered an accident which rendered him ever afterward less active. He was, therefore, the more confined to his home and to the association of his wife. They grew old together most beautifully. His papers and books seemed to become dearer to him in his last days, and his many friends were held in ever-growing affection as they neared the parting time.

At last his children were hurried to his bedside one night, by the announcement that he could last but a few hours. With perfect composure and in possession of all his faculties, he looked upon them and repeated clearly and in triumph:

> "My latest sun is sinking fast,
> My race is nearly run;
> My strongest trials now are past,
> My triumph is begun."

He motioned to the children to join in the chorus, which they sought to do, but failed from their uncontrolled emotions and inexpressible grief. He suffered and grew tired—so very, very tired. On Sunday, May 7th, 1899, God came and took him home.

Sleep on, Father in Israel, faithful and true. Peaceful be thy slumber until the Resurrection Morn. Many be they who, inspired by thy ministry and saved by grace, shall greet thee in the home of thine inheritance.

Brother Inlow was buried at Little Union Church, midway between Palmyra and Philadelphia. Sister Inlow died February the 3d, 1908, and was laid by his side.

WEST CUIVRE BAPTIST CHURCH.

By Mrs. S. E. Moore.

This body was constituted April 5, 1845. Eleven members comprised the original number and Elders W. H. Vardeman and J. G. Sweeny organized them. Elder W. H. Vardeman was the first Pastor. He was succeeded by Elder J. N. Griffin, W. M. Jesse, B. B. Black, L. C. Musick, J. F. Smith, R. S. Duncan, J. T. Wheeler, W. R. Wigginton, J. D. Robnett.

The constituent members were: J. N. Griffin, Sarah Griffin, Lida Fuqua, John N. Fuqua, Sarah H. Fuqua, Nancy Fuqua, Nancy Adams, Walter S. Adams, Elizabeth Adams, Lyda Liney, Emily Dulang. They held their meetings in a schoolhouse, had some revivals and when the church numbered one hundred they decided to build. In 1860 the church built a frame house 40x60 feet, which was erected at the cost of $2,000. In August of the same year it was dedicated. The dedicatory sermon was preached by James F. Smith. The meeting was protracted for five weeks and there were seventy-six additions; the revival continued for months. Other preachers assisted, L. C. Musick, the Pastor of the church, J. F. Smith, M. T. Bibb, J. N. Griffin. Through the efforts of these noble workers of God much good was accomplished; they had a good Sunday School. They have never been much on missions and education. There have been some preachers sent out. Thomas Musick was ordained, did good work, did not live but a few years; J. J. Griffin was ordained and is still in the work; Walter Gossett was ordained, sent to William Jewell College and died in a few years. B. B. Moore was Deacon at one time. W. W. Wise, J. J. Griffin were clerks. The church-book could not be found up to 1883, therefore, I cannot give much of history and dates. In 1856 some of the preachers wanted to hold a meeting, J. M. Johnson, M. M. Modisett; some of the church thought it was too busy a time, the people would not attend; it was beginning of wheat harvest. Monday morning they began harvesting, cutting with cradles; worked in the field till eleven o'clock, hitched up and all went to church. The ladies had their dinner baskets well filled, had one sermon, then their dinner, then another sermon, went home and to work; continued that way for three weeks. There were thirty-two additions, the church greatly revived, sinners converted, and all the harvest saved. The church met in a house, the frame of which was weatherboarded, had the sleepers for seats, dirt floor, built up a stand of scattered pieces of lumber, but that did not keep the Lord from meeting with the people and blessing them. There are but very few that attended that are living. I am one of the few, am seventy-four years old. Am sorry I can not assist you more in collecting the history. I can remember many circumstances, but cannot date them. I was a member of Cuivre Church for thirty-eight years. After my husband died I moved away. There I enjoyed many gracious revivals. J. C. Moore, my husband, was treasurer and Deacon of the church when he died. I am now a member of Brookfield Church.

These brethren have been pastors: M. L. Bibb, G. B. Smith, W. K. Estell, D. P. Dwire, H. B. Rice, P. H. Hally, Luke Kertly, Emmett Cole, J. N. Barbee.

MARION BIGGS.

Marion Biggs, of Gridley, California, was born in Pike county, Missouri, May 2, 1823; received a common school education; elected sheriff of Monroe county, Missouri, in 1852, re-elected in 1854; elected to the California Legislature from Sacramento county in 1867, and from Butte county in '69; elected to the State Constitutonal Convention from the State at large in 1878; was elected to the Fiftieth Congress as a Democrat; was re-elected to the Fifty-first.

In Fiftieth Congress he served on Committees on Agriculture, Mines and Mining and Indian Depredation Claims.

In Fifty-first Congress he served on Committees on Pacific Railroads, Expenditures in State Department, Indian Depredation Claims.

In the Fifty-first Congress he spoke on the tariff on olive oil, and once on supplying representatives with clerks.

In early life he was active in church work. He was a son of Hon. William Biggs.

DUNCAN ELLIS.

One of the strong and constant Christians in Baptist propagandism in Lincoln county was Duncan Ellis, one of the founders of Mill Creek Church. He gave the ground for the house; he was a leader in the construction of the house and used his large possessions for the welfare of the church, which became one of the best churches in the land. In his old age he moved to the vicinity of New Hope, and he became even more useful there, for he grew in grace and was active in personal Christian work. He would go to the homes of the wayward and plead with them and he was wise in giving advice.

ELDER JOHN M. JOHNSON.

Wayne county, Kentucky, was Brother Johnson's birthplace, and January 5, 1804, was the date of his birth. In August, 1820, he was baptized by Elder Matthew Floyd, who J. H. Spencer, the author of "A History of Kentucky Baptists," says, "was one of the most popular, beloved, and efficient preachers in Kentucky, in his generation." The day he was baptized he preached his first sermon. He was ordained May 26, 1821. In 1831 he moved to Marion county, Missouri, having married Sally Kelly, daughter of Joseph and Jane Kelly, May 23, 1822, in Pulaski county, Kentucky. "He was an industrious, energetic man, and a hard student all his life." His income from his ministry was small and his family of children numbered fifteen. In secular business he prospered while he preached about three sermons each week. He would not employ men given to swearing, to work with his boys. "He was a man of learning and ability to which was added the most devoted piety. He won the esteem of all who knew him. He was a man of an unusually even temperament, kind in his family. He was never heard to use coarse or harsh language." He organized Sugar Creek Church, Pike county. The church started with eight members. He preached as the Pastor for twenty years, and, under God, brought them to a membership of one hundred and eight. He was Pastor of various other churches and he did a vast amount of missionary labor. He estimated that in a certain eighteen years of his ministry he rode horseback 24,339 miles, preached 7,421 sermons, and baptized 243 persons. For many of his last years Brother Johnson lived in Pike county, where he died, March the 27th, 1866. The end was peaceful. Elder A. P. Rodgers preached the burial sermon. His body was buried with Masonic rites.

JUDGE ALEXANDER PHILLIPS MILLER.

By Dalton Biggs, Esq.

Judge Miller was born in Nelson county, Kentucky, August 12, 1821; emigrated with his parents to Marion county in 1835, and after remaining there about nine months, removed to Pike county, where he lived till his death, April 10, 1886. His father, Alexander Miller, was a native of Virginia, born April, 1784, and removed to Kentucky with his father in 1803. His mother, Sarah Phillips, was born in Kentucky, in 1787, and was married in 1809. There were five children, of which A. P. was the last survivor. Judge Miller received only such an education as the facilities of the times afforded. He married April 2, 1846, Miss Fannie Peay, a daughter of Geo. W. Peay, an old and highly respected citizen of Pike county. Although a farmer by choice and occupation, yet he has been called several times to discharge the duties of important political and judicial stations. He was commissioned a justice of the county court by Gov. John C. Edwards in 1847 and again commissioned a few years after the expiration of his first term of office. He was elected to the State Legislature in 1876, serving on some important committees.

In 1839 he joined the Peno Baptist Church and was baptized by Eld. A. D. Landrum. Shortly afterwards he brought his membership to Mt. Pisgah Church, of which he was subsequent clerk for twenty years. At the time of his death he was an honored Deacon of that church. Out of forty-seven sessions of the Salt River Baptist Association since he joined the church he attended all but two, and it was on account of Providential hindrance that he was not present at every meeting. For twenty years he was clerk of that body and Moderator for five years. He was also at one time a member of the Southern Baptist Convention, When stricken down by disease he expressed himself as having no fear of death, and talked about the great change as cooly as one would of ordinary affairs. By his death the community lost a valuable citizen and the Association a highly important and worthy member.

CHAPTER VI.

SEPARATING FOR SERVICE.

RELATION OF BEAR CREEK ASSOCIATION TO SALT RIVER.

By R. S. Duncan.

The First Baptist Church of St. Charles. This church, formed in November, 1818, had nine constituent members. It was the fruit in part of the labor of J. E. Welch. For want of preaching, and after struggling with insurmountable difficulties for several years, the church disbanded.

The Second Church, St. Charles, was planted by Elder William Hurley in 1832. In the spring of said year, Elder Hurley visited St. Charles and began preaching. He found there a few Baptist families, at whose solicitation he continued his labors once a month for a year. Within a few months from his arrival, he had baptized ten or twelve converts. These with those whom he found there, he organized into a church in the summer of 1832. This was the *Second Baptist Church* in St. Charles. About the end of the year Eld. Hurley left them, and being now without ministerial succor, the church, after a brief period, disbanded.

The Third Baptist Church, St. Charles, was organized by Elder W. R. Rothwell, corresponding secretary of the State Mission Board, and Eld. J. H. Tuttle, Missionary of Bear Creek Association, in 1870 or '71.

CUIVRE.

In the oldest record it was denominated "Upper Cuivre Creek," but this was too long and in a few years they called it simply *Cuivre.* This was the pioneer Baptist Church of Lincoln county. The date of its organization is placed at 1815, or '16, as it was one of the six churches that organized the Missouri Association in 1817. It then had thirteen members. Charles Hubbard and M. Springston were the messengers to the Association. This church was in a community some six or seven miles westerly from Woods' Fort (now Troy). First of any denomination in the county, so far as records show. The church dissolved after some twenty years. Eld. Bethuel Riggs, who settled in St. Charles county in 1809, and in Lincoln county in 1817, was, by tradition, the first, and for eight or ten years, Pastor of Cuivre church, she being the pioneer church and he the pioneer preacher of the county. Darius Bainbridge was second, and for seven or eight years, Pastor. The Cuivre Association was organized at this church in 1822. Its name disappears from the Association minutes in 1838.

Charles Hubbard, above named, who was the father of David Hubbard, who became a Baptist preacher in 1824, settled in Saint Louis county in 1809, and became an influential member and Deacon in the Old FeeFee Church. Subsequently he removed to Lincoln county, and joined at Cuivre.

Darius Bainbridge was a Kentuckian, settled in St. Charles county in 1822, son of Dr. Absalom Bainbridge. His wife, Mary, was sister of Elder Thos. J. Wright, for years a preacher in Lincoln county. Ordained a preacher about 1824. Labored in Missouri 12 years, moving thence to Wisconsin, thence back to Clay county, Missouri, in 1847, where he spent the residue of his life. He died in 1865. He became what was called an "Old School Baptist" in the Schism, but was not so "hard" as some others of this school. It is related of him that while preaching on one occasion he became very earnest and commenced exhorting sinners to repent. Stopping suddenly, he said, "Brethren, I feel like doing what I ought not to do." But why not exhort sinners? Let any who will, answer the question.

Major Christopher Clark, the first white settler of Lincoln county, visited the spot where Troy now stands in 1799, and the year following he returned, built a cabin, and, not long afterward, a stockade fort, called Clark's Fort, three miles southeast of Troy. In 1802, Joseph Cottle and Zadock Woods settled the town of Troy, and built a fort, called until 1819, Woods' Fort. Lincoln county was established in 1818, up to which time it was a part of St. Charles county. Troy was incorporated in 1826, and made the county seat in 1829. In the territorial period of the State, and prior to 1818, immigration to this section of north Missouri was comparatively light, the settlements being much more frequent on lands contiguous to the Missouri River. We find the names of no Baptists among the immigrants to Lincoln county prior to the war of 1812-'15.

The date of the organization of the *First Troy Baptist Church* is somewhat obscure. Our minutes of the Cuivre Association in 1828 show that Troy church was then existent. The probabilties are that this church was in the organization of the old Cuivre Association in 1822. Not a word have we as to the early Pastors. Few records were kept in those days, and not a few of those that were, have been lost. The first house built by the Troy Baptist Church was a small, plain log structure, on Crooked Creek, two and a half miles south of Troy, some years after the church was organized. Here they met in summer time, but in winter from house to house. In 1835 or '36, they built a double log house farther south, near a small stream by the name of Sand Run, five miles south of Troy. Cuivre Association met with Troy Church in 1836. The minutes for 1838 have this entry, "Sand Run Church (formerly Troy)," which settles the question as to the first Troy church. It is now the Sand Run Church. Who was the earliest Pastor, we know not, but subsequent to 1830, Thomas J. Wright filled this office for a number of years.

Elder Thomas Jefferson Wright, a native of Clark county, Kentucky, settled in Lincoln county in 1830. He had fine natural ability. In the Schism, he took his stand against what he called the "men-made institutions of the day." He claimed that the Lord called him to preach *"To correct error."* His method of preaching, therefore, was controversial. His death occurred September 2, 1867.

An incident. Lewis Duncan, a member of Troy Church, wishing to move his membership to a church nearer his home, asked for a letter of dismission. A brother arose and said: "I object to the applicant's having a letter in full fellowship, because he believes in a general atonement." Lewis Duncan arose and said, "I believe in a general atonement, and am willing for my view of that doctrine, or any fact in this case, to be stated in my letter." The question was deferred, and next month, by unanimous consent, the letter was granted. This was about the time Troy Church moved to her new home on Sand Run, five miles south of the town; and the incident shows the trend of the anti-mission controversy.

This early Troy Church in the schism went with the so-called Old School wing, and never was a member of Salt River Association, but having occupied ground which subsequently was occupied by said Association, it deserved a place in this sketch.

The oldest Lincoln county church that became a member of the Salt River Association, was the one next to be considered.

Stout's Settlement (now New Hope) Church, one of the constituents of the Salt River Association in 1823, was organized June 16, 1821, in the vicinity of the present site of New Hope, by Elders Bethuel Riggs and Jesse Sitton, the latter of whom was Pastor until 1828, when he was dismissed by letter and removed from the State. Eld. David Hubbard succeeded Eld. Sitton as Pastor of the church, and so continued for two, three, or more years. The church, in 1831, changed her name from *Stout's Settlement* to *Union,* As early as 1828, Stout's Settlement Church had changed her membership from Salt River to Cuivre Association. Her name is on the list in the minutes of Cuivre in the said year. In May, 1835, Elder Ephraim

Davis became Pastor and so continued until his death in 1851. During this pastorial period, the church, by resolution, refused correspondence with any "society of Christians who hold to the present benevolent institutions of the day;" and, at the end of the period, the church was much divided on doctrine and the subject of missions. The majority called Eld. A. G. Mitchell as Pastor in 1852, and the minority withdrew, some with letters and some without, and united with Bryant's Creek Church. Soon after this, the church rescinded her resolutions against missions, and under Elder Mitchell's ministry soon began to increase in numerical and moral strength. In 1857, the church moved into New Hope, having built a commodious frame house of worship there, 40x60 feet. They re-entered Salt River Association soon after A. G. Mitchell became Pastor.

Sulphur Lick. This is one of the poineer Baptist churches of Lincoln county. It was organized in 1823, the year after Missouri was admitted to the Union, of four members, viz. Bethuel Riggs, Nancy Riggs, his wife, Armstrong Kennedy, and Polly, his wife. Eld. Bethuel Riggs preached and conducted the service of organization at his own private house, near a large spring called Sulphur Lick, not far from the north fork of Cuivre and five or six miles north of Troy. On the same day John Cox and his wife, Polly, were received by experience, and baptized by Elder Riggs, who was also chosen Pastor, and filled the office for some years. From her commencement, the church grew in numerical strength, worshipping for several years in private houses. In 1826 or '27, a new location was selected four miles west of the spring, and by 1830, the church had become strong enough to erect a substantial brick house of worship on the new site, on the left prong of the Salt River road, eight miles northwest of Troy, the county seat. This was the first church house in the county, and far surpassed any erected for well nigh twenty years after. Some years later this house was burned, and replaced by a frame building on the same site in 1856.

Robert Gilmore was among the early converts at Sulphur Lick, and was subsequently sent into the ministry by her. He was ordained prior to 1838. Lewis Duncan, who joined the church by letter in the thirties, was sent out to preach by her, having been ordained in 1838.

As to Pastors of the church, our records, in detail, are imperfect. Bethuel Riggs was first. Afterwards came David Hubbard for a number of years. Then Robert Gilmore, Lewis Duncan, W. D. Grant, Walter McQuie in 1854, and R. S. Duncan in 1856. In the second year of this pastorate (1857), a gracious revival was enjoyed, and, as a result, some twenty-five converts were added to the church.

Sulphur Lick was a member of Cuivre Association up to 1839. That year she entertained the Association and the proceedings were so unfriendly to missions, that two churches withdrew, viz., Salem, in Warren county, and Sulphur Lick, and, in 1841, Sulphur Lick joined the Salt River Association, and remained a member until, in 1854, when she united in organizing the Bear Creek Association. She then had sixty-four members. Her union with Salt River placed Robert Gilmore and Lewis Duncan on the list of ministers in said Association.

PASTORAL SKETCHES.

Bethuel Riggs. Born in the Colony of New Jersey in 1760, joined the army of the American Revolution in 1777, converted and joined the Baptists when eighteen years old, married in early life, Nancy Lee, whose brother, James Lee, a Baptist preacher of celebrity, used to preach under the trees with gun by his side, apprehending an attack from Indians. Bethuel Riggs was something of a rover. Not long after his conversion he removed to North Carolina, thence to Georgia, where he commenced preaching, and traveled extensively as an itinerant. While still camparatively young, with a colony, he made a hazardous, but successful trip across the mountains, and settled in the territory of Kentucky opposite Cincinnati.

An incident: A couple came one day to his house to be married, but because of some restrictions in the laws he could not marry them in Kentucky. They got into their canoes, rowed out into the Ohio river, and, when in mid-stream, he married them, and they went their way, happy.

He settled in St. Charles county, Missouri, in 1809, and in Lincoln county in 1817, near the spring which gave name to the church of 1823. Besides some pastoral work, he spent much of his time traveling and itinerating. "He preached over large portions of Warren, St. Charles, Lincoln, Montgomery and Pike counties." Subsequently he moved to Monroe county and preached to the settlements in the Salt River country. He moved thence to Illinois, thence to Ohio, and back to Missouri, and died in a good old age.

Brother David Hubbard had many devoted admirers, and, because they were such, they enjoyed the following anecdote: In 1843, the Salt River Association sat at Sulphur Lick. Several preachers were spending a social hour at William Moore's, near by the church. Conversation was upon the introductory sermon which merited severe criticism. Bro. Hubbard raised up and said, "Brethren, if I can ever outpreach myself it is when I have to follow a bungler." That night, a visiting brother was put up to preach. It was undecided as to who should follow him. The sermon was somewhat muddy and mixed. A. D. Landrum, sitting near Hubbard in the pulpit, whispered in his ear, "Now is your time, Brother Hubbard." The visiting brother finished and Hubbard rose to follow. He took a text, talked awhile, all was dark. He took another text, but utterly failed of any liberty on it, and sat down finally, having said but little. Marvelously does this exhibit the human side of a gospel preacher. "Not by might nor by power, but by my spirit, saith the Lord." We may learn a lesson.

Robert Gilmore, Pastor once at Sulphur Lick, was a Virginian, born 1792, married Mary Hansford in 1818, moved to Missouri in 1819. First lived in St. Charles county, then in Lincoln. Baptized by Bethuel Riggs at Sulphur Lick, and in 1829 the church gave him a license to preach, and ordained him probably about 1831. He was a good man, with a limited education, an old style preacher. His labors were confined chiefly to Lincoln and Montgomery counties. He was at one time Pastor of Zion church in the last-named county. I well remember his coming home with my father from an Association in 1847. I was a boy of only fifteen years.

Brother Gilmore died enroute to California at the head of Sweet Water, June 25, 1849.

Lewis Duncan, for twelve or more years, a member of Salt River Association, immigrated to Missouri with his young family, in 1828, settling near Troy. He was born in Culpeper county, Virgina, March 1, 1806. Married Harriet Kinnaird, of Virginia, September 11, 1827. Converted in 1828. For ten years after coming to Missouri, he taught school and cultivated the soil. Ordained a preacher at Sulphur Lick Church on May 23, 1838. In his preaching he was methodical and used no superfluity. His active career as a preacher was of twenty-five years' duration, during which he filled successively the pastoral office in the churches that follow: Sulphur Lick and New Salem, in Lincoln county; Zion, Montgomery county; Indian Creek, Pike county; and Pleasant Grove, Lincoln county. He "Fed the flock of God." His frame was feeble, his voice weak, and his manner deliberate. He studied a subject until he reached the bottom. He learned to think accurately, and his sermons were well nigh perfect. His preaching was genuine food and drink to souls hungry and thirsty for the truth. *He preached the gospel.*

Few churches, in his day, paid salaries. If any did, the Pastor was called a "money preacher," "hireling," etc. Little do we now appreciate, probably, what our fathers endured and sacrificed to build up churches able to furnish us comfortable pastorates. They removed prejudices, corrected wrongs, established precedents, thus preparing the way for the present generation.

I have known no one who possessed greater evenness of temper than Lewis Duncan. He was a model in uniformity of life. When others were wild with excitement he was cool and self-possessed.

He was author of the resolution in Indian Creek Church, in 1853, suggesting a division of the Salt River Association, and the formation of a new Association, which was done, and Bear Creek was formed the next year.

When he died there was no visible form of disease present. He fell asleep on Lord's day, December 15, 1872, and was buried in the family cemetery on the hill between his mother and my mother.

William Davis Grant, was of Scotch ancestry, born in Ohio, July 10, 1812; the family moved to Ralls county in 1820, and here and in Pike county he grew up and spent many years. While learning the tanner's trade he hired a man to give him lessons in the spelling-book.

In 1832, after conversion, he joined the Methodist Church and became a licensed exhorter. The study of the Bible made him a Baptist, and he united with Noix Creek Church, Pike county, in 1843. The church at once licensed him, and two years later ordained him to preach the gospel. Wm. Hurley, A. D Landrum and J. Bowers composed the presbytery. Not long after this he moved to Lincoln county.

He was of the class called "farmer preachers," and never received what would be now called a salary. To many of the Lord's poor did he break the Bread of Life. He served as Pastor of these churches: New Salem, Sulphur Lick, Cottonwood, Bethlehem, Mt. Prairie, Mt. Hope, Zion, Mt. Pleasant, Wellsville, and

Walnut Grove. He studied his sermons at the plow handle. In doctrine he was Calvanistic, and, as a rule, he was regarded a better preacher by his hearers than by himself.

Late in life, he died a very poor man, and was buried at Foley, in Lincoln county, Missouri.

Walter McQuie, Pastor of Sulphur Lick in 1854 and '55, was of Scotch parentage, born October 19, 1802, married Mary J. Baskett in 1835, converted in 1829, and entered the ministry in 1834. He participated in organizing the General Association in August, 1834, and a little later in the same year, his name was on the list of ministers in Salt River Association. This was his first appearance in Missouri, so far as our information shows.

He spent some years as missionary of the General Association, and traversed much of the territory of Eastern Missouri, preaching the gospel. Later on, when more permanently settled, he entered the pastorate in churches located in the counties of Ralls, Pike, Lincoln, St. Charles, Warren and Montgomery. During his twenty-five years of active ministerial life, he held many revival meetings and baptized hundreds of converts. He was a plain, earnest gospel preacher. Besides Sulphur Lick Church, he filled the pastoral office in Bethlehem, Indian Creek, Middletown and Montgomery City churches. He died in the sixties, near Middletown.

MOUNT HOPE CHURCH

was organized by Elds. Joseph Nicholls and Robert Gilmore in 1839, with Henry Ball, Littleton Cockerell, Horatio Ball and James Carr as constituent members. Its location was in St. Charles county, which then was, and is now, under a strong Roman Catholic influence. Baptists have not, to this day (1907) gained much of a footing in the county. Prior to 1839, two efforts at Baptist church organization had been made in the town of St. Charles, and at least two others in the county, in the territorial age of the State, for the same purpose, and, as shown by available records, all had failed. But Mount Hope Church has had a much more permanent and successful career. With feet firmly planted on the eternal Rock of Ages, she stood by the pure doctrines of a spiritual religion. Her early Pastors were old time preachers, who emphasized experimental Godliness; she early added to her membership Reuben and William Harris, and Charles Hutchinson and his wife; able and true.

For six or seven years the church met in West Liberty schoolhouse, then built themselves a substantial frame structure, some five or six miles easterly from Flint Hill. Here they worshiped for years, and enjoyed many a season in genuine fellowship.

First Pastor was Robert Gilmore, then, for a season, Lewis Duncan and Walter McQuie as alternate pastoral supply. Joseph Nicholls followed as Pastor, then R. C. Hill in 1848, who baptized several converts.

In 1843 they sent a letter and messengers to Salt River Association, and the church was received as a member of that body. Thus they were brought into closer touch with the brotherhood; and, in 1851, Eld. W. H. Vardeman, from Salt River, made the church a visit and held a meeting. A revival ensued, and, as a result, quite a number were added by baptism, among them Jane Carr, and Elizabeth Lindsey whom Eld. Vardeman married in 1852, and about that time he became Pastor of the church and so continued until 1855 or '56. After his marriage he removed to St. Charles county, and divided his time somewhat between the farm and the pulpit.

In 1854, Mt. Hope joined in the organization of Bear Creek Association, at which time there were forty members on her roll.

Eld. Robert C. Hill, once Pastor at Mount Hope, died in Caldwell county, Missouri, January 13, 1874. He was born in Virginia July 11, 1806, converted November 4, 1832; married Mary Hume in 1832; ordained a preacher at Mt. Horeb Church, Callaway county, Missouri, August 16, 1841; lived in Missouri from 1835 to 1863; lived in Kentucky from 1863 to 1867; in Missouri again until death. Did much preaching in Missouri; a faithful minister—a sound Baptist; was Pastor of many churches; the weather did not keep him from his appointments; old style preacher.

ZION CHURCH

the next in the list, is situated in the eastern border of Montgomery county, and near by the large expanse of prairie extending miles to the westward. The organization was effected on March 15, 1841, at the home of John H. Dutton, by five constituent members, viz.: John H. Dutton, Mary R. Dutton, Washington Graves, Mildred Graves and Jesse Watkins. In that early day, the settlements did not occupy the area of prairie country, but were confined chiefly to the timber lands adjacent to the watercourses. The settlement in which the church was located was on Bear Creek, ten or twelve miles east of the present site of Montgomery City.

Robert Gilmore was, for the first six years, Pastor of Zion Church, and was succeeded by Lewis Duncan, he by Mahlon Spyres, A. C. Davenport, W. H. Vardeman and others.

This church was a sufferer in the war of 1861-'65. Her Pastor, W. H. Vardeman, was made a political prisoner, and a little later some of her staunchest members were banished or otherwise compelled to leave the State, of whom Elder D. W. Nowlin was one.

Zion Church first identified herself with the Little Bonne Femme Association, whose churches then were mainly in Boone, Callaway and Montgomery counties; but in 1845, she united with Salt River Association.

In 1850, she enjoyed a very gracious revival, which added a number of new converts to her membership, among whom was J. B. Shelton, who is yet one of the substantial members. Again, in 1851, November, another revival followed, in a meeting held by W. H.

Vardeman, R. C. Hill and James N. Griffin, and twelve or fifteen converts were baptized, and among them, two, who became preachers of the gospel, viz.: D. W. Nowlin and R. S. Duncan.

Zion Church entertained the convention that organized the Bear Creek Association in May, 1854, in which year she had on her roll fifty-two members. She was one of the constituents of Bear Creek.

A. C. Davenport, once a Pastor at Zion, was, in or about 1850 or '51, a member of Troy Church. I had a slight acquaintance with him about the date above named, and know only that he had married into a family whose religious proclivities were quite out of harmony with Baptist principles and policy. His labors in the ministry were not extensive and not long after 1852, I think he moved from the State, and did not live very long afterwards.

TROY CHURCH.

The present Baptist church in Troy was organized in 1844, by whom we know not. She joined the Salt River Association in the year aforesaid, and so remained until it became a member of Bear Creek Association, ten years later. Among the early members at Troy were some of the prominent women of the community, namely, Mrs. James H. Britton, Mrs. Helen B. Woolfolk, widow of the late Dr. Woolfolk, and sister of Judge Carter Wells, and Mrs. Col. T. G. Hutt.

Late in the forties, R. C. Hill was Pastor, and the Salt River Association sent help to the struggling new church in the persons of Elds. Wm. Hurley and W. H. Vardeman. These men held a meeting, the fruit of which was a revival and the conversion and baptism of eight or ten, who were added to the church. In 1852 the writer moved to Troy and put his membership into the Baptist church, which, at that time, numbered thirty members, half of whom were negroes, and all the members were women except two. In addition to those above mentioned the following were active members at Troy in 1852: Mrs. Jordan Sallee, Miss Polly Wade and John Britton, who was father of Col. J. H. Britton, then a leading merchant of the community.

In the year of my removal to Troy James F. Smith, missionary of the Salt River Association, visited the church and held a meeting. Another gracious revival followed, such as had been before unknown at Troy, the fruit of which was fifteen baptisms and additions. Following this, for one or more years, Brother Smith visited them as Pastor.

Up to the revival of 1852, the Baptists, having no house of their own, held their services in the Presbyterian house. At the end of the first week of the Baptist revival, the Presbyterian Pastor occupied his pulpit on Sunday. At the close of the service he (Rev. Mr. Noel) announced meetings for the week to the astonishment of Brother Smith and his congregation. After consultation, the Baptists moved their meeting to a room under the Masonic Hall used for religious worship, and the revival continued. An interest in the Baptist meeting, which was making an inroad into some of the Presbyterian families, doubtless, is the explanation of the action of the Presbyterian Pastor. This episode opened the eyes of the Baptist people in Troy to the necessity of building a house of worship of their own, a thing they did several years later.

For not a few of her earlier years, the church had something of a struggle, yet she made progress, and ultimately found herself strong enough to erect her first house of worship, which was completed during the ministry of J. E. Welch as Pastor, beginning in 1857, and, save one or two years, continuing ten or eleven years, successively. The structure is a neat, plain and durable frame and is yet (1907) standing and in use.

Troy church was a member of the convention in 1854, which organized the Bear Creek Association, but, objecting to some of the Articles of Faith, did not return in 1855. She, however, waived her objections and sent a letter and messengers to the session of 1856, and became a permanent member of the body.

BETHLEHEM BAPTIST CHURCH.

In a settlement along the southern border of the West Prairie, and in the timber lands north of West Cuivre River, the missionary, in the early forties, found a few Baptist families. This settlement was about fourteen miles northwesterly from Troy, and four miles southeast from where Olney now stands, and was in Lincoln county. Eight of these scattered sheep of the fold met at the house of Mahlon Spyres on April 26, 1845, and were constituted into a church of "United Baptists," called *Bethlehem*. The organization was effected by Elders David Hubbard and Jacob Capps. The constituent members were Mahlon Spyres, Edward Moss, Jacob Capps, Elizabeth Capps, Sampson Wamble, Mary A. Wamble, David Capps and Sarah Capps. The same year the church sent messengers and joined the Salt River Association.

For some months, meetings were held at Brother Spyres' house. Then the church built a log house in which to worship. My first visit to this church was in 1854. I found the house then to be a primitive looking structure, with a stick chimney, a dirt floor, a clapboard door and split logs and slabs for seats. In August, 1846, a resolution was passed calling for the observance of "Foot Washing" as a church ordinance. No such custom, however, existed in 1854.

Succession of Pastors. Jacob Capps was first Pastor for one year. He was followed by L. C. Musick for a year, and, in April, 1847, Robert Gilmore was chosen Pastor. Mahlon Spyres became Pastor in 1848, he having been ordained by the church in May of that year the presbytery, consisting of Elders A. D. Landrum, David Hubbard, L. C. Musick, Lewis Duncan and W. D. Grant. The last named was Pastor from September, 1850, for one year or more, and he was succeeded by Walter McQuie, who continued in the office to the close of 1855.

A meeting was held in 1851 by T. T. Johnson and Mahlon Spyres which added six members to the church which is the first intimation of an ingathering shown by the records.

In July, 1854, the church gave a license to R. S. Duncan to "exercise his gift," and on the 26th of August, 1855, at her call, he was ordained to the ministry by Elders W. McQuie, W. D. Grant and Lewis Duncan, and the following year he was chosen Pastor and so continued until late in the year 1859.

The old log house was replaced by a new double log house of worship in 1854 and '55, forty-four by twenfour feet, well finished with shingle roof and a pulpit. This house was modeled after a plan common in those times, the two sections of the side walls being joined together in the middle by pens, with door in one pen and pulpit in the other. This house served a good purpose for worship until the erection of the present frame house which was completed in 1875, out on the prairie, some two miles northeasterly from the old site. In the meantime Old Bethlehem and Mt. Prairie churches had united and formed one church and called it Fairview.

In the second year of R. S. Duncan's pastorate, which was August, 1857, Old Bethlehem Church enjoyed a gracious revival, extensive in results. Such had not before been known in the community, and seldom, if ever, in all that section of the State. Elders T. T. Johnson, and Walter McQuie aided the Pastor in the first part of this revival meeting, and Lewis Duncan later on. The revival spirit continued through August, September, and October, the fruit of which was the baptism of thirty-seven converts, some of whom were enrolled at Indian Creek Church. This was an old time revival meeting, in which the "mourner's bench" was used. The year following its close (1858) the total membership was sixty-seven as shown in the Association minutes. The year preceding the revival the church reported only twenty-one on her roll.

In May, 1854, Bethlehem Church was a member of the convention that organized the Bear Creek Association, and her membership in the Salt River Association ceased.

Mahlon Spyres, the first to be ordained by Bethlehem Church, had only a short career as a gospel minister. He, however, filled his mission with fidelity. When he joined in the organization of the church, he was then an elderly man, with a large family. When and from where he emigrated to Missouri, we know not. He seemed built for a frontiersman—robust and strong. Well suited for a vanguard to those who must come after him. Probably he never went to school a day in his life, and knew little of books, but he studied men, and could preach to them, which he did for a few of the later years of his life.

Brother Spyres was a miller and a farmer. By the mill and the farm he lived and supported his family. I was with him at the Salt River Association in 1852, the last time I ever met him. He died between that date and 1854.

Jacob Capps, one of the constituents, and Pastor the first year, of Bethlehem, preached a few years in that section of the State, and moved thence to southwest Missouri.

The following additional churches were, for only a brief period identified with Salt River Association, then united with Bear Creek, viz.: Middletown, Indian Creek, Cottonwood and Mt. Pleasant. Their sketches will be brief also. The first is

MIDDLETOWN.

This church is in Montgomery county. When it was a mere village, a few Baptists, found there and in the community, met together and formed a church. The organization took place on the second Saturday in September, 1851, with fifteen constituent members, and, the new church united with the Salt River Association, and continued with that body until the formation of the Bear Creek Association in 1854, of which it was a constituent. That year the church had thirty-three members, and Walter McQuie was Pastor and filled the office successively until 1857.

In 1854, the church had in it not a few of the choice spirits of the community, and she has been one of our shining lights.

INDIAN CREEK CHURCH,

for two years in the territory of Salt River Association, was organized the 20th of September, 1851, at the Union schoolhouse in Pike county, located five miles south of the old town of Ashley. Eld. Walter McQuie superintended the organization, and was aided by Eld. Lewis Duncan, who was one of the constituents, eleven in all, as follows: Lewis Duncan, Levi Moore, Thomas Weatherford, James Shaw, Robert Shaw, Harriet Duncan, Nancy Moore, Matilda Weatherford, Julia Ann Shaw, Catherine Shaw, and Margaret Reeds.

They concluded their Covenant in these words: "To distinguish our church from others, our appellation and style of record shall be the *United Baptist Church of Christ called Indian Creek."*

Walter McQuie was chosen first Pastor in January, 1852, and served two years.

Indian Creek Church, from her earliest history, has been a fruitful garden—a light shedding its rays into and blessing homes in an extensive community, gathering into the fold a very substantial membership. On the day of the organization, Elizabeth Moss joined by experience, and on the following Sunday Sarah C. Duncan was received for baptism. Later in the fall of the same year—the church not having yet called a Pastor—James F. Smith, a missionary from Salt River Association, visited the young flock and held two meetings, adding eight or ten new converts to the fold; among whom were Jordan Motley and wife, J. W. Motley and wife, and James A. Motley and wife. The last-named brother served the church as Deacon for over thirty years. In 1853, Walter McQuie and Lewis Duncan conducted a meeting, resulting in several baptisms, of whom one was W. E. Duncan and another Sarah J. Duncan, the young wife, and the brother, of R. S. Duncan.

The Bear Creek semi-centennial sermon concludes thus: 'The eleven men and women who, in 1851, stood up in the old log house hard by, covenanting with each other to walk in a church compact, and by so doing, laid the foundation on which you have builded, have all long since gone to their reward. Not one remains. Let us ever cherish their memory, and hold as sacred the legacy they left us.

Besides these, there are the names of many noble men and women, sainted and pious, on this church roll, who have crossed over the river, entered through the pearly gates, and now dwell in the 'Land that is fairer than day.' To all these sainted ones, we owe an unpaid debt of love and gratitude for what they did in building on the original foundation; in prayer and in tears they sowed that we might reap. How blessed and how sweet their memories.'

COTTONWOOD CHURCH

was located six miles northwesterly from Troy, Lincoln county. It was organized in 1852 and had nineteen constituent members. A year or so later a hewed log house of worship was built, twenty-four by thirty feet, near by Cottonwood Spring, which gave name to the church. Two years after the organization the membership had grown to twenty-seven. Her history as a member of Salt River Association was very brief, she having sent messengers and joined said Association in 1853, and the year following united in organizing the Bear Creek Association.

W. D. Grant was the Pastor from the first year until 1867, a period of fifteen years, save two years, in 1860, when R. S. Duncan filled the pastoral office, and 1865 when the church was pastorless.

MOUNT PLEASANT CHURCH.

This church was gathered and organized by Elder Joseph Nicholls in June, 1853, at a house used for both school and preaching purposes, two miles north of High Hill and in a community that had been largely destitute of church privileges. There were eleven members in the organization. The number grew to seventeen the first year. Most, or all, of the earliest members were of the prominent families of the community—as the Talbots, the Diggs, Sharps, Badgers, etc. Two of the sisters—Mrs. J. H. Diggs and Mrs. John Sharp, were sisters of the renowned Baptist preacher of Virgina, Jerry B. Jeter. Mrs. Diggs is yet living (1907).

Mount Pleasant held membership in the Salt River Association only one year—the year of her organization, 1853. She joined with her sister churches in the movement and helped to organize the Bear Creek Association in 1854, in which she yet holds her membership.

Joseph Nicholls, who gathered this new fold, became first Pastor and served two years. He was succeeded in the pastorate by T. T. Johnson in 1855, who had, as itinerant from Salt River Association, rendered valuable service here in the earliest history of the church.

Joseph Nicholls, who for the first two years was Pastor of Mount Pleasant and one year a member of Salt River Association, was born in Worcestershire, England, November 8, 1789; married in 1815; emigrated to the United States in 1830, spent four years in Pennsylvania and New Jersey; moved to St. Louis in 1834, and thence to Warrenton, Missouri, in 1836. He was converted in England in 1810 and joined the Baptists. He learned to read and write after his conversion, and by hard study became a good English scholar. After his removal to St. Louis, he commenced preaching as an independent missionary, and was ordained by Salem Church, Warren county, in 1838, and continued his ministerial labors in the destitute country adjacent to Warrenton, working at his secular trade, carpentry, for his daily bread, and preaching the gospel on Saturdays and Sundays, traveling sometimes as far west as Loutre Island on the western border of Montgomery county.

He formed the churches at Warrenton and Wright City in Warren county, and of Warrenton, the county seat, he was the Pastor. Besides his pastoral work, he continued his independent missionary operations.

In 1839, the year after his ordination, he was a member of Cuivre Association, which met that year at Sulphur Lick. A measure was introduced in antagonism to missions. Nicholls pleaded, almost alone, for liberty of conscience. But the measure was passed, and he and the other messengers of Salem church withdrew, and the church subsequently joined Little Bonne Femme Association. Nicholls stood firm and immovable on Baptist ground.

Joseph Nicholls was a sound gospel preacher, calm, deliberate, logical. His sermons were scriptural and very instructive, well arranged. "In doctrine he was Calvinistic." He was able to continue his active ministry into his seventy-eighth year. He was once co-pastor at Union Church, ten miles east from his home at Warrenton. His custom was to rise early, walk the ten miles to his appointment, preach at the noon service and return home.

The last five years of his life he was cared for in the home of his son-in-law, Mr. Freymuth, of St. Charles county, at whose home he died the day he was eighty-three years old, November 8, 1872.

NOTE.—From the minutes I see that in 1843 Camp Creek Church, Warren county, united with the Salt River Association, the only church in said county that appears on the roll of churches in Salt River. I have an impression that this church was located eastward from the present site of Truxton some two miles, and on the highland near Camp Creek, which gave name to the church. Sometime in the forties, when I was a mere boy, I distinctly recollect attending, with my parents, a meeting at the locality above named on Camp Creek. On Sunday the services were conducted under a great arbor erected on the lowlands near by Camp Creek. I call to mind, at this distant day, that as we drove up to the grounds on Sunday morning, the woods seemed lined with horses and wagons, and the face of the earth was covered with people. To my boyish eyes it was an immense throng. These facts confirm my statements in the former paragraph relative to the existence of the Camp Creek Church at that place. I remember no detail as to the services, but there were a number of preachers on the stand, and the singing was, to me, grand.

CONCLUSIONS.

In tracing the results of gospel preaching and the implantation of gospel churches, there comes to me an exemplification of this fact; that through the local church and a living ministry we must seek and hope for the restoration of fallen humanity. *This is our only hope*—the *church* and the *ministry*. These are our Lord's instrumentalities. In these we have our New Testament model. Ignore them and failure may as well be written over every church door.

SOME SALT RIVER PEOPLE I KNEW.

By Belinda Nowlin Jones.

Until the Bear Creek Association was organized in 1854, Zion church, on North Bear Creek, Montgomery county, belonged to Salt River Association. Two of the men who represented the Zion Church in that Association were Rev. David W. Nowlin (1812-1865) and Washington Graves (1805-1870.)

JUDGE N. McDANNOLD.

COL. WM. G. HAWKINS.

ELDER J. H. KEACH.

SENATOR E. W. STARK.

During the Civil War Rev. D. W. Nowlin was banished. The provost-marshal was James O. Broadhead, with whom Rev. Nowlin had been associated in the law school of the Virginia University. Knowing of this old school friendship Rev. W. H. Vardeman went to St. Louis to procure the rescinding of the order. While he was engaged in this work a friend came to him and warned him to leave St. Louis, that an order had been issued for his arrest. Rev. Vardeman replied, "I came here to work for my friend, and as long as I have my liberty I intend to continue the work." Shortly afterward he was arrested and put into Gratiot Street prison. He found men crowded together like cattle in a cattle car, with no room for cleanliness or decency. Dirt and filth were everywhere. The prison was infested with vermin. Rev. Vardeman's neck, wrists and ankles became raw from body lice it was impossible to avoid. In the midst of this squalor and confusion Rev. Vardeman began to sing a hymn. His voice was deep and strong, and soon others joined with him in singing. They kept up the singing until all became attentive, then Rev. Vardeman began to preach. That was the beginning of a great revival. Rev. Vardeman said, when telling his friend, Rev. Nowlin, about his experience, that he had done more for the cause of his beloved Master in his six months of imprisonment than in six years of freedom.

Rev. W. H. Vardeman had baptized Rev. D. W. Nowlin and had assisted in his ordination for the ministry. As a preacher, Rev. Nowlin's manner was that of a man thoroughly self-controlled. His sermons were well planned and logical and he always kept close to his subject. Even in preaching a most impassioned sermon upon the text, "Father, forgive them, they know not what they do," his manner was calm. While the picture he presented of the divine spirit of forgiveness moved many to tears, his voice kept up the even tenor of the discourse, with only here and there an indication of his deep emotion.

He had spent the six months prior to his death in Litchfield, Illinois, and while there had preached repeatedly to the delight of the people. One of his sermons upon the text, "I would rather be a doorkeeper in the house of the Lord than to dwell in the tents of wickedness," attracted a great deal of favorable comment as presenting in such a convincing manner the excellence of the Christian religion.

Washington Graves was tall, slender and erect, with the bearing of a soldier, and a man of decided opinions. Hampered by ill health in his youth, he never attained a liberal education at school, and perhaps for that reason he valued the more highly the superior mental equipment of Rev. Nowlin. Never was one friend more devoted to another than was Washington Graves to Rev. Nowlin.

It was at the first meeting at Zion after Rev. Nowlin's death that Rev. J. E. Welch was preaching, and in speaking of the loss the church had sustained he said that Rev. Nowlin was ripe for the glory of the Lord, and hence his time had come to depart. Turning to Washington Graves, whose sad face was looking up at him eager for comfort in his desolation, Rev. Welch said, "Brother Graves, if you and I had attained to our growth in grace we would be now in glory." The last six months of his life Washington Graves was eager for death. He spoke of his going away as one would speak of going on a journey to one's old home and friends. At the deathbeds of others he had given courage and cheer; in sorrow he had given comfort and assurance, and when the death angel came to him he still had the firmness of will to help the loving ones bear the inevitable separation.

Here is a circumstance to illustrate the relation between Rev. J. E. Welch and Rev. W. H. Vardeman: They were the guests of Rev. Nowlin. One morning as Rev. Vardeman entered the room where all were ready for family worship, Rev. Welch said, "Billy, where did you sleep last night?" "Above stars," answered Rev. Vardeman, waving his hand toward the stairway. "Above stars! The nearest stars are so many millions of miles away that it takes a ray of light from them three years to reach the earth, and yet Billy has made the journey before breakfast. Ah! you are a most wonderful traveler, Billy."

Rev. W. H. Vardeman and Rev. D. W. Nowlin were great admirers of Rev. Wm. Hurley. They often said that for brilliance of ideas and perfect mastery of language they had never known his equal. Rev. Hurley had familiarized himself with the oriental surroundings of the life of Jesus, and was an artist in picturing the scenes of that life, and his rare ability in that particular was often the subject of conversation between his friends, Rev. Nowlin and Rev. Vardeman.

Another Englishman whom those two friends revered and loved was Rev. Joseph Nicholls, a man of gentle manner and affectionate disposition. His look of pleasure and admiration when he met those friends is a thing worth treasuring in memory.

As a preacher Rev. Nicholls emphasized the resurrection of Jesus, holding that to be the pivot of the Christian doctrine, and he oft repeated the words of Paul, "If Christ be not risen from the dead, then is our preaching vain." No one who ever knew Rev. Nicholls intimately could doubt that Christ had risen in his nature; the spirit that was in Rev. Nicholls was so evidently the spirit that was in Christ Jesus.

Another brother in the ministry about whom those friends often talked was Rev. R. S. Duncan. While they revered Elder Nicholls as a father, they talked of R. S. Duncan as of a son. They admired his studious habits, his earnestness, his ambition to serve the Lord. They said of him, "He has never yet known a great sorrow. When such an experience comes to him, and he has drunk the bitter cup, he will be a power in the church. It is a hard thing to say, but only thus do men learn sympathy with human nature in others and can become 'fishers of men.'"

Rev. J. T. Williams was at one time associated as partner of Rev. Jesse A. Hollis in the management of what is now Stephens College, Columbia, Missouri. He was loved and admired by his pupils. When my class graduated, Rev. Williams delivered the address to the class. The point that I remember was the emphasis put upon what the world needed and expected from educated women. He made us feel a weight of responsibility, the gravity of our position, the necessity of coming up to the expectations of our families, the church and society, and yet it had a ring of triumph; for we left that platform like soldiers ready for battle.

On one occasion Rev. J. E. Welch and Rev. Thornton T. Johnson were together at Zion. Rev. Johnson's favorite hymn was "Amazing grace! How sweet the sound," and the chorus he sang was: "I want to live a Christian here, I want to die a shouting." Rev. Johnson's face would become radiant with joy as he sang that chorus. I heard Rev. Welch say aside to my father, Rev. D. W. Nowlin, "I don't join in that chorus of Brother Johnson's. When I die I want everything quiet." I recalled this circumstance when Rev. Welch passed over. He came through St. Louis on his way to the Centennial celebration of July 4, 1876—was present at the Democratic convention when they nominated Hendricks as vice-presidential candidate with Tilden. He seemed in excellent health and spirit. After being at the World's Fair he went into the ocean bathing, was taken with cramps and died on the beach amid the roar of the Atlantic. Rev. Johnson's death occurred in the quietude of home, surrounded by his family.

One of the women of Zion Church who could sit hour after hour deeply interested in every detail of the business of the Association was Mrs. Mary Dutton. She was one of the constituent members of the church. One radiant June morning when the writer of this sketch was thrilling through and through with the beauty of the sky and fields and groves, Mrs.

Dutton looked up from reading her Bible and said, "The earth is full of the glory of God." Her eyes were directed toward a grove of oaks whose leaves were glistening in the sunlight and looking in the same direction I replied, "Yes, I see and feel that, too." She looked at me tenderly and said, "Child, you have been converted."

CHAPTER VII.

STRENGTHENING THE STAKES, 1854-1860.

The Association met with Sugar Creek Church, September 7 and 8, 1855. The introductory sermon was preached by Elder A. D. Landrum. His text was Matt. 3. Salt River Church, Pike county, was received into fellowship; the messengers were J. J. Brown, W. Defoe and W. T. Spencer. Elder W. C. Busby was a visitor. One missionary had been employed and seventeen conversions were reported. Eld. W. W. Mitchell was encouraged in efforts to distribute religious literature. The same executive committee was continued.

In 1856 Adiel was the place of meeting and September 12th and 13th the time. Elder A. G. Mitchell preached the sermon. His text was: "For I am not ashamed of the gospel of Christ: for it is the power of God unto salvation to every one that believeth; to the Jew first, and also to the Greek." Pleasant Grove Church, Audrain county, came into the Association; W. H. Birch was the messenger. The visiting brethren were J. J. Bradley, J. Culbertson, J. Dowell, W. Finley, J. McPike, James F. Smith, R. S. Duncan. There had been two missionaries in the field; thirty-one conversions were reported, also four hundred volumes of denominational books sold. The Association took up the question of establishing a male and female seminary at Bowling Green. Hon. James O. Broadhead addressed the body on the subject and a committee, consisting of A. P. Rodgers, A. P. Miller, Charles Bacon, Wm. Penix and George W. Peay, was appointed with instructions and authority to act and report the following year. The ministers were A. D. Landrum, T. T. Johnson, W. McGuire, J. J. Gipson,

J. F. Hedges, Stephen Fisk, C. B. Lewis, E. Autery, W. H. Vardeman, John H. Keach, J. M. Johnson, A. G. Mitchell, W. D. Grant, D. V. Inlow, David Hubbard. The new board was the same as before.

The following resolutions were adopted on the death of Elder Wm. Hurley:

"*Whereas,* An all-wise God, in the dispensation of His providence, has, since our last anniversary, removed by death from our midst to that rest prepared for all who love His appearing, our much-loved and highly esteemed brother, Willam Hurley, and

"*Whereas,* Brother Hurley had been for more than twenty years an able and efficient minister of the gospel in the bounds of this Association:

"*Resolved,* That while we deeply regret the loss of our esteemed brother, and say that the will of the Lord be done; yet in the death of Elder Hurley our denomination has been called upon to part with one of her ablest and most useful ministers, while society has lost an interesting and valuable citizen.

"*Resolved,* That this tribute of respect be sent to the *Watchman* for publication and also be entered upon the records of this Association.

"M. M. MODISETT,
"JOHN M. JOHNSON,
"WILLIAM PENIX,
"Committee."

Martinsburg, Pike county, Illinois, entertained the Association September 1 and 2, 1857. Elder M. M. Modisett preached the introductory sermon. His text was: "And they continued steadfastly in the apostles' doctrine and fellowship, and in breaking of bread, and in prayers." A. G. Mitchell was elected moderator and A. P. Miller clerk. At this time Brother Landrum had moved from the bounds of Salt River Association. Pleasant Hill, Pike county, Illinois, was received into associational fellowship; the messengers were Dr. J. A. Thomas, W. E. Smith, L. Turner and D. Wilson. The visiting brethren were Eld. J, F. Smith, Eld. E.

Kinman and G. G. Sitton. Elders Landrum and Modisett had done missionary work. The committee on the Bowling Green school was made to consist of A. P. Miller, John M. Johnson, G. W. Peay, J. E. Shannon and A. P. Rodgers.

Ashley and Pleasant Grove are dismissed from Salt River Association. The same mission board was continued. The Association asked the churches to prohibit their members from visiting groceries and dramshops, or using intoxicating drinks as a beverage.

Providence, Pike county, was the place of meeting September 10 and 11, 1858. Elder J. M. Robinson, of Boone county, preached the sermon from the scripture: "The same came to Jesus by night and said unto him, Rabbi, we know that thou art a teacher come from God: for no man can do these miracles that thou doest, except God be with him." New Providence, Ralls county; Concord, Pike county; West Cuivre, Audrain county; Pleasant Vale, Pike county, Illinois, and New Hartford, Pike county, Illinois, were the churches that came in this year. Their messengers were: From New Providence: J. S. Doke, C. B. Hicklin and J. Ralls; from Concord: Thomas Stanford and J. J. Mitchell; from West Cuivre: J. C. Moore, W. Birch and H. M. Brown; Pleasant Vale: J. Gates, J. C. McFall, J. Rafferty and J. R. Williams; New Hartford: J. J. W. Place. Visiting brethren: Nathan Ayres, J. W. Mitchell, J. S. Green, James Culbertson and John M. Robinson. Two missionaries had been in the field; eighty-one conversions reported. One dollar per day was paid the missionaries in previous years, but $1.50 was paid these.

The committee on the Bowling Green school reported the movement impracticable and recommended that support be given a school in Louisiana in the hands of Elder J. T. Williams. A Ministerial Education Society was organized with Elder J. F. Smith as president, Col. John Ralls as vice-president, Elder J. T. Williams as secretary and Judge John D. Biggs as treasurer, and $100 was raised. The committee on Sunday schools, J. T. Williams, John D. Biggs and Wm. Penix, said: "That we recommend to every church in the Association to establish a Sunday school in her midst, and that every member of our churches are hereby earnestly entreated to give countenance and support to the worthy enterprise." The old mission board was continued.

Union Church, Lincoln county, entertained the body on September 9 and 10, 1859. Elder J. T. Williams preached the annual sermon from the text: "Hearken to me, ye that follow after righteousness, ye that seek the Lord: look unto the rock whence ye are hewn, and to the hole of the pit whence ye are digged." Elder A. G. Mitchell was chosen moderator and Elder J. T. Williams clerk. Hamburgh Church, Illinois, was received into the Association; J. McLean was the messenger. The visitors were Elders Henry M. King, W. H. Vardeman, R. S. Duncan, Wm. Cleaveland, Lewis Duncan and Brethren James Carr, J. J. Sitton and J. L. Moore. Elders L. C. Musick and C. B. Lewis had been the missionaries, blessed with twenty-eight conversions. The Association asked for an average of fifty cents from each church member for district missions. An announcement was made of the establishment of a male and female seminary in Louisiana, Elder J. T. Williams principal. Eight of the twenty-three churches had Sunday schools. Salt River Church, Ralls county, is reported dissolved. There was no change in the men of the mission board. The Association took steps to have her history written and Judge A. P. Miller was to receive the material sent by the churches for that purpose and then to send it to Dr. S. H. Ford. The Association advised against receiving Pedobaptist and Campbellite immersions.

Buffalo Knob Church entertained the Association September 7 and 8, 1860. Elder W. F. Luck preached the sermon. His text was: "He saith unto them, but whom say ye that I am? And Simon Peter answered and said, Thou art the Christ, the Son of the living God." Elder A. G. Mitchell was chosen moderator and Judge A. P. Miller clerk. Two new churches came into the Association: Bethsaida, Lincoln county, whose messengers were T. Halley and W. Simpson, and Mt. Zion, Pike county, whose messengers were H. Salling and N. Smith. The following brethren accepted seats in the body: Elders H. M. King, Wm. Cleaveland, Lewis Duncan, R. S. Duncan, J. H. Thomas, J. N. Griffin and Brethren Gibson, Moore, Collins, Motley and Sharp. Two men had been in the mission field, the conversions reported were thirteen. There were six Sunday schools reported. Hamburg Church was dismissed by letter. The mission board continued to be G. W. Peay, W. W. Waddell and Henry Sisson. The ministers were A. G. Mitchell, J. H. Keach, J. M. Johnson, H. M. King, E. Jennings, J. J. Gipson, J. F. Hedges, A. P. Rodgers, J. T. Johnson, L. C. Musick, A. B. McElfresh, W. W. Mitchell, W. F. Luck, J. B. Johnson, E. Autery, J. P. Smith. The committee on obituaries, John M. Johnson, A. B. McElfresh and J. G. Sitton, reported: *"Whereas,* We have learned of the removal of our much esteemed brother, Elder C. B. Lewis, by death since our last anniversary, therefore

"1. *Resolved,* That while we mourn our loss we bow in humble resignation to the will of an all-wise Providence in this removing from our midst a brother in the prime of life and in the midst of his usefulness.

"2. *Resolved,* That we sympathize with the family and friends of the deceased and commend them to the guardian care of God the Father of the fatherless and the widow's everlasting friend.

"3. *Resolved,* That while an all-wise God is removing some of our ministers from their fields of labor we will not cease to pray the Lord of the harvest to send more laborers into His harvest."

ASHLEY CHURH.

By J. W. Riggs.

In 1854 they organized a church, bought a machine shop and fitted it up very nicely for those times as a church house; Simeon P. Robinson, John J. Mitchell and Barzel Riggs were the Deacons and trustees. They had Brother John M. Johnson for Pastor a short while, then Brother Walter McQuie; also J. F. Smith, and Thornton Johnson served them as supply. And Brother Hurley preached regularly for about one year. I think they kept up the organization only about three years.

BOWLING GREEN BAPTIST CHURCH.

By Deacon T. J. Ayres.

The First Baptist Church was organized in 1853 or 1854, with some fifteen or eighteen members, under whose counsel or advice, is not known, and it is thought that of the original or constituent membership there is not a single survivor.

Time passed, bringing prosperity and adversity, and we find among the ante-bellum Pastors that champion of evangelical religion, Elder William Hurley, succeeded by M. M. Modisett and he by W. F. Luck. Also that Rev. Albert Mitchell and Rev. Martin T. Bibb, uncle to our Brother E. T. Bibb and great uncle to our Brother Byron Bibb, held a revival meeting prior to the war which resulted in a number of conversions, and greatly strengthened the struggling body. The war came on, bringing trouble to churches as well as to individuals, and the adoption of a new State constitution, embodying a test oath for ministers as well as teachers and others, found J. Frank Smith at the helm as Pastor, whom many of the present membership remember well. He was a remarkable man in many respects, among which was the fact that he was a strong, able preacher. His conscience would not allow him to subscribe to the test oath with the result that regular services were discontinued. Divisions followed, so that, in 1865, thirty-five members of the old First Church took letters and were organized into the Second Baptist Church by Rev. John M. Johnson, who served them as Pastor for a short time, the original or First Church shortly becoming extinct. We retain in our membership to-day a number of this constituency, among whom are Sister Reynolds, Sister Wm. Kincaid, Sister Dickerson, Brother John R. Wise and wife, Brother J. D. Frier and wife, Brother J. J. Peay and wife, and there may be others. The second Pastor was Rev. A. P. Rodgers for two or three years; third Pastor, Rev. A. F. Randall for only a few months, during which time he held a revival meeting resulting in sixty-four additions to the membership. Following him came the lamented J. T. Williams as fourth Pastor. The fifth was Rev. T. N. Sanderson for one year. The sixth was the second pastorate of Rev. A. P. Rodgers of two or three years, he being succeeded by Brother J. D. Biggs in a two years' pastorate; followed by Dr. J. F. Cook as a supply for a few months, who was succeeded by W. H. Burnham, when Brother J. D. Biggs was recalled and served the church for eight years, succeeded by Rev. J. D. Hacker for six and one-half years.

The first property owned by the organization was begun to be builded in 1867 and completed in 1868, involving untold anxiety and sacrifices of the then membership of perhaps fifty, and bringing to them a brick building thirty-four by forty-five feet, with the real joys and hopes that would naturally fill the breasts of those who toil and sacrifice for the Master. Time went on until the year 1885, when the communicants numbered about one hundred and fifty, with proportionate increase in attendance, so that the old building became inadequate for the accommodation of the congregation, and the brethren began to discuss the enlargement of the building, which resulted in the appointment of a ways and means committee, and later a building committee composed of Brethren J. E. Sanderson, who remains with us, and W. N. Gibbs and E. T. Smith, both of whom have passed to their reward, yet are still held in loving remembrance by those with whom they labored and sacrificed, as is evidenced by the memorial windows which bear their names in this beautiful edifice.

Up to this time the body had enjoyed religious services but one Sabbath in each month, for which the Pastor was scantily paid, and the meager salary was hard to provide. Indeed, but a short time prior to this, the county held a lien on the property to secure money borrowed to liquidate a debt, due on Pastor's salary. Closely following the building of the addition, however, some brethren, doubtless led by the Spirit, began to agitate an increase of service, but were met by discouragement from others, with an argument based on the difficulty before mentioned. But by persistence arrangements were made for services for half time. The means being more easily provided than for one-fourth time, gave encouragement. So the service was soon increased to three-fourths time, with the same result, which encouraged to full time.

And what shall I say of the results flowing out of these heroic efforts, largely the struggles of those whom the Master has called up higher? It must not be thought that the trials and discouragements already mentioned constituted the sum total to be borne by this struggling band, for ever and anon the grim monster crept into our midst and removed one after another of our faithful band, and left an aching void, and we wondered who would fill his or her place in the church and our hearts were sad. But still the Master knew, and raised up others, and the good work went on, until the old house became untenable, or at least discreditable to the cause for which it stood, and we found it necessary to arise and build.

The result we see in the comfortable, commodious and handsome building which we now enjoy, and of which we are justly proud. The trials, struggles and sacrifices which gave it to us are fresh in every mind, and it is fitting to give thanks to the Master for the mercies and blessings which have crowned our effort to serve him in this beautiful temple.

The new house was built during the pastorate of Rev. J. D. Hacker, and largely through his labor and instrumentality. He was followed by Rev. W. D. Bolton in a successful pastorate of five years, during which the debt on the house was paid, a goodly number added to the membership, and general prosperity prevailed. He was succeeded by the present pastor, Rev. J. B. Crouch, under whose ministry the general work, including contributions to the various missions, is prospering. Present membership, three hundred and sixty-one, June, 1909.

MT. ZION CHURCH.

By Elder W. A. Bibb.

Mt. Zion Church was organized April 25, 1860. Brother Ed Jennings, prior to this date, had held some meetings in a schoolhouse near where the church was built and a presbytery was called consisting of Brothers Ed Jennings and J. T. Willams. A call for members to constitute the body was made and fifteen brethren and sisters responded and the church fully organized. Brother Ed Jennings was called and served as first Pastor, and on the 5th day of May the church in a business meeting voted to locate and build a house of worship, which resulted in the construction of a log house on the present site. Brother Jennings served the church thirteen years as Pastor. Brother A. P. Rodgers was Pastor for five years, Samuel Noel for seven years, Brother S. G. Givens one year. Brothers J. B. English, E. J. Sanderson, M. M. Modisett, J. W. Trower, R. D. Robertson and W. M. Tipton were Pastors. During Brother Tipton's pastorate he encouraged the church to build the present commodious little house of worship. E. J. Sanderson, J. D. Watson and W. A. Bibb, the present Pastor, have all served the church. The church's first Deacons were Brothers Henry Salling and N. R. Smith. N. R. Smith was also the first church clerk. The present Deacons are James Johnson, Benjamin Williams, Harvey Boyd and Worth Baxter. Others that have served as clerks and Deacons are J. D. Warner, T. J. Gibson, Gillum Phelps, J. T. Ayres. The Ingram family have been a great factor in the church, but many of them have gone to their eternal reward. Among those that remain are the Dodds, Hendersons, Williams, Warners, Johnsons, Ingrams, Sears, Ayres, Adams, Baxters, Shys, Boyds. The dawn of a brighter day is hoped for.

Mt. Zion Church has enjoyed many precious revivals. All of the regular Pastors have assisted other pastors at times in meetings and other brethren have helped us, contributing in this way to the good of the church, the salvation of man and the glory of God.

ELDER WILLIAM HURLEY.

By Judge Thos. J. C. Fagg.

The great man of the Baptist Church in Missouri when I came to the State in 1836 was William Hurley. He came to America to take charge of a Baptist congregation in the city of New York. He told me at various times during our acquaintance a few incidents in his life after coming to the United States. His history was a singular one. My decided conviction for nearly seventy-five years has been that he was much the greatest man intellectually that I have ever seen in a western pulpit. In many respects he was peculiar. He was rather indolent and to a certain extent, indifferent as to the applause of the populace, and yet he always felt himself highly complimented by the presence and the attention of well educated and intelligent people in his congregation. The profound respect and attention of such men as Judge Carty Wells of Lincoln, James O. Broadhead of Pike, Samuel T. Glover and others of the Palmyra bar, were his on all occasions when court was in session. On one occasion when the Salt River Association was in session at Mt. Pisgah Church by common consent every member of the bar in attendance at Bowling Green from a distance, including R. S. Blennerhassett, the noted criminal lawyer and advocate from St. Louis, went out to hear Mr. Hurley preach. He recognized the compliment at once and he exerted himself to the full measure of his capacity. The subject of the sermon was "The Healing of Naaman the Syrian." It was the third or fourth time that I had heard him on the same subject, but I never got tired of it. His powers of description were so graphic and so attractive that the most careless listener was carried along irresistibly to the end of the discourse. Mr. Hurley's power to entertain an audience did not depend upon any of the tricks and devices so common among public speakers and especially among the class known as revivalists. His logic was clear and simple, yet always forceful and convincing. On this occasion he seemed to be aroused to the full measure of his great abilities, and in my experience of more than threescore years and ten I never listened to a public address of any character that was quite so effective as this sermon. At the beginning the group of distinguished men whose names I have given, occupied positions some distance from the pulpit. As the sermon progressed they gradually arose to a standing attitude and involuntarily advanced nearer and nearer to the stand until the last sentences found them as near to the pulpit as was possible to get, eagerly catching every word and syllable that fell from the lips of the eloquent speaker, and apparently greatly dissatisfied at the end. No one knew better than the old man eloquent himself what the effect of that sermon was. He had read it in the countenances of all his hearers—he had seen and understood it thoroughy in the eagerness of these intelligent, distinguished men as they crowded around him to catch his last words, and he was preeminently pleased and gratified. In talking with me afterwards about the occasion and the character of his audience, he said, "I like to preach to men who can understand and appreciate what I say. It stimulates my powers of thought and gives me an utterance that I do not have on ordinary occasions."

He was a man much below the average height. He was inclined to be fleshy and awkward in his gait; yet he had a magnificent head and face, and was always careful and neat in his dress and personal appearance. He never walked abroad without a silk hat upon his head, nicely brushed and in good order. His history in the United States briefly told is that after preaching in the city of New York for a time he received a letter from a business man in the city of New Orleans inviting him to come to that city and make his house his home and guaranteeing to him the charge of a church that would give him an ample salary. It was the sort of opening that seemed to afford him the opportunity that he was looking for. He wanted to see more of this great country than he could ever hope to see by remaining in the large city in which he was then located. Above all he wanted sooner or later to get into the great wild west about which he had read and heard so much in his native district, and without hesitating he made up his mind to take a sailing vessel and make his way to the city of New Orleans, and there to make his home. He informed the unknown friend of his decision. A check was promptly sent him to meet all expenses with full directions about finding the business house and residence of the donor. He made the trip, found the friend upon landing at New Orleans and was soon domiciled at this man's house and in a short time commenced preaching in that city. It was a sort of romantic history, but he was most delightfully situated and highly pleased with his new friends and new field of labor. Still he was not satisfied. His residence in the city of New Orleans only increased his desire to see the great valley that was tributary to it. He never got tired of going down to the wharf and looking at the great steamboats that carried down the iron and glass from Pittsburg, the flour and pork from Ohio, and the hemp and grain from Kentucky, and the great bales of fur and peltries from the Rocky Mountains. He thought this valley of the Mississippi must be the greatest region of country upon the globe. That country he must look upon with his own eyes. Then, too, he thought of the Indians. He had never seen them, he had no real conception of them, of what their real character was. He must see them in their own country, and form his own opinions as to their real character, modes of life and habits. He procured a small one-horse wagon and with an outfit that would enable him to camp out in case of absolute necessity, he started out to hunt the Indian country. How long he remained within their territory or what amount of experience he had in the study of Indian habits and character I do not know. His desire to see and know more about the resources of the Mississippi Valley induced him to turn his course northward. He drifted on until he reached northwest Missouri. Here he found a country with a soil so fertile, with advantages of location so great and a population so warm hearted and congenial that he determined to fix his permanent home somewhere within its limits. He was fond of homelife and the comforts and associations that clustered about a well-ordered, well-regulated family in a country home. Strange to say he never married, and so far as I know he never contemplated such a step in life. I have never known a man about whom there was such a great variety of opinions. It was generally conceded that he was a man of great intellectual force and ability, yet his eccentricities of character were such at times as to produce the impression that his mental faculties were somewhat impaired. But nothing of that sort was ever apparent in his pulpit utterances. I have several times heard Henry Ward Beecher, and other preachers of national reputation, but it is my deliberate conviction that no one of them was superior to Mr. Hurley. I may safely go farther and say that I have never heard any one that was quite equal to him. His manner in the pulpit was dignified and impressive, his diction almost faultless, and his gestures few in number, but always appropriate. He seemed on all occasions to be impressed with the sacred character and absolute truth of the message he was delivering, and the almost unanimous judgment of those who heard him was that he was a great preacher.—*The Central Baptist* of January 5, 1906.

After the death of Elder Hurley, letters were received from his friends in England, giving some facts in his life. These facts are given in the "Supplementary Memoir," written by William Crowell and published in the "Memoir of Rev. William Hurley, by Stephen Fisk, M. D." I quote: "Rev. William Hurley was born at Ryton, in Warwickshire, February 5, 1795. He was the eldest in a family of six children, two sons and four daughters. The records of the Baptist Church at Queenshead, near Halifax, Yorkshire, show that Mr. Hurley was invited on the 17th of August, 1819, to serve the church as its preacher, on probation; that on November 26th, the same year, he was invited to become its minister; and that on the 2nd day of July, 1822, he was ordained to the pastoral office in that church. On the 27th of July, 1829, he resigned his office of Pastor of that church."

Mr. Hurley's early life was spent in a center of intellectual activity, he being born in the native country of Shakespear, and which is the seat of Rugby Grammar School, whose influence stirred those who were responsive to such force.

His labors in Salt River Association were abundant and edifying. His social life was marked by personal oddities, usually of a humorous kind. Sometimes these oddities would crop out in the pulpit and then they must have made his ministrations less effective.

His death occurred in Troy, Missouri, about 4 o'clock Sunday morning, August 15, 1856, according to my information. In his last illness, he was lovingly cared for by his friend, Mr. John Snethen and family. He was buried in the Troy cemetery and a beautiful monument was erected at his grave. By this monument I have often stood and thought on William Hurley and his life work.

ELDER A. P. RODGERS.

By Himself.

I was ordained by the church at Mt. Pisgah, Pike county, Missouri, October 5, 1858, and a short time afterwards was called to serve that church as Pastor, which I did for several years. For about the first twenty years of my ministry, I was engaged mostly in pastoral work, partly in the bounds of Salt River Association and partly elsewhere. I was Pastor for two years on a distant field. In this twenty years I was Pastor of twelve churches in this Association, ranging in time from two to eight years.

In the year 1880, my home was broken up by death and my own health was so completely broken that I was confined mostly to my room for about three years I have tried to do something in the way of preaching the gospel. But as long as God permits me to stay here below I want to do anything that He is pleased to give me grace and strength to do, to help build up His cause and to point sinners to the Savior.

ELDER GREEN BENJAMAN SMITH.

By Himself.

I was born in North Carolina, in Iridel count June 8, 1830. Father moved from that State to Ter nessee. I was one year old then, and we lived ther one year. Then moved up into the State of Indian Wayne county; we lived there ten years; then, in 184 moved to this State, Warren county, where we locate about three miles from Warrenton, the county seat, where I grew to manhood. We settled in the woods on Congress land, like nearly every one else did. I was the oldest boy and had to help father all I could to clear up ground to raise something to live on. The country was wild and new, sparsely settled, with plenty of game such as deer, wild turkey; also wolves and some bears. When I grew to manhood I learned the blacksmith trade, and I followed my trade for quite a number of years.

I united with Noix Creek Baptist church, November 28, 1852. Bro. J. Frank Smith was Pastor and baptized me. The 26th day of December of the same year I was united in marriage with Miss Margaret Hedges, by Rev. John F. Hedges. My wife died, leaving me with two little boys. This was the hardest stroke that ever befell me. I afterwards was united in marriage with Miss Drucilla Price, of Pike county, Missouri. My wife and I are all alone now; we have raised a large family.

I was licensed to preach by Noix Creek Baptist Church the third Saturday in January, 1859. I then moved back to Warrenton. I worked all the week in the shop and preached every Sunday and Sunday night. I was requested to protract my meeting at one of my points and did so, working in the shop in day and then going to my meeting six miles away at night. There were some eight or ten conversions. I put my church letter in the Warrenton Baptist Church. This church called for my ordination, and I was ordained on the day of the presidential election, 1860. I have been in the pastoral work the most of my ministry, was elected once as missionary in Bear Creek Association. In all my preaching I have tried hard to know what the gospel was and then preach it earnestly as the only way of salvation for lost souls. I believe with all my heart that God saw fit by the foolishness of preaching to save them that believe.

I was Pastor four years at Middletown. There we built a house forty by sixty feet. I organized the Wellsville Baptist Church with only the aid of two Deacons. I was called to its pastorate and preached there five years.

Rev. L. C. Musick helped me in a protracted meeting at New Hartford; a church was organized, and I was called to its pastorate, I then moved there. I preached to them six years and the house that is there now was built. I was Pastor at Olney Lincoln county, Laddonia, Farber, Zion Church, Audrain county, Grand View, Boone county, Walnut Grove, Warren county, and West Cuivre. At all these churches I held meetings with fair results. I have helped Pastors in meetings.

ELDER JAMES FRANK SMITH.

"As Rev. Smith has been a most useful minister in the Baptist pulpit in northeastern and central Missouri for more than forty years, a short biographical outline of his life and labors in the ministry will be read with interest by his many friends scattered broadcast over the land. He was born May 7, 1811, in Jessamine county, Kentucky, and grew up under pious parental influence and under the ministry of Edmund Waller. Yet, despite these influences, he lived outside of the church. On the 7th of March, 1833, he was united in marriage with Miss Mary A. Dingle, of Kentucky, a daughter of Elder Edward Dingle. Not long after this event he removed to Missouri, and settled in Marion county, and in 1835 he and his wife were both converted, under the ministry of Elder Jeremiah Taylor, by whom they were baptized in March of that year. Elder Smith continued for several years with no special indications of anything above an ordinary interest in the progress of Baptist principles, but at a meeting in 1841, held at the old Bethel Church in Marion county, he became very much revived, and here he delivered his first exhortation, though at the time he had no thought of becoming a preacher. His church (Mount Zion, in Shelby county), however, licensed him to preach in the following December. He continued his labors in the gospel, which became more and more fruitful, and in November, 1843, he was endowed with full powers of a minister of the gospel, by ordination at the hands of Elders Gentry, Keach and Stevens. Of this period of his life Elder Smith says: 'I had but little education; was very poor; my knowledge of the Bible was limited, and a growing family made my prospects anything but promising; but the encouragement of friends, who never faltered, enabled me to persevere. I soon saw and felt the need of education. It was now too late for me to think of obtaining one, but I must use all the means within my reach to acquire knowledge. I studied English grammar on horseback, in going to and from my appointments. I have read thousands of pages while in the saddle. At one time I went to school with four of my children.'

"Besides being Pastor at different times of an almost innumerable number of churches, he has abounded in itinerant labors, having done more work, perhaps, in protracted meetings than any other man in this section of the State—from Lewis county on the north to Warren county on the south, and from Pike county on the east to Howard and Chariton counties on the west. He has baptized about 1,500 converts into churches, and witnessed as many more baptisms by the Pastors with whom he has labored.

"Down in Pike county in December, 1865, about the close of the 'late unpleasantness,' Rev. Smith says that while he was in the midst of a glorious revival he was arrested by the constable of the township in which the meeting was being held, and carried before a justice of the peace for preliminary trial. The charge was having preached the Gospel without taking the prescribed oath. Wm. H. Biggs, a prominent attorney of Pike, volunteered to defend him.

Several witnesses were examined and Elder Smith was required to give heavy bond, in default of which he must go to prison. Two friends, Mason Rose and Asa James, went on his bond, thus saving him from being placed in durance vile. Of the subsequent proceedings in the case his own language is used:

" 'I appeared at the next circuit court at Bowling Green. I do not think the judge—T. J. C. Fagg—wanted me arraigned, but the clerk (I forget his name) reminded him that I had not been called. So I was brought before the court with four others—three negroes and a white man—all charged with stealing, except myself. My crime was "preaching the Gospel and baptizing." I gave bond to appear at the next term of the court and sat down near a group of lawyears, one of whom remarked, "Parson, this is pretty hard, I tell you." "Yes," said I; "but there is no Patrick Henry here." Just then I thought of Christ being numbered with the transgressors, and felt that I had but done my duty.' "

"However, before the case finally came up for trial the Supreme Court of the United States passed upon the 'Missouri test oath,' declaring it unconstitutional, and Elder Smith was relieved from further annoyance and cost.

"The subject of this sketch is a minister well known throughout this and adjoining States, and hundreds now active in church work in the field of his labors have been brought in under his ministrations.—*The Globe-Democrat.*

In 1889, Brother Smith went on a visit to his old Kentucky home. In June, before starting, he preached at Hopewell Church, Audrain county, administered the Lord's Supper and baptized three persons. He visited familiar scenes of his young days and his earth journey ended in Kentucky, where it began. He died in Lexington, June 27, 1889. His body was brought back to his home, Mexico, Missouri, and memorial services were held in the church, Governor Hardin being one of the speakers. We laid the body to rest at Richland Church, Callaway county. His brethren in the ministry were the bearers of his remains.

James Frank Smith was a preacher of great power; his knowledge was large, his thought was clear, his heart was warm, his speech was mighty. At the throne of mercy he was as a little child.

JOHN THOMAS WILLIAMS.

By Mrs. J. T. Williams.

Rev. J. T. Williams was a Virginian by birth, and came to this State with his parents at the age of ten years. He was converted in early manhood and united with the Baptist church at Hannibal. Received a five-years' course of study at Georgetown College, Kentucky, and was licensed to preach by the Georgetown Baptist church, July 13, 1850. Finishing his course of study there he returned to Missouri, and began his life work as preacher and teacher in his home county. He was called by Providence church to his first pastorate and was regularly ordained and set apart to the solemn office of the ministry by order of that church on the fourth Saturday in October, 1853. He was also called about that time as Pastor of Bethel Church and he taught in Bethel College in Palmyra. His work in Salt River Association, began in 1857. He then became Pastor of the Louisiana Baptist church and taught a private school in the basement of that church for one year, when he purchased school property there and continued till the fall of 1860, when he became president of what was then known as Baptist Female College of Columbia, Mo., now Stephens College. He remained there, serving both the church and school during the troublous period of our late Civil War. In 1865 he returned to Louisiana and resumed his labors there both, teaching and preaching. His labors in the Salt River Association covered a period of fifteen years, though not consecutive. He held pastorates in quite a number of churches during that time; Noix Creek, Ashley, Sugar Creek, and some others.

As a minister of the Gospel he was ever true to the teachings of God's word, and was not afraid to preach its doctrines, though never in a controversial spirit. While to him was given a good measure of success in soul winning, and he had the privilege of baptizing many converts in his various pastorates, yet it was as teacher that he left his deepest impress for good in forming the character of the many young men and women who gathered in our home from year to year as students. Never boastful, in a quiet way he used the many opportunities thus afforded him to help those who were struggling with many difficulties, to gain an education. I hope I may be pardoned for using an extract from a private letter received a year and a half ago which will show better than any words of mine the thought I wish to convey. This dear friend and old pupil writes: "I have never failed to appreciate the unusual and unmerited kindness of Mr. and Mrs. Williams toward me in those days when I was struggling on in my effort to get an education. I have sometimes asked myself what Mr. Williams saw in me which moved him to do so much for me, and have always reached the conclusion that he must have done it out of the genuine goodness of his heart. Of one thing I am sure, it has made me thoughtful to assist young men in similar circumstances of need when the opportunity has offered" Adding at the close of the letter, "It is strange that a man has to get beyond fifty years of age before he realizes to the full the helpfulness of the influences of his early years."

It is gratifying to me to receive such testimony after all these years and I feel that I can truly say "his works do follow him." This is only one of many, and it enables me, too, to realize that the godly influence of a Christian home, while almost imperceptible at the time is often deeper and more lasting than that exercised by preaching alone. When called to other fields of labor it was with regret that his connection with Salt River Association was severed, and he oftentimes recalled to mind the friends and pupils that endeared to him that noble organization. His labors elsewhere were generally along the same line, either the pastorate, or teaching, or both, as was the case at Grand River College, Edinburg. On leaving there he expressed himself as feeling that they were four of the best years of his life—that he could see better results. Be that as it may, the close of his labors were drawing near, and the consciousness at the last that God had put upon them the seal of His approval was a fit closing of his useful life.

CHAPTER VIII.

TRIED BY FIRE, 1861—1869.

The Association held her session of 1861 on September 13th and 14th in Louisiana. Elder A. P. Rodgers preached the annual sermon from the Scripture: "And salute no man by the way." Elder J. M. Johnson was chosen moderator and Judge Miller clerk. The former moderator was absent. One missionary had been in the field and fifty conversions were reported and one church organized. The Sunday School interest was made a part of the regular work of the body. The Sunday School committee for this year was J. J. Gipson, J. Haynes and Judge Newton McDannold. The mission board was Wm. Penix, G. W. Peay and J. E. Shannon.

The Association passed a resolution to not put a missionary in the field because of the troubles consequent from the Civil War, which began in April preceding. In this the brethren seemed to have shown a faltering faith. The Prince of Peace is needed most when carnage and devastation are at their worst. There was never a time, a place or condition when the Gospel is powerless and should not be preached. The greater the peril the mightier should be the gospel call.

The committee on obituaries reported the following obituary:

Elder E. Autery.

"In presenting to you, dear brethren, our report, we call attention to the death of our beloved brother, E. Autery, whom God in His providence hath called away from our fellowship, to join that of His companion in singing the praises of his Redeemer; therefore,

"*Resolved*, That while we mourn our loss, we bow in humble submission to the will of an all-wise God, and mourn not as those who have no hope.

"*Resolved,* That we sympathize with the bereaved family and friends of the deceased, and commend the orphans thus left to the care of Him who has declared that He will be a father to the fatherless.

"*Resolved,* That while an all-wise Creator is removing laborers from His vineyard, we pray Him to raise up others throughout the Gospel field.

"J. G. SITTON,
"J. J. W. PLACE,
"J. J. GIPSON,
"Committee."

In 1862 the place of meeting was West Cuivre, the time was September 12th and 13th. Elder M. M. Modisett preached the sermon. His text was: "Cease ye from man, whose breath is in his nostrils; for wherein is he to be accounted of?" Elder M. M. Modisett was chosen moderator and Judge Miller clerk. R. S. Duncan and B. S. Tucker accepted seats as visitors. On district missions the Association took this action: "In view of the unfavorable circumstances for systematic operations in the mission work,

"*Resolved,* That this Association requests their ministers to assume the work of evangelists, as far as their circumstance will allow, taking up collections, and soliciting funds for the object, and report the same to the next Association; and out of which said ministers shall be paid for their services as far as it goes."

The Association dispensed with the executive board. A circular letter is issued in which they say, "We cannot write you of refreshing seasons in revivals. We write in the pavilion of sorrow, in the garments of heaviness. Ministers and members, we fear, have lost their wanted zeal." The letter expresses confidence that "the powers that be" will protect them in their constitutional rights to worship and it urges attendance at the next session. The committee on Sunday Schools was Brethren Carstarphen and Lefever.

In September, 1863, Mt. Pisgah entertained the Association. Elder H. M. King preached the introductory sermon from the scripture: "But he who was of the bondwoman was born after the flesh; but he of the freewoman was by promise. Which things are an allegory; for these are the two covenants; the one from Mount Sinai, which gendereth to bondage, which is Agar." Dover Church, Pike county, was received into associational fellowship; H. T. Ogden and J. A. Sanderson were her messengers. Elders James S. Green, Robert Kaylor and Brethren James McPike, Levi Moore, J. Motley and M. E. Motley accepted seats. There is no record of mission work done. The same plan as last year was adopted for the work of evangelization. The state of humiliation and unrest of the brethren is expressed in this action of the Association, appointing the 15th of the following month in connection with Bethel Association, "As a day of humiliation, fasting and prayer to Almighty God for peace in the land and for spiritual peace and a revival of His work in all the churches."

The *Western Watchman* was recommended to the brethren. Elders J. D. Biggs and J. H. Keach were the committee on Sunday Schools. The ministers were A. P. Rodgers, J. F. Hedges, J. J. Gipson, E. Jennings, J. M. Johnson, J. H. Keach, L. C. Musick, A. G. Mitchell, W. W. Mitchell, W. F. Luck, J. N. Griffin, J. J. W. Place, Jas. F. Smith, J. G. Davenport, Thos. H. Musick, R. Vermillion, M. M. Modisett and J. B. Fuller.

New Salem Church was the hostess of the body, September 9 and 10, 1864. Elder A. G. Mitchell was the preacher for the occasion. His text was: "For if the first fruit be holy, the lump is also holy; and if the root be holy, so are the branches." Elder A. G. Mitchell was chosen moderator, Elder W. W. Mitchell clerk; brothers in the flesh, yoke-fellows in the Lord's service. Spencerburg Church, Pike county, was received into fellowship, with F. M. Wicks, T. P. Woodson and W. Fuqua messengers. Elders R.

S. Duncan, J. Thomas, W. H. H. Vardeman and Brother J. T. Overall were visitors. Many churches had been blessed with revivals. The corresponding letter said: "Dear Brethren: Though we are in the midst of wars and corruptions that seem to threaten the destruction of social and religious liberty, and the very existence of the Church of Christ, there yet remains abundant reason to bless the God of all grace." Two men in the field reported one hundred and five conversions. An executive board was again appointed. It consisted of S. A. Edwards, J. Major and Duncan Ellis.

September 8 and 9, 1865, the Association held her annual session with Noix Creek Church. The opening sermon was preached by Elder J. T. Westover. The text was: "And ye are not your own. For ye are bought with a price; therefore glorify God in your body and in your spirit, which are God's." Judge John D. Biggs was elected moderator and Judge Miller clerk. The visitors were Elders W. J. Patrick, J. T. Williams, Lewis Duncan, J. H. Horner, J. T. Westover, R. Holman and Brethren E. Hayden, G. Smith, and D. M. Wilson. There had been one missionary in the field. The committee on Sunday Schools, W. W. Mitchell and H. M. King, made an earnest report. The new executive board was S. A. Edwards, Duncan Ellis and Newton McDannold. The corresponding letter said, "Although coldness, dreariness and in many cases immoralities and vices seem to prevail among us, yet we are thankful that there are some signs of vital piety in our midst." They seemed to take heart because, "Since we last corresponded with you, the blasts and commotions of war which were sweeping over the country, have passed away. One of the "commotions" left by the war was the Test Oath, which attempted to place the authority of the State above the call from God to preach. But those preached on who could say with Peter and John, "Whether it be right in the sight of God to hearken unto you more than unto God, judge ye. For we cannot but speak the things which we have seen and heard." Elders James F. Smith, Henry M. King and others were true to God and true to our Baptist history. "So when they had further threatened them, they let them go, finding nothing how they might punish them, because of the people." The oath was declared unconstitutional by the Supreme Court of the United States. Justice Field delivered the opinion of the court in which it is declared that "The Test Oath imposed by the Constitution of Missouri is a violation of that provision of the Constitution of the United States which provides that 'No State shall pass any bill of attainder, *ex post facto* law, etc.'" (Constitution of the United States, Art. I, Sec. 10.)

During the incoming year many ministers were arrested and some were imprisoned for preaching without taking the Test Oath.

Dover Church entertained the Association September 7 and 8, 1866. Elder J. T. Williams preached the sermon from the Scripture: "Then spake Jesus again unto them, saying, I am the light of the world." The visitors were Elders Horner, Smith of the Southern B. C., Williams, Rodgers, Gipson and Bibb, and Brother Harlow. It was voted to raise money "that the poor and destitute of our Association may have the gospel preached unto them." There was $500 raised on the occasion. The executive board was increased to the number of five and was made to consist of W. W. Waddell, W. G. Hawkins, W. W. Wise, N. McDannold, A. P. Miller.

At the suggestion of Mt. Pisgah Church, a committee was appointed to advise what steps to take as to the Test Oath. They reported: "Your committee recommend the Association to appoint a committee of five members—in case it should become necessary—to memorialize the next Legislature to repeal or abolish the 'Test Oath,' or at least so much as relates to the ministers, many of whom are debarred from prose-

ELDER M. S. WHITESIDE.

DEACON LUKE LEWIS.

ELDER F. M. BIRKHEAD.

SENATOR M. R. K. BIGGS.

cuting their duties, duties which they dare not disregard, and which the State should vouchsafe securely, as a sacred duty, on account of the commission they hold from Jesus Christ himself to preach the Gospel to every nation."

The report was adopted. The committee consisted of H. G. Edwards, W. G. Hawkins, J. D. Biggs, M. R. K. Biggs and A. P. Miller.

A strong report was made in favor of Baptist education by committee: J. T. Williams and M. M. Modisett.

The Association endorsed the course of the *Missouri Baptist Journal,* published at Palmyra.

Ramsey Creek received the Association to her hospitality again September 13 and 14, 1867. Elder James F. Smith preached the sermon from the text: "For ye are bought with a price; therefore glorify God in your body and in your spirit, which are God's." Four churches came into the Association at this time: New London, whose messengers were Ezra Carstarphen and J. Caldwell; Ashley, the second time, whose messengers were F. Williams and B. Shipp; 2nd Church, Louisiana, whose messengers were J. T. Williams, G. W. Foster, J. J. Gipson and J. T. Overall; and Star Hope, whose messengers were M. S. Whiteside and David P. Gilliland. The visitors were Elders W. C. Busby, J. H. Thomas, W. H. Vardeman, —— Horner, and Brother Wilson. Three conversions reported and three churches organized in the mission field.

The body met with Salem Church, September 11 and 12, 1868. Elder W. F. Luck preached the sermon. His text was: "As we have, therefore opportunity, let us do good unto all men, especially unto them who are of the household of faith." Elder A. G. Mitchell was elected moderator, Judge Miller clerk. Salt River Church, Pike county, came into the Association; her messenger was E. M. Wheeler. The visitors were Elders J. S. Green, W. C. Busby, —— Place and Brethren P. H. Rudesell, J. B. Mayhall and Edw. Hay-

15

den. Elders Luck, Grant and Whiteside had done missionary work at $2 per day. The committee on education, J. T. Williams, M. M. Modisett and J. H. Keach, recommended that help be given to William Jewell, just re-opening after the war. Elder J. T. Williams was invited to canvass for a proposed endowment. The *Central Baptist,* St. Louis, edited by J. H. Luther and Norman Fox, was endorsed. The committee on Sunday Schools was J. T. Williams, A. F. Randall and E. A. Wyman. The body voted to organize a convention. The new board was G. W. Hawkins, A. P. Miller, J. E. Shannon, M. R. K. Biggs and H. G. Edwards.

In 1869 the Association met at Providence, September 10 and 11. Elder J. T. Williams preached the introductory sermon from the text: "Lest any should say that I had baptized in mine own name." Elder A. G. Mitchell was chosen moderator and Elder J. T. Williams clerk. Three new churches were received. The second church, Bowling Green, whose messengers were W. P. Lowry, D. M. Kimball, A. P. Rodgers; Walnut Grove, whose messengers were B. A. Jennings, W. J. Zumwalt, E. K. Howell and W. Bland; and Ebenezer, whose messengers were J. Bradley and J. A. Edwards. The visitors were R. S. Duncan, W. H. Vardeman, J. F. Smith, B. F. Hixson, J. McPike, G. B. Smith and W. F. Luck. The committee on Education, J. H. Keach, R. Gibson and W. B. McPike, recommended Wm. Jewell College, and Baptist College, Louisiana, of which Elder J. T. Williams was president. There had been three missionaries in the field, and eighty-nine conversions were reported by them. The amount of money on hand for the incoming year was $1,120.40. The ministers are J. T. Williams, G. W. Foster, M. M. Modisett, S. G. Givens, E. Jennings, A. P. Rodgers, E. Noel, J. G. Davenport, J. J. Gipson, J. F. Hedges, R. Vermillion, J. H. Keach, J. N. Griffin, A. G. Mitchell, W. F. Luck, B. F. Hardesty, M. S. Whiteside, J. F. Smith, J. T. Wheeler, R. Gibson, J. B. Hawkins.

DOVER BAPTIST CHURCH.

By M. E. Broaddus, D. D.

This church was organized September 8, 1862, at Goodman's Grove in Pike county, Missouri. This grove was in the field just opposite the site of the present church house. The following were the constituent members of this church: James A. Sanderson and wife, James Anderson and wife, Nathaniel R. Smith and wife, John R. Smith, Edwin B. Smith, Henry T. Ogden, Mary E. Goodman and two colored persons, Mary and George. On the same day James A. Sanderson and Henry T. Ogden were elected Deacons of said church. These Deacons were ordained by Rev. J. B. Fuller, Rev. A. G. Mitchell, and Rev. M. M. Modisett. At the same meeting N. R. Smith was elected church clerk, Rev. M. M. Modisett was also elected Pastor and served the church as such, until April, 1873, when he resigned, giving up this pastorate entirely. During his ministry the church was very much strengthened by additions to its membership from year to year, and there were several good meetings held in this time, the Pastor being aided by other brethren and many were baptized. It was also during his pastorate that the commodious building now occupied by the church was erected at a cost of some two thousand dollars.

In February, 1874, Rev. A. G. Mitchell was elected Pastor and accepted the charge. He was Pastor from this date to November, 1876, when he gave up the pastorate, and was succeeded by Rev. J. F. Cook, D. D., who remained as Pastor until August, 1896. During the pastorate of Brother Cook the church was greatly enlarged in membership, reaching the one hundred and fifty mark. Several good meetings were held and the church very much built up numerically and spiritually. During his pastorate, also, very many of the best members, at the present time, were induced by him to go to LaGrange, where they were educated and are now among the most useful members.

Rev. J. D. Biggs became pastor November, 1896, and continued as such for ten years, up to December, 1906. During the pastorate of Brother Biggs the church was very much built up. From year to year they held very successful meetings and many of the saved were added to the church. In May, 1907, Rev. M. E. Broaddus, D. D., became pastor and is still the Under Shepherd, with deacons J. M. Duncan, W. H. Edwards, L. F. Mackey and William N. Goodman; with Hon. John W. McIlroy as church clerk. The church has recently sustained a great loss in the death of Deacon H. T. Ogden, he having died and gone to his reward, March 27, 1909. He was one of our most faithful members, indeed, his Pastor called him the "Line Tree," on the occasion of his funeral service. He will be a great loss to the whole Association.

The church begins the holding of services two Sundays per month on May first of this present year. Holds Sunday School every Sunday in the twelve months, and now numbers almost two hundred members.

EBENEZER BAPTIST CHURCH.

By Ida Dawson Lahr.

Ebenezer Baptist Church was organized the fifth Saturday in July, 1869. J. J. Bradley and his wife, Rhoda, J. A. and R. B. Edwards, T. J. Smith, T. E. Johnson, Miss Lucy Lilley and Miss Bettie Bradley were the constituent members. Revs. Albert G. Mitchell, M. S. Whiteside and M. M. Modisett composed the Presbytery. Rev. M. S. Whiteside was chosen Pastor and served the church four years. R. B. Edwards church clerk; Thos. Page and J. J. Bradley were elected Deacons.

This church, composed of five men and three women, sent their first letter to Salt River Association, which convened with Providence church, 1869, and asked to be admitted into the Association.

The church met at Smith schoolhouse for several years when the place of meeting was changed to Smith Chapel (Methodist) church house. God gave the church a rapid increase. During a meeting conducted in 1872 by Revs. G. C. Sparrow and M. S. Whiteside, thirty members were added to the church.

The fourth Saturday in March, 1875, seventeen members, including four of the above named constituent members of Ebenezer Church, were granted letters and became constituent members of Oak Ridge Baptist church. The same year John Wright, J. J. Bradley and James L. Dawson were appointed as a building committee. Clem. B. Lindsay donated a large lot from the southeast corner of his farm. The lot is shaded by beautiful trees, "Monarchs of the Forest Primeval," and is located one mile south of Sledd, Missouri.

At this time there were no railroads in Lincoln county or the southern part of Pike, so most of the material for the church was hauled from Clarksville, Missouri, where it had been transported by boats that plied the Mississippi river. The church house, valued at $1,000, was completed in 1876, and dedicated by Dr. W. Pope Yeaman, the fourth Sunday in August, 1877.

Dr. Chas. Gilbert, Thos. Ogden and James L. Dawson were ordained as Deacons in 1876. James L. Dawson served continuously as Deacon from 1873; as church clerk from 1875 and as church treasurer from 1876 to the time of his death, April 25, 1903. His long and faithful service in the church of Ebenezer, and in the Associations of which Ebenezer became a member, is his best memorial.

Lewis Mitchell was elected deacon March, 1878, Robert A. Crank, January, 1879, and both were ordained as Deacons the fourth Sunday in February, 1879. Paulus Watts and John Wright were ordained Deacons the fifth Sunday in April, 1882. Revs. Pascal W. Halley and Thomas R. Campbell were licensed and ordained by Ebenezer Church. Rev. Web P. Bibb was licensed by this church, but ordained at Anada Baptist Church. Ebenezer had the pleasure of welcoming and entertaining Salt River Association August, 1886.

Revs. M. S. Whiteside, Wm. W. Mitchell, W. H. Burnham, J. D. Robnett, M. P. Matheny, Chas. A. Mitchell, Bland Beauchamp, W. M. Tipton, W. N. Maupin, W. H. Stone were the Pastors, in order named of Ebenezer Church while she was a member of the mother Association.

Ebenezer Church and fourteen sister churches withdrew from Salt River Association and met at Cornerstone Church, September 18, 19, 1891, and organized Cuivre Baptist Association, of Lincoln county, Missouri.

GRASSY CREEK CHURCH.

By Z. T. Smith.

Grassy Creek Baptist Church was organized in August, 1870, with twelve constituent members, mostly coming from the old Noix Creek Church. There are only two constituent members living at the present time: W. B. Smith and Z. Taylor Smith. John J. Smith, known as Uncle Jack, who died on the morning of January the first, 1908, being ninety-five years, two months and two days old, was one of the constituent members of the church. I think he was the oldest member of any of the churches of the Association.

Brother G. W. Foster was called as Pastor of the church in August, 1870, he being the first Pastor. We built the present house in the year 1877. Being poor financially it was hard to get the means to build with, but finally we succeeded in building. Brother J. D. Watson is pastor.

CHURCHES IN ILLINOIS.

These churches began coming into the Association early, Quincy being the first to come. They continued in fellowship with Salt River Association for many years. At this writing I have not the record of their withdrawal, but it seems to have been in 1863. I will mention them severally.

Quincy. When the Association was in session with Bethel Church, Marion county, the 7th and 8th of October, 1827, Quincy Church, Adams county, Illinois, was received into fellowship. William Roberds and James G. Wooton were the messengers. The membership numbered eleven. In 1830 the church was reported as dissolved.

In 1829, *Atlas Church,* Pike county, was received into fellowship. Ozias Hale was the messenger, the membership was five; the following year she had increased to ten. In 1831 Brother Hale is given as an ordained minister. At this time Atlas Church is dismissed by request "with a view of joining a new Association."

Six Miles Church, Illinois, was received into the Association in 1836, W. Foreman, J. Samson and F. Colland being the messengers. In 1837 Six Miles numbered forty-one members. In 1838 Elder David Hubbard was the messenger and the church had grown to number fifty-four. Brother Hubbard was the Pastor. The church sent messengers in 1846 for the last time. The messengers then were S. Applegate, J. D. Garnett, J. Stark and W. Mitchell.

Martinsburg became a member of Salt River Association in 1845. The messengers were David Hubbard and J. Hubbard. The membership was twenty-eight. Martinsburg Church was organized February 15, 1845, by Elders David Hubbard and Jacob Capps. The new church had sixteen members. Brother Hubbard preached on the subject of a gospel church. John Hubbard was chosen clerk at the March meeting.

A. Standley was his successor. In February, 1847, J. G. Sitton was chosen clerk. J. D. Garrett was a licentiate in this church. In August, 1848, the church invited the Association. In July, 1849, David Capps and A. Mosher were elected Deacons. Also a committee was appointed to select a site for a house of worship. In February, 1851, under the ministry of Elders Hubbard and Capps there was a gracious revival in Martinsburg Church. The services were then transferred to Pleasant Hill, where the interest grew and great grace was upon the people. The church began regular services at Pleasant Hill in addition to the home services. In a work of triumphant grace in Pleasant Hill a large number of members were received into Martinsburg Church, the services beginning in April, 1852. In May, 1852, the church elected Elder David Hubbard as Pastor. He accepted. The messengers elected to go to the Association in 1852 were Elder David Hubbard, Elder Eli Hubbard, J. G. Sitton, C. A. Felton and Joseph Hubbard. David Willson was chosen deacon. D. H. Simpson was elected Deacon in May, 1853. At the same meeting Elder L. C. Musick was elected Pastor and accepted. The month following Eld. F. W. Ingmire was elected "as Pastor for one year." Elder James Frank Smith helped in a revival at Pleasant Hill, where the work was done under the direction of Martinsburg Church. The results were gracious and abundant. In 1854 Elder Ingmire was elected Pastor. Elder A. D. Landrum accepted a call to the pastorate in April, 1855. In August, 1855, there was a revival in Pleasant Hill under the ministry of "Brother Smith from Texas." August 9, 1856, was a day of great interest in Baptist circles in Pleasant Hill. On that occasion C. B. Lewis and Elijah Autery were ordained to the ministry and a house of worship was dedicated. These services were had under the jurisdiction of Martinsburg Church; Pleasant Hill brethren had not yet organized. Elder A. D. Landrum and M. M. Modisett were the ministers in these services. At the March meeting, 1857, Martinsburg Church granted to a large number of members letters to organize in Pleasant Hill. For many years the church had maintained a sort of dual existence, vibrating between the two towns.

Pleasant Hill. The Baptists at Pleasant Hill were members at Martinsburg until the spring of 1857. The minutes of Martinsburg Church has this record for March 28, 1857: "The following named members were dismissed by letter to constitute a separate church at Pleasant Hill by the name of Pleasant Hill United Baptist: I. A. Mosher, Lucy V. Mosher, William Mitchell, Susan Mitchell, J. D. Brooks, Mary J. Brooks, Lawson Turner, Susan Turner, John Sapp, Frances Sapp, Joe Ernest, Eliza Ernest, Mary Collard." It is a matter of regret that I have no more material on the history of this excellent body of Christians. I did not know them in the period contemplated by this history. Later I knew Dr. John A. Thomas, who must have belonged to Pleasant Hill in the period of 1857-1863. He was a godly man, cultured and informed. He accepted Christ and His church at Pleasant Hill February, 1851. He was a leader in church work, eminent in Sunday school work and a representative American citizen. He could have easily stood in the front rank in any assembly of men with which he was identified. If this imperfect effort to get information from the churches in our former territory in our sister State, bestirs some one to get the obscured Baptist history of that favored land I shall be grateful.

Hamburg was received into the fellowship of the Association in 1859. J. McLean was the messenger and they had ten members. Elder C. B. Lewis was the Pastor. They gave that year $10 missionary fund.

NEW LONDON CHURCH.

By Mrs. Blanche Megown.

New London Baptist Church was organized on the second Saturday in March, 1867, with nineteen members, three of whom are living, Mrs. LaRue Jones of Novinger, Mrs. Bettie Briscoe and Mrs. Kittie Carstarphen of New London. Mrs. Carstarphen has been an invalid for seven years. The council was composed of delegates from Salem, Bethel, Hannibal and Providence churches. Ministers present: Rev. John H. Keach of Salem, B. F. Hixson of Providence, Bro. W. C. Busby of Hannibal, and Bro. J. Frank Smith. The first protracted meeting was held by Bro. H. M. King; several came into the church. In 1869 Brother Hixson held a meeting and twenty-three came into the church. During the forty-one years we have had twelve pastors. Brother Busby served us eight years and Brother Biggs about fifteen. These are our longest pastorates. Brother Patrick followed Brother Busby and served six months. Brother Colvin one year, Brother Hixson two years, Brother Biggs two years, Brother Morgan two years, Brother Wm. H. Vardeman six months, Brother Beauchamp two years. Brother Biggs was called in 1888 and remained three years, Brother Smith two years, Brother Simms one year, Brother James Reid six months. The church then called Brother Biggs for the third time and he faithfully served us till December, 1906. In June, 1907, we called Brother T. R. Campbell, of LaGrange.

We have had many good meetings. I recall a meeting held by Rev. Sanford M. Brown during Brother Beauchamp's pastorate, when we had a large ingathering; one very old man past sixty came into the church. Brother Reid was with us in a meeting when he was State Evangelist, in which twenty came into the church. In 1897 he was with us in another meeting, when we had a large ingathering from our Sunday school. At the close of the meeting he organized our first B. Y. P. U. In recent years we have had Evangelists Dew, Taylor, Houser and Wells. Brother Dew's meeting stirred our town as no other ever did. We all agree Brother Dew taught us more of the Bible than any minister who was ever with us. Brother Patrick held several meetings with us. Brethren Hatcher, Tate, I. W. Reid and Throgmorton have been with us during meetings. Our Sunday school was organized in the courthouse in 1868 and has never taken a vacation. For a number of years we had a Methodist superintendent, but we were a Baptist Sunday school. To-day we have a fine school; Brother Jack Briscoe is our efficient superintendent. We have entertained the Association twice; twenty-three years ago we entertained for the first time and again nine years ago at the seventy-fifth anniversary. We are ready to have it again.

In 1868 Brother Ezra Carstarphen, our Deacon and leader, undertook to build a church house. Had he not been a man of great faith and Christian zeal he would have been discouraged from the very first, so much opposition did he meet. But so enthusiastic was he that he went about the work to succeed. He was heard to say: "I will build the house if it takes all this world's goods I have," and had he lived he would. The lot was donated by Mr. Sam Caldwell, circuit clerk of Ralls county, but not a Christian, and the building was begun. The cornerstone was laid by the Masons on the 20th of May, 1868. In September, 1869, the walls were completed and Brother Carstarphen, Brother John T. Brown and Brother Caldwell were sent as messengers to Salt River Association, which met at Ramsey Creek, and instructed to ask the Association for funds to help finish the building. Brother Carstarphen was taken sick at the meeting, came home and lived only a few days. But after many years of toil the church was finished and stands to-day as a memorial of Ezra Carstarphen. For two years after Brother Carstarphen's death no effort was made to finish the church; then the women, a noble few, concluded to finish the edifice. Mr. J. W. Buchanan gave time and means to help these women and finally raised enough money to roof the church. Mrs. Buchanan and Mrs. Nichols went to Hannibal soliciting aid and succeeded. The work went on little by little, and all these years Brother Busby coming once a month and preaching in the courthouse. God bless him, we love him yet. In 1871 the women made a supper, clearing $395.95. With this they plastered and floored the house. Now it must be seated. For several years the sisters served dinners during circuit court and were well patronized, until at last enough was raised to put in seats. Then a bell was needed. Mr. Nichols solicited funds, purchased and superintended the hanging of the bell. A few years later he provided the old church clock in the same manner. Many who worked in those days have been called home. Sister Nichols and Sister Brown never tired of the work and were always hopeful. Only a few who were in the early struggle are left, Sisters Jones, Buchanan, Briscoe, Carstarphen, Elzea, Brother Brown, now past eighty years, and Brother J. O. Caldwell. We were children then and are now filling the places of the sainted ones gone before, but the memory of those days will always be sweet to us.

SPENCERBURG CHURCH.

By T. J. Ayres.

The United Baptist Church at Spencerburg, Pike county, Mo., was constituted March 3, 1864, largely as result of a protracted meeting held in August, 1863, by Revs. H. M. King and W. J. Patrick, by a presbytery composed of Elder G. W. Robey and Brethren John Ford, John S. Ford and John Ferrell. Elder G. W. Robey served as moderator and Brother John Ford clerk. After enrollment of proposed constituency, Constitution, Articles of Faith and Rules of

Decorum were adopted. Rev. Henry M. King was elected Pastor and Brother K. A. Laird clerk.

After a diligent inquiry no records can be found from date of organization until the July meeting in 1872, which record shows Rev. S. G. Givens Pastor and T. J. Ayres clerk.

It is impossible to determine definitely the constituency of the church, but all have passed away, except Sister Martha Bondurant, now of Vandalia, Mo., and Sister Sarah Guthrie, now of Curryville, Mo. Among the early additions we find Miss Sallie E. Kessler, Miss Ann E. Read, Dr. F. M. Wicks, T. J. Ayres and others who still survive. This congregation has had as Pastors the services of Revs. H. M. King, S. G. Givens, M. L. Bibb, J. D. Biggs, W. J. Patrick, James Reid, M. M. Modisett, E. Jennings, S. W. Tucker, S. S. Keith, A. P. Rodgers, J. W. Trower, R. E. McQuie, W. N. Maupin and George T. Baker, the present Pastor, and others as temporary supply.

The record shows a membership since the organization of something over three hundred. The present membership as reported at the last meeting of the Association is one hundred. Brother J. M. Liter is now clerk. The church has been greatly revived and has been strengthened in efficiency.

STAR HOPE CHURCH.

By Elder E. Anderson.

The organization of this body was Saturday before the third Sunday in May, 1867, with nine members: M. S. Whiteside, Mary A. Whiteside, David P. Gilliland, Virginia Gilliland, Lucy McClellan, John McClellan, Elizabeth Hopkins, Nancy Bell, John W. M. Palmer. Elder Wm. F. Luck preached the sermon. The next month Elder M. S. Whiteside was elected Pastor. Brethren Gilliland and Palmer became Deacons and Brother Gilliland clerk.

Mr. Francis Worthington gave a building lot and in January, 1868, a building committee was appointed, consisting of Brethren Whiteside, Palmer and Gilliland, and the spring following a house thirty-five by fifty was built at a cost of $1,500. October, 1868, the house was dedicated; the sermon was preached by Elder J. F. Smith. In June, 1870, a Sunday school was organized. The Pastor's salary was fixed at $125. The rod was used early and often in the vigorous young church. In February, 1868, it was resolved to "handle the male members for non-attendance."

In October, 1868, Elder J. F. Smith helped Pastor Whiteside in a revival and in October, 1870, Elder B. F. Hixson helped him. Elder W. H. Burnham became pastor in May, 1875; Elder A. G. Mitchell in January, 1879; Elder C. A. Mitchell in January, 1883; Elder Wiley J. Patrick in March, 1887; Elder J. D. Hacker in December, 1888. In 1893 Star Hope Church became a member of Cuivre Association.

WALNUT GROVE BAPTIST CHURCH.

By Wm. Maddox.

Organization. At a meeting held by appointment at the Walnut Grove schoolhouse in Pike county, March 17, 1869, for the purpose of organizing a Baptist Church, after a sermon by Rev. Ed Jennings it was agreed to organize, whereupon Rev. Ed Jennings acted as moderator and Alex McDannold as clerk. The Articles of Christian Faith and Church Covenant were then read and unanimously adopted.

An invitation was then given to the brothers and sisters hereafter named, who presented themselves and gave their names as follows: Edmond Jennings, Frederick Hanson, Alexander Todd, James A. Jennings, Eli M. Howell, William J. Zumault, Tillman T. Headrick, John Taliaferro, Wm. H. Price, C. Columbus Price, Wm. Dillender, Jesse Bland, Larkin D. Howell, John L. Zumault, Wm. H. Bland, James T. Bland, Stephen Bland, Wm. Harris, Andrew H. Noble, Alex McDannold, Jr., Tillitha A. Headrick, Lucinda C. Harris, Lucy Taliaferro, Lizzie Bland, Mary

V. Luck, Permelia Howell, Sarah Cowhard, Emily A. Todd, Elizabeth Humphry, Martha M. Cornell, Susan E. Cook, Mary J. Howell, Mary S. Taliaferro, and, after constitution, Caroline Noble by relation. The church elected Rev. Ed. Jennings as Pastor and appointed Brother B. A. Jennings, S. G. Jennings and Alex McDannold to serve as a building committee for house of worship. The church elected Brother William J. Zumault church clerk and Brother B. A. Jennings Deacon.

Sunday following the first Saturday in December, 1869, the Lord's Supper was observed. At this regular meeting the first protracted meeting was held by Rev. Ed Jennings, assisted by Rev. Hanes. It resulted in the conversion and baptism of five souls. Brother John Steward was elected Deacon. A meeting held in November, 1870, conducted by Rev. Ed Jennings lasted nine days and resulted in the conversion and baptism of six souls.

In 1871 a few days' meeting held in August by Rev. Ed Jennings resulted in the conversion and baptism of one. October, 1871, W. J. Zumault resigned the office of church clerk. W. A. Waugh was elected to fill the vacancy.

In February, 1874, B. A. Jennings resigned his office as Deacon and Charles R. Huntington was elected to fill his place. March, 1874, W. A. Waugh resigned his office as church clerk and Charles Huntington was elected to fill the vacancy.

A series of meetings in 1874, conducted by Revs. Ed Jennings and M. M. Modisett, continued two weeks and resulted in twelve additions. There had been other revivals with good results in conversions and general advancement.

February, 1876, Rev. M. M. Modisett was elected Pastor of the church. In 1877 Brother James Reid was elected Pastor.

Brother Alex Todd was elected clerk in 1878. Brothers Wm. Cook and C. C. Price were elected Deacons.

Rev. Ed Jennings was again elected Pastor. A. G. Raufer was elected as church clerk in 1880. The December meeting was continued thirteen days, conducted by Revs. Reid and Patrick, thirty-five uniting with the church by experience and baptism.

February, 1882, Brother Luther Edwards was elected Deacon and council called to ordain Deacons, Revs. W. J. Patrick and M. S. Whiteside. Rev. M. S. Whiteside, assisted by Rev. James Reid, conducted a two weeks' meeting, resulting in twelve conversions and baptism of same. Rev. James Reid resigned as Pastor and Rev. M. S. Whiteside was elected in his stead.

In June, 1884, Rev. W. A. Bibb was elected Pastor, a meeting continued fourteen days, seventeen uniting with church by experience and baptism. Brother R. J. Martin was elected Deacon in February, 1885. In December of same year a series of meetings continued twenty-three days, conducted by the pastor, Rev. W. A. Bibb, assisted by Rev. Wm. M. Tipton.

A meeting conducted by Pastor W. A. Bibb, assisted by Rev. S. G. Givens, in 1886, continued seventeen days and resulted in twelve additions by experience and baptism. A meeting continued fifteen days in November, 1887, and was conducted by Rev. W. A. Bibb, assisted by Rev. Emmet Sanderson, resulting in nine additions by experience and baptism. January, 1888, Rev. W. A. Bibb conducted a several days meeting at McCune Station, which resulted in seven by experience and baptism and two by relation. In February thirteen were dismissed by letter to unite with new church at McCune. In January, 1889, a several days meeting conducted by Pastor W. A. Bibb, assisted by Revs. W. M. Tipton and W. J. Patrick, resulted in eight additions. Brother W. L. Maddox was elected church clerk. Rev. F. M. Birkhead was unanimously elected Pastor in 1890. A series of meetings conducted by Rev. Maupin (Pastor F. M. Birkhead being absent on account of sickness) resulted with two uniting with the church. In 1893 a series of meetings conducted by Pastor F. M. Birkhead continued two weeks, resulting in two additions by letter, the church being greatly revived. In January, 1894, a series of meetings conducted by Pastor F. M. Birkhead, assisted by Rev. James Downing, continued twenty days with six additions. In October, 1894, a revival meeting was conducted by Pastor F. M. Birkhead, assisted by Rev. J. S. Eames. It continued nearly two weeks, much interest was manifested and five additions to the church by experience and baptism.

Rev. W. N. Maupin was elected Pastor in March, 1897. A meeting conducted by Pastor W. N. Maupin in December of same year continued several days.

Rev. F. M. Birkhead was elected unanimously as Pastor of church in December, 1899.

In October, 1900, a series of meetings conducted by Pastor F. M. Birkhead, assisted by Revs. Tucker and W. J. Patrick, resulted in twenty-eight additions. October, 1902, a series of meetings conducted by Pastor F. M. Birkhead, assisted by Rev. W. J. Patrick. This meeting we believe accomplished good, strengthening the church. That the gosped was preached in purity and there were seed sown that will bring forth fruit to the honor and glory of God.

January, 1904, a series of meetings conducted by Pastor F. M. Burkhead, assisted by Rev. Chas. Mitchell, some sermons by Rev. W. J. Patrick, resulted in twelve additions. At the regular business meeting in January, two Deacons were elected: Bros. Dan W. Maxfield and J. W. Wood. Those present at their ordination were F. M. Birkhead, Charles Mitchell, Deacons David Hettich and C. C. Price. Preparations to repair house, clean well and build fence were made.

In December, 1905, a series of meetings, conducted by Pastor F. M. Birkhead, and Rev. Luke Kirtley resulted in two additions by experience. Rev. E. W. Chewning was elected Pastor in August, 1906. A series of meetings conducted by Pastor E. W. Chewning in December, 1906.

Series of meetings conducted by Rev. Luke Kirtley in 1908 resulted in five additions by experience. Rev. W. A. Bibb was elected as Pastor in March, 1908, after an absence of several years, beginning with the fortieth year of Walnut Grove's existence as a Baptist church.

MCCUNE COLLEGE.

Elder J. T. Williams made a strong effort to establish in Louisiana an institution of learning with the safeguards of Christianity in it and Baptist support under it with such a mold of life and teaching as would bring honor and advancement to the denomination he loved. He had the active and vigorous support of Salt River Association. After he had laid a foundation in a personal movement to build up a high order of institution, Louisiana Baptist College was incorporated and he was made president. This was in 1869. Sister Williams had charge of the home department. They did great service in awakening the spirit of education and they gave thorough intellectual and religious training to the hundreds of young men and young women who came into their college home. Scores of them are still living and they may be found filling most honorably the higher walks of life for which they had been fitted. After Professor Williams, came others who held the presidency with varying success. Elder James D. Biggs accepted the presidency. He had received a most thorough elementary and classical education. He and his able associates accomplished all that seemed possible under the limitations of an unendowed institution. Prof. W. B. McPike was associated with Brother Biggs and was principal in 1874-5. Dr. Williams returned to the presidency in 1875.

Prof. A. Slaughter was elected president in 1880, and he gave energy and efficiency to the enterprise and was rewarded with large success. In 1881, the name was changed to McCune College in honor of Deacon A. J. McCune. Dr. H. T. Morton, a distinguished scholar and educator, filled with honor the presidency for several years. There came a time of obstruction and discouragement. Prof. Beeson and Prof. Musgrove each found the presidency, which he accepted a hard task. Prof. E. W. Dow had the school one year and had large prosperity, but a death in his family caused him to go out. Prof. Grenwell took the presidency and struggled on a few years and returned to the scenes of his former labors in Kentucky. The college closed.

ELDER DAVID HUBBARD.

A figure that stands out prominent, strong, constant and evangelistic is that of Elder David Hubbard. He was one of the builders of our Baptist temple in these regions. His record in Salt River Association shows ability and co-operative fellowship. March 12, 1853, Martinsburg Church took the following action: "Know ye, that our beloved brother and Pastor, Elder David Hubbard, has been a member in our church ever since we were constituted (in A. D. 1845) and we know him as a man to possess a good moral character not surpassed by any man; that he is a devout, humble Christian and as a minister of the gospel he is fearless, able, faithful and efficient, apt to teach, always abounding in the work, possessing preaching talents of a high order. And during his ministration, (since 1845), by the grace of God, has been a blessing to us. And we know of no other minister in our denomination whom as a Pastor of a church that we could so cheerfully recommend." At this meeting Elder A. G. Mitchell was moderator *pro tem* and John G. Sitton clerk.

In the first years of the church Elder David Hubbard seems to have done the work of the Pastor with the co-operation of Elder Jacob Capps, who often ministered to the church. As the church grew in years it was more effectively organized by giving Brother Hubbard the full office of Pastor. I take this also from the records of this church of date, September, 1856: "Agreed to send Elder David Hubbard, our former pastor, some help for his faithful ministerial labors to this church from the time she was constituted till his removal to Oregon." At this service Elder C. B. Lewis preached and served as moderator and J. C. Sitton was clerk.

ELDER J. D. BIGGS.

By his son, Dalton Biggs, Esq.

The subject of this sketch was born in 1843. He is the son of John D. Biggs, and great-grandson of Davis Biggs. In early life he farmed with his father on the old homestead near New London, and went to school in the old Salem schoolhouse. He had the benefit in early life of instruction from an old master who was educated in the University at Edinburgh. Afterward he attended and graduated in Georgetown College, Kentucky. He began his pastorate at Millersburg, Kentucky, and afterwards moved back to Missouri. He has been Pastor at different periods of his life of a number of the churches of this Association. He was Pastor of Springfield Baptist Church from 1874 to 1877; Pastor at Kirkwood, Missouri, for one year; moderator of Salt River Association four years. He has been successful as a Pastor of these various churches. He is full of energy and power as a preacher. He was recently Pastor of the following churches: Dover, Ramsey Creek, Bethany and New London. He is, in May, 1909, Pastor of Odessa Church.

In 1876 he was injured in a wreck on his way home from the Centennial, from which he has suffered a great deal since. He married Miss Lucy Hatch in 1868.

MRS. MARTHA J. CASH.

By T. J. Ayres.

Mrs. Martha J. Cash, the subject of this sketch, was born in Shelby county, Kentucky, November 13, 1823, is therefore well along in the eighty-sixth year of her age. She came with her parents, Thomas J. Ayres and Elizabeth Ayres, nee Lewis, in the fall of 1829, in the sixth year of her age, to this State and has spent about eighty years of her life in Missouri, the greater part in Pike county. At her coming the country was almost a wilderness, sparsely settled, abounding in game of almost every variety, turkeys and deer being much more abundant than rabbits, squirrels and quails at the present day, hence she has seen the country develop from the crudest state of civilization (if indeed, it could have been called civilized, as Indians roved at their will through this section at that time) to the splendid state of civilization and general improvement, along all lines of to-day. She was married in her fifteenth year to Mr. James A. Kesler, who being seized with the general gold fever of that date, crossed the plains to California in 1849 to seek his fortune in the gold fields then but recently discovered, where he soon sickened and died, leaving her with three small children, all girls, and with little means.

She, with her husband, had made profession of religion, and united with Mount Pleasant Church, October 22, 1842. The division in the church on the question of missions occurred in 1843, when she with her husband, took letters, with the idea of uniting with the anti-mission wing, but not being well satisfied on that question, they held their letters, investigating and praying over the matter, finally reaching the conclusion that the commission "Go ye into all the world and preach the gospel to every creature," etc., carried within itself the doctrine of missions, she (her husband having died), returned to a mission church.

On the death of her husband she, returned with her three children, to the home of her parents, reared and educated them, remaining a widow for twenty-five years, until her daughters were all married, after which she was married to Mr. A. J. Cash, with whom she lived about fifteen years, when he passed away, leaving her, for a second time, a widow, in her old age. She now resides with her second daughter, Mrs. Rebecca B. Brown, also a widow, who conducts a hotel in New London, Missouri.

She has been a consistent, faithful church member for sixty-seven years, and bids fair to remain a member of the church militant for some years to come. She retains her physical and mental faculties to a remarkable degree, takes a lively interest in all the work of the church, as well as household affairs, being on terms of cheerful intimacy with boarders and transient customers of the hotel as well as neighbors, to all of whom she responds to the endearing name of "grandma."

She has seen much of life, has passed through many changes, borne many sorrows, as well as enjoyed many of the pleasant, cheerful things of life. Two husbands, parents, four sisters, two brothers and hosts of other relatives and friends have passed to the other shore. Only herself and three brothers of the ten remains on earth's side. Through all, never having lost faith in the Savior she trusts, she serenely, cheerfully, awaits the summons, which sooner or later comes to all.

REV. S. G. GIVENS.

By J. D. Biggs and Wiley J. Patrick.

A man of God has gone to rest. Brother Samuel Green Givens died at his home in Louisiana at 3 o'clock p. m. February 15, 1900, aged 64 years, 1 month and 20 days.

The birthplace of our brother was the old homestead on Noix Creek. His parents were John Green Givens and Mary A. Givens, the former being a South Carolinian. His education was received at the schools of the neighborhood and the education received there was carried forward in subsequent active life. His early boyhood was spent on the farm, where he developed into a sturdy, healthy young man. His remarkable physical strength fitted him for the hard service in the Master's vineyard. September 19, 1856, he married Sarah E. Stewart. Four children were born to them, three of whom with their mother preceded our brother to the spirit world. One—Mrs. Mary Winnie Ayres—survives him. On March 18, 1875, his second marriage was with Mrs. Louisa M. Hunter, who died August 25, 1892. She left one son, Edward Dudley Hunter, who affectionately watched with the deceased who was to him a father and friend. He married again September 5, 1895. This companion, who was received to his heart and home, ministered to him through fourteen months of suffering, and now mourns his loss, was Miss Sallie A. Waddell. She is a great-granddaughter of Rev. Davis Biggs, whose old family Bible she now possesses, bearing date of 1792.

Brother Givens was born of God in a revival at Noix Creek in November, 1862, and uniting with the church he was baptized by the Rev. M. M. Modisett. In this revival there were some three score souls brought to Christ. On the baptismal occasion Brother Givens and Deacons Ambrose Beckher and Thornton Stark went down into the water together. The Rev. James Frank Smith did most of the preaching in this revival.

In 1865 Noix Creek church gave Bro. Givens license to preach. He began at once. His first sermon was preached at the old house of Noix Creek church. About 1866 the same church ordained him to the ministry of the gospel, the Presbytery consisting of Elders E. Jennings, J. M. Johnson, J. F. Hedges and M. M. Modisett. In the time of his ministry Bro. Givens was a Pastor at Frankford, Mt. Pleasant, Spencerburg, New Hartford, Providence, Adiel, Oak Ridge,

Pleasant Hill; Nebo and New Canton, Illinois. Also others. And he did a good deal of evangelistic work. The manuscripts that Brother Givens left show that he was a continuous and growing student to the last of his days of strength. They embrace the general scope of revealed truth and emphasize the preciousness of the blessed Savior, the Holy Spirit's work in the Christian's heart and life and the love of God for a lost world. One of his texts was, "No man cared for my soul;" another, "Thou shalt call His name Jesus, for He shall save His people from their sins;" another, "There is therefore now no condemnation to them which are in Christ Jesus;" another, "The Lord knoweth them that are His;" another, "These things I have spoken unto you, that in me ye might have peace." The subject of one sermon, the one on John 15:5, "Without me ye can do nothing," is "What Christ is to the soul." His papers were in intelligent order and may be studied to the edification of those who are seeking the better things. He had a library of about 175 volumes. Among our brother's papers is a sermon on the subject of "Treasure in Earthen Vessels" from the text, "But we have this treasure in earthen vessels." He treats the subject as one who had seen, therefore spoke. The last sermon Brother Givens preached was on the occasion of the burial of Mariah Miller, a colored sister who was said to be 103 years of age. This was on Thanksgiving day, November, 1898. Brother Givens had looked after her temporal effects and the family, finding him a friend true and honest, sought consolation from him in the final sorrow.

Brother Givens was a Christian gentleman in the service of the King of Kings. He had the true dignity which becomes a minister of the gospel of Christ. He was chaste in conversation; clean in his life, with no stain of imprudence or indiscretion. He leaves thus a precious legacy to his family and his brethren in the ministry. His character was symmetrical, his life faithful, his preaching instructive and safe. The excellency of the power was of God. The earthen vessel we lay in the bosom of Mother Earth, while the spirit rejoices in the rest that remaineth to the people of God.

ELDER C. H. CALVIN.

By Himself.

I was licensed by the Louisiana church September, 1901, and have preached regularly ever since. I moved the following October to LaGrange, where I attended LaGrange College. My health gave way and I moved from LaGrange to Franklin county, Missouri, bought a small farm and preached for the Sullivan Baptist Church eighteen months, then moved to Illinois. My time was soon all taken in this State in the ministry of the gospel. The Lord has blessed my work, having baptized something over two hundred converts in four years.

While in Louisiana, Missouri, I married Miss Mary Olive Ross.

ELDER R. E. MCQUIE.

By Himself.

I united with the West Cuivre Church when fifteen years old, and remained a member there for several years. I was baptised by Bro. J. F. Smith. I did my first preaching at Noix Creek Church. I had been attending the Baptist College at Louisiana while Dr. J. T. Williams was president and through him secured the Noix Creek school, and taught the first school in the schoolhouse after it was built.

It was about this time I began to try to preach. I was Pastor of Spencerburg five years and assisted in several meetings in the bounds of Salt River Association.

DEACON HENRY TAYLOR OGDEN.

Bedford county, Virginia, was the native place of Deacon Ogden and February 25, 1826, was the day of his birth. When twenty-three years of age he came to Missouri. The following year he returned to Virginia and married Miss Margaret Eliza Hobson, February 27, 1850. In December, 1860, Brother Ogden accepted Christ as his personal Savior and united with Buffalo Knob Church. He was baptised by Elder A. G. Mitchell.

He was one of the constituent members in the organization of Dover Church. He was at once elected Deacon and was ordained in August, 1862. The ordaining Presbytery consisted of Elders J. B. Fuller, A. G. Mitchell and M. M. Modisett. Brother Fuller preached the sermon from the text, "Watchman, what of the night?" For forty-seven years he used the office of Deacon well. His elevated character, his symmetrical life, his sense of equal justice to all, his firm faith all combined to fit him for the high degree of spiritual service to which by the grace of God he had attained. His presence was an exhortation to the Christian life. He reared his family in honor and in the fear of the Lord, and he left them the rich inheritance of a good name, upright citizenship and the testimony of redeeming grace.

Deacon Ogden was a cousin to the well known and eminently useful minister, Elder Armstead Ogden, of Virginia. Monday, March 10, Brother Ogden was stricken with paralysis while at breakfast. He lingered, without speaking, until 2:30 p. m., Saturday, March 27, 1909. The funeral service was Monday following, at Dover Church. The Pastor, Dr. M. E. Broaddus, preached from the text, "He being dead yet speaketh." The remains were interred beside his faithful companion who died September 6, 1896.

ELDER M. S. WHITESIDE.

By Himself.

I was born in the year 1836, united with the Mill Creek church in 1853, licensed to preach by that body in 1862, ordained in 1863. I was married twice. My first wife was Margarett Damaron, who lived about five years. After her death, I married Mary A. Johns in 1866. They were both helpmeets for me, always giving me a self-sacrificing support in my efforts to preach the gospel.

Immediately after my ordination I went to Nebraska, where I remained for two years. Soon after my arrival there, I was appointed missionary by the New York Board, which position I held until I left the State. I returned to Missouri in the spring of 1866, and I have since lived in Lincoln, Pike, Audrain, Ralls and St. Louis counties, and about five years in the State of Tennessee.

I was missionary for Salt River Association, also for Audrain Association. Was one year under the appointment of the State Board. I organized Star Hope, Foley, Ebenezer, Laddonia, Farber, Pleasant Plains and Benton City Churches. I preached at many other places where I afterwards assisted in the organization of churches. I visited, under the direction of Salt River board, and assisted in the organization of churches at Rush Hill, Corinth, Oak Ridge, Ashburn and Annada.

ELDER F. M. BIRKHEAD.

This efficient minister of the gospel was born and reared in Lincoln county, Missouri, near New Salem church. He has been Pastor of New Salem, Adiel, Walnut Grove, Prairieville, Elm Grove, Silex, Harmony Grove, Foley and Highland churches. He is an honorable citizen, a genial gentleman, a correct man in his business relations, a faithful head of his family and an impressive, scriptural preacher with superior powers of exhortation. His labors have been blessed of the Lord in a large degree.

COL. JOHN RALLS.

This gentleman was a son of Daniel Ralls, for whom Ralls county was named. Col. Ralls was a lawyer by profession. He was an efficient Deacon in the church at New London. He was active in politics, a personal friend of Governor Hardin. Under date of February 10, 1908, Mark Twain says that Colonel Ralls buckled a sword on him in New London when he was starting to the Confederate army. Mr. Clemens said, "Colonel Ralls of Ralls county fought with credit in the Mexican War." Brother Ralls loved his church and was a strong support to his Pastor.

ELDER THOMAS NEWMAN SANDERSON.

By his son, Robert B. Sanderson.

Rev. T. N. Sanderson was born May 4, 1819, in Bedford county, Virgina. His ancestors were from Scotland. He married in same county, Miss Martha Jane Crews, February 28, 1839. To this union one child was born, Wm. A. After a short time his wife died. February 15, 1844, he married Miss Mary J. Drummond, and to this union thirteen children were born. Sarah C., Thomas E., John E., Henry L., James M., Virgina A., Emmett J., Robert B., Samuel M., a daughter who died in infancy, Mary C., Amanda B., and Daniel T. He had at his death fifty-two grandchildren, twenty-six boys and twenty-six girls. About fifteen years of his early life was spent in business and he met with much success. He was industrious, careful and above everything else, strictly honest, and upright in all his dealings. He was at one time in his early life an officer of the law.

When a young man he accepted Christ as his Savior and united with Hunting Creek Baptist church and was baptised by the Pastor, Rev. William Harris. He soon felt called to preach the gospel of God to a lost world and after he was clearly convinced that God had called him he entered into the great work of preaching the gospel under some difficulties. He had only the start of sixty days of school life; therefore, to prepare himself for the great work of preaching the gospel, he was impressed with the essential need of more book knowledge. He lost no time in home study. He was always firm in the right as he saw it, believing that God had fixed ways and it was not for man to change but rather seek the truth through divine guidance. At the call of Difficult Creek Baptist church, Bedford county, Virginia, August 17, 1855, he was ordained to the ministry. The presbytery were William Harris, Thomas C. Goggin, Alexander Eubank, George W. Leftwick and David Staley.

At this time he entered upon colporteur and pastoral work. To Beaver Dam he preached until he left Virginia. By Beaver Dam Baptist Church the following expression was given: "That we can but express with pleasure our heartfelt gratitude for that union and kind feeling which have existed between us as Pastor and people for the last fourteen years, and that the separation which now necessarily takes place so unexpectedly to many of us, produces more or less sadness in many of our hearts. We highly esteem our brother and believe him to be an earnest and faithful minister of the gospel, and that his labors have been useful to us as a church and the community at large." While Rev. T. N. Sanderson lived in Virginia he served as Pastor of the following Baptist churches: Shady Grove, New Hope, Morgan's Bend, Liberty, Glade Hill, Rocky Mount, Hale's Ford, Flint Hill, Fair Mont and Surch Springs.

He came to Missouri in December, 1869, and lived in Pike county. He accepted the pastorate of the following churches from time to time: Adiel, Spencerburg, Mt. Zion, Bowling Green, Silex, Troy, Sugar

Creek, Auxvasse, Noix Creek, Providence, Mt. Pleasant, and Prairieville. In 1880, he moved to LaGrange to educate his children and while there he was Pastor of the following Baptist churches: New Prospect, Antioch, Alexandria, Gregory's Landing, Ten Mile, Dover, Gilead, Monticello, New Ark, Durham and Lewistown.

After he came to Missouri he had many calls to go back to Virginia and hold special meetings. About 1873, 1878, 1884 and 1895, he visited Virginia and held meetings with his old churches. In his 1884 trip at Beaver Dam church the Lord blessed his labors with fifty-one converted souls; Shady Grove, twenty, New Prospect, twenty-one, Morgan's Bend, twenty-seven, and Surch Springs, three.

In 1895, when he visited Bedford county, in several revivals the Lord blessed his labors by saving eighty-six souls under seventy-eight sermons. In his revival ministry he grew in the graces bestowed by the Holy Spirit.

The esteem in which he was held in his Virginia ministry is shown in a letter from Rev. J. M. McManaway of Fayette, Mo., under date of December 21, 1900:

"I am grieved to hear that Bro. T. N. Sanderson has left us. He was a good man and true. I remember him as among the first preachers I ever heard. He was Pastor in New Hope church in Bedford county when I first went to preaching. That must have been as far back as 1852 or '53. He continued there until he declined re-election to come to Missouri. He was very fond of music. We were always glad to see him at my father's because of his singing, especially. On his visit back to the old State he held some great meetings. He seemed to have returned in the fullness of the blessing of the gospel of Christ. My brother, Rev. A. G. McManaway, recently deceased, and I both made profession of religion in his meeting at New

Hope and he baptised us together. He was held in highest esteem back in Virginia to the last."

Rev. Harvy Hatcher wrote from Atlanta, Georgia, December 29, 1900, of him: "Our relations as brethren were delightful."

At the time of his death he was moderator of Cuivre Association. Rev. T. N. Sanderson spent his last days at Edgewood, Pike county, where he knew all and all knew him. On December 18, 1900, he fell asleep. About twenty-four hours previous, he said to his son, Robert: "It is only a few steps across; I will be here only a short time."

Rev. T. N. Sanderson believed in preaching the Bible in its purity and simplicity, leaving it with God to convince and convict the world. His request was that the remarks made at his funeral should be from the Scriptures, "By grace are ye saved." His Pastor, Rev. J. S. Evans, Rev. W. J. Patrick and Rev. R. D. Robertson were the ministers who spoke at his burial, which was at Edgewood cemetery. When these three brothers who had known him so long stood declaring his great aim to lead souls to Christ, his son, Rev. E. J. Sanderson, viewing the children and grand-children and his father's wonderful care to try to leave things in such a way that his beloved wife, who survives him, shall not want, was moved with a sense of responsibility resting on the living.

Having borne the cross, the sainted man of God is now wearing the crown and beckoning us all over that way.

SENATOR E. W. STARK.

The *St. Louis Republic* of Wednesday, June 17, 1909, said:

State Senator Eugene W. Stark, of Pike county, Missouri, died Tuesday afternoon at 4 o'clock in St. Luke's Hospital. Senator Stark, whose home was at Louisiana, Mo., was one of the leading Democrats of

Missouri, and during the last session of the Legislature was a conspicuous lawmaker at the State capital. He was the author of many bills which were passed.

He was formerly county judge in Pike county and was a member of the Stark Bros. Nursery and Orchard Company, the largest nursery in the world. He was a native of the county in which he resided, being born at the Stark home, which is one of the historical places of Pike county.

He married Miss Anna Withrow, of Troy, Mo., who survives him, together with three sons. He was 46 years old.

Elected to the State Senate last fall he was a leader of the conservative element in the Senate and spoke in favor of the Missouri immigration bill and the Springfield Court of Appeals, doing much to get these measures through the Senate.

A delegation of business men from Pike county arrived in St. Louis yesterday to accompany the body home.

Senator Stark was a member of Dover Church. His pastor, Dr. M. E. Broaddus, preached the burial sermon in the church at Louisiana. Business houses were closed and there were many public men present.

His mother is living. Hon. J. O. Stark is his brother. The Senator was a fine mold of manhood, generous, broad, honest, progressive.

RECOLLECTIONS OF PIONEER BAPTISTS OF SALT RIVER ASSOCIATION.

By LaRue (Caldwell) Jones.

Among my first recollections of the Baptist people of Salt River Association is that of Rev. William Hurley. He came horseback from St. Charles to Bethel Church in Ralls county. He would stop at New London, preach at the home of my father, my mother being the only Baptist in the town. He would always go to the barn and attend to Billy, a large dapple gray horse, himself before coming to the house. Uncle Ben Stevens, father of Dr. B. Q. Stevens, of Hannibal, as a preacher of distinction, I remember well. Also father Keach's memory is vivid in my mind. Under the preaching of him and H. M. King I was converted at old Bethel Church January 3, 1863. I was baptized by Brother King January 7, 1863, at which time seventy-three others were baptized.

Rev. William Vardeman was another preacher of great note whom I have heard preach the gospel fluently. He went to Wentzville, St. Charles county, and died there after years of effectual labor in the Master's service. Rev. J. D. Biggs is not one of the pioneer preachers of Salt River Association, yet he has been in the Association for years, a true, devoted Christian Pastor and preacher, a combination very seldom found in one man. Brother John Ralls was a man much loved by his church members. While not a preacher he was always found at his post of duty, ever ready to perform the duties of a Deacon's office.

Brother Ezra Carstarphen, also a Deacon of the New London Baptist Church, was a devoted Christian, one of God's best workers, a noble man. He practically built the meeting house at New London, never tiring in his efforts to see it completed. Yet the Lord called him home before he saw it completed. He leaves two sons, who I hope will follow in their father's footsteps. Brother J. T. Brown, now ninety-two years old, has served his Master faithfully since early youth, is seldom absent from his seat at church, always listening attentively. Brothers George and Burgess Lake, both passed away, were earnest, consecrated Christians, ever ready with the hand of charity to aid the cause of the pioneer Baptists of Salt River Association.

Uncle Dabney Jones, of Ralls county, was one of the first members of the Baptist Church organized at New London in 1822. Rev. R. A. Jones, of Novinger, is a descendant of his of the fifth generation.

RECOLLECTIONS OF SALT RIVER ASSOCIATION.

By H. M. King.

In the fall of 1859, at Paynesville, Pike county, Missouri, I first met with the Salt River Baptist Association. Brother Albert Mitchell, of sainted memory, was moderator, and the scholarly J. T. Williams was elected clerk. Other brethren, in the ministry, present besides these were Brothers Wm. Mitchell, Cleveland, A. P. Rogers, Johnson, Wm. Luck and L. C. Musick. I think also that Brother Whiteside was a preacher.

It was the second Association the young preacher had ever attended, and as at the first one, he was deeply interested in everything said and done. He had been told that the Baptists were an ignorant and bigoted people. These people did not appear to be either ignorant or bigoted; they seemed to be grand men and attractive women. After the introductory sermon the business of the meeting was transacted in the house, and there was preaching morning and evening at the stand.

The morning of the second day the moderator gave out preaching at the stand by Brother Cleveland, followed by the young brother, who when he went into the stand and saw in it the man he was to follow, was so scared that he came near running to the woods instead of going into the stand to preach—but—well, he still lives at this writing in 1908. At this meeting I began to get a revelation of this Baptist folk in the sphere of fellowship and friendship. The "dinner on the grounds" (but we ate from one long table), the meeting of old friends, making new ones and, no doubt many young people promised to go together as long as they lived. Where is there on earth the fellowship and good comradeship with true friendship, as at the "dinner on the grounds" of a Baptist Association in harmony? Letters have been read, reports made, sermons preached, prayers offered and songs sung. Only beyond the river is anything better.

At the home of Brother Whiteside at night were, I don't remember how many ministers, Deacons and brethren, happy as Christians, playful as boys, and as talkative as women.

In the room where we slept (a little while) the bedsteads overflowed, but on the floor good, comfortable pallets received all who came to them. Reminiscent narratives prevailed to the "wee small hours." William Vardeman, the whole souled Christian and prince of good fellows, said: He nearly always dreamed of catching fish just before being in a great revival, and told a number of dreams and of the revivals which followed. When he ceased and was perhaps going to sleep, Deacon Hayden, of Adiel Church, said: "Brother Vardeman, you haven't told one fish story and I will tell it. Brother Vardeman was helping Brother Johnson, the Pastor at Adiel; at the close of his sermon one night, he gave an opportunity for persons to join, and a man by the name of Scott, an eccentric man of the neighborhood, and a daughter, a very worthy and sensible young woman, came forward to unite with the church. Brother Vardeman said, 'Brother Johnson, you talk to the young lady and I will talk to the old man.' When Miss Scott had told a tender and clear experience of hope and been received, Brother Vardeman said, 'Now, Mr. Scott, what have you to say?' who promptly replied, 'Well, all I have to say is, I belonged to the church once and they turned me out for nothing and I said then "I will never join again," and I say so yet."'"

In 1860 the Association met with the Prairieville Church. I was there as a messenger from the Louisiana Church. Though there was in progress the canvass of a presidential election of unparalleled conditions and excitement, the meeting was entirely harmonious and pleasant. There were mutterings of a coming storm, but none could then conceive its terrible realities.

The terrible storm of civil war broke in fearful fury over our unhappy country in 1861. Of course the membership of the churches were greatly divided on the issues involved. The preachers differed warmly in opinions and action. Our men young and old volunteered, some in one and some in the other army.

This condition of things made the work of the Pastors very difficult during the war and for some time afterward. In the fall or winter of 1862 a military order from headquarters at St. Louis required all church houses to have a "United States Flag" above the front door. *After the winds had torn* these to pieces the order was changed, and smaller flags must be at the right and front of the pulpit. If troops found a preacher holding services without the flag he was taken prisoner, perhaps with others, and the congregation dispersed. This continued for some time after the surrender of the armies in the field.

Often during these dark, dark days the congregations consisted of men usually over sixty, the women greatly in the majority, and boys under fifteen. Difficulties and hinderances became more and more pronounced as the war continued, until, during the winter of 1864 and 1865 a State convention made a new State Constitution, which prescribed and required of all ministers in the State an oath (known as the "Ironclad Oath") which they must take, subscribe and file in the office of the clerk of the circuit court. The substance of the oath was that they had not been in the (so-called) rebel army, aided or abetted any one in it, or sympathized with the South, or in any way given comfort or encouragement to any friend of the South.

The penalty for preaching without taking such oaths was a fine of not less than five hundred dollars or imprisonment of not less than six months in the county jail, or both fine and imprisonment. The limit of time to take the oath was the first of September, 1865.

The Association met that fall at historic "Noix Creek Church," on Saturday before the second Sunday. One Sunday (the first) had passed. The law, with its new and "iron-clad" qualifications to the ministry, was in force. As the brethren greeted each

Tried by Fire.   261

other they looked earnestly each into the other's faces. Who had taken the oath? Who had preached without taking it? It was learned that two or three had taken "the oath," but the greater number had not. Only one had preached without taking it.

The brethren were filled with gloom and sadness. It was the first time that distrust and fear had ever been felt among them. Only those who had taken "the oath" were appointed to preach. Those who favored taking it held that to take *any* part in the meeting or business of the Association was a violation of "the law" if the "oath" was not taken. They made an exception of a visiting brother from the North, who preached several times. Dr. Holman, of the "Home Board" of the Southern Baptist Convention, was present, but did not preach or take any public part in the meeting.

The brethren who had not taken the "oath" made no contention in the Association, but maintained their convictions and manhood. Quite a number of these spent the evening and night at the hospitable home of Brother John E. Shannon, near the church. Well into the hours of the night they engaged in worship, mutual encouragement and prayer. Brother James F. Smith, full of experience, wisdom and good fruits, led this delightful meeting of the brethren. The next morning, which was the second day of the Association, they started on the return to their homes, determined to follow their conscientious convictions in the fear of God.

Brother Smith adopted the expedient of holding prayer-meetings, instead of preaching at his appointments. But a short time afterwards, while holding daily prayer-meetings in the "Rose schoolhouse," and a number being converted whom he baptized, coming up out of the water he was arrested by a constable, on the charge of administering a religious ordinance contrary to law and put under bond to appear at circuit court.

H. M. King, who had been filling all of his appointments, had not taken the oath, and going to his appointment, in the Cumberland Presbyterian Church at Madisonville, on Sunday, January 10, 1866, found a large crowd, with six ex-soldiers in uniform with revolvers, sitting on the front seat. They had come to arrest him. He told them there was a law in the State making it a criminal offense to disturb public worship; if they arrested him before he began the service he would not use that law against them. But when the service was begun, if they interfered he would prosecute every one of them to the limit of the law. This deterred them and they left the house. The large house was full of people from all the country around. The text was Phil. 3:8: "Yea, I count all things but loss, for the excellency of the knowledge of Christ Jesus my Lord: for whom I have suffered." At the close of the sermon, as by one impulse the people stood up and sang, "Am I a soldier of the Cross?" and rushing to the preacher they took both his hands, weeping, praising and thanking God. They almost bore him off his feet, but how they sang. As a winter's storm was increasing in violence they were advised to get to their homes as quickly as possible. Toward night, the storm still raging, the soldiers with a constable and two magistrates returning to the house of the minister, they arrested him, the constable reading a warrant charging him with "preaching the gospel contrary to law against the peace and dignity of the State." They took him some fifteen miles that night to the house of one of the magistrates for trial. But getting into a dispute among themselves, at three o'clock Monday morning, they let the prisoner go with his promise to appear for trial at Madisonville on the 16th of the month, when they dismissed the case.

The Baptist people of Salt River Association, ministers and members, were as noble men and women as the writer has ever known; his esteem for them has had no limit. He asks their prayers and prays for blessings on their children and their churches.

CHAPTER IX.

ENLARGEMENT AND TRAINING, 1870-1884.

Sugar Creek Church was the meeting place in 1870. Elder A. G. Mitchell preached the sermon from the scripture: "And this gospel of the kingdom shall be preached in all the world for a witness unto all nations; and then shall the end come." A. G. Mitchell was elected moderator and J. T. Williams clerk. The following new churches were received into fellowship: Haw Creek, Hickory Grove, Prairieville and Grassy Creek, all of Pike county. The messengers: Haw Creek, H. H. Hostetter, J. Nichols, J. S. Bradley, J. Unsell; Hickory Grove, T. J. Kendrick, J. W. Woodson; Prairieville, W. T. Jacobs, Z. W. Mosby; Grassy Creek, W. W. Waddell, Jr., W. H. H. Johnson, J. J. Sparks.

Brother James Buford, of Ralls county, had left a legacy of $500 to Baptist missions. The matter at this session was referred to a special committee. A. P. Miller and M. M. Modisett were made the committee. This money never came into the hands of the mission board for whom the generous donor intended his gift. The courts decided that the designations in the bequest did not sufficiently specify the beneficiaries of the bequest. The effect of this loss was far more than the amount involved. It left an impression that making bequests was an impractical form of benevolence, which is an error. Bequests to missions, education, orphans' homes and other worthy objects are wise, legal and appropriate forms of doing good. There are those who need the productive use of their property while they live and desire it to descend to some object that will wisely use the property in doing good when the giver has passed beyond the use of earthly possessions. Brethren B. F. Hixson R. S.

Duncan, G. B. Smith, David Wilson accepted seats in the body.

That which was called the executive committee is now called the executive board. A collection of $66.35 was taken for the foreign mission board of the of the S. B. C., Elder R. S. Duncan agent. The missionaries of the year were S. G. Givens, E. Jennings, J. B. Hawkins, M. S. Whiteside, W. H. Bibb, J. M. Wheeler, L. R. Smith. They reported, days given, 206; baptisms, 35; churches organized, 2; papers and tracts distributed, 500.

J. F. Smith presented home mission of the Southern Board. Education and Sunday school work received good consideration. The whole number of baptisms for the year was 290 in the bounds of Salt River Association. The ministers at this time are given: J. D. Shelton, G. W. Foster, M. M. Modisett, J. T. Williams, S. G. Givens, J. G. Davenport, J. J. Gipson, J. F. Hedges, R. Gibson, E. Jennings, S. Noel, A. F. Randall, R. Vermillion, J. F. Smith, L. R. Smith, J. H. Keach, J. B. Hawkins, J. N. Griffin, A. G. Mitchell, W. F. Luck, B. F. Hardesty, M. S. Whiteside, J. M. Wheeler, W. H. Bibb, T. N. Sanderson. The American Baptist Publication Society was commended.

The Association "*Resolved,* That we commend *The Central Baptist,* published at St. Louis by Luther and Yeaman." A pure Christian journalism extends and strengthens the ministry of the gospel. By divine appointment the saving message was made permanent and transmittible by giving it the written form. It has served as a mighty multiplier in gospel propagandism. When the editing is such that no evil is concealed or winked at, no worthy deed discounted, so that all men are treated with justice and every righteous cause is promoted and no personal ambitions or sinister claims are given a place, so that righteousness shall rule and wickedness shall be overthrown; when the periodical stands for "whatsoever things are true, whatsoever things are honest, whatsoever things are just, whatsoever things are pure, whatsoever things are lovely, whatsoever things are of good report; if there be any virtue, if there be any praise," such editing, such a journal should be sustained. Such a Baptist paper should be in each home even if the windows have to go uncurtained or the floor uncarpeted. Such a paper should be part of the fixtures when the couple goes to housekeeping, and aged saints in sight of the heavenly dawn may have such a paper read to them by their grandchildren.

And a good book takes a place even higher than the place of the periodical, and so it was Christian business to commend the Publication Society. For intellectual growth and spiritual edification the book surpasses. And it is a storehouse of knowledge. Choice literature should be read over and over. Valuable information should be where one can lay his hands on it. In the book well preserved these advantages may be had. The book read in early life may be a lifetime companion, and if one is wise in selecting the companion it will be chaste, agreeable and elevating. We all need help in the selection of books. In a few minutes we may get the name of a book, the recommendation of which is based on the reading of many days. Therefore the benefit in buying from a house that publishes only the best. A collection of good books ought to be in every family; and they can be. If books are classed among the necessities of life, like bread and clothes, as they should be, some money will be found to buy them or some kind hand will give them. We are largely what our reading makes us.

A. P. Miller was made *president* of the Sunday School Convention, J. T. Williams *secretary*, and C. W. Williams *treasurer*.

In 1871 Salt River Association met with Mill Creek Church. The sermon was preached by Elder J. F. Smith from the passage: "But seek ye first the kingdom of God, and his righteousness; and all these things shall be added unto you." New Michigan Church, Audrain county, was received into associational fellowship, and the messenger, Elder S. T. Noel, took his seat in the body. Brethren W. J. Jesse, W. R. Wigginton, E. Hayden, L. B. Seaton, W. H. Vardeman, J. R. Keith, J. H. Tuttle, J. G. Sitton, J. Shelby, J. R. Graves of Tennessee and A. Van Hoose of Mississippi, accepted seats in the Association. The executive board says, "From the reports of our evangelists we cannot give you as favorable an account as heretofore." The work as given was: Days given, 211; sermons, 69; baptisms, 36; churches organized, 2; Sunday schools organized, 4. The board paid the evangelists $310. A. P. Miller, W. G. Hawkins, M. R. K. Biggs were continued as the executive board. August the 9th "the Association adjourned at 11 o'clock a. m. to hear Brother J. R. Graves preach, after which a subscription of $500 was raised for the 'Southern Baptist Publication Society.'" Baptist College, Louisiana, J. T. Williams, A. M., president, was recommended.

A student learns what is taught him as the eater eats what is set before him. What the teacher is counts for more than what he says before his class. Hence the need of schools whose teachers are what we want the students to become, the religion fervent, the character upright, the ethics pure. It is desirable that the school be Baptist. The Baptist position gives the largest catholicity. The doctrine of regeneration being our distinguishing ecclesiastical doctrine enables us to think well of the saved soul wherever found and he can feel at home in a Baptist school. A Baptist school worthy of support teaches all who willingly listen the Baptist interpretation of the scriptures.

The Sunday School Convention held a session. There were reported: Sunday schools, 16; teachers, 96; scholars, 849; expenses, $226.50.

Elder Van Hoose represented the domestic board of the Southern Baptist Convention.

Louisiana Church entertained the Association September 13 and 14, 1872, and Elder T. N. Sanderson preached the sermon from the scripture: "That they all may be one; as thou, Father, art in me, and I in thee, that they also may be one in us: that the world may believe that thou hast sent me." Frankford and Corner Stone Churches were received into fellowship. The messengers of Frankford were S. G. Givens, R. Vermillion and N. B. Hogan; those of Corner Stone, H. Hall, C. Bibb and R. J. Chasten. The visitors were Elders G. W. Hyde, W. T. Russell, S. W. Marston, J. H. Luther, T. W. Barrett, W. C. Busby, W. H. Steadman, J. M. Oliver and Brethren J. Wilson, L. B. Seaton and William Carson. $1040 was raised for Baptist College, Louisiana. G. W. Hyde represented William Jewell College. *The Central Baptist* was strongly endorsed. The new executive board were A. P. Miller, W. G. Hawkins, M. R. K. Biggs, A. McPike, J. E. Shannon. There had been five missionaries in the field. The board closed the year with $433 on hand.

The place of meeting in 1873 was Bethel Church. There was a fall of rain that made the attendance small. Elder James D. Biggs served as moderator *pro tem,* and W. B. McPike as clerk *pro tem.* Organization was effected by the election of A. P. Miller moderator and W. B. McPike clerk. The introductory sermon was preached in the afternoon by Elder W. F. Luck. His text was: "Ask of me, and I shall give thee the heathen for thine inheritance, and the uttermost parts of the earth for thy possession." Highland Church, Lincoln county, was received as a member of the Association. J. O. Allen was the messenger of the church. The committee on Sunday schools spoke of "the want of success of our Sunday School Convention." But steps were taken to advance the work. T. M. Colwell, S. M. Marston, William Carson and J. T. Williams accepted seats in the body and spoke in the interest of denominational work. *The Central Baptist,* represented by J. T. Williams, was commended. Baptist College, Louisiana, now under the presidency of J. D. Biggs, A. M., was given the support of the Association. The missionaries reported: Days of labor, 366. It was required of the missionaries for the incoming year to report quarterly. There was preaching by W. F. Luck, M. S. Whiteside, A. P. Rodgers and J. T. Williams. The executive board for the new year was A. P. Miller, W. G. Hawkins, M. R. K. Biggs, A. McPike, J. E. Shannon.

The Association met with Mt. Pleasant Church in 1874. Elder James D. Biggs preached. His text was: "Even so hath the Lord ordained that they which preach the gospel should live of the gospel." J. T. Williams, A. C. Goodrich, B. F. Hixson, R. S. Duncan, D. J. Motley, R. E. McQuie, L. C. Musick, B. Baker, William Ferguson, David Wilson, F. H. Lewis, D. C. Bolton, L. M. Berry, Lewis A. Dawson, W. H. Bibb, D. B. Ray, S. W. Marston and S. H. Ford accepted seats.

Since the previous meeting of the body Elder J. J. Gipson had died. The Association adopted this report, made by T. N. Sanderson:

"*Whereas,* Since our last meeting Bro. J. J. Gipson, of Louisiana, has been summoned from us by death.

"*Resolved,* 1. That in the death of our brother we feel that we have lost a precious man and a faithful minister.

"2. That his family have lost a kind husband and an affectionate father.

"3. That while we humbly submit to the will of God, we mourn his loss and deeply sympathize with his family."

One of the good things of this session was the report on ministerial education, which was signed by J. Ralls, James D. Biggs, A. P. Rodgers. I quote: "Who is able for the task? Shall we spend millions for the education of men for all positions except the pulpit? We answer, we need and must have a ministry thoroughly furnished. Our fathers were able for the work of their day. They did it well and have left us a glorious heritage. They raised up our churches, organized our missionary societies, built up our colleges, whose halls of learning are open to God's poor in purse but rich in faith, whom he has called to the sacred office. They anxiously desire culture equal to the task. If we do not aid them, are we not in danger of hearing Christ say to us, 'As ye did it not unto these, ye did it not unto me?'"

A. P. Miller, M. R. K. Biggs and W. G. Hawkins were made the executive board. There was preaching by W. F. Luck, B. F. Hixson, R. S. Duncan, J. T. Williams, D. B. Ray, J. D. Biggs, A. G. Mitchell, L. M. Berry, S. H. Ford.

New Hope was the meeting place in 1875. The sermon was preached by Wiley J. Patrick. from the text: "Except I shall see in his hands the print of the nails, and put my finger into the print of the nails, and thrust my hand into his side, I will not believe." Two new churches were received into fellowship: Clarksville and Oak Ridge. The messengers from Clarksville were W. H. Bibb and James Major; those from Oak Ridge were J. A. Edwards, J. H. Mitchell and W. L. Smith. The executive board reported that the missionaries had labored thirty-four days, for which the board had paid them $68.

The committee on obituaries, consisting of J. F. Smith, E. Jennings and B. Lake, reported: "Since our last meeting Brother Mason Rose, who for many years served the Adiel Church as one of her Deacons with great acceptance, has passed from earth to heaven. In the death of Brother Rose the church has lost one of its best members, the community a good citizen, the aged wife a kind husband, to whom we tender our sympathy. Also Brother John A. Rose, Deacon of Spencerburg Church, has died. He was truly a good man." At this time there was a general movement in the United States to celebrate the centennial of the nation's life by strengthening our educational work. The Association took this action: "That we acknowledge our gratitude to God for the privilege of worshiping Him according to the dictates of our own consciences; and that as a suitable way of doing so we give as we are able, during the centennial of our American Independence, for strengthening and endowing of our denominational educational institutions." A special committee composed of A. P. Miller, James D. Biggs and A. P. Rodgers was appointed to carry the action into effect. Something was done in making known the history and opportunity of Baptists and some money was given. G. J. Johnson presented the work for the American Baptist Publication Society and received $102.25 for that purpose. Brethren R. S. Duncan, L. S. Moore, D. J. Motley, H. T. Pendleton, James R. Gilliland, B. F. Hixson, David Wilson, J. R. Moore, C. N. Ray, S. W. Marston and G. J. Johnson occupied complimentary seats in the body. There was preaching by J. D. Biggs, B. F. Hixson, R. S. Duncan, M. M. Modisett, J. F. Smith, G. J. Johnson, J. T. Williams, W. J. Patrick, A. P. Rodgers. A. P. Miller, M. R. K. Biggs and W. G. Hawkins were made the executive board for another year.

In 1876 the session was held with Dover Church. Elder M. S. Whiteside preached the annual sermon from the scripture: "The church of the living God, the pillar and ground of the truth." A. P. Miller was re-elected moderator and A. P. Rodgers was elected clerk. The former clerk was absent. Curryville Church, Pike county, was received into fellowship. The messengers were W. M. Brandon and George W. Wylie. The executive board reported: "We think that good has been done in advancing and promoting our principles, the strengthening of our chuches, the conversion of sinners and consequently thereby is God honored and glorified." The missionary had been instructed "to labor as much as possible in the destitute regions" and "labor with the churches to be at the expense of the congregations where the labor might be performed." There were eight months and ten days of labor. Wiley J. Patrick was the missionary. R. S. Duncan, D. T. Morrill and J. F. Smith accepted seats in the body. A resolution having been introduced concerning the fellowship of Walnut Grove Church in the Association, growing out of a disputed question of discipline between Walnut Grove Church and Dover Church, a special committee was appointed to report on said resolution. The committee consisted of A. G. Mitchell, A. P. Rodgers, J. Reid, M. R. K. Biggs and Wiley J. Patrick. This committee reported: *"Whereas,* The Walnut Grove Church received into her fellowship M. M. Modisett, a member of the Dover Church, without a letter; and he the said Modisett, was afterwards excluded from the said Dover Church;

"Whereas, Said Modisett has been and still stands charged with habitual drunkenness; and

"Whereas, Said Walnut Grove Church still retains him in her fellowship without investigation and has appointed him a messenger to this Association; therefore,

"Resolved, That these acts on the part of Walnut Grove Church are disorderly, and, therefore, that we require of her a correction of this disorder in order to a continuance of fellowship with us." Soon after this session of the Association Walnut Grove made specific charges against Brother Modisett as to his habits of drinking, set a day for trial and summoned witnesses. At the time set the church met in business session, Elder Modisett appeared for trial but no witnesses came. The case was informally dismissed and subsequently Elder Modisett took a letter from Walnut Grove Church and united with a sister church outside of Salt River Association.

The corresponding letter, signed by W. H. Bibb, R. W. Unsel and N. McDannold, said: "Our heavenly Father has been very gracious to us during the past year. He has revived His work in some of our churches and many have been added to our numbers." President J. T. Williams presented the claims of Baptist College and raised for the institution some money. N. McDannold, J. E. Griffith and A. Beckner were made the executive board. There was preaching by J. Reid, J. F. Smith, A. P. Rodgers and W. J. Patrick. The ministers in the Association at this time were: W. H. Bibb, F. M. Birkhead, W. H. Burnham, G. W. Foster, S. G. Givens, J. N. Griffin, J. B. Hawkins, E. Jennings, J. H. Keach, W. F. Luck, M. M. Modisett, A. G. Mitchell, W. W. Mitchell, W. J. Patrick, T. N. Sanderson, J. F. Smith, J. Reid, J. D. Robnett, A. P. Rodgers, J. M. Wheeler, M. S. Whiteside and J. T. Williams.

The Association met with Star Hope Church in 1877. J. T. Williams was elected moderator and A. P. Rodgers was elected clerk. The following accepted seats in the body: M. T. Bibb, Joshua Hickman, J. G. Sitton, M. V. Shives, J. A. Sitton, A. F. Sitton, William Ferguson, B. F. Hixson, John Smarr, E. D. Owen, J. E. Mosley, B. Capps, D. J. Hancock, E. H. Sawyer. Baptist journalism received attention. Brother W. H. Burnham reported on foreign missions that "the solemn obligation to occupy this great field and to bear this extensive and effective testimony for Christ still rests on the churches." Brother J. D. Robnett, reporting on correspondence, said, "During the past year some of our churches have enjoyed gracious revivals and their numbers and efficiency have been increased." Brother J. Reid, reporting on education, said, "It is a false idea that induces many of our people to send their children abroad to be educated, when we have just as good schools of our own, and at home." W. W. Mitchell had been the missionary. The board had expended $180, days of labor 90. The same board was continued. There was preaching by B. F. Hixson, J. D. Robnett, J. Hickman, M. T. Bibb, E. H. Sawyer, A. G. Mitchell.

The introductory sermon was preached by J. T. Williams from the text: "I can do all things through Christ which strengtheneth me." The ministers at this time were: W. H. Bibb, F. M. Birkhead, W. H. Burnham, G. W. Foster, S. G. Givens, J. N. Griffin, J. B. Hawkins, E. Jennings, J. H. Keach, W. F. Luck, M. M. Modisett, A. G. Mitchell, W. W. Mitchell, Wiley J. Patrick, T. N. Sanderson, J. F. Smith, James

ELDER JAMES D. BIGGS.

ELDER A. G. MITCHELL.

DEACON H. T. OGDEN.

JUDGE A. P. MILLER.

Reid, J. D. Robnett, A. P. Rodgers, J. M. Wheeler, M. S. Whiteside, J. T. Williams.

The session of 1878 was held with West Cuivre Church. Elder W. H. Burnham preached the introductory sermon from the Scripture: "Were there not ten cleansed? but where are the nine?" In the reorganization, W. J. Patrick was made moderator and W. B. McPike was made clerk. There being at this time a scourge of yellow fever in several of the southern states, a motion prevailed to spend a half hour in prayer for "the suffering of the south." Also a collection of $45.63 was taken for the sufferers. The visiting brethren were: R. S. Duncan, M. E. Motley, R. E. McQuie, E. D. Owen, A. P. Oliver, B. Smith, A. Haverill, W. White, M. T. Motley, B. F. Hixson, M. L. Bibb, M. T. Bibb, James Carroll, J. C. Maple, Barnabas Baker, M. L. Laws, L. B. Ely, J. D. Murphy, J. Hickman, S. H. Ford, W. R. Wiggington. Spencer Creek Church was received into fellowship; J. L. Higbee was the messenger. Elder James F. Smith, reporting for the committee on correspondence, said, "Many of our churches have enjoyed refreshing seasons within the last year; nearly all have had additions by baptism. The total number baptized is 177." The claims of various denominational interests were presented. S. H. Ford represented the *Christian Repository*. L. B. Ely, William Jewell College, J. D. Murphy, the *Central Baptist*, Joshua Hickman, State missions. J. L. Dawson, reporting for the committee on foreign missions, said, "This department of Christian labor is great; truly, the field is great. The seed is the word of God, and since the command to preach the gospel to every creature is given to us, we do cordially recommend foreign missions." Brother E. Jennings had been the missionary the past year. He labored forty-four days. The Association increased the number constituting the executive board to ten. The new board were: A. P. Miller, J. T. Williams, Jas. W. Riggs,

John Cockerell, Isaac Cannon, Jas. E. Griffith, H. T. Unsell, J. D. Robnett, Jas. Reid, J. C. McGrew.

Elder J. H. Keach had died since the previous session. The committee on obituaries, consisting of A. P. Miller, J. F. Smith and A. G. Mitchell, said, "We know of no death among us, save our venerable brother, John Hawkins Keach, one of the oldest ministers of the Association. Elder Keach was born in Prince William county, Virginia, the 29th day of March, 1807, was baptized in Kentucky, by Elder Edmond Waller in March, 1826, and entered the ministry in Marion county, Missouri, about the year 1840. He was a sheaf ripe for the harvest. In early life his labors in the ministry were abundant throughout northeast Missouri. He labored long and faithfully for William Jewell College and kindred educational institutions, having always been a fast friend of education and especially of an educated ministry. Conservative in temperament, he made but few enemies; kind and simple in manners, he made many friends; instructive in his preaching, the thoughtful listened to him with profit; evangelical and fervent, his labors were blessed among saints and sinners. We do express our sympathy with his bereaved family, and commend them to an all-wise God, who alone can give that comfort which the gospel affords. The Association will miss his counsel, but we bow with humble submission to Him who doeth all things well."

In 1879 we met with Spencerburg Church. The sermon was preached by Elder J. Reid. The text was: "For ye are not under the law, but under grace." Laddonia and Farber churches, of Audrain county, were received into the fellowship of the Association. The messengers from Laddonia were J. H. Baskett, J. A. Gilliland, J. N. Cartmell and R. Gilliland; those from Farber were N. H. Sutton, G. T. Bondurant and S. Ross. The time of the annual meeting having become agitated in view of various business interests, a special committee was raised, consisting of A. P. Miller, W. H. Burnham, G. R. Waddell, S. G. Givens, S.

Enlargement and Training. 275

Guttery. This committee recommended "Tuesday before the second Sunday in September." That time, or about a week earlier, has been the date for the sessions since to the present time. The question of the care of infirm ministers and ministers' families unprovided for came up by a motion made by Elder J. T. Williams. This is an essential question in healthy denominational movement. The Scriptures teach that, "Even so hath the Lord ordained that they which preach the gospel should live of the gospel." But a *living* seems to be all that is here ordained. Laying by in store does not seem to be contemplated in the minister's income and in current ministerial operations the income is sufficient for only a living when economically used. The minister who is faithful will find numerous demands in the spiritual and temporal needs of the people to take all the money that comes to him above the judicious expenditures in home life. Hence the wisdom of providing for ministers and their families. This may be done by sending them money in their place of private abode or by providing a minister's home. Dr. W. Pope Yeaman's favorite idea was a home, provided with a library and such other accommodations as would contribute to the welfare of these men of God. At the time our Heavenly Father took him home he was maturing a plan for such a home, which he wished to present to Missouri Baptists. Whatever is done should be done in the spirit and character of service rendered to comrades and fellow-laborers worthy of the highest honor that the sons of men may receive. And it should be done openly, cheerfully, generously. In this instance at Spencerburg, it was the case of Elder W. W. Mitchell's family. He had labored long and stood for God and his churches. The amount raised was $36.

Brethren M. S. Whiteside, E. Jennings and Jas. D. Biggs had been the missionaries of the Board during the outgoing year. They reported days of labor, 141. The board says, "We adopted the plan of having a missionary sermon at the place of meeting, which, we think, contributed to the interest of the meeting. Bro. J. D. Biggs delivered the sermon at Curryville, and Bro. W. H. Burnham at Mt. Pisgah. God has blessed us with prosperity, and as we are his servants, shall we not devote a large share of our means to the advancement of his cause?" The report was signed by A. P. Miller as president, and J. T. Williams as secretary. J. W. Riggs was treasurer. The new board were A. P. Miller, J. Reid, J. W. Riggs, Isaac Cannon, Jas. E. Griffith, H. T. Unsell, Jas. C. McGrew, J. L. Higbee, A. P. Rodgers, F. D. Hardesty. There was preaching by W. Pope Yeaman, B. F. Hixson, J. T. Williams, A. P. Rodgers, M. S. Whiteside, W. H. Burnham, R. S. Duncan, J. D. Biggs. Dr. Yeaman took a collection of $60.90 for the work of State Missions. Elders W. F. Luck and W. W. Mitchell had died. Brethren M. S. Whiteside, H. N. Baskett and J. E. Shannon, committee on deceased brethren, said, "We have to report the death of aged brother W. F. Luck, the oldest minister of our body. He died on the 26th of December, 1878, at the age of 77. He was in the ministry fifty-five years. Thirty-four years of his ministerial life were spent in the State of Tennessee and the remaining twenty-one years with us in abundant labor as Pastor and evangelist. By his faithful labors many of our churches were much strengthened in membership and greatly built up in the faith of the gospel. We may, in truth, refer to him as one able, earnest and successful in every branch of ministerial labor. He fell like a soldier, he died at his post. While we miss him from our midst, and while our hearts are sad that he is no more on earth with us, yet we rejoice that he died in the triumphs of faith and in the firm hope of a glorious resurrection. We report, also, the death of Brother W. W. Mitchell. He was not at the time of his death a member of our body, but as the greater part of his life was spent with us the committee think it but just that his name appear in the report. Brother W. W. Mitchell died in Illinois, April 4, 1879, in his fifty-fifth year. He was thirty-five years in the gospel ministry. Through all this period, in weakness of constitution and often in extreme feebleness of health, he preached faithfully the gospel, which he seemed to realize as fully as any one with whom the committee ever were acquainted, and that it was the power of God unto the salvation of sinners. He seemed to watch for souls as one that must give an account. Many sad hearts have been comforted, and many fainting ones have been cheered on their way by the words of love and counsel that fell from his lips. He did as much as any one who ever lived among us to settle difficulties in churches and communities and we believe he has gone to realize the blessedness of the peacemaker. To the bereaved families of these brethren we offer our heartfelt sympathy, and we commend them under God to the attention and care of this Association. The committee would recommend to this body that steps be taken by which the families of our deceased ministers be cared for."

The visitors at this time were B. F. Hixson, Nathan Ayres, M. E. Motley, D. W. Motley, M. T. Bibb, J. C. Maple, W. Pope Yeaman, F. H. Lewis, R. S. Duncan.

In 1880 we convened with Vandalia Church. Elder J. D. Biggs preached the annual sermon. His text was: "He that believeth and is baptized shall be saved; but he that believeth not shall be damned." Harmony Grove Church, Lincoln county, was received into the Association; T. H. Admire and J. Nichols were the messengers. Visiting brethren were M. T. Bibb, J. F. Smith, W. J. Jesse, Edward Hayden, W. R. Wigginton, B. F. Hixson, J. A. Thomas, M. V. Shives, R. S. Duncan, G. B. Smith, J. D. Robnett, B. Smith, L. C. Musick, Milton Cox, W. Pope Yeaman, L. B. Ely, M. L. Laws, J. F. Cook, D. B. Ray. On the second day Dr. Yeaman preached before the body at eleven o'clock. He took a collection for State Missions of $122.65. Sister Jane Barker, returned missionary from Assam, represented womans' missionary work in foreign lands. L. B. Ely raised $250 for

William Jewell College. The committee on education, J. Reid, J. C. Biggs and A. M. Tinsley, said, "Your committee on education is glad to report that Baptist College at Louisiana is to be re-opened this fall. We trust Brother Slaughter, with his able corps of teachers, will make it a success." The committee then repeated former recommendations of William Jewell College.

The men employed in mission work were F. M. Birkhead, E. Jennings, M. S. Whiteside, A. P. Rodgers and J. D. Biggs. The board says, "At each meeting we have had a missionary sermon and as many ministering brethren as could be induced to come. So that they have been really missionary gatherings, which we trust the Lord has blessed." The committee on the state of the churches, consisting of J. D. Biggs, J. R. Bondurant and William Penix, said, "The home mission work, we believe, is in better condition than for many years previous. . . . Seven churches have built or begun to build houses of worship." There was preaching by W. Pope Yeaman, J. T. Williams, T. N. Sanderson. The ministers at this time were J. D. Biggs, F. M. Birkhead, J. B. English, S. G. Givens, J. F. Hedges, E. Jennings, M. P. Matheny, A. G. Mitchell, W. J. Patrick, J. D. Robnett, A. P. Rodgers, W. M. Tipton, J. Reid and M. S. Whiteside.

The committee on obituaries, consisting of J. D. Robnett, W. S. Luckett and A. J. McCune, said, "Your committee would report thirty-four deaths in the churches composing the Association, during the past year. Among them we find the names of Brethren Jas. N. Griffin, of West Cuivre church, G. W. Foster, of Louisiana, and E. D. Whiteside, of New Hope. Brother Griffin was born in Pulaski county, Kentucky, June 12, 1809. He moved to Missouri in 1830 and married in 1837 Miss S. M. Vardeman, by whom he had eleven children, all of whom are now living, except two, and are members of the church, one of whom is preaching the gospel. Brother Griffin was converted in 1842 and was baptised by W. H. Vardeman. He began to preach the same year, and was ordained in about twelve months. He was actively engaged in the ministry for about twenty years, during which time his labors were richly blessed and many converts made and added to the churches, some of whom are now preaching the gospel. He fell asleep in Jesus last July, leaving his family the heritage of a godly life.

"Brother G. W. Foster departed this life November, 1879. In the early part of his ministry over one thousand two hundred converts were baptized by him. In the latter years of his life, he practiced law, giving only a portion of his time to the ministry. He died, leaving his family in a destitute condition.

"E. D. Whiteside died March 7, 1880. He was licensed to preach the gospel by New Salem church, and he always longed for the opportunity to engage fully in the work. He was deeply pious and maintained a godly walk and pious conversation. Though suddenly cut down in the morning of life, his friends should not weep for him as those who have no hope."

We met in the session of 1881 with New Salem church. Brother J. D. Robnett preacher the sermon from the words: "Who his own self bore our sins in his own body on the tree, that we, being dead to sins, should live unto righteousness; by whose stripes ye were healed." Pleasant Hill church was received as a member of the body. The messengers were John Ardery, G. C. Jeffries, Mary Busby, Angeline Weldy. The visitors were R. S. Duncan, J. D. Robnett, T. R. Bowles, L. B. Ely, J. H. Tuttle, T. W. Pierce, J. T. Williams, George Steel, N. H. Zumwalt. The Association being informed that there was great destitution in Calhoun county, Illinois, several ministers volunteered to go to specific places and hold meetings, and a voluntary collection was taken to pay the expenses of these ministers. J. T. Williams represented the Southern Baptist Theological Seminary, Louisville, Ky., which has from the first had the co-operation of

Salt River Association. R. S. Duncan presented Foreign Missions. The missionaries had been J. D. Biggs, F. M. Birkhead, D. W. Morgan, A. P. Rodgers, W. J. Patrick, M. S. Whiteside, and $229.40 were expended.

The question of Sabbath observance was taken up and the Association said: "We recommend to the churches that they have religious services of some kind and, if possible, the public preaching of the gospel on the Lord's day." The report on this subject was by J. D. Robnett, W. O. Shannon and R. W. Unsell. It was discussed with ardent interest and marked insight into this great need. The report on education was made by J. D. Biggs, Isaac Whiteside and W. M. Tipton. The name of the school at Louisiana had been changed to the name McCune College. The committee said, "We would recommend to the brethren McCune College, Louisiana, Mo., under the efficient management of Prof. A. Slaughter. This school is more successful than at any former period of its history. . . . We would also recommend William Jewell College to those who are seeking a higher Christian education. The report on obituaries was made by A. G. Mitchell, C. F. Burk and H. T. Ogden. They said: "Your committee would report forty-three deaths in the churches composing this Association; among them we find the names of Newton McDannold, of Ramsey Creek church, J. F. Hedges, of Noix Creek church, and G. C. Merrill, of Louisiana Church." Brethren McDannold and Merrill were Deacons who used the office of deacon well. "Brother Hedges was a minister of the gospel, a member of Noix Creek church when he died, being in his eighty-fourth year. He was often a member of our Association. The fruits of his labors have helped the churches." Three Sunday School conventions had been held during the year. The new board were A. P. Miller, J. Reid, J. W. Riggs, Isaac Cannon, J. C. McGrew, A. Beckner, H. T. Unsell, William Lake, D. T. Killum and J. L. Dawson. There was preaching by D. W. Morgan, T. W. Pierce, J. T. Williams. A Sunday School board was appointed, consisting of M. P. Matheny, D. W. Morgan, R. W. Unsell, W. D. Major, Frank L. Dawson.

Noix Creek church was the place of meeting in 1882. Elder W. M. Tipton preached the opening sermon from the text: "If we have sown unto you spiritual things, is it a great thing if we shall reap your carnal things?" Pleasant Plains church was received into the fellowship of the Association. The messengers were J. F. Harrelson, Mrs. Harrelson, Henry Grafford, Mrs. Grafford. The visitors were J. T. Williams, J. F. Smith, W. H. Zumwalt, P. R. Clare, F. H. Lewis, L. B. Ely, A. M. Johnson, M. P. Matheny, D. B. Ray, S. H. Ford, J. B. English, John D. Biggs, James D. Biggs and J. F. Cook. Brother James D. Biggs took a collection for State Missions. Brother J. F. Kemper took a collection for Foreign Missions. This resolution, introduced by D. W. Morgan, was adopted: "That this Association declares itself unequivocally in favor of the movement looking toward a State constitutional amendment prohibiting the manufacture, importation or sale of alcoholic liquors, except for use in medicine and the mechanic arts. The committee on education, A. P. Miller and J. R. Bondurant, reported: "That education should be Christian. It should be so Christian that it will bring bread to the eater, purity and power to the character and glory to God. When the minds of the young are seeking intellectual treasures, they will the more readily receive the knowledge which comes from above, or imbibe prejudices against it."

The executive board reported: "Our plan during the past year has been, as in years past, to help weak churches and supply the destitute with the gospel. . . . As in the past we have held our meetings in different parts of the Association inviting some brother to preach a missionary sermon. We have usually had good congregations and we trust the meetings have been profitable." The employees were J. D. Biggs, D. W. Morgan, F. M. Birkhead, W. J. Patrick, A. G.

Mitchell, W. N. Maupin, J. J. Griffin, Green B. Smith, E. Jennings, M. S. Whiteside. The committee on State Missions, A. Slaughter, J. D. Biggs and J. V. Moxley, reported: "A large number of weak churches aided in supporting their Pastors, and the gospel was preached to thousands of the destitute." A special committee on religion in the family, reported: "We recommend that we agitate this subject until every household in which we have a member shall have set apart some time in which God shall in some way be regularly and publicly acknowledged the God of that house." The special committee on Sunday Schools reported: "Employed Brother W. N. Maupin as Sunday School missionary for three months at $33 1-3 per month to visit churches and destitute places, organize Sunday Schools, preach the gospel, sell Sunday School and other good literature, by which or by collections to raise means for his own support. We are glad to announce that Brother Maupin has done great good in the Sunday School work and has won some precious souls." The committee on state of the churches, J. E. Shannon, J. H. Baskett and T. M. Rose, reported: "That the news from the churches is more cheering than for several years." The committee on McCune College, W. B. McPike, Jas Reid, J. D. Biggs and R. W. Unsell, reported: "We find it under excellent management and well patronized. There were enrolled one hundred and fifteen pupils, thirty-four of whom boarded in the school. . . . The home department, under the direction and control of Mr. and Mrs. Slaughter, is a model of domestic management." The committee on obituaries, M. R. K. Biggs, Geo. A. Lake and F. M. Birkhead, reported: "Bro. John Ralls, of New London church, a man of much ability, having a large experience in civil as well as in military affairs, particularly in the Mexican War, has passed away. Truly he was a good and a useful man, active in church matters, and a warm-hearted Christian gentleman. Brother Charles R. Huntington, of Mt. Pisgah church, was a zealous, modest Christian whose memory will long be cherished by his church and neighbors. We have lost, also, one of the constituent members of Mt. Pisgah church, Brother Diggs Luck, aged over ninety years. He was a good and useful man. The Clarksville church mourns the death of Brother James Major, 'a good man and full of the Holy Ghost.' His final words were, 'Not a wave of trouble rolls across my peaceful breast.' Deacon Corbin Benn of Mt. Pleasant church, died at about eighty years of age. His life was full of faith and good works." The executive board for the incoming year were W. O. Shannon, J. Reid, J. W. Riggs, Isaac Cannon, H. T. Unsell, J. L. Dawson, J. C. McGrew, William Lake, A. Beckner, D. T. Killam. The Association raised the question of getting a song-book at a price permitting every worshiper to have one. A committee, consisting of James Reid and R. W. Unsell was appointed to lay the matter before the General Association. Favorable action was taken by that body. The effort in this thing was based upon the belief that every one who comes into an assembly of worshipers should receive recognition and should have help to actively join in the services.

In 1883 the session was held with Corner Stone church. D. W. Morgan, of Clarksville, who had been chosen to preach the sermon was absent, and J. F. Kemper, the alternate, preached the sermon. Corinth, Elm Grove and Rush Hill Churches were received into Associational fellowship. The messengers of Corinth were W. T. Fuqua and G. T. Bondurant; Elm Grove, messengers absent; Rush Hill, messengers absent. The visitors were Harvy Hatcher, J. M. P. Martin, D. B. Ray, A. G. Mitchell, T. H. Duncan, S. S. Grimmet, W. L. Dawson, M. M. Motley, T. H. Lewis.

Brethren M. S. Whiteside, J. J. Griffin, W. A. Bibb and A. P. Rodgers had been in the employment of the board. The year had been one of substantial growth in the vineyard of the Lord. The committee on State Missions said: "Every time the gospel is preached to those who have it not, there is additional evidence given of the Messiahship of Christ. . . . Many new churches have been planted, weak churches have been strengthened, the word preached in churchless districts; souls have been converted and baptized and general strength and courage given to the denomination in Missouri." This committee was A. P. Miller, J. R. Smith and W. A. Bibb. The committee on education, M. S. Whiteside, J. F. Kemper and A. M. Johnson, reported, "That education is not only of inestimable advantage in life, but that it is also a duty which we owe to God, who gives intellectual faculties and opportunity for their development. We would further emphasize the importance of having our children educated under Christian influences." The committee on obituaries, S. G. Givens, chairman, reported the deaths of Deacons Benjamin King and Barzel Riggs; also, Brother Reason Vermillion, who "tried to preach the gospel and was very warm-hearted and earnest in his appeals to sinners." They gave, also, the death of "Elizabeth J. Unsell, aged ninety-two. Sister Unsell was one of the constituent members of Peno church." The board continued the same, except that T. J. McDannold was put in the vacancy caused by the removal of Isaac Cannon from the Associational limits. The committee on nominations were A. J. McCune, M. C. Biggs, J. V. Moxley. The ministers at this time were E. Jennings, C. W. Alexander, W. A. Bibb, J. D. Biggs, S. G. Givens, W. N. Maupin, J. F. Kemper, J. Reid, G. B. Smith, M. S. Whiteside, N. T. Allison, F. M. Birkhead, A. M. Johnson, J. B. English, J. J. Griffin, C. A. Mitchell, W. J. Patrick, A. P. Rodgers, W. M. Tipton and J. N. B. Hepler. The question of dividing the Association having been raised, Judge Miller introduced a resolution to the effect that such questions belonged solely with the churches. It is greatly promotive of denominational welfare that Associations, conventions and councils confine themselves to the specific work for which they are organized. A Baptist church is the highest religious authority on earth and her prerogatives may not be infringed upon by any man or set of men.

The Association met with New London church September 10, 1884, Elder C. A. Mitchell preached the sermon from the words: "Who gave himself for us, that he might redeem us from all iniquity, and purify unto himself a peculiar people, zealous of good works." W. J. Patrick declining re-election, the reorganization was effected by the election of James D. Biggs as moderator and W. B. McPike clerk. Winfield and Elsberry churches, of Lincoln county, were received into the Association. The messengers from Elsberry were J. W. Waters, J. W. Taliafero, Ada Mayes, Landy Waters. Those from Winfield were D. S. Killam, J. B. Nelson, L. McClay and F. D. Hardesty. The visitors were H. Hatcher, B. F. Hixson, J. T. Smith, D. W. Morgan, W. H. Vardeman, S. W. Marston, J. F. Cook, J. B. Hawkins, John D. Biggs, T. M. Zumwalt, L. L. Hobbs. Several churches asked for letters of dismission that they might go into the organization of a new Association to be formed in Audrain county. They were Corinth, Farber, Laddonia, Pleasant Plains, Rush Hill, Vandalia and West Cuivre. The request was granted and the parting hand was given by the members of the Association to the messengers of these churches.

The executive board reported: "We have, as in the past, held our meetings in different parts of the Association, and had some brother to preach a sermon prepared for the occasion, which we think has done good. In obedience to a recommendation passed in the report on Sunday Schools at our last meeting, we called a Sunday School Convention to meet at Clarksville, March 28, 29 and 30, which was well attended and was the source of new and increased interest in the Sunday School work." In the mission field the board had the services of A. P. Rodgers, W. A. Bibb, E. Jennings, M. S. Whiteside, J. J. Griffin, C. A. Mitchell and W. M. Tipton. The committee on State Missions, J. D. Biggs, W. T. Fuqua and J. J. Griffin, said, "Nearly every church in Salt River Association has contributed or will contribute to the State Mission work." The committee on Foreign Missions, H. N. Baskett and O. B. Hicklin, said, "'The field is the world,' said our Lord and He laid His final obligation on the hearts of His redeemed people to carry the glad tidings of great joy to every nation." The committee on obituaries reported that, Geo. W. Peay died, aged eighty-three years. "Thus another good man has fallen; one who had the confidence of every person who knew him." Deacon Luke Lewis was called from his earthly labors. "Brother Lewis was a Christian of firm and elevated character, a man of culture and intelligence, a citizen of integrity and worth. He was converted in the great revival near Spencerburg in 1832-3, and was a Baptist of extended usefulness." Ephraim M. Bondurant was born in 1800. "For sixty-two years he was a faithful servant of Christ, a tender-hearted Christian gentleman." These three were Deacons." The committee on correspondence, S. P. Dawson, J. W. Waters and J. M. Keach, said, "Brethren, let us continue in and contend for the faith once delivered to the saints." The new board were A. J. McCune, C. A. Mitchell, J. W. Riggs, A. Slaughter, J. C. McGrew, T. J. McDannold, D. T. Killam, J. L. Dawson.

CURRYVILLE BAPTIST CHURCH.

By T. M. King.

In writing this history, we must go a little back of the organization of the church, and note some of the circumstances leading up to the building of a house of worship. Prior to 1875 there was no regular preaching by the Baptists in Curryville. Occasionally, however, a Baptist preacher passing through would stop and preach, there being a few Baptists in and around the town. In the spring of 1875, a few of the brethren counseled together and determined to make an effort to have preaching once a month in the school building, there being no other house suitable for public worship. In that conference it was suggested by Deacon Luke Lewis, that we correspond with Elder S. A. Beauchamp with the object of securing his services for awhile. He was, therefore, written to and invited to come and preach a few sermons for us, which resulted in a visit by Elder S. A. Beauchamp, at which time he preached several times and greatly endeared himself to the brethren. At this time arrangements were made by which he agreed to preach once a month, for which service he was to receive $200 per year. In June, 1875, he began his regular monthly services, and began the agitation of the subject of building a house of worship. No one denomination being strong, a union church house was built during the summer and fall of 1875, one-half owned by the C. P. church, one-fourth by the Missionary Baptists and one-fourth by the anti-missionary Baptists.

The third Saturday in November, 1875, a presbytery was called. The Presbytery consisted of Elders S. A. Beauchamp, of Huntsville, Mo., H. M. King, Fayette, J. T. Williams, of Louisiana, A. P. Rodgers and E. Jennings, of Bowling Green. Bro. J. T. Williams, was chosen moderator and T. J. Ayres, clerk, when the following eighteen names were enrolled, going into the organization: Benj. King, Luke Lewis, Rachel King, Wm. K. Biggs, Martha Biggs, Emma Biggs, Anna Biggs, James W. Riggs, Lucretia Riggs, M. J. Trabue, Wm. Brandon, Ann Brandon, Jas. E. McPike, H. P. Lewis, Lou Lewis, Geo. W. Wylie, T. J. Ayres, Mollie E. Ayres. A committee appointed for that purpose reported a church covenant, and articles of faith which were adopted. The organization being completed, T. J. Ayres was elected church clerk, Luke Lewis and Benj. King were elected Deacons, each of whom had been ordained and served in that office. Elder S. A. Beauchamp, by a unanimous vote, was called as Pastor; call accepted. Then the Baptist church at Curryville was organized with eighteen constituent members, seven of whom have since gone to their reward, leaving their work to follow them. This leaves eleven that went into the organization living, five who still hold their membership with us. Immediately following the organization of the church, a series of meetings were held, conducted by Rev. H. M. King. In these meetings God graciously blessed his message to the people. The little church was greatly revived, and thirteen were added to her number, five by letter and relation and eight by experience and baptism. On the very threshhold of its existence, God gave His approval by graciously blessing the newly organized church in their meetings. Bro. H. M. King greatly endeared himself to the church and community.

In May, Bro. Beauchamp offered his resignation as Pastor, as he was thinking of moving to the State of Texas. In July, 1876, Bro. W. J. Patrick, by request, preached for the church, at which time he was called as a supply until Bro. S. A. Beauchamp should be heard from, which call was accepted. In August, 1876, the church clerk, having been instructed at a previous meeting, had prepared a synopsis of the Articles of Faith, adopted by the church, and a letter to the Salt River Association. In September, following, the church was admitted into the Association. In November, 1876, a series of meetings were conducted by Rev. W. J. Patrick, who was still serving the church as supply. In this meeting the church was greatly blessed and three added to the church by experience and baptism. The Pastor, Bro. S. A. Beauchamp, having moved to Texas, at its meeting in December, 1876, the church, by unanimous vote, called Bro. W. J. Patrick, as Pastor of the church. The call was accepted. Bro. Patrick served the church faithfully, in the work of the Master for ten years. His resignation was accepted in December, 1886, with the deepest regrets of the church. At same meeting Dr. H. P. Lewis was elected church treasurer. In January, 1877, the committee on contributions recommended that the church give aid regularly to denominational interests as follows: Christian education, District Missions, State

Missions and Foreign Missions, which was adopted, and has ever been adhered to.

But to make the work more efficient, in December, 1879, the church resolved to have a special committee of two to solicit aid for these various denominational interests. Since the adoption of that report, in 1877, no year has passed so far as we can ascertain, without a contribution from the church to each of the named denominational interests.

Arrangements were made for a protracted meeting January, 1878. One of the writers of this history remembers well the more than usual interest taken by several of the members in preparing for this series of meetings. In these meetings was secured as ministerial help Brother L. M. Berry, of Salisbury, Mo. Precious, indeed, to the hearts of God's People were these meetings. The church was greatly revived and permitted to rejoice at seeing sinners awakened and converted. In these meetings there were added to the church ten by letter and relation and twenty-two by experience and baptism. A remarkable incident on this occasion was the baptism of four brothers on the same day, sons of Deacon Benj. King, deceased. How exceedingly rich in goodness and mercy is our Heavenly Father.

In February, 1879, the Pastor, assisted by Bro. J. Hickman, held a series of meetings. In these meetings the church was edified and strengthened by the faithful preaching of the word of God. Sinners were awakened and converted. Three united with the church by experience and baptism. Same year the church was invaded by death, when Elijah Harper, an aged man who had been a member but a short time was called to his reward. The meeting in December, 1879, was protracted in which the Pastor was assisted by Bro. J. D. Biggs, of Louisiana, Mo. The church was again revived. The gospel was preached with power, accompanied by the Holy Spirit. Sinners were converted and the church received into her membership three by letter and eleven by experience and baptism. Brother Biggs greatly endeared himself to the church by his faithful work in these meetings. The baptizing on this occasion took place on the 24th day of December, a very cold day. Twelve had offered themselves for membership by experience and baptism. But one of the number fearing sickness, declined to be baptized and the next morning the only sick one of the twelve was the one unbaptized; surely not from immersion. At the January meeting in 1880, J. S. Ayres was elected as an additional Deacon, and at the February meeting following he was ordained to that office. Ordination sermon by Bro. Jas. Reid; charge to candidate and church by Bro. J. D. Biggs; prayer by Bro. J. D. Robinett. In December, 1880, J. W. Hawkins was elected church treasurer. In 1881, Bro. J. C. Maple, of Mexico, assisted a few days in a meeting, but taking sick the meeting closed with but little interest manifested. In 1882, Bro. L. M. Berry again assisted in a series of meetings. The church was blessed with a revival and four were added to the membership by experience and baptism.

In March, 1882, a committee consisting of P. H. Routen, J. C. Biggs and H. P. Lewis was appointed for the purpose of buying another one-fourth interest in the church building. Said committee was continued from time to time, until in December, following, when the one-fourth owned by the anti-Missionary Baptists was purchased. The two Deacons, Benj. King and Luke Lewis, having grown very infirm, at their request, the church at the September meeting in 1882, elected and ordained two additional deacons, P. H. Routen and J. C. Biggs. Ordination sermon by Bro. A. M. Johnson; prayer by Bro. W. J. Patrick; charge by Bro. J. B. English.

On January 4, 1883, Deacon Benj. King, one of the constituent members of the church was removed by death, and at the February meeting the following resolutions of respect to him were adopted by the church: "Deacon King was a man of more than ordinary intelligence and attainments. He was a practical surveyor in North Carolina, from whence he came to Missouri. He was tendered positions of honor and trust during the Civil War in the Confederate army. He was unswerving and retiring in disposition, yet strong in his convictions of right and firm in purpose." February 21, 1883, William Brandon, another of the constituent members was called to his reward. At the March meeting, following, the church adopted resolutions of respect to him. By energy and economy, Wm. Brandon had accumulated a good estate. Of these means he contributed at one time $500 to the Southern Baptist Theological Seminary, then located at Charleston, South Carolina. Ed. Biggs was elected clerk.

The meeting in January, 1884, was continued, Bro. P. R. Ridgely, of Palmyra, assisted. Eleven were added to our number, two by letter and nine by experience and baptism. The meeting closed with interest unabated. In March, following, two by letter and two by experience and baptism united with the church. In April, one by letter and one by experience and baptism. At this meeting the church granted to J. N. B. Helper the privilege of speaking and teaching in public. On April 24, 1884, Deacon Luke Lewis, one of the constituent members, was called to his reward.

At a call meeting of the church in April, 1884, J. N. B. Helper was ordained to the gospel ministry. Ordination sermon by Bro. J. Reid. Charge by Bro. S. G. Givens. In a series of meetings held by the church in January, 1885, Bro. Bland Beauchamp did most of the preaching. God blessed his preached word to the upbuilding of the church. Five were added to the church.

The second Saturday and Sunday in October, 1885, the church held a reunion, it being the tenth anniversary of the organization of the church. This reunion was followed by a series of meetings in which the Pastor was assisted by our first Pastor, S. A. Beauchamp. The church was greatly revived, and three were added to the church, at the November meeting, the result of that meeting. At the February meeting, 1886, Bro. B. R. Patrick was granted the privilege of speaking and teaching in public. At the November meeting, 1886, Pastor W. J. Patrick tendered his resignation as Pastor of the church, to take effect in December, which was accepted. Thus closed ten years of a faithful and fruitful pastorate. Brother Reid held a short series of meetings with the church in February, 1887, with one addition to the church. In 1887, Bro. M. L. Bibb was elected Pastor; call accepted.

In August, 1887, the Salt River Baptist Association met with the church. In January, 1887, the Pastor M. L. Bibb, held a series of meetings. The church was revived spiritually. Much good was accomplished during this meeting. Fourteen were added to the church—four by letter and ten by baptism. On the 27th day of February, 1889, Bro. C. M. Williams was unanimously called as Pastor and the call was accepted. Special meetings were conducted by the Pastor, assisted by Bro. A. M. Vardeman, in December, 1890. The church was awakened to her duty and six were added to the church—four by letter, two by experience and baptism. In December, 1891, a series of meetings was conducted by Bro. C. W. Dicken. The Lord blessed him and our Pastor in their work. Two united with the church by letter and five by experience and baptism. At the same meeting the church called Bro. J. S. Dingle, of Palmyra, as Pastor, which call was accepted. Death, on December 26, 1902, called Sister Rachel King, wife of Deacon Benj. King, deceased, to her reward, and her works do follow her. During a series of meetings conducted by Pastor, assisted by Bro. L. M. Berry, in October, 1893, five were added to the church. Deacon P. H. Routen, one of our beloved deacons, was called to his reward by death, and at the following meeting resolutions of respect to him were adopted, as follows: "Resolved, that in the death of Bro. P. H. Routen, whose piety was deep and practical, whose service as a Deacon, in fidelity and benevolence was eminently satisfactory, we suffer great loss." Deacon Routen was a man of firm convictions; his wise counsel in church affairs are hushed forever on earth. At the request of the Deacons, J. S. Ayres and J. C. Biggs, the church at its meeting in March, 1894, elected H. P. Lewis and J. W. Riggs as two additional Deacons for the church. On the 5th Sunday in April, 1894, the ordination sermon was preached by Bro. W. J. Patrick. Prayer by Bro. J. S. Dingle. Charge by Bro. C. M. Williams. In December, 1894, the Pastor, assisted by Bro. O. L. Bronson, conducted a series of meetings which strengthened the church and twelve were added, one by letter and eleven by experience and baptism.

At the August meeting in 1895, Bro. J. D. Hacker was called to the pastorate of the church. He served only three months. In October, 1895, the chuch celebrated her twentieth anniversary. The day was one of a spiritual feast to those that love the Lord. In December, 1895, Bro. Bland Beauchamp was called as Pastor of the church.

On May 27, 1896, a destructive tornado swept over our town and community, destroying much property and the cause of one death. Our church, the "union church," was damaged so badly that the services could not be conducted in it. A building and finance committee were appointed, consisting of brethren J. W. Hawkins, H. P. Lewis, J. S. Ayres, J. C. Biggs and T. M. King. Said committee labored earnestly and persistently to the end. All praise and honor was given to Him, who said, "I will not leave you comfortless, I will come to you." He came and manifested Himself in sanctioning the work that was done in his name. The church was dedicated the second Sunday in December, 1896. The dedicatory sermon was preached by Bro. Bower R. Patrick, free from debt at a cost of $1,926.59. Bro. Bower was converted and united with the church by experience and Baptism, January 12, 1882; was licensed to speak and preach in public February, 1886. Immediately following the dedication a series of meetings were conducted by the Pastor, assisted by J. L. Downing. The church was greatly revived and much good was done. Fourteen were added to the church during this meeting; six by letter and eight by experience and baptism. A Baptist Sunday School was organized with J. W. Hawkins, superintendent; T. M. King, assistant superintendent; H. E. Lewis, secretary. It may be well to say here that Bro. J. W. Hawkins has served as superintendent all the time even under the times of discouragements; he has ever been faithful and conducted an evergreen Sunday School.

In February and March, 1898, a series of meetings were conducted by the Pastor, assisted by Bro. N. R. Pittman, seven were added to the church. The church was greatly strengthened and Bro. Pittman endeared himself to the church and community. Bro. J. L. Downing was called as Pastor; call accepted. He served the church as Pastor only three months, when he was called to go to Brazil, in April, 1899. Bro. C. A. Mitchell was called to the pastorate of the church; the call was accepted. In October, 1900, a series of meetings were conducted, the Pastor, Bro. Mitchell, delivering the message of the dying Savior to the people. The church was edified and he was blessed in his efforts by seeing so many confess Jesus as their Savior. Ten were added to the church—two by letter and eight by experience and baptism.

In February, 1902, a series of meetings were conducted by the Pastor assisted by Bro. S. M. Brown, which resulted in seven being added to the church. In October, 1902, the Pastor again conducted a series of meetings. The church was spiritually revived and much good was accomplished. Seven were added to the church. Bro. W. K. Biggs, who went into the organization of the church and who was a regular attendant at all church work and took an active interest in the work until broken down in health, died June 26, 1903. His faith failed not. In October, 1903, at a series of meetings conducted by the Pastor, assisted

Enlargement and Training. 295

by Rev. T. C. Carleton, fourteen were added to the church membership—one by letter and thirteen by experience and baptism.

In April, 1904, the church called Bro. R. R. Maiden as Pastor; call accepted for an indefinite time. The fifth Sunday in July, 1904, Bro. C. A. Mitchell was again unanimously called for an indefinite time.

(Dr. M. E. Broaddus has just closed a two years' pastorate with Curryville Church.—Author.)

FIRST BAPTIST CHURCH, CLARKSVILLE.

By Mrs. Doctor Story.

Organized January 22, 1874, the records give Rev. J. D. Biggs, A. G. Mitchell, S. W. Marston as the ministers on the occasion. The constituting members were: James Major, W. D. Major, Kate Major, B. F. Yates, Margaret Yates, G. W. Pendleton, Susan Pendleton, S. A. Edwards, Mary J. Edwards, Emily Limerick, C. C. Runkel, Mary Runkel, Martha Berry, Theodore Berry, W. H. Bibb, Martha J. Bibb, Elizabeth Beamer, Jethro Ferrell, Elizabeth Ferrell, Maducia Edwards, W. H. Nicklin. The church worshiped in the Presbyterian and also Methodist churches. A house was erected in 1876 and dedicated by Rev. M. H. Pogson, April, 1877. Size of building is forty-two by fifty-four feet, built of brick, conveniently located on Main street, and carpeted and comfortably furnished.

W. D. Major was for years the clerk and he was also the beloved superintendent of Sabbath school. He and his family were staunch supporters of the organization. The first Deacons were S. A. Edwards, B. F. Yates and W. D. Major. The Pastors have been: W. H. Bibb, first supply; W. H. Burnham, 1875-1880; J. B. English, 1880-1881; D. W. Morgan, 1881-1883; W. M. Tipton, 1883-1886; J. D. Hacker, December, 1886-April, 1888; J. F. Kemper, August, 1886-January, 1890; Charles A. Mitchell, supplying meantime; W. H. Stone, November, 1890 to 1891; J. D. Hacker, June, 1892-October, 1892; W. M. Tipton,

May, 1893-May, 1895; W. H. Stone, July, 1896-June, 1899; J. T. Nevins, March, 1900-August, 1901; J. D. Biggs, May, 1902-May, 1906; M. E. Broaddus, May, 1907—. George H. Ferrel is church clerk. The Deacons are Charles Middleton, J. E. Riggins and G. H. Ferrel.

The officers Baptist Ladies Aid Society are: Mrs. Charles Middleton, president; Mrs. Edward Wigginton, vice-president; Mrs. J. H. Story, secretary and treasurer.

Sunday school officers: J. E. Riggins, superintendent; Mrs. J. H. Story, assistant superintendent; Miss Lily Young, secretary and treasurer; Miss Lillian Riggins, organist.

The present membership is sixty.

CORNER STONE CHURCH.

By W. B. Palmer.

Corner Stone Baptist Church was organized May 10, 1872, at the Pea Ridge schoolhouse. Feeling the need of preaching on Long Arm Prairie some six or eight persons of Baptist churches decided to organize that they might the better promulgate Baptist principles in this part of the county. Accordingly on the above date a Presbytery consisting of Elders A. G. Mitchell, T. N. Sanderson and Wm. H. Bibb was called, and after appropriate services the following persons were organized into a church: Hiram Hall and Fanny, his wife, Robert J. and Sarah A. Chasten, James R. and Dulena A. Gibson, Adam Hall and Jenny Estes. Jenny Estes, Sarah A. Chasten, Jas. R. Gibson and wife are the only members living that helped to organize the church, but none of them are members with us at present.

The church called for its first pastor Elder Wm. H. Bibb and elected Robert J. Chasten clerk. Others soon came by letter. After a good deal of sacrificing and toil $850 was secured in money and pledges and the present meeting house was built on Long Arm Prairie. The church has had since its organization eleven Pastors: W. H. Bibb, M. S. Whiteside, Jas. Reid, F. M. Birkhead, J. N. B. Hepler, W. N. Maupin, E. B. Dillard, O. A. Gordon, D. E. Mellechamp and W. J. Patrick, serving the church in the order named. The Deacons have been Hiram Hall, James R. Gibson, H. Atkins, B. F. Blackwell, Robert Harris and Alphonzo Noah. But one of these, B. F. Blackwell, serves the church at present. The clerks have been Robert J. Chasten, John Moxley, S. S. Hall, E. M. Atkins, W. T. Hall and W. B. Palmer.

The church received into its membership in all two hundred and thirty-five persons. During the last decade the church has lost nearly all of her members, principally by death and removal, until her present membership is only forty-two, with but about a dozen members living close enough to the church to attend her services.

This body from the first has been missionary through her Pastors supplying at various points where there was but little or no preaching. During the first year of her history the church was received into the fellowship of the Salt River Association. This fellowship continued until the year 1890, when the following resolutions were offered by J. S. R. Gregory and adopted by the church:

"*Whereas*, Salt River Association has become so large and unwieldy, therefore the Baptist Church at Corner Stone at her regular meeting June 14, 1890, adopted the following resolution:

"*Resolved*, First: That for the good of the Baptist cause and convenience of the churches it is best for us to withdraw from said Association and form an Association in Lincoln county.

"*Resolved*, Second: That we send eight brethren to visit sister churches in Lincoln county and contiguous thereto and ask them to adopt the above resolutions and send delegates to a convention to be held at Corner Stone on the 7th of August, 1890, at 11 o'clock a. m., to carry into effect and select a place and set a time to convene an Association as soon after the meeting of Salt River Association as practicable."

According to the intention of the church the new Association, known as Cuivre, was then organized and held her first session with this church the following year.

WINFIELD CHURCH.

By Deacon F. D. Hardesty.

Winfield Baptist Church was organized April 6, 1884, by Elder C. A. Mitchell and Elder F. M. Birkhead, in the new meeting-house, with fourteen members, whose names are as follows: F. D. Hardesty, Mary M. Hardesty, D. T. Killam, Kate Killam, W. S. Killam, Mary D. Hardesty, Amina Fielder, R. C. Magruder, S. A. Magruder, Anna Meadows, Lewis McClay, Girty McClay, Sarah Nelson and W. R. Admire.

The following brethren have been the Pastors of Winfield Baptist Church: C. A. Mitchell, five years; E. J. Sanderson, four years; W. M. Tipton, three years; Charles E. King, one and one-half years; J. P. Stewart, one and one-half years; W. J. Patrick, four years; Charles E. King, two years. J. H. Terrill is the present Pastor. Brethren Calloway, Clayton and King have preached for us at various times when we had no Pastor. Clerks of Winfield Church: F. D. Hardesty, twenty years, C. F. Miller, present clerk.

ELSBERRY CHURCH.

By Elder Abe C. Jones.

The Elsberry Baptist Church was organized October 27, 1883. The constituent members were: J. W. Waters, Mrs. Mary Waters, J. R. Cannon, Mrs. Ida G. Cannon, Landy Waters, Robert Waters, Miss Lela Waters, C. L. Gennie, Mrs. Rosie E. Gennie, Mrs. Ada Mayes, Mrs. Anna Powell, Dr. J. W. Taliafaro. Rev. W. A. Bibb, moderator, and J. R. Cannon, clerk, in organizing. C. A. Mitchell was first Pastor, then

J. D. Hacker and W. H. Stone to the time of withdrawal from Salt River Association.

FARBER CHURCH.

By J. D. Sutton.

The Farber Baptist Church was organized by Rev. Whiteside in February, 1879. The constituent members were N. H. Sutton and wife, E. L. Grigsby and wife, George W. Adams and wife, A. B. Toliver and wife, Joe Toliver, Z. T. Burch and Mildred Farrington. In 1882 a frame house of worship was erected, the cost of which was $1,800.

HARMONY GROVE CHURCH.

By Mrs. Mack Fielder.

Harmony Grove Baptist Church was organized February 1, 1880, with twelve members. Brother James Nickolds and Brother Morgan Turnbull were the Deacons and Brother Turnbull served until he died. Brother F. M. Birkhead was first Pastor and preached for the church nearly ten years; he resigned June 1, 1889. Brother P. W. Halley was next Pastor; he preached two years, and was followed by Brother C. W. Davis. Brother J. S. Eames was next Pastor; he preached his first sermon November 19, 1892, and resigned July 13, 1895.

Brother James Nickolds, Brother James H. Norton and Brother S. D. Alexander are the present Deacons. Brother W. N. Maupin is our Pastor now. We have a good house of worship.

HAW CREEK CHURCH.

By Mrs. W. H. Caverly.

This church was organized in 1870 with eleven members: J. Bradley and wife, Henry Hostetter and wife, William Caverly and wife, J. Nichols and wife, Tib Mefford and wife, and Betsey A. Davis. Elder S. G. Givens was the first Pastor, afterward Elder G.

T. Colvin filled that office. Elder E. Jennings was the last Pastor. The clerks were, first, Wm. Caverly, then Joseph Bradley. Services once each month were held in the Haw Creek schoolhouse. There were some revival services. The church lived five years and had twenty-nine members when she dissolved.

OAK RIDGE BAPTIST CHURCH.

By Elder Abe C. Jones.

This church was organized on Saturday, May 29, 1875, at the Edwards schoolhouse, with seventeen members, who had taken letters from the Ebenezer Church. Their names: James Barrett, J. A. Edwards, Annie G. Edwards, R. B. Edwards, Lina E. Edwards, W. L. Smith, T. J. Smith, Lucy Lilley, Davis L. Key, Ella Key, Mahala Thompson, Lydia A. Robinson, John, Sarah, W. N., Albert and Martha Mitchell. The church elected J. A. Edwards, R. B. Edwards and T. J. Smith, Deacons, who were ordained the following day; Rev. Albert G. Mitchell, W. W. Mitchell and M. S. Whiteside assisting in the same. In 1892 Leland V. Edwards was licensed to preach, and on May 18, 1893, he was ordained to the ministry by this church.

The following have served as pastors: W. W. Mitchell, M. S. Whiteside, A. P. Rodgers, S. G. Givens, W. N. Maupin, C. A. Mitchell, E. J. Sanderson, S. W. Clay, Wm. Calloway, Charles E. King, L. V. Edwards, O. A. Gordon and Abe C. Jones.

The church edifice is located three miles northwest of Elsberry; was built at a cost of $1,000 and dedicated free of debt, on the first Sunday in June, 1880. The same year a mission house was built at Damron, at a cost of about $200, where there have been some good revival meetings at different times; also now and then regular preaching services and a Sunday school. Only two of the constituent members are now members of the church, namely: W. L. Smith and Mrs. Annie G. Edwards. The church maintains a cemetery, well fenced and cared for, on adjoining lots.

A BRIEF HISTORY OF PLEASANT HILL CHURCH.

By J. D. Biggs.

In the spring of 1881, as nearly as I can remember, I was passing through the community in which Pleasant Hill Church now stands. A gentleman, Mr. Geo. Ford, accosted me and asked me if I would stop and preach a funeral. I told him yes. It was in the afternoon. I preached and after the sermon he asked me if I could not come again the next Sunday afternoon and I said, yes, again. Thus the work began. For a few times we held the meetings at private houses, but finally moved the place of meeting to the top of the hill, near the Pleasant Hill burying ground. We held the services under some large trees for awhile. Toward the end of the summer we built a house and before the winter had come on fully we were worshiping in a very comfortable house.

The community which for many years had been considered ungodly, was really transformed by the power of the gospel of Christ. Hunting and fishing and any kind of manual labor were engaged in on the Sabbath day. There were several followers of infidelity. They were certainly well posted on their views. They frequently opposed me in my gospel ministrations, but usually listened to me when I began to preach. They had much to say in regard to "the mistakes of Moses," following the infidel's line of thought. The preacher had much to say about the perfection of Jesus the Christ. The sins of men and the sacrifice for sin were continually held before them. The love of God for sinners and his hatred for sin; the person, the character, the teaching of Jesus the Nazarene, his ability to save and his willingness, were all kept before them. God was pleased to convert some of them and use them for the advancement of His cause.

There were also a few desperate young men in the community. They drank and fought among themselves, but they were especially pugnacious toward the residents of another community. Somebody was almost sure to be killed when the two communities came together. Some of them once threatened to ride the preacher on a rail; he told them that he would have to ride free if he rode at all, for he had no money. Some of the good people were afraid that the preacher would be waylaid and killed; the answer came back that he was going to preach or fall with his head toward the church. I think every one of these were converted. Two at least of the number have crossed over the river and are now at rest with the Lord they once reviled. One, I know, still lives and labors for the Master.

In regard to building the house of worship, I may add, never did a people work more earnestly than they did when once they had put their hands to the work. There are two cases that were remarkable in the church there. The first was the case of Brother George Weldy. His name ought to be preserved in history. Brother Weldy lived in a neighborhood that was grossly wicked and yet he was a very upright man. Often men would refer to Weldy as an outsider and say he was as good as any member of the church. Shortly after we began to preach at Pleasant Hill he came forward one day to unite with the church. He told practically this story: "Twenty-five years ago I was attending a meeting at Salem, in Ralls county. Under the preaching I felt myself to be a sinner. I prayed God to forgive me and I felt a peace that I cannot describe. I went home hardly knowing what to do. I did not know whether it was conversion or not, and yet I kept up praying. I did not feel like carousing as I had done before. There was a peace that I had never known. I had an earnest desire to do good and be good. Soon after this the war came on and I joined the army. I tried to do my duty to my God and my country as I saw it. I went through the war trying to keep a good conscience. Sometimes the hope I had would be brighter and sometimes weaker, but there never was a time when I would have parted with it for all the world. I am still trusting Jesus Christ and hope to till I die. My life is so unworthy that I hardly dare to ask a place among His children, and yet I want to be with them." Weldy was elected a Captain soon after he went into the service. His fellow soldiers said that he was one of the bright lights in the army. His life amidst the surroundings was like a light in a dark place, or like a beautiful lily growing in the marshes.

The other case was Brother George C. Jeffries. Jeffries was a bachelor. Perhaps fifty years of age at the time of which I write. He was lame in both feet. Very large and, to most of us he seemed, almost helpless. He had to use crutches and moving around was a hardship to him. He moved, however. George Jeffries had been a Christian for several years before he began the work at Pleasant Hill. He went into the organization of the church. He was a noble man of God; pure in heart and zealous in the work of the Master. Two brief incidents in his life will suffice to show the character of the man. He asked the Pastor one day what he could do for the Lord. A suggestion was made that he could get some tracts and distribute them with judgment among the people, especially the children. Immediately he sent for some tracts that would be useful in pointing sinners to Christ. Then he sent for some small Testaments. These he distributed with his own hands. He had no buggy, he could not ride horseback, so he harnessed up the horses to the wagon and drove from house to house giving away the little Testaments. One day he met a little girl to whom he had given a Testament and stopped to ask her if she had read it. She stood for a moment and looked at him and then as the tears came to her eyes she said, "Papa burned it up." Uncle George said, "Well, I'll give you another one and I don't think it would be wrong to keep the next one hid from your papa." Year in and year out Uncle George drove around in his two-horse wagon. He climbed in and out as best he could, he hobbled around on his crutches and he was a blessing to the community. I think he led many precious souls to Christ.

The second incident in his life was a very touching one. When the house was to be built Uncle George, who was not very wealthy, gave very liberally. He gave so cheerfully of his means to build that it was a pleasure to see him take from his hard-earned store, and withal so small, the money for the house of God. One day as we were going through the community and turned aside to see how the building was progressing we saw a sight that might have moved the heart of the hardest. Uncle George had tried to get some one to dig out the rest of the foundation, which had been begun. He was so anxious to have the house up and enclosed before the weather got bad. When he could find no one to do the work he hobbled down into the trench and began digging himself. For a time he was unconscious of our presence and digged away as if his life depended on his digging. I don't know how he could dig under the circumstances, but he did. There were many noble men and women in that church at that time, but most of them have crossed the flood.

SPENCER CREEK CHURCH.

By Mrs. J. J. Laylin.

On April 28, 1878, the following named brethren and sisters presenting letters of dismission from sister churches, organized themselves into a regular Baptist Church at Fowler's schoolhouse, in Ralls county: John S. Clark, Thomas H. Self and Sarah A. Self, Eleven Hitch, Pauline Hitch, John C. Hitch and Hester F. Hitch, Jennie Hitch, Mary Ferguson, Joseph L. Higbee, James A. Brown and Susan A. Brown, twelve in number. Elder E. Jennings, missionary of Salt River Association, acted as moderator. A committee was appointed to select a name for the church, resulting in the name Spencer Creek Baptist Church.

Brother E. Jennings supplied the church with preaching until October, 1878. At this date Brother M. S. Whiteside was called as their first regular Pastor. Rev. S. G. Givens was called as Pastor and re-

ELDER S. G. GIVENS.

E. T. SMITH, ESQ.

DEACON EZRA CARSTARPHEN.

DEACON C. G. DANIEL.

mained in that capacity until January, 1882, after which Rev. A. P. Rodgers was called and held that position one year.

The house of worship was built in the summer of 1881. The building was a substantial frame twenty-four by thirty-six feet. The cost of the building was about $800. This building was found to be sufficient for a few years, but as the church prospered and the congregations grew the church was compelled to enlarge on the original building, which was done in 1890. During this interval the church had several Pastors. Rev. S. G. Givens was called again to fill the pastorate, and remained in that capacity until August, 1884. At this time Rev. James Reid became Pastor and remained until April, 1886. We called Rev. Bland Beauchamp, who retained this position until December, 1887. During his pastorate the church experienced a grand revival and ingathering, which is only one of many such revivals during the period covered by this history. The next Pastor called to the church was Rev. J. W. Neff; and in March, 1889, Rev. S. T. Hudson became Pastor and remained in that capacity until January 24, 1891. In February, 1891, Rev. W. S. Tucker was called and served in that capacity until his death in 1893. In January following the church called Rev. W. W. Brown. In March, 1895, Rev. C. A. Mitchell was secured as Pastor. February, 1896, Rev. F. M. Shoush was called and remained as Pastor until March, 1900. In November, 1900, Rev. A. M. Vardeman accepted the call of the church as their Pastor and remained in that capacity until his death October 24, 1901. The church called Rev. E. L. Rogers, January, 1902, who served as Pastor for two years, after which in March, Rev. Luke Kirtley was called. He remained until November, 1907.

During this period the church has had many changes as to Deacons and clerks. In August, 1878, J. L. Higbee and John C. Hitch were elected the first Deacons of the church; Deacon Hitch filled the office until his death, January 7, 1880. J. S. Clark was elected Deacon in 1880. G. A. Lake was elected Deacon in 1881 and A. F. Manzke and Luke Kirtley were elected in 1887, and on the fifth Sunday in May the last three named brethren were ordained to the office of Deacon and Thomas J. Kendrick was ordained to the ministry. Again in 1894 S. K. Caldwell and J. B. Clark were ordained to the office of Deacon. In May, 1896, G. C. Cole and K. A. Cobbs were ordained Deacons, the former still filling that office. During this period there came to the church two Deacons from sister churches, Deacon D. D. Ellis in August, 1899, and Deacon H. L. Elzea in January, 1900; both were received as active Deacons. Deacon Elzea is still occupying that position.

The first clerk was James A. Brown, being elected in May, 1878. J. W. Maupin and J. V. McGrew each served as clerk. Also J. B. Clark and O. W. Lake. K. A. Cobbs served two years, then Henry Lake was elected. At this date the present clerk was elected, J. J. Laylin.

ELDER WILLIAM ALBERT BIBB.

By Himself.

Bedford county, Virginia, near Lynchburg, was my birthplace. My parents, Benjamin and Mary Bibb, brought me to Pike county, Missouri, in infancy. I was reared upon a farm and was blessed with a common school education. I attended the high school at Clarksville one year; was five months in the Paynesville Academy, also was two years in the LaGrange College. I was converted at the age of fifteen years and joined the Ramsey Creek Baptist Church, was baptized by Uncle A. G. Mitchell. At the age of twenty I felt the call of God to the ministry of the gospel, but did not yield for some time, but when I fully realized the only way to happiness was obedient to God's call, I entered college, spent what means I had in preparing for the life's work. In the year 1882 four churches called me to serve them as Pastor, and

Ramsey Creek Church called a Presbytery and ordained me, in company with C. A. Mitchell, to the full work of the ministry. From 1882 to date I have never had an idle Sunday. I have served as Pastor twenty-eight churches, labored eighteen months as missionary for Salt River Association, have baptized 3,287 men and women and witnessed many other conversions in Christ; also organized the church at Center, Ralls county, and Peno at McCune Station. I have married 298 couples, preached many funerals. Am now pastor of New Salem Church for half time; also Mt. Zion once a month.

Married Miss Mary A. Givens when quite a young man. It was a happy union; to us were born six children—one boy and five girls. Great afflictions came to us in the loss of a sweet little girl. The afflictions and death of this sweet spirited wife, who had been my greatest earthly help, was a severe trial. The deep sorrow had hardly passed until the only boy, then a man, was suddenly cut down in death. Grief-stricken and lonely, I looked up to heaven and said, "Though thou slay me, yet will I trust Thee." I married my present wife, who was Miss Margaret I. Lindsey, in January, 1898. One little daughter has been given us and the home is happy.

I was in Audrain county six years. Have held meetings in Illinois and Kansas. It has been my greatest joy to labor in the work of soul saving and God has greatly blessed these labors in this work. In the early part of my ministry I purchased a good library and this is my workshop. Wise and good brethren have helped me much. J. D. Biggs, James Reid, W. J. Patrick and Wm. Tipton all contributed by way of needed counsel. I have sought a loving relation with my brethren; I love men, and thus love God and the lost of this world.

I was made moderator of Salt River Association in the year 1907 and am moderator at this writing. My highest ambition is not for fame nor riches, but to glorify God and help others to God, realizing the days for soul-winning with every man are numbered and few; also the inevitable result to those who are not won to God, stirs my heart much every day, and as the evening-tide begins to come and the shadows fall lower, how I wish for this old world that they come and go to the land of the blessed.

ELDER WILLIAM HENRY BIBB.

By his son, Charles A. Bibb.

My father was a native Virginian, born May 18, 1810. He entered the ministry when past middle age and was ordained at Timber Creek Baptist Church, Marshall county, Iowa, in March, 1859. In Iowa he organized three churches and did other regular work of the ministry. After coming to Missouri he organized three churches in Salt River Association. He relied largely on his income in business for a support for his family. He engaged in farming and merchandising. Late in life he removed to Southwest Missouri, where he organized a church in Vernon county and two churches in Lawrence county.

He was an influential Christian worker, loved most by those who knew him best. His death occurred February 15, 1891.

ELDER C. A. MITCHELL.

By Himself.

Charles Albert Mitchell, now residing in Mexico, Mo., was born on a farm in Lincoln county, January 18, 1854. He is a son of the sainted Rev. Albert Gregory Mitchell, who spent about thirty-five years of his life in Salt River Association as Pastor of churches, preaching for one church thirty-three years.

C. A. Mitchell was of a family of nineteen children, being the sixteenth child. At the age of sixteen my father moved to Paynesville, Pike county, where I was given the advantages of the school then known as the Paynesville Academy. At the age of twenty-two I married Miss Nancy J. Ferguson, a daughter of

David and Leanna Ferguson. To this union were born three children. My wife died December 23, 1889. November, 1890, I married Miss Annie B. Dixon, daughter of J. J. Dixon, of Montgomery City, Mo. To this union were born two children, one of whom is living.

I was converted in a meeting held with Ramsey Creek Church in 1877, conducted by my father, Pastor of the church, assisted by Rev. J. J. Hickman, of St. Louis. I was chosen superintendent of the Sunday school in the spring of 1878 and served two years. Having moved some distance from the church I gave up the Sunday school superintendency and organized a neighborhood prayer meeting, which by the aid and encouragement of others had a great deal to do in developing the gifts of him whose heart was throbbing with a desire, yet with a fearful trembling, to undertake such a responsible duty as preaching the gospel. In August, 1880, the church at Ramsey Creek having seriously considered the matter licensed me to preach. Having farmed for the few years past I sold my possessions and spent a half term in school at Paynesville. In January, 1881, I moved to LaGrange. Mo., and spent two years in LaGrange College under the venerable Dr. J. F. Cook. In April, 1882, the church at Ramsey Creek called for my ordination and on the 30th of the month I with my fellow companion, Rev. W. A. Bibb, who had been licensed two years before and who had spent the same time at LaGrange College, was set apart to the full work of the gospel ministry. The council consisted of the Pastor of the church and Rev. Wm. Tipton and the Deacons of Ramsey Creek and Clarksville Churches. The ordaining sermon was preached by Rev. Tipton. I had been called to the Ebenezer Church in Lincoln county, and I readily accepted the call and began the pastorate of the church the following month. In the fall of the same year I accepted work offered by Star Hope, New Hope and Highland churches, all in Lincoln county. I located at New Hope, near the field. In the spring of 1884, as the new towns were springing up along the Burlington railroad, I preached at Winfield and organized a church, assisted by Rev. F. M. Birkhead, and later organized a church at Foley, assisted by Rev. M. T. Whiteside. I was chosen Pastor of the new church at Winfield and preached for her five years and a half.

In September, 1889, I received a call to work in Callaway county, and located in Auxvasse. I was instrumental in building a neat church house at New Hope, which took the place of the one built through my father's influence during his early ministry at the same place. I held revival meetings with the following churches, then in Salt River Association, apart from those of which I was at that time pastor: Ebenezer, Oak Ridge, Elsberry, Winfield, New Salem, Harmony Grove, Mill Creek, Prairieville, Edgewood, Grassy Creek, Sugar Creek and Mount Pisgah. In some of these meetings the power of God was manifest and we had gracious revivals. The first meeting I held after my ordination in February, 1883, was at Star Hope, in which God seemed to pour out His spirit in abundance. Disappointed in the help promised to assist in the meeting, the meeting continued three weeks and as a result the ordinance of baptism was administered to thirty-seven professed believers, among whom was six from the Stirmlinger family, who were devout Catholics, the father, mother, two daughters, two sons, one of whom, Rev. Joseph Stirmlinger, is Pastor of Oakwood.

The mission interest then was not so well worked as to-day, but the churches to which I preached stood closely identified with each department of the work. In 1899 I became identified with Salt River Association, again having accepted a hearty call extended to me by the Curryville Church.

JOHN J. SMITH.

John Johnson Smith, one of the oldest and most highly respected citizens of Pike county, died at the home of his son, Joe H. Smith, on Grassy Creek, Wednesday morning at six o'clock, December 31, 1907, aged ninety-five years, two months and three days.

John J. Smith was born in Bath county, Kentucky, in 1812, and came to Missouri with his parents, Joe Ab and Nancy Smith, in 1817, and stopped near St. Charles. In 1818 they came on up the river and settled near Salt River in what is now Pike county. In 1817 he married Martha W. Yeater and bought the farm on which his son, Joe, now lives. Soon after his marriage he built the house which still stands on the farm.

Mr. Smith came to Pike county before Missouri was a State and lived to see it the fifth State in the Union in population. He was one of the early pioneers who helped to change the wilderness into cultivated farms.

Uncle Jack, as he was called by his many friends, was an upright, Christian gentleman and brought up his children in the way they should go. He had been a member of the Baptist Church for more than seventy years and was a constituent member of Grassy Creek Baptist Church.

The funeral was conducted at the Grassy Creek Baptist Church Thursday at two p. m. by Rev. W. A. Bibb, of this city.

We do not believe there is a man living in the county to-day who was here when Mr. Smith came to the county. He had lived a long and useful life and has now gone to his long home.—*Louisiana Times.*

THE ASCENT OF GRASSY CREEK.

By Dr. G. W. Hyde, Lexington.

Sometime in the early eighties it fell to my lot as assistant secretary of Rev. Dr. W. Pope Yeaman, corresponding secretary of the General Association, to make a canvass of Salt River Association in behalf of the State Mission Board. I put myself under the command of Rev. Wiley J. Patrick to make my appointments, and to give general direction to my labors while in the bounds of Salt River Association. The weather was intensely hot at the time. But it was arranged for me to preach twice daily on week days and three times on Sunday for a change. To accomplish this work I usually had to travel from fifteen to thirty miles a day. We invariably traveled in a buggy. And as I remember it this campaign lasted about two and a half or three weeks.

Among the churches designated for a visit was Grassy Creek Church, located near the waters of that classic stream, thence we were to go over the highlands to Walnut Grove Church on the waters of Noix Creek. A very heavy rain had just fallen and removed several small bridges on our road. But to the indomitable Patrick, who accompanied me on this trip, that was a very small matter. On several occasions we had to unhitch our horses and then let the buggy down the banks of the branches or creeks as best we could; and then hitch up again. This was done a time or two before we reached Grassy Creek. But upon reaching Grassy Creek itself I found that our road for many miles went right along the bed of Grassy Creek. That is to say, the bed of Grassy Creek and the road was one and the same thing. Sometimes for short distances the traveling would be moderately fair, but then again our buggy would encounter rocks from the size of a man's head upward. In fact several times immense boulders would lie right in our pathway, and could not be avoided, having been dislodged from their resting places and washed down the creek bed by the strong currents of water. Several times did we have to unhitch our horses and lift our buggy over or around these immense rocks. In my time I had seen many roads, but this road for roughness and peril exceeded anything I had ever seen. Frequently I thought, "Well, our buggy surely will be smashed to pieces, or the horses or ourselves killed." But strange to say, and thanks to a kind Providence, we actually ascended Grassy Creek for many miles and finally reached Walnut Grove on Noix Creek, with our buggy intact and our horses and ourselves alive and unharmed!

Recounting this experience leads me to make a remark or two: I remember the Master said, "One soweth and another reapeth . . . other men labored, and ye are entered into their labors."

Our secretaries complain now that the churches don't sympathize with the great missionary movements of the times, and that they don't contribute to the cause of the Lord. And this is too true to-day. But there is much more unity and harmony, and the spirit of cooperation is much stronger now than it was twenty-five or thirty years ago.

Some of the largest and strongest district Associations in the State in annual session would then vigorously and solemnly protest against any of their churches making any sort of contribution to State missions. As agent I was opposed and rejected several times by district Associations, and not allowed to make any plea for the cause I represented. Evil disposed men had sown the seeds of discord, and the minds of the brethren for the time were beclouded and poisoned against the truth.

And withal in presenting the missionary cause to our churches and Associations we had to be "wise as serpents and harmless as doves." We tried to speak the "truth in love," and so to present the matter that we would be welcome if we ever made a future visit.

The secretaries of our boards have a hard time now, but the agents and secretaries of our boards had a much harder and rougher experience twenty-five or thirty years ago. The secretaries now ride in Pullman palace cars. I don't criticise them for this. Perhaps they ought to do this in order to save unnecessary wear and tear. But in my many years of agency work I never knew the luxury of riding or sleeping in a Pullman car. I tried to avoid this expense, and often paid personally dearly for it. After a tiresome day's work I have often ridden all night long in a crowded, common passenger car, and then had to preach the next day, though tired and weary, dusty and sleepy. Now our agents or secretaries go to the hotel, where their expenses are paid, or have a bed in a private home. But a generation ago a bed for a traveling secretary was almost an unknown thing during the sessions of the District Associations, which lasted for about three months during the summer and fall. We then slept on the floors of houses, often twenty or thirty in a room, or in lofts, or wherever we could.

This generation, I am sure, will never understand the trials and heartaches of the men who in the later sixties and seventies tried to do the work of the Lord in Missouri. Sometimes the Board of Trustees of Wm. Jewell College or the State Mission Board would sit up the larger part of the night, praying and planning, and sometimes weeping in order to know how best to carry on the work of the Lord. Happily those trying times have passed, and a better and brighter day has dawned upon Zion. But let us not forget to appreciate the sacrifices and labors of those who have gone before.

RECOLLECTIONS OF SALT RIVER ASSOCIATION.

By Elder W. M. Tipton.

I was in Louisiana two years and then with country churches twenty years, minus three years in western Missouri. I was five and one-half years at New Salem, Sugar Creek five years, Edgewood fourteen and one-half years in all, Clarksville five years, Elm Grove and Salem six years, Cyrene, Corner Stone, Mill Creek, Frankford and Mt. Zion. During my pastorates at Cyrene, Salem and Mt. Zion, new houses were built. I raised nearly all the money for these three houses.

CHAPTER X.

HELPING THE WEAK, 1885—1892.

September 9, 1885, we met with Edgewood church. Elder S. G. Givens preached the opening sermon. His text was: "He that hath an ear, let him hear what the Spirit saith unto the churches." The following brethren accepted seats: W. H. Burnham, W. H. Williams, D. B. Ray, T. N. Sanderson, William Lake, J. B. Moore, M. S. Whiteside, M. E. Motley, A. G. Mitchell, Ernest Cook, F. H. Lewis, William E. Smith, J. Fortune, Emma Fortune, G. W. Hyde, J. Reid, W. H. Vardeman. The moderator appointed A. P. Miller, W. J. Patrick and B. Beauchamp, committee on the home mission work of the Southern Baptist Convention, represented by Elder G. W. Hyde. The report was favorable to the work. The board reported that E. Jennings had been employed as missionary. And the colportage work had been taken up and put into the hands of J. N. B. Hepler. They appeal for money "to enable the board to employ a preacher for his whole time—one who, Paul-like, will seek the destitution of Salt River and break to them the bread of life." The committee on obituaries reported the name of Brother G. C. Jeffries, a good and useful Christian. The board was continued as before, except that W. J. Patrick succeeded C. A. Mitchell. The committee on foreign missions, W. J. Patrick, J. B. Vardeman and P. P. Waddell, said, "Our missionaries are of a high type of Christian character and they are laboring in wisdom and faithfulness." The committee on correspondence, T. J. McDannold, A. G. Gordon and J. A. Freeman, said, "Some of our churches report through messengers and letters, that God has graciously blessed them in His work, and has given them many precious souls who have realized the power of the Spirit in converting the soul."

September 8, 1886, we met with Ebenezer church. The clerk, W. B. McPike, being absent, George C. Wise was chosen clerk *pro tem.* Elder Bland Beauchamp preached the sermon. His text was: "Blessed are the pure in heart; for they shall see God." Reorganization was effected by the election of James D. Biggs as moderator and Geo. C. Wise as clerk. Two new churches, Union Hill, of Lincoln county, and Pleasant Hill, of St. Charles county, were received into associational membership. The messengers of Pleasant Hill were W. H. Vardeman and D. H. Richards; those of Union Hill were R. G. Hopkins, D. P. Lockheart, S. E. Page and B. G. Gammon. The visiting brethren were: J. M. Hunt, G. L. Black, G. W. Hyde, A. G. Mitchell, R. E. McQuie, Jas. Williams, Jeff. Williams, B. F. Hixson, I. N. Clark, J. D. Hacker, J. Hickman, J. E. Cook, H. T. Morton. Collections to the amount of $331 were taken during the session. The executive board had the services of S. G. Givens, F. M. Birkhead, W. H. Williams, E. Jennings, C. A. Mitchell and W. M. Tipton. The board said: "We have also had in the field laboring for a per cent., two special colporteurs, P. W. Halley and B. R. Patrick, the former in the south half and the latter in the north half of the Association." Each one visited all the churches assigned him. B. R. Patrick said: "I and the work have been kindly received. I must express my gratification at the co-operation of all the Pastors." The report on Sunday Schools, made by W. J. Patrick, S. P. Dawson and L. C. Bibb, says, "We need, 1. Every Pastor to thoroughly prepare the lesson and be always in the Sunday School; 2. Godly teachers who prepare the lesson and regularly meet their classes; 3. To keep strictly before us, that the purpose of the Sunday School is the salvation of souls; 4. Baptist literature in every school; 5. Regular attendance of every member of the Sunday School on the preaching and as many of the church members as possible in the school; 6. Libraries consisting of at least maps, Bible dictionaries and the best commentaries; 7. To look after the illiterate and friendless." The new board were A. J. McCune, J. D. Biggs, W. J. Patrick, J. W. Riggs, T. J. McDannold, H. T. Unsell, J. C. McGrew, D. T. Killam, J. W. McIlroy, J. L. Dawson. The committee on the state of the churches, W. A. Bibb and J. M. Terrell, said: "We learn from the reports of the many churches of our Association that during the past year, the Lord has greatly manifested His power in our midst in the outpouring of His Holy Spirit in many of our churches." R. T. Ellis, Edgar McDannold and C. A. Mitchell made the report on obituaries. They said: "Brethren A. P. Miller, of Mt. Pisgah church, Samuel Guttery, of New London, David McIlroy, Louisiana, J. B. Vardeman, Bethel, William Culbertson, Bethel, have been called to their reward. While we mourn their loss and miss their presence, let us remember that our loss is their gain." The ministers at this time were Bland Beauchamp, W. A. Bibb, J. D. Biggs, F. M. Birkhead, Dr. Cole, S. P. Dawson, S. G. Givens, J. B. Hawkins, E. Jennings, J. F. Kemper, C. A. Mitchell, H. T. Morton, T. J. Musgrove, W. J. Patrick, A. P. Rogers, E. J. Sanderson, W. M. Tipton and W. H. Vardeman.

Curryville church was our place of meeting, August 31, 1887. Elder W. A. Bibb preached the annual sermon. His text was: "Behold the man." The visiting brethren were W. H. Williams, G. W. Hyde, Ernest Cook, J. J. Griffin, Jas. McQuie, J. T. Smith, L. B. Ely, I. N. Clark, D. B. Ray. A letter from Elder H. M. King, of St. Augusta, Florida, formerly a member of this body, was read by W. J. Patrick. He asked for money to help build a church in this old city and $37.05 was sent him. The board had the services of W. J. Patrick, P. W. Halley, J. F. Kemper, E. Jennings, J. D. Hacker and E. J. Sanderson as missionaries, and of Harvey Beauchamp, W. A. Bibb and E. J. Sanderson as colporteurs. The work was blessed of the Lord of the harvest. Cyrene church, of Pike county, was received into fellowship. The messengers were J. T. Lindsay and J. E. Bailey. The meeting time for the Association continued to be agitated. In view of that, a motion was carried to raise a committee of one from each county to report on the question. G. S. Lake of Ralls, G. R. Waddell of Pike, B. M. Vance of Lincoln, and D. H. Richards of St. Charles, were made that committee. They said, "Your committee beg leave to report, in our judgment, Tuesday before the first Sunday in September as the most favorable time for such meeting." $1,000 was raised to be used in paying for McCune College. The new executive board were J. D. Biggs, T. J. Ayres, J. W. Riggs, A. J. McCune, T. J. McDannold, H. T. Unsell, J. C. McGrew, D. T. Killam, J. L. Dawson, J. W. McIlroy. To the list of ministers, J. D. Hacker and T. J. Kendrick had been added. And a list of men licensed to preach is given. They are E. W. Dow, P. W. Halley, B. R. Patrick, W. S. Tucker, J. L. Downing and S. A. Douglass.

August 28, 1888, the Association convened with Bowling Green Church. The introductory sermon was preached by Elder J. D. Hacker from the Scripture: "They that gladly received His word were baptized." The Association re-organized by electing James Reid moderator, J. D. Biggs having put him in nomination, and by electing Geo. C. Wise clerk. Two new churches were received into fellowship, St. Charles of St. Charles county, and Bethany of Pike county. The messengers from St. Charles were James Reid, Sister Bettie A. Reid and G. W. Jones; those from Bethany were J. D. Biggs, J. E. Shannon, J. C. Stewart and A. Beckner. The visitors were A. M. Vardeman, J. W. Neff, J. L. Applegate, J. F. Smith, A. G. Mitchell, G. W. Hyde, D. B. Ray, W. H. Williams, T. N. Sanderson, S. M. Brown, W. L. Boyer, W. R. Manly, M. V. Shives, Mrs. Dr. Thomas, Mrs. Browning, S. H. Ford, J. J. Griffin and R. E. McQuie. James Reid raised $400 for the purchase of a house of worship in the city of St. Charles. For the first time the Association elected a messenger to the Southern Baptist Convention. W. J. Patrick was chosen to go.

The executive board reported and it said that the Association had undertaken, perhaps, the greatest work in her history. The board had kept up the regular missionary services by employing C. A. Mitchell, S. T. Hudson, E. J. Sanderson, H. T. Morton, E. Jennings and M. S. Whiteside, who had done good service in their respective fields. And M. S. Whiteside had done colporteur work. W. J. Patrick had held a Sunday School Institute in each county which paid their own expenses with a balance. The supreme effort had been at St. Charles. Here was a city over one hundred years old without a Baptist church. The set time seemed to have come for the crowning day of church advancement. The board of the General Association and the board of Salt River Association jointly employed Brother James Reid to enter the field at a salary of $1,000, each board to pay half. At this session the board made the first report of this work. They say: "J. Reid has labored at St. Charles seven months, preached eighty-three sermons, baptized two, conducted sixteen prayer meetings, ten Bible readings, organized one church and one Sunday School, and collected towards paying for the church property $903.55, missionary fund $8.50. He bought property, the prime cost of which was $2,000, which property could be disposed of at a handsome advance." The records of Salt River Association say again and again that they are giving the gospel to the weak and destitute and now they are making their word doubly good. I must here insert the dying words of Thomas J. McDannold. He had looked into the field, his heart was moved, his hand was helping and among his last words were these: "Don't give up St. Charles."

We met with New Salem church August 27, 1889, when the introductory sermon was preached by Elder W. M. Tipton, from the text: "But God, who is rich in mercy." Two new churches were received. Whiteside and Foley, both of Lincoln county. The messengers from Foley were W. N. Crenshaw, C. S. Alloway, John Tiller and A. M. Binnin; those from

Whiteside were E. Magruder, W. M. Magruder, J. R. Gibson and J. W. Luck. The following brethren accepted seats in the body: G. W. Hyde, W. H. Stone, A. G. Mitchell, John E. Mosely, F. M. Ray, J. W. Swift, Claud Kelly, J. J. Griffin, J. T. Williams. Elder J. D. Biggs was elected to go to the Southern Baptist Convention. The executive board reported: "We have assisted one church and kept two missionaries in the field. Bro. M. S. Whiteside has labored in the employ of the board 280 days at $25 per month, organized one church at Foley with forty members, assisted in the organization of a church at Whiteside, organized a Sunday School at Highland. Reports twelve additions at Pleasant Hill, St. Charles county. He has sold about $90 worth of books and has made some benevolent distributions. We helped Winfield church the first four months, at the end of which time they reported seven baptisms and say: 'Brethren, as we believe, there are others who need and deserve your help, we do not ask you to aid us any longer.' Bro. J. Reid has been in the employ of the board for the entire year in St. Charles, city and county, at $500 per year. He has preached one hundred and four sermons, held thirty-one prayer meetings, received by letter five, by baptism seven, ordained one to the gospel ministry, to-wit: Bro. A. Konzelmann, who is known to many of you. They had the misfortune to have their house damaged by fire, which caused an expenditure of near $600, so that there is now due on the house near $350. He held Sunday School institutes under the direction of the board in Pike and Lincoln counties, which more than paid expenses." A contribution was made towards the payment of this house debt of $476.60. Elder J. W. Swift presented the claims of the St. Louis Baptist Sanitarium and raised $50. The committee on State Missions, W. J. Patrick, J. E. Shannon and F. D. Hardesty, said: "The past year has been one of wise planning and faithful prosecution. There is a call for the cup of cold water and the great possessions. Let the widow give her mite and the rest give their mightiest." The committee on Sunday Schools, E. J. Sanderson, A. Konzelmann and J. C. McGrew, said, "Since there are twelve or fifteen hundred children under the direct influence of our Sunday Schools, we would recommend that the churches under whose watchcare those Sunday Schools are would assume a relation similar to that of the mother to her child." J. C. Mackey succeeded T. J. McDannold on the executive board. A. Konzelmann was added to the list of ministers.

The committee on obituaries reported as follows: "Deacon Thomas J. McDannold died April 4, 1889, aged fifty years and twenty-eight days. His life was spent in the community of Ramsey Creek church. In early life he was baptized into the fellowship of the church, and for several years was one of the Deacons. At the time of his death he was on the committee to write the history of the first seventy-five years of the church. For many years he superintended the Sunday School. Brother McDannold was president of the executive board of Salt River Association. He was a man, a gentleman, a Christian gentleman.

"Duncan Ellis has finished an eventful life that was prolonged to an honored age. His useful career began in Kentucky, where he received the riches of earth and the riches of grace. In Missouri he was the leading spirit in building up Mill Creek church, which was built on ground given by him. He helped to establish William Jewell College. In age he honored God and God crowned his life with a radiant end.

"Horatio Nelson Baskett was a Christian patriarch. A history of his life would be a history of the Baptist cause in his community. He was wise in counsel, firm in purpose, just in decisions and faithful to the end of his long journey. For a great number of years he served New Hope church both as Deacon and clerk. He served his county in a judicial capacity. His extensive information and his ability with the pen made him a useful contributor to church history.

"Ira T. Nelson was the most aged of our comrades who have fallen during the past year. Born and reared in Virginia, he brought to his Missouri home business habits and social culture, which made him a leading citizen. He loved to talk of the good things in the Bible. He was a friend to his Pastor.

"Dennis Magruder died at home, March 3, 1889, aged forty-eight years, one month and four days. As a church member Brother Magruder was ready to do his duty whether in things great or things small. He served the church as treasurer and Sunday School superintendent. He took a leading and commendable interest in establishing a cemetery at Mill Creek and in laying it out and maintaining it in order.

"Henry L. Luck died February 24, 1889. In Christian fervor, zeal, steadfastness and soundness in the faith, Brother Luck was blessed in a high degree. His bouyancy and cheerfulness made it a joy to meet him. He was for a while superintendent of Mill Creek Sunday School. Brother Luck left a fragrant memory.

"Edward T. Smith died in Bowling Green, Mo., December 22, 1888, aged forty-six years, eight months and twenty-six days. Brother Smith was a man of high spirit, a firm believer in Christ, and he was constant in his religious duties. His mind was strongly of a literary cast, he had a genius for the law. As a lawyer he stood with the head of the profession in his judicial district and his mind was bent towards yet higher attainments. He was a Confederate soldier. He was State's attorney. I visited him on his deathbed. He said to me, 'I pray that God may bless your labors wherever you preach.' A leading judge, speaking of him to me, said, 'His integrity was unquestioned in all his business in court.'

"Elder James F. Smith, at the time of his death, was not a member of Salt River Association, but he was for so many years identified with this body that it seems proper to record his name with our honored dead. He stood high on Zion's wall. His eagle eye was one of the first to descry the enemy. A blast from his trumpet often awakened the army of Israel to battle and sent dismay to the army of the aliens. Loving hands laid his body to rest at Richland church, Callaway county, Missouri.

"John Davis Biggs, for many years deacon of Salem church and superintendent of the Sunday school, died in Ralls county, surrounded by all of his living children and many of his grandchildren, and his body was laid away in the old churchyard. He was a man of intense energy, imperious will and determined purpose. He loved his church and gave largely to her support. He befriended the poor. At one time he was a justice of the court of Ralls county, at another he was a member of the Missouri House of Representatives. He belonged to a family of whom, in direct line of generation, were four moderators of Salt River Association. They were Davis, William, John Davis and James Duvall Biggs.

"James Briscoe lived and died a member of Bethel church. For fifteen years he was a sufferer and at times a helpless sufferer. His faith was strong and his death triumphant.

"William G. Hawkins was one of nature's noblemen. He was a Kentuckian by birth and impress, and a Missourian by adoption and long citizenship. In early life he gave his heart to the Saviour and united with the church. He was first a member of Peno church. He succeeded his father as clerk of Mount Pisgah church, of which he had become a member. He also served this church as Deacon. In the sessions of the Association his influence was great and salutary. When a member of the Twenty-seventh General Assembly he served on the committee on Retrenchment and Reform. He was held in high honor."

The Association held her session of 1890 with Grassy Creek church, beginning September the second. The annual sermon was preached by W. J. Patrick, from the text: "Whereof I am made a minister, according to the dispensation of God which is given to me for you, to fulfill the word of God; even the mystery which hath been hid from ages and from generations, but now is made manifest to His saints; to whom God would make known what is the riches of the glory of this mystery among the Gentiles; which is Christ in you the hope of glory." Re-organization was effected by the election of J. Reid moderator and R. N. Gilbert clerk. Center church, Ralls county, was received into fellowship. Dr. J. B. Hawkins was the messenger. The visitors were W. B. Fuqua, J. F. Cook, J. J. Griffin, J. E. Chambliss, D. B. Ray, F. M. Ray, S. F. Taylor, T. M. S. Kenney, S. M. Brown, W. T. Campbell, W. L. Boyer, J. T. Daniel. The executive board reported that they had had the services of E. W. Dow, S. S. Keith, Joseph Stirmlinger and James Reid as missionaries and of R. D. Robertson as colporteur. "Each of them reports favorably of the work." The house at St. Charles had been paid for and six had been brought to Christ. The committee on State Missions, W. P. Throgmorton, J. V. Moxley and J. W. Tredway, said, "As an Association, we are under special obligation to contribute largely to the work of our State board. It has contributed to work in our bounds for some years past." The committee on Sunday Schools, S. G. Givens and Isaac Cannon, said, "During the past year four Sunday School institutes have been held in the Association by Brethren W. L. Boyer and W. A. Bibb. We need: First, a Baptist school in every Baptist church and every member in the school; second, Baptist literature in every school." The committee on the sanitarium, W. J. Patrick and W. E. Wiatt, said: "Your committee would report that the St. Louis Baptist Sanitarium should be incorporated into our permanent work. Dr. W. H. Mayfield commands the confidence and assistance of leading physicians in the city. We commend the sanitarium to the prayers and bounties of those who love our Lord Jesus Christ in sincerity." The committee on state of the churches, W. N. Maupin, A. Hall and R. N. Gilbert, say, "We note with gratitude to God some seven or eight special revivals in our bounds and most of our churches report a fair state of prosperity." The committee on woman's missionary societies, E. Jennings, I. Whiteside and E. J. Sanderson, said, "We have a list of nine societies actively engaged, these represents nine churches, and we would recommend that the sisters in all the churches organize for effective missionary work." The committee on obituaries, F. M. Birkhead and J. E. Shannon, reported the death of Sister Jane Caldwell. The new executive board were T. J. Ayres, W. J. Page, J. W. McIlroy, J. C. Stewart, T. J. Smith, J. W. Riggs, D. T. Killam, W. A. Bibb, J. T. Hutcherson, J. C. Mackey. The resident ministers were W. A. Bibb, J. D. Biggs, F. M. Birkhead, Dr. Cole, S. P. Dawson, S. G. Givens, P. W. Halley, J. B. Hawkins, E. Jennings, T. J. Kendrick, W. N. Maupin, T. J. Musgrove, W. J. Patrick, J. Reid, A. P. Rodgers, E. J. Sanderson, T. N. Sanderson, W. P. Throgmorton, W. S. Tucker, W. H. Vardeman and M. S. Whiteside.

Clarksville was the meeting place and September the first the time in 1891. The sermon was preached by W. P. Throgmorton from the Scripture: "Watch ye, stand fast in the faith, quit you like men, be strong." Farmer church was received into the Association; the messengers were A. P. Rodgers, E. W. Hepler. The visiting brethren were R. Harrison, R. S. Duncan, M. V. Shives, W. H. Williams, A. C. Rafferty, G. W. Hyde, W. H. Burnham, J. Stirmlinger, B. G. Tutt, W. O. Shannon, S. S. Keith and F. C. Tate. The executive board reported that they had in the course of the year the services of E. Jennings, C. W. Davis, A. P. Rodgers, W. A. Bibb, R. D. Robertson, J. Reid, F. M. Birkhead, B. R. Patrick and S. F. Thompson. Brother Robertson did also colporteur work. It had been a year of abundant labors and general advancement. For the purpose of organizing a new Association, Oak Ridge, Whiteside, Harmony Grove, Silex (Union Hill), New Hope, New Salem, Ebenezer, Pleasant Hill, Corner Stone and Winfield asked for letters of dismission. The request was granted and the parting hand given them. The report on missions, made by W. J. Patrick, recommended that the centennial of the Cary mission movement be made the occasion for advance work. This was done. Geo. S. Lake and W. J. Seaman were put on the executive board to fill vacancies caused by some brethren having gone into the new Association. The committee on Sunday Schools, A. P. Rodgers, P. W. Halley and Pike Lindsey, said: "Each local church has a home field to cultivate." The committee on obituaries, W. A. Bibb and T. R. Mitchell, reported: "Bro. B. M. Vance, of Star Hope, has passed away. Sister Elizabeth Mackey, of Ramsey Creek, has been taken home. Brethren Clark Owen and Thomas Clark, of Salem, have gone to their reward." The following was adopted: "Elder John Thomas Williams is at rest; he was for many years a laborer in this vineyard as Pastor, College president, instructor and moderator of our Association. We honor his memory."

CENTER CHURCH.

By C. W. Jenks.

The Center Baptist church was organized December 3, 1889, after a series of meetings, in which nine professed their faith in Jesus Christ. The council met in the Methodist church in Center. The ministers were Bros. S. S. Keith, J. D. Biggs and W. A. Bibb, of Bowling Green, and J. W. Neff, of Vandalia. Bro. J. C. McGrew was moderator and M. C. Biggs clerk of council.

They were organized with twenty-four members as follows: Sisters Maggie Rice, Melly Frazer, Susan Rice, Missouri Pimbly, Fannie Hawkins, Lizzie Frazer, Mary Lucas, Ann Rice, Laura Nutgrass, Polly A. Shultz, Flora Hendrix, Anna Shultz, Susan Smith, Rachel Ellis and Bros. John Rice, John P. Briscoe, A. J. Rice, J. B. Hawkins, Isaac Rice, Daniel Nutgrass, Wm. Shultz, Peter Shultz, John Hendrix, C. W. Jenks. In the afternoon of the same day, the first business meeting was held and nine were received for baptism and membership, Geo. E. Frazer, Geo. P. Rice, Moses Frazer, Charley Martin, Ursa Hawkins, Mollie Jenks, Nettie Morley, Ruth Schultz, Gertie Hawkins, and Mrs. Hesket by relation.

At the next business meeting three Deacons were elected as follows: John Rice, Geo. P. Rice and Geo. E. Frazer. John P. Briscoe was church clerk. Rev. W. A. Bibb was the first Pastor, resigning after six months, and Rev. J. D. Biggs was Pastor the next six months.

In 1890 a meeting-house was erected at a cost of $2,000, placing a debt of $900 on the church. Rev. W. S. Tucker was Pastor for the year 1891. Rev. W. A. Bibb was the next Pastor, serving from June, 1892, to April, 1893. The next Pastor, Rev. S. F. Thompson, served one year. During 1894 the church house was paid for and dedicated the 5th Sunday in September. Rev. E. B. Dillard was Pastor during 1895. Rev. W. J. Patrick in 1896 was Pastor. In 1897, Rev. J. A. Riney became Pastor. In December, 1897, the church building was damaged by a fire so that it was thought best to build again, and in 1898, the present home of the Center Baptist church was built and dedicated, free of debt, October 2, 1898. The next Pastor, H. B. Rice, served four years from September, 1900. In 1905, Rev. Dotson supplied for six months. Rev. J. W. Crouch, of LaGrange, was the next Pastor, serving about one and one-half years. He was followed by Rev. George T. Baker in 1907, and Rev. G. W. Wright, the present Pastor, in 1908. The church has preaching the third Sunday, Sunday School all the year, and prayer meeting weekly.

CYRENE CHURCH.

By S. O. Craig and D. T. Sanderson.

Cyrene village was founded in April, 1879, and was without religious organization until the spring of 1885, when a Sunday School and prayer meeting was organized in the Cyrene schoolhouse and conducted for two years, chiefly by members of the old Knob church, which had been recently moved to Edgewood.

About January, 1887, sixteen of the Cyrene people withdrew their membership from Edgewood church in order to form a church at Cyrene. These original members were as follows: J. E. Bailey, R. P. Burkholder, Betty Burkholder, Sallie B. Farmer, Pike Lindsey, Martha Lindsey, Maggie Lindsey, Mollie Lindsey, W. C. Lindsey, M. B. Grafford, Dr. W. E. Wiatt, J. M. Blackwell, Sallie F. Farmer, Jas. Bryant, J. T. Lindsey and Dove Witten.

On February 1, 1887, a presbytery was convened, composed of the following: Elders W. J. Patrick, W. A. Bibb, E. J. Sanderson, H. Beauchamp and W. M. Tipton, also Prof. A. Slaughter, Wm. H. Smith and C. M. Tipton. Dr. W. J. Patrick was elected moderator and Cyrene church was formally organized. J. T. Lindsey was church clerk, Pike Lindsey and J. E. Bailey, Deacons, and J. M. Blackwell, superintendent of Sunday School. Rev. W. M. Tipton was unanimously called as Pastor.

During the summer of 1887, they solicited funds for a church building, which was erected during the fall of that year, church services having been conducted throughout the summer in the schoolhouse. A revival meeting was held by the Pastor in January or February, 1888, before the building was entirely completed. It was a fruitful meeting.

Rev. W. M. Tipton resigned as Pastor March 1, 1889. Rev. Richard Harrison was next called, taking charge in March, 1890.

Cyrene church was dedicated on the second Sunday in April, 1891. Dr. A. C. Rafferty preached the sermon. R. A. Henderson was elected Deacon. Rev. Harrison resigned February, 1893, and Rev. B. W. N. Simms was called as Pastor. Rev. Simms was a most excellent Pastor and did much in advancing the church work. Resolutions of respect were adopted on the death of Deacon Luther Edwards, January 20, 1894. Rev. Simms resigned June, 1894, and Dr. J. E. Chambliss was called in July. Sometime after, one of the best revival meetings ever held here was conducted by him, which lasted nearly four weeks. It was a season of God's blessings, both to church and community, and resulted in twenty additions. Also a number professed Christ and united with other churches. License to preach was granted Walter E. Wiatt, March 16, 1895. D. C. Smith was made Deacon in 1895 and J. C. Burks in 1898. Rev. Simms accepted the pastorate again in October, 1896, and Dr. Chambliss accepted the pastorate again in July, 1897.

Rev. Richard Harrison, the former Pastor, moved to Cyrene in the fall of 1897, in very poor health, and after a lingering illness, he died at the home of Dr. W. E. Wiatt. Rev. W. A. Bibb was called as Pastor in April, 1898. During the six years of his pastorate, Rev. Bibb moved into our community and he and his family placed their membership with us.

Dr. W. J. Patrick began his labors as pastor April, 1907. He needed no introduction, having served as president of the presbytery that organized the church; also, he had assisted Rev. Bibb in a revival meeting in which he did some most excellent preaching. In November, 1907, Dr. Patrick was assisted in a meeting by Rev. Russell Whiteside, resulting in twelve conversions, one restoration and two added by letter. J. G. Phelps was licensed to preach in July, 1908. Rev. J. W. Keltner assisted in a meeting in October, 1908, which resulted in eight conversions. The preaching was good and brought great benefit to both church and community. We consider Dr. Patrick, our Pastor, one of the most able ministers in this section. He has been a delegate to the Southern Baptist Convention for many years.

Cyrene church maintains Sunday School and prayer meeting throughout the year, and is doing good work.

Pike Lindsey.—Born February 19, 1826, in Pike county, Missouri; crossed the plains to California in 1850, returning via. Panama; married Martha Scott, April 6, 1853. Eight members of his family composed one-half of the sixteen constituent members of Cyrene church. His prompt and constant presence and participation in all the services of the church gives to him a commendable prominence in the history of religious influence in Cyrene community. He was a son of Hon. John Lindsey.

Prof. A. Slaughter.—Born near Woodville, Virginia, August 12, 1828; married Laura Abbott, December 19, 1850; taught school in Louisville, Ky., 1854-'57; taught school in Western Missouri till 1870, and at Louisiana, Mo., till 1885. He resided at Cyrene with his son-in-law, Dr. W. E. Wiatt, till 1898. It was in no small measure to his mind and energy that Cyrene church achieved her high spiritual influence during the pastorates of Rev. Simms and Dr. Chambliss. He was grandfather to the Rev. Walter E. Wiatt and Mrs. Fannie Wiatt Darrow, the two missionaries sent into the foreign field in Burmah, Asia. They were converts from Cyrene Sunday School and were members of the church throughout their youth until 1898.

Samuel M. Patterson.—Born October 18, 1823, in Pike county, Missouri; reared and educated in the vicinity of his home; married Martha Johnson, April 15, 1858. Professed religion under the preaching of Rev. M. M. Modisett, uniting with Dover church in 1864. He settled on his farm near Edgewood in 1864. Moving his membership to the old Knob church a short time after, he lived a devoted member there for many years. His first wife died June, 1881. He married Mrs. Catherine Turner, April 26, 1886. In 1892 he moved to Cyrene and united with this church. He has always been a liberal contributor. At the advanced age of eighty-five years, he is now a devout member of Cyrene church, and an honored citizen, loved by all who know him.

The present Deacons are C. A. Bibb, S. M. Sanderson, J. C. Burks and Guy Edwards. Organists have been Mrs. Dr. Wiatt, Misses Roberta Grafford, Elsie Simpson, Jessie Bibb and Vella Sanderson. C. A. Bibb has been superintendent of Sunday School for almost twenty years.

SILEX CHURCH.

By Mrs. James W. Green.

July 10, 1886, Union Hill Baptist church of forty-six members, with Eld. F. M. Birkhead as Pastor, met and elected messengers to Bear Creek Baptist Association, asking for a letter of dismission from that body, which was granted them. August 14, of the same year they sent messengers to Salt River Baptist Association, desiring membership with them, which request was granted.

In February, 1887, Elder C. A. Mitchell assisted Elder F. M. Birkhead in a very precious meeting, which resulted in twenty-five happy converts, with the church greatly revived, and earnestly hoping the revival would continue.

In 1889 the name of the church was changed from Union Hill Baptist church to Silex Baptist church. Elder F. M. Birkhead remained Pastor of the church until July 1890, at which time he tendered his resignation, which was accepted.

At a special meeting, August 16th, Elder T. N. Sanderson was elected Pastor. At the same time the church resolved to withdraw from Salt River Baptist Association and unite with other churches to form an association in Lincoln county. She then sent messengers to Salt River Baptist Association for a letter of dismission from that body with a view of uniting with what is now called Cuivre Baptist Association.

September 2, 1891, Salt River gave to Silex church a letter, at which time Elder T. N. Sanderson is Pastor with a membership of forty-eight. The Deacons were J. L. Gibson, S. E. Page and A. R. Luck. A. M. Stevens was chosen clerk. The church has had a varied experience of growth and losses since entering Cuivre Association.

ST. CHARLES CHURCH.

By Mrs. Bettie A. Reid.

In January, 1888, the mission boards of Salt River Association and of the General Association employed Mr. Reid at a salary of $1,000 per year, to go to St. Charles and look after Baptist interests in city and county. He found a few Baptists in the city, and on June 28, organized a church of nineteen members. The council to organize was appointed by the two boards, and were Brethren L. B. Ely, W. J. Patrick, M. S. Whiteside, J. D. Biggs, S. M. Brown and C. A. Mitchell. He found a church house belonging to the German Methodists who were anxious to sell. It was a substantial brick building, which they offered very reasonably. He told them "he had not been sent to buy churches," but would confer with the boards and they advised him to buy and canvass the State to pay for it, which he did. The house had cost them more than $10,000, they offered it for $2,000, just what the stone wall had cost them that was in front of the church. In October, 1889, he reported at the meeting of the General Association all paid. The house was deeded to Brethren W. M. Senter, J. J. Brown and D. T. Killam, trustees for the State Mission Board. We seemed to be doing well, God was with us while many were opposing us.

On November 18, 1888, Rev. Andrew Konzelman and wife were received into the church and baptized same evening. Brother Konzelman was the Pastor of the German church whose house Mr. Reid had bought. Brother Konzelman was ordained as a Baptist minister and was employed by the board of the Southern Baptist Convention to labor among the Germans in different parts of the State, and afterwards he was employed by the city mission board of St. Louis. Soon after this, there arose trouble in the church. Mr. Reid resigned his work there, but the two boards were not willing to release him, but sent committees to investigate the condition of affairs. Committees were W. F. Elliott, J. H. Guthrie and J. C. Armstrong, of the State Board and W. J. Patrick, J. F. Kemper, J. D. Biggs and D. T. Killam, of Salt River board. They met April 4, 1889. The church at this time numbered thirty-one members. After a full investigation of all things the committees reported, sustaining Mr. Reid in all his work. This caused quite a commotion. Ten members withdrew, leaving twenty-one members. We struggled on and on; it was a warfare all along.

In August, 1889, Brother Jno. P. Charles was received into the church and in August, 1892, he was ordained to the gospel ministry. He preached for a time to country churches, but finally left St. Charles and went to Staunton, Illinois. The ladies kept up an aid society, by which means was raised considerable money which was spent for the benefit of the church. The church has surely had a hard struggle and is struggling yet, though prospects are better than at first. But prior to the above in 1891, the discussion occurred between a Catholic priest and Mr. Reid, and it is needless to say it was a period of great excitement and uneasy moments for me, though Mr. Reid seemed to fear nothing; he felt he was in the right, and truly it was good for our cause in St. Charles.

WHITESIDE CHURCH.

By John F. Whiteside, Esq.

The town of Whiteside was built on the farm of William Whiteside, who was a member of Mill Creek Baptist church, and a very large part of the first settlers of the town were Baptists. As soon as they could get a room to worship in they began to have preaching. The first sermon was preached in the railroad depot, by Elder Wiley J. Patrick in the spring of 1886. Soon after this a schoolhouse was built, and the same minister was engaged to preach at intervals on his way home from Mill Creek, where he was Pastor.

Elder M. M. Modisett preached at intervals in the same house.

In the spring of 1888 steps were taken to build a house of worship. E. Magruder, D. J. Moxley and J. R. Gibson were the building committee. A building site situated on the south side of the railroad was bought. They built a house twenty-eight by forty-four feet, with seating capacity for two hundred and fifty. The pulpit was in the rear. There were two doors in front and one in rear. This was in the year 1889. A Sunday School was organized in the schoolhouse in the spring of 1887, with J. M. Terrill as superintendent; it was moved to the house of worship in the spring of 1889 with Elias Magruder as superintendent.

A church was organized March 25, 1889, with Elder Wm. M. Tipton as Pastor. At a meeting held at the Baptist church at Whiteside for the purpose Brother M. S. Whiteside was chosen moderator. The church was organized with twenty-one members from different churches of Salt River Association and to be known as the Baptist Church at Whiteside. E. Magruder and J. W. Luck were chosen Deacons and A. B. Magruder church clerk. The council was composed of M. S. Whiteside, W. J. Patrick, W. N. Maupin, P. W. Halley and S. S. Keith.

Helping the Weak. 335

The church was admitted into the membership of Salt River Association in 1889, and remained with them until the organization of the Cuivre Association.

THE COLPORTEUR AND OTHER WORK.

By P. W. Halley.

I was colporteur in Salt River one year. I was Pastor at Owen Station when church was built and Bro. J. S. Eames and I held a meeting at a schoolhouse six miles northwest of Troy. I think we had forty-five additions. Preacher Tucker is one of them. They organized a church, called me, and we built Mt. Pleasant church. I preached two years for them. I preached six years for Fairview and six for Mount Gilead.

THE COLPORTEUR WORK.

By R. D. Robertson.

I began the work first in the summer of 1890, under the direction of the mission board of Salt River Association. I had a letter of credit to the American Baptist Publication Society to furnish me books to the amount of one hundred dollars, and I had on hands at different times, a stock of books amounting to $125, consisting of Bibles, Testaments and other books, most which set forth the Baptist doctrines. The work was done principally in Salt River Association. I found it a very profitable work so far as the moral good was concerned; from a financial point the profits were small. I gave away Bibles and Testaments and some other literature where people were in need and were not able to buy. As a general thing I met a hearty welcome whether with saint or sinner. I remember of only one occasion where I had to put up at a public boarding house for want of a Christian home. I meet people to-day who are glad to see me because they remember a good book that they bought from me. I continued under the direction of the Salt River board for about two years, during which time I sold and gave away thousand of pages of valuable tracts on various subjects of interest to both believing and unbelieving people.

I have done considerable work along this line in four counties, namely, Lincoln, St. Charles, Pike and Ralls, with lesser labors in other parts. One feature in my experience always impressed me and that was that I met with churches that objected to me as their settled Pastor because I sold books, and I have a distinct recollection of two pastorates where I was turned down on that account after I had served one year.

So far as I know, I did the last work that has been done in Salt River Association under the direction of the board, having finished up a remnant of a stock of books about the summer of the year 1897.

B. R. PATRICK.

His Colporteur and Other Work and Experiences.

Bower Reynolds Patrick is the son of Wiley J. and Elizabeth Ann Patrick. His mother's maiden name was Withers. He married Miss Jane D. Serpell. In the summer of 1886 he was employed by the Salt River board to sell books and preach. Writing from the Naval Training Station, San Francisco, under date of March 9, 1908, he said, "I shall endeavor to write you briefly about my colporteurship." Instead of a letter on that subject, however, I have from him the following:

"THREE MONTHS ON THE PACIFIC.

By Chaplain B. R. Patrick, U. S. Navy.

Three months and a day is a long time to spend in getting from America to Tutuila, but it took that long a time for us to make our memorable trip just recently ended. When we sailed past the long and splendid column of American battleships in San Francisco Bay and out through the Golden Gate on July 6th last, we expected to arrive in Pago Pago in about twenty days.

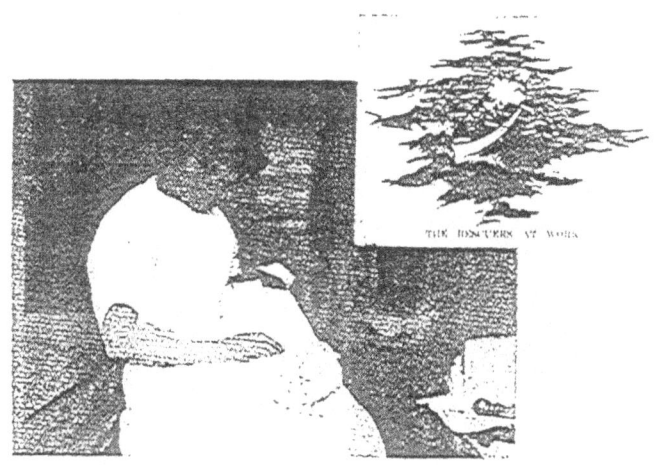

THE NURSE, MISS CAMPBELL, AND THE BABY.

THE SHIP MANUKA AND THE RESCUE.
THE AEON IN THE DISTANCE.

For twelve days the Aeon steamed bravely along on her course, and six or seven days more would have put us in Apia, but on that day the ship was carried twenty-five or thirty miles out of her course by the wind and the current and at 9:34 p. m. she ran upon the coral reef on the northerly side of the southeast point of Christmas Island, about five miles from the end of the point. There was considerable excitement for a few minutes, especially among the men of the Chinese crew, but after that, all hands worked faithfully and well. The life boats were lowered to the rail and replenished with food and water, and other needed preparations were made for abandoning ship if that should become necessary. This work was all finished before midnight, when everybody composed themselves to wait for morning or for whatever might happen sooner than that.

The ship struck bow on, with her engines going full speed astern. The engines were kept going astern until they were so badly twisted that they would not run. By 11:30 the wind and current had carried the ship broadside on to the reef where she was caught hard and fast amidships. It was the pounding on the rocks that twisted and broke the engines. We had then become a hopeless wreck and knew that our safety depended on the chance of a passing ship or the near proximity of land.

All through the night we did not know whether we had struck an island or a submerged reef; so that it was with anxious eyes that we waited for morning, peering into the darkness to make out, if possible, some indication of land. Toward daylight we could see objects that appeared to be a long ways off and we thought them to be cocoanut trees. When good daylight had come, we found, much to our joy, that two ship's lengths away was an island with a good beach and that it was approachable through the breakers. It looked like nothing but a desert island, but we thanked God for dry land so near, and began at once to make more thorough preparations for landing.

A line was sent ashore about six o'clock. It was safely landed and secured on the beach, after which the ladies and children were sent safely ashore along this line in a small boat. The day was spent in landing provisions and water and material to make shelters out of. By nightfall we had tents erected that were fairly comfortable and food enough to last us a short time. Every one was tired and we went to bed early to get as much rest as possible, for we knew that we had to face days of hard work that would keep every one busy.

Day after day was spent in landing additional provisions and in the effort to make our habitations more comfortable, until by and by enough stores had been landed and put in our provision tent to have lasted us from six months to a year; and our camp had been made as comfortable as the place and the material at our disposal would permit.

The surrounding water was full of edible fish; there were plenty of crayfish and land crabs, and, if we had needed them, no doubt we could have secured many eggs from the numerous sea birds that were all over the island. But the Aeon had several hundred tons of foodstuffs on board and so long as she did not break up we were in no danger of starvation. There was no sickness and we were very thankful for good health. For twelve days we were short of fresh water, but at the end of that time the ship's engineers completed a distiller on the beach and on the same day the carpenter found good drinking water about five hundred yards from the beach at a depth of seven feet in a bed of fine coral sand.

When we had been on the island one month the Captain, second officer and two engineers started to go to Fanning Island in one of the life boats that had been fitted up with a gas engine. But they had an accident that night, the boat shipped a heavy sea that so injured the wires that the engine would not work, and the boat drifted all night. In the morning they found themselves near the ship and as soon as repairs had been made they returned to the wreck. It was almost another month before the boat was ready to go to sea again. This time it had better luck. The Captain and his party got away on September 15th on a fine calm morning. That afternoon they reached the site of the old station on Christmas Island and found that it had been long since deserted; they did not even find cocoanut trees there. On the third day after leaving the wreck the life boat reached Fanning Island and sent away our messages for help and the news to our homes that we were safe. In a few days the Royal Mail Steamer Manuka stopped at Fanning Island, picked up our Captain, his party, and boat, and brought them all back to Christmas Island.

It was a very exciting moment when we looked out across the island and saw such a fine steamer coming to rescue us. Just twenty-four hours previously a little daughter had been born to Mrs. Patrick and we were afraid that it would be hard on the mother and child to move them so soon. The Manuka reached the wreck about dark on September 23, 1908, and spent the night taking the six hundred bags of mail from the Aeon. During the night the people on shore got their baggage off to a life boat that was moored under the lea of the Aeon, and early in the morning of the 24th Mrs. Patrick, the baby and the other ladies and children were safely and comfortably removed to the Manuka, and before noon we were on the way to Suva, where we stayed for a few days and were then brought comfortably to the pretty harbor of Pago Pago by the United States Steamer Solace. Here we were delighted with the reception given us by the officers and their families of the station, and by the cordial good will shown us by all the Samoan people.

We have thanked God many times for His kind providence that cared for us throughout all our perilous adventures. No shipwrecked people ever had more comforts than we had. We were thankful for good weather, good health, good food, good water, a Captain who was kind and thoughtful, and for many other mercies of God, including the kindness of the officers, crew and passengers of the steamers Manuka and Solace. And now forward to the pleasure of living and working on the charming Island of Tutuila and among her generous people."

Bower was Pastor in Hannibal and five years at the First Church, Duluth, where his mind was drawn toward the work among the naval men. But he always shows a kindling joy on his return to Missouri and especially to the scenes of his first Christian love and labors.

REV. JAMES REID.

The ministry of James Reid is now a completed career. Like Paul, the Apostle to the nations, he was "separated unto the gospel of God." He had the Christian graces and the personal attainments that enabled him to accomplish his career and the ministry which he had received of the Lord Jesus to testify the gospel of the grace of God.

In early life he believed on the Lord Jesus Christ. Salvation wrought through his inner and outward life. He soon felt called of God to preach his gospel. He became well equipped for this calling. His Godliness was sincere, his scholarship was thorough, his bearing was gentle and prudent, his sense of honor was superlative, and his acceptance of revealed truth was firm and intense.

Brother Reid was born in the home of his parents, Mr. and Mrs. James Reid, in Lincoln county, Missouri, near Auburn, February 18, 1838. It is a beautifully embowered farm house, characteristic of Missouri country life. The home was one of industry, prosperity, intelligence and strict religious training. The family belonged to the Associated Reformed Presbyterian Church, Mt. Zion, which was in the vicinity. Under their teaching Brother Reid became a Christian and received his sense of duty to preach. He never ceased to love these Christians and they showed him distinguished consideration. In quoting the Psalms, he usually quoted them in the metrical form that he learned in their worship and he left the request that the twenty-third Psalm should be sung at his burial. This was done. Soon after he entered upon the active duties of manhood, he became associated in teaching in Clarksville, Missouri, with Prof. M. S. Goodman, whom he ever held in the highest esteem. I want Prof. Goodman to speak for himself of his friend. He says: "I never knew any one who combined more of the essential elements of true Christian manhood than the late James Reid. He was simple in his tastes, sincere in his convictions. Firm in his religious opinions, he was big enough to be tolerant of the beliefs of others. The public knew his labors in the cause of his Master, his associates knew as well the sympathies of his wondrous heart. His was a nature which sorrowed with the sorrows of his fellow man. Sickness and personal cares often weighed heavily upon him but never, when able to think and act, did he permit either to keep him from the bedside of the afflicted or from relieving the burdens of others. Endowed with high and holy ideals, he sought continually their realization. Honor was his brother and duty his dictator. With him sacrifice was the price of success and he never hesitated to lay his dearest hopes upon the altar of duty. His strong will and love of justice made him a bulwark of defense to the defenseless, and his tender sympathy, broad as our common humanity, led him to minister to the heart of affliction. The world is poorer since he left it, but one loving legacy he has left us—the necessity for charity and kindness while in this life. After a pilgrimage of sixty-seven years his confiding spirit has gone to the God who gave it. His simple and abounding faith assures the peace he has so justly earned."

In 1867 Brother Reid united with Dover Church, Pike county, Missouri, and was baptized by the Rev. M. M. Modisett. He was here ordained. Soon afterward he accepted his first pastorate, Jackson, Cape Girardeau county, where he remained eight years.

January 19, 1869, he married Mrs. Bettie A. Rodney. God gave them two sons, T. Lacey Reid, who died in infancy, and James Albert Reid, M. D., of Foristell, Missouri, who recently accepted the professorship of bacteriology in Barnes Medical College, St. Louis. Sister Reid's daughter, Anna Rodney Shaw, of Louisiana, Missouri, shared in Brother Reid's love equally with his own children.

Dr. J. C. Maple, a true friend and a fellow-helper in Southeast Missouri, can best tell the story of the labors in that great field, rendered by this man of God.

Brother Reid's Work in Southeast Missouri.

"I have not at hand the exact date on which I first met Rev. James Reid. He was living in Jackson, Cape Girardeau county, and as Pastor was then engaged in a protracted meeting. Being on a visit to Southeast Missouri, while Pastor at Owensboro, Kentucky, Rev. J. H. Clark and I drove to Jackson to meet the Pastor and gather some crumbs of truth from the gospel there preached. We met Brother Reid at the home of a mutual friend. He was a young man yet single, full of zeal and overflowing with the vigor of his cheerful, fun-loving but consecrated manhood. For a number of years we only met on occasions of my annual visits to that portion of Missouri.

"In his active duties the Lord led him to Charleston, where he met the good woman who was his destined wife. This union was to him the greatest and best of all the gifts of God, after he had received that eternal life which is, of course, God's greatest gift to any human being.

"As Mrs. Reid and Mrs. Maple had been brought up in the same locality and had always been very much devoted to each other, this tie increased and cemented the friendship of the two preachers.

"Brother Reid went everywhere in a number of counties in Southeast Missouri, and as he went he preached the gospel of the Son of God. He found much difficulty in some localities in finding some one to lead the singing. He began industriously to learn how to sing. After great labor he learned to sing one "common meter" tune. And when there was no other leader he used that tune until he had by hard work acquired two other tunes, one a "long meter" and the other "short meter." He then drilled himself upon Greenville, until he could sing "Come Thou Fount of Every Blessing." He held many meetings in the most destitute parts of the country and was instrumental in establishing several churches. There was also quite a number of young men converted who entered the ministry. He was Pastor at Jackson and at Goshen church afterward consolidated with Oak Ridge, Hubble Creek and many others. During almost all the period that he was engaged in this widely scattered and varied work he was also engaged in school teaching.

"He bought a farm just west of Jackson and for several years conducted an academy in his own home. It must not for a moment be forgotten that in all this work he had in his scholarly wife an invaluable helpmeet. The work he did would not have been possible but for her skillful and polished management.

"Brother Reid was an original thinker and could not move along in the old ruts. He had too much sense to think of creating a new law of gravitation or forming another world than the one in which we live. He knew that our mission is to investigate what is here found. And he no more sought to inject new truths into the word of God than to create new laws for the material universe. But he did try most diligently to discover what the Divine mind had stored away for us in both the book of nature and the Bible. He constructed his own system of teaching English Grammar, and had printed an outline. That his influence was far-reaching for good need scarcely be uttered. While the structure of his mind made him one incessant joker, yet never did he use his wit, nor did the inherent humor of his make-up induce him to make light of any sacred thing or to fail to encourage any desire for the better life on the part of a human soul. However awkward the way in which an inquirer seemed to approach the great question of personal salvation, he was sure to find sympathetic response and solid instruction from Brother Reid. His great common sense and varied gifts were well adapted to the work needed in Southeast Missouri at the time he located in that part of the State.

"The churches had been scattered by the civil war. The demoralization was general and everything was prostrated. The need was for a man who could construct and rebuild out of the scattered and broken material left upon the desolated field. Rev. James Reid was the man whom God selected and sent to that field, for that work, and no one could have done better. So well did he build that there has been constant growth up to the present hour."

In 1875 I attended the meeting of Cape Girardeau Association, which held her session at Oak Ridge Church. I went home with Brother Reid, spent the night with him and his family. And a delightful home it was; a home of love, culture and religion. The next morning he and I went to the sight of the old historic Bethel Church. While there we got the block from one of the old logs, out of which was made the gavel that was subsequently presented to the General Association. Brother Reid cut out the block.

He moved back to Lincoln county in 1876. I was then preaching at Mill Creek Church, near the old homestead where his mother was still living. We were then thrown a great deal together in pastoral duties, revivals, councils, associations, board meetings, in sickness and in death. He taught the Prairieville and Bowling Green schools, but most of the time he gave himself wholly to the ministry. He was Pastor at Prairieville, Noix Creek, Walnut Grove and elsewhere and he did a vast amount of revival preaching. Walnut Grove and Noix Creek churches had wide-spread-ing, all-conquering revivals under his ministry. He and Brothers J. D. Biggs, J. Frank Smith, S. G. Givens and others were closely associated in their ministry, and their labors together were greatly blessed. He was an intimate friend of Gov. C. H. Hardin and Dr. W. Pope Yeaman. He was called to the church at Vandalia. I desire that one who was himself blessed under his ministry at that place speak for Vandalia:

"Vandalia, Mo., February 20, 1905.

"Brother Reid was called to the pastorate of the First Baptist Church at Vandalia in 1880 for half of his time and continued as Pastor for eight years until 1888. When first called the church was weak, few in numbers and down in spirit, but under his administration the church was builded up along all these lines, so much so that after the second year he was called for all his time, and so continued until the Salt River Association in 1888 laid its hands upon him as one especially fitted and qualified to build up the cause at St. Charles, where no Baptist Church existed and where much destitution abounded, and called him to that field and, just like him, he could not resist this Macedonian call and asked the church here to release him that he might go there. This was done after much prayer and deepest regrets on the part of the entire membership, and he left us beloved by every member of the church and beloved and respected by the entire community. Their love and respect for him have continued through all these years since, and his coming to us when called on special occasions was always looked forward to with brightest anticipations for a good time while Brother Reid was with us.   C. G. DANIEL."

Under the ministry of Brother Reid there was at one time in Vandalia a pervading, triumphant revival that shook the powers of darkness and empowered the Christians for life and service.

God seems to have had Brother Reid in training for these twenty-one years for the great and arduous task to which He called him in 1888 in St. Charles, Mo. Here was a city more than one hundred years old;

growing, the metropolis of a great county, without a Baptist Church. On the invitation of the boards of the General Association and Salt River Association jointly he went to St. Charles without an organization or a house of worship. He had business capacity. He found a house that could be had at a great advantage by his advancing $500. Having no time to advise with others, on his own judgment and responsibility he met the conditions, by wiring to a bank at his former home (Vandalia) for permission to make draft for the amount (though he had no funds in the bank), which the bank promptly granted. Thus he secured the house. From the start the work prospered and the church became self-sustaining. Brother Reid went then into other work for two years. The church had reverses. Then he was recalled to the church and he remained with her till his course on earth was ended.

In connection with this church after his return, he preached at Wentzville and Jonesburg churches. None of them were strong. He was offered better salary but he said, "No, those who are strong can get some one else, I'll preach to churches that are not able to pay much." At St. Charles a great work has been done; God did it and he used James Reid as his weapon of righteousness. And Sister Reid and their children have nobly shared with him in the heroic deeds and labors of love.

In 1891 he preached a series of sermons on Roman Catholicism, which were published in the city papers and also in pamphlet form. In doing so he answered some public utterances of a priest. Brother Reid was courteous, incisive, Scriptural.

The subjects he treated were: "The Bible Doctrine of the Church;" "The Bible as the Sole Rule of Faith;" "God's Word Our Lamp and Light and Our Only Infallible Guide;" "Baptist Churches Possess Not Only Four but All the Marks of New Testament Churches." I have just read parts of these sermons, which I read with great interest when they first appeared. They are scholarly and conclusive and I could wish to see them given permanent form.

Brother Reid was the author of a grammar entitled, "An English Grammar for the Use of Schools of Every Grade." He published this in 1872, while principal of Fairview Seminary, Jackson, Missouri. It shows a mastery of the principles of English language.

For four years he was the moderator of Salt River Association. For many years he was a member of the Ministers' Conference, St. Louis, and he served one term as the presiding officer of the body. He was on several college and mission boards and for many years he was recording secretary of the State mission board. He insisted on integrity and righteousness in public institutions as in private character.

A letter from Bower R. Patrick, written from Philadelphia, February 19, 1905, says: "I was deeply grieved to learn of Brother Reid's death. I wish that I could have seen him recently. He has held a place in my affections from my boyhood till now as one of less than half a dozen friends who have all along stood to me as types of what is best in manhood."

Brother Reid preached his last sermon at Jonesburg at eleven o'clock on Sunday, February 5, 1905. A letter from Brother H. C. Begeman, Jonesburg, Mo., dated March 4, 1905, says: "Brother Reid's last Sunday morning sermon was from the text Luke 12:15. His subject was 'Giving Up All for Christ.' One of the songs was, 'I'll go where you want me to go.' He sat while he preached. He spoke against selling whisky, beating others in a trade and all such things. He said we ought to do good, relieve the suffering, give to the poor. I do not know how often the past year I have heard him say that his desire and prayer more and more were to be like Jesus. His patient and calm life will help me to be more like Jesus, I trust. The last time he was here he stayed with us all the time."

He remained in Jonesburg until Tuesday and married a couple. He was taken down with pneumonia but was able to reach the home of his son, Dr. Reid, in Foristel. Sister Reid came at once. He was conscious to the last and gave directions as to his burial. He died Sunday, Feburary 12th, about 10 a. m. We laid his body to rest in the midst of a snowstorm about one o'clock p. m., Tuesday following his death, at Mt. Zion Church, Lincoln county. Four generations lie there: Brother Reid's son, Brother Reid, his father, James Reid, and his father's father, Alexander Reid.

"Them also which sleep in Jesus will God bring with him."

RECOLLECTIONS OF SALT RIVER ASSOCIATION.

By E. W. Dow, Ph. D.

Early in the summer of 1886 I landed at Bowling Green, coming from Knoxboro, New York, where I had been teaching after leaving college. I was to take the position of teacher of languages at "Bowling Green College," as Pike College was then called. I met with a kind and hospitable reception by the people, and especially by my Baptist brethren. Two of my children were born at Bowling Green, Ernest H., who died at McCune College of scarlet fever and is buried in the Bowling Green cemetery, and Grove S., who is of the class of 1909 at William Jewell College. At the end of the college year I was elected president. I raised a debt of $2,500, in which the Baptists of Salt River Association, and especially Bowling Green, contributed generously. Although the college was non-sectarian I always received a courteous hearing at Salt River Association and was most kindly received and recognized. Oftimes the brethren rendered voluntary help in securing students.

Brother Ed T. Smith, one of Pike county's most able lawyers, was a loyal, true friend. On his death I mourned him as a brother. Brethren Reid, Musgrove, Jennings, Whiteside, Charles A. Mitchell, Sherman Tucker and W. A. Bibb are kindly remembered. Brothers Patrick and J. D. Biggs are remembered by me among my dearest friends, and I shall ever treasure in mind and heart their many kindnesses and deeds of love to me and mine; especially in the dark hours when companion, sister and dear children were taken from me. Pike county is a home county to me, and Salt River Association is a part of the picture. I shall ever remember the kindly words of the presbytery, which meeting at McCune College on February 21, 1894, ordained me to the gospel ministry. Brother Wiley J. Patrick was president of the presbytery and J. D. Biggs secretary. The names of J. Reid, S. F. Thompson and E. Jennings are also upon my ordination papers. Methinks I can still feel the hands of the brethren upon my head as they sought God's blessing upon me and my work. To me, Dr. Patrick is a prince of men, and he has written his name upon the history of Salt River Association and stamped it upon the hearts of her people. With him I have journeyed to many of her churches, sometimes preaching as best I could. Mt. Pisgah, Ashley, Cyrene, Edgewood and other churches whose names I cannot recall, were places we visited together.

While at the college I served the Association at Ashley as missionary for several months. Brother W. T. Jacobs, for many years superintendent of the Bowling Green Sunday School of the Baptist Church, opened his big heart and his home to me. It was in Salt River Association I found a true helpmate in Carrie A. Reneau, who was converted under the preaching o J. D. Biggs and baptized by him into Ramsey Creel Baptist Church. So Salt River Association gave t(me one who, as the years have passed, has always fille(worthily the various places which she has been calle· to occupy.

T. J. Ayres was another friend, true and trie(thoughtful and full of kind deeds. At the time I live in Salt River Association he was beginning to be or of the leading spirits of the Association among th laymen, a position that he continued to occupy.

When I returned to the Association after two years absence, as president of McCune College, I did so with the desire to spend my days there. With our one hundred students in the literary department alone, I was looking forward to a still larger success when again death's cold hand was stretched forth and my beautiful boy, Ernest, fell by that dread disease, scarlet fever. Discouraged and overwhelmed, God sent me forth to preach. The call came to go to Troy, New Hampshire, my native State. Four years I labored there and God richly blessed my labors. Though since that time I have been engaged again in educational work as president of Pierce City College and Southwest College, I have always continued my work as a preacher. At Osceola, Mo., I welcomed one hundred and eight into the church, seventy-six by baptism. Again I found work in the east in the midst of Unitarianism and Universalism, but I cling to the old faith and desire in closing to express my deep appreciation of all that Salt River Association and her noble ministers have done for me, both directly and indirectly.

CHAPTER XI.

BAPTIST HONOR, 1892-1900.

The Association met with Mill Creek Church August 30, 1892. The introductory sermon was preached by W. T. Campbell from the words: "Say not ye, there are yet four months, and then cometh harvest? Behold, I say unto you, lift up your eyes, and look on the fields; for they are white already to harvest." The Association reorganized by electing T. J. Ayres moderator and R. N. Gilbert clerk, Brother Reid having asked to be relieved from the moderatorship. Frankford Church was received into associational fellowship. The messengers were J. T. Hutcherson, S. C. Truitt, Lee A. Hutcherson, R. F. Draper. The visiting brethren were W. T. Campbell, F. T. Shore, C. W. Davis, J. S. R. Gregory, T. N. Mitchell, William Whiteside, J. J. Bradley, R. D. Robertson, M. C. Harris, G. C. Harris, J. S. Eames, S. S. Keith, M. E. Motley, P. W. Halley, R. H. Boney (colored.) The board had, during the outgoing year, employed Brethren A. P. Rodgers, J. Reid, W. A. Bibb. Brother Rodgers preached thirty-five sermons, baptized 2; Brother Reid preached one hundred and ninety-seven sermons, baptized ten; expended $400 on the house. There are forty members in the Sunday School; besides which the church at St. Charles has ordained to the ministry Brother John Charles and Brother Reid has organized a church at Pauldingville. Brother W. A. Bibb preached three hundred and forty-four sermons and baptized seventy-seven. And the board had in the colporteur work Brethren R. D. Robertson and B. H. Bibb, who did some good work. W. J. Patrick reported that under the direction of the board several foreign mission centennial meetings were held. $117.07 was raised and expended in the movement. The cooperation of minister and churches was general.

The Association held a centennial service: Devotional half hour; lecture on missionary map, W. J. Patrick; Salt River missionaries and the foreign field, by J. Reid; address by J. D. Biggs on self-denial for missions; report on home and foreign missions with an address by W. A. Gibony; State missions, by W. T. Campbell. Brother Johnson Clark had charge of the singing. For use during the year the following song and music were generously contributed by Professor R. P. Rider, A. M,. and they were used with good results.

4 We asked great things of Thee in sadness,
Thy glorious power Thou wouldst make known;
And now we come to Thee in gladness,
For Thou hast claimed the earth Thine own.
Blest pre-emption!
For Thou hast claimed the earth Thine own!

5 Dear Lord, centennial honors bringing,
We offer Thee exultant praise,
Approach thy throne with joyful singing,
For Thou hast crowned our waiting days!
Blest fruition!
Thou'st richly crowned our waiting days!

* Theme in the Tenor responds to Soprano. Let the response be made with marked effect.

The committee on obituaries, John Cotter, C. S. Burks, W. J. Patrick, reported: Sister Susan Hawkins was an Israelite indeed in whom there was no guile; Sister Susan Patterson was quiet, constant, Godly; Sister Sarah Smith had the spirit of Christ and was active in His work; Brother Otha Pool brought forth fruit in his old age; Brother Wash Burch lived a faithful Christian life; Brother Ernest Edwards lived a life that was a model to his associates; Sister Alice Lewis walked worthy of the Christian calling; Brother George W. White was humble and zealous; Sister Linnie Morris was a choice Christian character; Sister Mary Parsons was gentle, truthful, placid; Brother Robert Bently was a zealous Christian man; Sister Louisa Givens, wife of Elder S. G. Givens, was a warm hearted, cheerful, true Christian. The new executive board was T. J. Ayres, J. C. Stewart, J. C. Mackey, J. D. Biggs, J. W. Keach, W. T. Jacobs, J. C. Biggs, J. A. Goodman, J. T. Hutcherson and W. J. Seaman. At this session Mill Creek and Elsberry churches called for and received letters to go into Cuivre Association. A collection of $524.50 was taken for the support of disabled ministry.

August 29, 1893, the body met with Spencer Creek Church. Elder W. A. Gibony preached the sermon. His text was: "And he said unto them, go ye into all the world, and preach the gospel to every creature. He that believeth and is baptized shall be saved; but he that believeth not shall be damned." The visitors were C. M. Williams, J. M. P. Martin, E. J. Sanderson, S. M. Brown, W. D. Cave, W. N. Boney (colored.) The board report that they had employed in the mission work A. P. Rodgers, J. C. Harris, W. A. Bibb and S. F. Thompson. The board said, we "are able to report only meager results. We have not been able to secure a colporteur this year." The committee on obituaries, S. G. Givens, R. Anderson and Dan L. Rose, reported: Sisters Nancy H. Penix and Cynthia A. Penix, dear sisters of precious memory; Sister

Sarah M. Hedges trusted the Lord; Sister Maggie Thurmond was ready; Brother J. A. Emerson died in the faith; Brother Addison Tinsley said, "Meet me in Heaven;" Sister Alvin Tinsley died a Christian; Sister Bessie Jones gave evidence of going home; Sister Jane Worsham has gained by our loss; Brother Williamson Shaw requested us to meet him in Heaven; Sister Laura Warner died trusting in a Saviour's love; Col. O. C. Tinker was taken home to rest. The new executive board were T. J. Ayres, J. D. Biggs, J. C. Biggs, J. A. Goodman, J. C. Stewart, J. M. Keach, J. T. Hutcherson, J. C. Mackey, W. T. Jacobs and J. N. Price. Star Hope Church received a letter to unite with Cuivre Association.

The Association met with Ramsey Creek Church August 29, 1894. The introductory sermon was preached by Elder J. M. McManaway. His text was: "And no man putteth new wine into old bottles: else the new wine doth burst the bottles and the wine is spilled, and the bottles will be marred; but new wine must be put into new bottles." Saverton Church, Ralls county, was received into the fellowship of churches in the Association; messengers not given. These visiting brethren accepted seats: James Reid, J. F. Cook, F. M. Birkhead, F. L. Dawson, J. S. R. Gregory, James L. Dawson, W. N. Birkhead, William Whiteside, P. W. Halley, D. B. Ray, J. P. Greene, B. G. Tutt, A. W. Payne, Joseph Stirmlinger. The board reported that they had in the course of the associational year the services of W. M. Tipton, C. M. Williams, J. D. Biggs, S. F. Thompson and J. L. Downing. The mission interests are represented as prosperous. The labors were well distributed over the field. The committee on Sunday Schools, W. J. Patrick, L. T. Patterson and J. B. Clark, said: "The Sunday School demands the heads and the hearts of our maturest men and women. The young people may find work by their side, the aged will give sweetness and hopefulness as they keep their company, but only the men and women who are at their best can bear the burdens and blasting winds of to-day. If the Sunday School is to outgrow its swaddling clothes and stand forth as a factor for good, and never for evil, it must be fed by strong, loving and holy hands." The committee on obituaries, W. M. Tipton, C. S. Burks and W. T. Sisson, said: "Our dear brother, W. S. Tucker, died at his home in Bowling Green, November 17, 1893, in the faith which he had embraced and which he so much delighted to preach. Brother Tucker was a young man of brilliant talent, which he cheerfully contributed to the cause he so much loved; we miss him." The committee on state of the churches, A. W. Stewart and A. P. Rodgers, said: "Of the twenty-nine churches, one has regular preaching every Sunday; two have preaching by Pastor twice a month; twenty-four once a month, and two have no preaching at all." When the Association was holding her sessions, in time of an intermission, August 30, 1894, brethren from various counties and Associations organized the Riverside Scripture Institute. Elder J. Reid was made president, Elder William Callaway secretary. An executive committee was appointed with Elder J. M. McManaway as chairman. The ministers were J. D. Biggs, W. J. Patrick, A. P. Rodgers, W. M. Tipton, M. S. Whiteside, E. Jennings, S. G. Givens, S. F. Thompson, J. M. McManaway, S. P. Dawson, S. S. Keith, R. S. Cole, J. W. Trower. Licensed for the ministry were W. P. Bibb, Luke Kirtley, Eugene Edwards, Charles Turner and Henry Peyton.

Adiel Church was the place of meeting and August 28th the day in 1895. The sermon was preached by Elder W. W. Brown from the text: "If a man's work shall be burned, he shall suffer loss: but he himself shall be saved; yet so as by fire." The reorganization was effected by the election of T. J. Ayres moderator and W. T. Jacobs clerk. At the request of the clerk the body elected Brother E. B. Omohundro assistant clerk. These brethren accepted seats in the Association: E. Anderson, —— Duckworth, R. D. Robertson, James Reid, N. R. Pittman, J. S. Conner,

B. H. Cox, Byron Bibb. Immanuel Church, of Ralls county, was received into the Association. The messengers were C. L. Yager, Thomas P. Norton, H. C. Cox and A. Robinson. The board had in the course of the year the services of S. F. Thompson, S. S. Keith and W. J. Patrick. The report of the board says: "It would be difficult to overestimate as mission fields the great importance of Ashburn, Saverton and Annada. There are houses of worship in progress of erection at both Ashburn and Annada at this present time." Brother S. F. Thompson was the missionary Pastor at these places. In July and August W. J. Patrick, assisted by C. A. Waters, held a meeting at Cross Roads which resulted in the organization of Immanuel Church." J. M. McManaway, committeeman for home and foreign missions, said: "An eloquent writer in a recent periodical said of the home mission board of the Southern Baptist Convention, 'It is the heart of a vast system of Christian evangelism; sends its life-giving blood through the arteries to many a destitute, parched and withered section over immense territory; it thus quickens into life many a desolate and dismal scene. It causes the beautiful flowering and fruitage of Christian virtues to adorn, to fructify and redeem the dreary place where once the dark shadow of death held his sombre sway.' The same may doubtless be truthfully said of the Baptist Home Mission Society. It is estimated that only about one-third of the world's population is even nominally Christian; that is, 500, 000,000 out of a total of 1,500,-000,000. We must remember that in this estimate every man, woman and child is counted as a Christian." The committee on State missions, W. M. Tipton, A. F. Manske and J. W. Treadway, said: "One chief work of the board is that of developing non-contributing churches into active contributing churches, thus helping every denominational enterprise." The committee on Sunday Schools, S. G. Givens, A. W. Stewart and Worth Baxter, said: "The aggregate number of pupils is 1,219; the amount contributed for the support of the schools is $250.25; the amount given to the different missions is $51.60." The Association held a memorial service in view of the death of the twenty-seven members who had passed away. The report made did not give the names. Brother M. S. Whiteside led the service. The incoming executive board were T. J. Ayres, J. D. Biggs, J. C. Biggs, L. F. Mackey, G. W. Emerson, J. M. Keach, J. T. Hutcherson, J. C. Mackey, W. T. Jacobs, George Harvey.

September 2, 1896, the Association met with Sugar Creek Church. The introductory sermon was preached by Elder E. Jennings. His text was: "And the key of the house of David will I lay upon his shoulder; so he shall open, and none shall shut, and he shall shut, and none shall open." The visitors were A. W. Payne, W. T. Campbell, J. L. Downing, S. H. Ford, J. T. Muir, J. N. Barbee, J. S. R. Gregory, J. W. Trower, W. L. Boyer, —— Duckworth, H. N. Boney (colored), Sam Ford, S. H. Ford. Ashburn and Annada Churches, Pike county, were received into the fellowship of the Association. The executive board reported: "At the beginning of the year we found two church houses, one at Ashburn, the other at Annada, just completed and looking to this board for payment of a debt aggregating $1,967.59. This has necessarily interfered with our missionary efforts. We have assisted Frankford Church $80, Immanuel Church $100, Mt. Zion $10, Saverton $25; have supplied Ashburn, Annada and Saverton with such missionary labor as we could at a cost of $139.59; balance last year, $40.35; printing minutes, $30.40; making total expenditures on the field $425.34. We have collected and paid on the above debt $733.09, making a total expenditure of $1,158.43. This leaves a debt remaining on the two churches of $1,234.50. We have had efficient missionary services rendered by Brethren S. H. Ballard, E. E. Blasdel and S. T. Hudson, entirely free of cost to the board, save actual expenses, and in some cases even these have been donated. We recommend that our efforts be unabated until the debts on Ashburn and Annada churches are fully cancelled. We have not been able to secure the services of a colporteur, and as the fund, now invested in books, is unemployed capital, we recommend that they be disposed of on the most favorable terms obtainable and the proceeds invested as you may direct." This was a crucial hour in the life of the Association. The material and work that went into those houses were furnished on the basis of the confidence that men had in Salt River Baptists. Would they be disappointed? The Association had never before been under financial responsibilities so heavy. Would our men stand fast? Yes, every messenger of every church. I did not hear of one who faltered. When they were told that *Baptist honor was on trial* they rose as one man and cancelled the debt. It was a time of God's power. "Thy people shall be willing in the day of thy power." That year was the supreme period in the life of Salt River Association unto this day. And to the board, who having done all, stood; and standing, prayed and watched and then got closer to the burden until the honor of Salt River shone as the morning star; to that board, to every member of that board be the gratitude of a grateful brotherhood.

Brother J. D. Biggs reported on obituaries: "Sister Nora Thurmond Edwards was developing beautifully in Christian womanhood; Brother and Sister Samuel P. Inlow were in their eighty-second year; Sister Harrison Fry bore her sufferings patiently; Sister Samuel M. Sanderson was a praying mother, a loving wife and a gentle Christian; Brother Resin D. Ellis was always ready to help with his presence, prayers and means; Sister Almeda Johnson was faithful in her attendance at all her meetings and enjoyed greatly the assembly of the saints; Sister Elizabeth Ann Snyder and Sister Alexander McDannold were sheaves ripe for the Master's garner; Brother James Scroggins gave promise of great usefulness in the Master's kingdom; Sister Maggie Stark was a bright, consecrated Christian girl." The new executive board were J. D. Biggs, T. J. Ayres, L. F. Mackey, S. K. Caldwell, Geo. W. Emerson, J. M. Keach, J. T. Hutcherson, J. C. Mackey, George Harvey, A. M. McGee. The ministers at this time were Bland Beauchamp, C. E. King, B. W. N. Simms, C. A. Waters, J. D. Hacker, S. S. Keith, A. P. Rodgers, W. J. Patrick, J. D. Biggs, W. M. Tipton, C. W. Davis, R. D. Robertson, R. S. Cole, S. G. Givens, W. W. Brown, E. Jennings, M. S. Whiteside, J. M. McManaway, S. P. Dawson, J. W. Trower, P. W. Halley and Henry C. Cox.

The Association met with Bethany church, September 1, 1897. Elder W. T. Campbell preached from the Scripture: "Verily, verily, I say unto you, He that believeth on me, the works that I do, shall he do also; and greater works than these shall he do; because I go unto my Father." The visitors were M. J. Breaker, S. M. Brown, W. T. Campbell, A. W. Payne, J. L. Downing, J. S. R. Gregory, J. L. Dawson, T. N. Sanderson, L. T. Alexander, President Bush, J. P. Sanson, M. V. Shives, and W. P. Brooks (colored). The board reported that $771.50 had been paid missionaries. J. N. Barbee, W. M. Tipton and W. J. Patrick had been employed, and there was good manifested. Brother Bland Beauchamp had held Sunday School institutes of a high order and with good results. The board recommended that the seventy-fifth anniversary of the Association be observed with special services.

The committee on home and foreign missions, J. D. Biggs, L. T. Patterson, J. W. Hawkins, said: "Burma, Assam, India, Siam, China, Japan, Africa, Sweden, Norway, Germany, Austria, Italy, Hungary, Russia, Finland, Poland, Denmark, France, Spain, Bulgaria, Belgium, Switzerland, Brazil and Mexico are receiving through these agencies the word of life. Many of our strongest preachers and some of our best churches were supported or helped by the Home Mission boards, North or South." The committee on education, John D. Hacker, O. B. Hicklin, A. J. McCune, said, "The Bible and Christian history under a thoroughly competent instructor must have a permanent place in the proposed course of study in our schools, before such are entitled to our patronage as Christian schools." The committee on obituaries, W. J. Patrick, C. C. Price and A. G. Raufer, said, "Brother James H. C. Bondurant was a godly man and worthy citizen; Brother John J. Arthur was godly, intelligent, prompt and liberal; Sister Lizzie C. Penn was a gentle Christian and a lovely daughter; Brother Elijah L. Kirtley was constant, exemplary and kind; Sister Catharine Caldwell has passed to immortal youth in her Heavenly Father's house; "It has pleased our Heavenly Father to remove from our companionship our beloved friend and Sister, Jennie Drake Smith." Elder R. S. Cole "seemed strong in the faith and he had been laboring long in the cause." Sister Caroline Lowe was "a devoted Christian." Brother L. D. Howell was a faithful servant of God; Sister Myra Tanner was always present at her regular church meeting; Brother Joseph W. Carr was growing into Christian usefulness; Sister Sallie Mosby lived a consecrated member to her death; Sister Eliza A. Inge was an humble, consistent Christian; Sister Jane Winn bore her trials with faith and courage; Sister H. T. Ogden "was a quiet, devoted servant of the Lord and loved her church."

At 5 o'clock p. m., Tuesday, October 13, 1896, there occurred the transition from earth of a brother and sister in a way that touched the hearts of thousands and that made the time and the place memorable. Death came to them when "life's volume lay open at" the fairest page. They were members of Salem church, faithful in the prayer meetings and Sunday School, constant in their church duties, adorning the doctrine of God, their Saviour. They were a son and daughter of Brother and Sister W. B. Guttery. The son was Demas E. Guttery, the daughter was Miss Jennie E. Guttery. Having been on a visit in the vicinity of

Emerson, Marion county, they returned through Hannibal in a buggy. They left this city about 3 p. m. for their home, a distance of some sixteen miles. The animal they drove was young and spirited, the roads were good, the day was pleasant; the brother and sister were bouyant with life and happy in each other's company. Nothing occurred to awaken apprehension of danger. No evidence of local rains or rising waters appeared to signal danger. It was now four o'clock. The hour and the nine miles yet before them would urge them on. They were on the New London road which crosses Salt River at the old Caldwell Ford. To the westward there had been a heavy rainfall and the tide had reached this ford. At this point the river runs in an east-northeast direction. The entrance to the water from the road-level was through a cut about five feet deep, which came from the northwest and touched the water at a sharp angle. The Hannibal road, now coming from the southwest, then met this cut at an angle of about thirty-five degrees. Along the north bank of the river and extending from the low water level to the general level of the bank was a border of sycamore trees with a heavy fringe of willows. The buggy top was up, limiting the view. The excellence of the road as it then approached the bank inviting speed, they seem to have gone on and into the descending cut before they saw the danger. When the waters had gone down, remaining buggy tracks showed the unavailing efforts which they had made to retrace their steps. The resistless floods now had control of the home-bound twain. They called for help. Two men who were near the railroad bridge below hastened to the southern bank, but were powerless to give relief. They witnessed the end of the struggle. Demas was out by the side of the horse, making a heroic effort to save his sister, but the death struggle of the horse and the fury of the waves carried him down. Jennie was then heard to exclaim, "O, God! have mercy on me! He's gone." In about one minute Jennie followed Demas beneath the flood. Their bodies were recov-

ered. On Demas' body was found a card with these words printed on it: "For God shall bring every work into judgment, with every secret thing, whether it be good or whether it be evil." Also, these words:
"This day!
I shall never see it again.
Am I using it well?"

Demas was manly, straight-forward, sincere. Jennie was womanly and she had the most gentle manner and a sweetly childlike face. Brother and Sister Guttery have five surviving children, who may say:
"Seven boys and girls are we;
Two of us in the churchyard lie,
Beneath the churchyard tree."

We met, August 30, 1898, with the church in New London. The sermon was preached by Elder W. J. Patrick from the Scripture beginning, "And it came to pass about an eight days after these sayings, He took Peter and John and James and went up into a mountain to pray;" the transfiguration as given by Luke, The hand of fellowship was given to the messengers of Annada church, which had re-organized. They were Belle Stewart, Jas. Crank and E. L. Lewellen. On the 31st, seventy-fifth anniversary services were held as follows: A list was presented of those who had been church members forty or more years, namely John T. Brown, J. T. Hutcherson, Mrs. N. R. Anderson, W. T. Jacobs, John S. Martin, Mrs. Susan B. Briscoe, James D. Biggs, Julia B. Owen, Geo. A. Lake, G. W. Ledford, M. S. Whiteside, J. R. Powell, E. Jennings, John Ford, M. E. Motley, H. C. Cox, Milton Cox, L. C. Bibb, Mrs. Lucretia Beckner, Ambrose Beckner, Mrs. Elizabeth Brashears, Mrs. S. V. Jinks, J. C. Stewart, John Barkley, Mrs. Susan Barkley, Mrs. P. F. Draper, Jeptha Lake, Mrs. Sarah Lake, Mrs. Martha J. Cash, Mrs. Martha Brashears, G. W. Wylie, Lizzie Cox, Mrs. Mattie Maxfield, Mrs. Lucian Buchanan, Mrs. Sallie Keach Wood, Mrs. Amanda Brown, R. B. Caldwell. Elder M. S. Whiteside led the devotional service. A fraternal address on behalf of Salt

River Association was made by Elder James D. Biggs. Fraternal responses were made by Elder B. F. Hixson, of Bethel Association, Elder James Reid, of St. Louis Association, Judge Milton Cox, of Bear Creek Association, and a letter was read from Elder R. S. Duncan, of same Association, Elder F. M. Shoush, of Audrain Association, Elder W. N. Maupin, of Cuivre Association, Elder E. Jennings, on behalf of Bay Creek Association, and by President J. T. Muir, of LaGrange College. A letter from Sister J. S. Green, of Palmyra, was read concerning her father, Hon. William Carson, who was the first clerk of Salt River Association. Eld. F. M. Shoush read a paper in honor of Elder James F. Smith. "A historical paper was read by Brother Dalton Biggs, full of information and pleasant memories." The standard old songs were used and singing and prayer were given large place. W. J. Patrick presented a gavel, made from a cherry tree growing near the spot where the Association was organized. On motion the gavel was accepted, with thanks."

Additional visitors: J. C. Stewart, W. L. Boyer, T. N. Walton.

The executive board reported: They had the services, in the course of the outgoing year, of B. Beauchamp, J. D. Biggs, R. T. Campbell and J. S. Eames. There was good work done but men were employed for brief periods. The committee on Sunday Schools, B. W. N. Simms, J. W. McIlroy and Worth Baxter, reported: "We believe the Institute work, inaugurated by the board of this Association, conducted so wisely and efficiently by our Brother Bland Beauchamp, has already produced fruitful effects, greatly strengthening the Sunday School sentiment." Brother J. J. Penix reported for the committe on obituaries. He said, thirty-six of our members have passed away. Brother G. R. Waddell was a worthy citizen and a devoted Christian; Sister Ida B. Lewellen was a good Christian woman; Sister Jennetta Anderson was useful and pious; Sister Harriet Paxton was a consistent member of the church; Sister Gabrella McGee was among the most faithful members of her church; Sister Sarah A. Smith was a devoted servant of the Lord; Brother Joseph L. King was a living epistle, known and read; Sister Hesket was a consecrated Christian; Brothers W. H. Smith and M. B. Grafford had willing hearts and open hands, ready to every good word and work; Sisters Mattie B. Smith and Harriet Mitchell have gone to their reward; Brother Enos Hostetter gave many years of faithful service in the Master's cause; Bowling Green church has lost seven, Sisters E. A. Ogden, Catharine Luckett, Rebecca Roberts, Ann Rodgers, Martha Shepherd, Rebecca Dalton, M. F. Frier and Mrs. H. S. Willis; Brother Samuel P. Dawson was an ordained minister and had the confidence of those who knew him. The Constitution was so changed as to make the executive board consist of one member from each church, that one to be elected by his church. The executive board to act until the churches elect are; J. D. Biggs, T. J. Ayres, J. W. Hawkins, A. C. Truitt, Geo. W. Emerson, J. M. Keach, L. F. Mackey, J. C. Mackey, Joseph McCune and A. M. McGee.

We met at Dover, August 30, 1899. The sermon was preached by Elder J. W. Trower. His text was: "And he shall stand and feed in the strength of the Lord, in the majesty of the name of the Lord his God; and they shall abide; for now shall he be great unto the ends of the earth." Re-organization was effected by the election of J. C. Mackey, moderator and L. T. Patterson clerk. The former officers desired to be relieved. The visiting brethren were: M. J. Breaker, J. C. Armstrong, Dr. Tyzzer, J. T. Muir, E. Barkley, —— Shives, J. L. Dawson, Thomas Smith, Byron Bibb, Isaac Cannon, J. R. Cannon, John W. Waters, Mrs. John W. Waters, John F. Whiteside, Mrs. John F. Whiteside, H. N. Boney (colored), J. M. McManaway.

The executive board reported: R. T. Campbell, F. M. Walton, W. A. Bibb and W. J. Patrick had done work. The ground had been held and some advancement was made. "We hope and pray, as well as have reason to believe, that with the church debts (which hampered our efforts) out of the way, that greater success may attend the labors under the new management."

The committee on obituaries gave no names. The new executive board consists of one man elected by each church.

The Association met with Ramsey Creek church, August 29, 1900. Elder J. C. Armstrong preached the sermon from the Scripture: "Who shall lay anything to the charge of God's elect? It is God that justifieth."

These visitors accepted seats: J. T. Nevins and wife, J. P. Stewart, J. L. Dawson, Misses Killam, J. W. Waters and wife, H. Bibb, T. N. Sanderson, C. A. Mitchell, H. M. Shives and wife, James Reid, C. C. Long, B. E. Anthrobus, J. C. Armstrong, Charles Rhodes, S. M. Brown, A. M. Vardeman, J. T. Muir. The committee on home and foreign missions, Will S. Hall, R. A. Jones and J. S. Martin, said, "As far as the east is from the west, and the north from the south, lies the field in which we are to work." The executive board reported: R. T. Campbell, J. W. Trower, J. A. Riney and E. Jennings had been employed in the various missions. The ministers did good service. The committee on state of the churches, W. M. Tipton, A. G. Raufer and W. M. Waters, says, "One hundred and thirteen have been our net increase. Our Sunday School work is encouraging, there being maintained a Baptist Sunday School in nominally all of the churches."

A collection of $90 was taken to help build a house of worship for Mt. Zion church. A Sunday School convention was organized with W. A. Bibb president, J. S. Megown secretary, and William S. Hall treasurer.

ANNADA BAPTIST CHURCH.

By W. A. Bibb.

The following persons, having just been baptized by Rev. J. S. Eames, went into the organization of a Baptist church: Mary Stewart, Annie Stewart, E. L. Lewellen, Nettie Steel, Luta Crank, Walter Brown, Beula Reed, Wesley Reed, Manervil Beauchamp, Laura Taylor, Cora Taylor, Elisha, Button and Dolly Beatty, Alton Hopke, George Alexander, Jas. Crank, Bertha Hammond, Richard Hammond and Mattie Williamson.

Brethren of Louisiana, Ramsey Creek, Dover, Ebenezer, Oak Ridge and Elsberry churches were with Thomas Campbell and J. S. Eames organized into a presbytery. They proceeded to organize the church. Bro. J. E. Griffin was made moderator, Bro. S. F. Thompson, previous to this organization, under the employment of the Salt River Association board, had preached and done much efficient work, also he built the present house of worship. Bro. Campbell was continued Pastor for three years. Bro. Jas. W. Callaway was called and served three years; W. P. Bibb, a part of a year; A. E. Lower, two years. W. A. Bibb followed them. Brethren who helped in meetings: Fitch Millerchamp, W. W. Brown, J. S. Eames, Luther Smith, Antherbus, Burkhead, S. F. Thompson, Barbee, Abe C. Jones.

The church has on her roll sixty-eight members, but many of them have moved away without taking letters. The district board of Association renders help to the church. The field is hopeful but difficult.

IMMANUEL CHURCH.

By Charles L. Yeager.

Immanuel Baptist church was organized in August, 1895, with seventeen members. September 28, T. P. Norton and C. L. Yeager were elected Deacons. Bro. W. J. Patrick was called as Pastor and continued as same two years. Brother H. B. Rice, of Laddonia, was then called and served six years, since which we have had no regular preaching.

ELDER J. N. BARBEE'S MISSION WORK.

By Himself.

Rev. Jas. N. Barbee was called to the mission work of Salt River Association by the board at its annual session held at Sugar Creek during the Association of August, 1896. He was present and accepted the work.

His work was at Ashburn, Annada and Saverton, where regular monthly meetings were held; and these, in addition to holding protracted meetings, occupied his time during the year. Ashburn and Annada are still maintaining the stated preaching of the word.

In the winter of 1897 the missionary held a meeting with the Ashburn church, which resulted in a number of additions, and the expending of some money on the meeting-house, organization of a Sunday School, buying an organ, seating the house and making it possible for the Baptist church there to live. And it is pretty well alive today, though there have been seasons of heaviness, discouragement and gloom.

He assisted Pastor Wm. Tipton in a meeting at Frankford during the time he was missionary and also conducted a fine meeting with Bro. Halley at Silex, Lincoln county. Also assisted pastor, Rev. J. D. Biggs, in a most excellent meeting at Bethany in the fall of 1897; also assisted at Noix Creek, and put in some time at Farmer.

One very peculiar and exciting experience related by Rev. Barbee, was while he was Pastor at Annada in 1897, and March of that year, or probably 1898. He was being assisted in special meetings by Elder Birkhead, of Winfield. The prospects were most encouraging for a good meeting. On Thursday night after the meeting began on Sunday, rain began to fall, and such was the downpour during the night that the levee above town broke, and Friday morning the town and immediately surrounding country were flooded—water

ELDER H. M. KING.

J. T. WILLIAMS, D. D.

ELDER G. B. SMITH.

ELDER JAMES REID.

running through the streets from two and one half to four feet deep. Bro. Birkhead was taken out of a house by getting astride of a horse. I was taken out of another house on a raft. Of course, the meeting came to an abrupt termination.

During my pastorate at Annada quite an interesting meeting was held, the object of which was to raise some money to pay off a small indebtedness. Bro. Biggs and I preached. An elegant dinner was served, some money was raised and the work has gone steadily on. At this meeting Dover, Ramsey, and Edgewood, and possibly Clarksville were represented.

The church at Ashburn has had a checkered career ever since the church house was erected by the lamented S. F. Thompson, who was my immediate predecessor as missionary in Salt River. The population of the town in the main has been very much of an unsettled character, and to a certain extent of different nationalities, on account of the great powder plant located just a mile north, a good many of the employees of which reside in Ashburn and have no affiliation with churches or care for religion. Consequently the church has always had to struggle hard for existence, never having had at any time a large or prosperous membership, but always some warm friends and supporters, both preachers and laymen, who have never lost sight of the struggling band.

Rev. Robt. Smith, a resident minister, consecrated and faithful, and a good preacher and minister of Jesu Christ, is breaking the bread of eternal life and meet ing with fine success.

CHAPTER XII.

STRENGTHENING THE THINGS THAT REMAIN, 1901-1908.

Salt River Association had now been shorn of vast territory to the east, to the west, to the north and to the south; a large number of churches and ministers had gone into the newer organizations. The territory came to be limited to the larger parts of Ralls and Pike counties. The call to us was to do intenser service and strengthen the things that remain. The limits of Salt River Association now are about one-fourth the limits of the land of Judea, say, thirty by fifty miles.

August 28, 1901, we met with Salem church. The annual sermon was preached by Elder R. D. Robertson, from the Scripture: "And the Lord said unto Moses, wherefore criest thou unto me? Speak unto the children of Israel that they go forward." The visiting brethren were S. M. Brown, A. W. Payne, Dr. Tyzzer, W. P. Brooks (colored), Jas. Reid, W. C. Busby, Everett Gill, R. N. Gilbert, Miss Olive Blunt, returned missionary from Japan, was also present.

The missionaries of the board had been R. T. Campbell, J. A. Riney and T. P. Todd. The work done was good and the results gratifying. The committee on State missions, W. J. Patrick and S. C. Truitt, said, "State missions serves as a reserve power to move forward when a district Association is weak or hesitating or in case there is territory not claimed by any local mission force."

The committee on obituaries, S. M. Sanderson and J. D. Biggs, reported that there had been fifty deaths in our churches. The executive board for the incoming year were J. M. Smith, Jas. M. Keach, B. F. Ball, J. C. Mackey, L. F. Mackey, A. J. McCune and George W. Emerson. The committee on Sunday Schools, W.

A. Bibb and Will S. Hall, recommended the organization of an institute with R. D. Robertson as president, J. S. Megown as secretary and Edgar McDannold as treasurer.

The Association held her session of 1902 with Bowling Green church, beginning August 28. Elder W. D. Bolton preached the opening sermon. The text was: "And the Lord said unto Moses, wherefore criest thou unto me? Speak unto the children of Israel, that they may go forward."

The visiting brethren were R. K. Maiden, J. F. Kemper, S. F. Taylor, C. A. Waters, W. P. Brooks (colored), J. F. Muir, A. W. Payne, Charles Rhoads, J. R. S. Gregory and wife, Sister Nelson, R. E. McQuie, Miss Eva Hudson, Miss Lou Parsons, G. A. Lake, —— Rogers, J. W. Trower, Miss Mollie Kirtley, T. L. West. The report of the board showed that W. A. Bibb, T. P. Todd, W. P. Bibb, J. D. Biggs, W. D. Pulis and F. G. Rogers had been doing mission work. The work of the Lord had prospered in their hands. The committee on Sunday Schools, J. W. Lacy, A. M. Edwards and D. T. Sanderson, said: "The Sunday School work is increasing slightly in interest among all the churches." The ministers at this time were W. D. Bolton, S. S. Keith, A. P. Rodgers, W. J. Patrick, J. D. Biggs, W. M. Tipton, R. D. Robertson, W. A. Bibb, Henry Cox, W. W. Brown, C. F. J. Tate, E. Jennings, P. W. Halley, Jos. N. Barbee, J. W. Trower. The newly appointed board, which had been increased to ten, was L. F. Mackey, J. E. Thompson, S. C. Truitt, Geo. E. Mayhall, W. D. Bolton, A. J. McCune, J. C. Biggs, H. G. McDannold, W. J. Patrick and C. F. J. Tate.

In 1903, September 2d, the Association met with the church in Louisiana. Elder J. W. Long preached the introductory sermon from the Scripture: "She hath done what she could; she is come aforehand to anoint my body to the burying." Reorganization was effected by the election of Edward Biggs moderator and Lem. T. Patterson clerk. Invitations to seats were accepted by the following brethren: M. J. Breaker, T. L. West, J. C. Armstrong, W. P. Brooks (colored), S. M. Brown, H. T. Morton, J. E. Cook, J. T. Muir, J. R. Pentuff, M. V. Shives.

The executive board reported that they had the services for various periods of time during the year of R. T. Campbell, J. D. Biggs, W. A. Bibb, J. W. Long, W. P. Bibb, J. W. Trower and R. E. McQuie. The work was done in Pike county. J. D. Biggs made the report on state of the churches. He said, "Eighteen of the churches self-sustaining, two have preaching every Sunday, two have preaching twice a month, several have no Sunday School, about eight have Sunday School all year."

The new board were L. F. Mackey, J. E. Thompson, J. J. Nichols, J. S. Megown, J. D. Biggs, A. J. McCune, J. C. Biggs, J. C. Mackey, Edward Biggs and C. F. J. Tate.

August 31, 1904, Salt River Association convened with Spencerburg church. Elder C. F. J. Tate preached the annual sermon. The text was: "Unto the angel of the church of Ephesus write; These things saith he that holdeth the seven stars in his right hand, who walketh in the midst of the seven golden candlesticks."

The visiting brethren were: A. W. Payne, James Reid, Sister Leona Mann, S. M. Brown. The executive board reported that R. T. Campbell, W. Callaway, J. D. Biggs, J. W. Trower, W. A. Bibb, R. E. McQuie, C. F. J. Tate, J. T. Nevins and D. E. Millichamp had been employed. Some churches were helped in Pike county. The executive board for the incoming year was Edward Biggs, L. F. Mackey, J. E. Thompson, W. D. Bolton, J. C. Mackey, David Hettich, J. R. Weaver, A. J. McCune, J. C. Biggs, J. J. Nichols, J. D. Biggs, C. F. J. Tate, S. M. Sanderson and Geo. E. Mayhall.

August 30, 1905, we met with Bethel church. Elder Sanford M. Brown preached the opening sermon from the text: "Ye have not, because ye ask not."

The visitors were M. J. Breaker, S. M. Brown, J. M. Crouch and W. P. Brooks (colored). The executive board reported. The report showed work done in Pike county at Annada, Mt. Zion, Peno, Prairieville, Spencerburg, Ashburn, Pleasant Hill, Eolia, Grassy Creek, Elm Grove, Adiel, Edgewood, Frankford, Bowling Green and Mt. Pisgah. The ministers employed were James W. Callaway, A. E. Lower, L. P. Smith, J. W. Trower, W. S. Wilburn, W. A. Bibb, R. E. McQuie. W. S. Wilburn, was general missionary.

He reports sixty-five baptisms as a result of his meetings. There was effective work done by the missionary pastors. The committee on temperance, T. J. Ayres and A. J. McCune, said, "Our country at large is to be congratulated on the growth of public sentiment in favor of temperance, and our State especially on having a Governor who is fearlessly enforcing the Sunday closing law." The committee on home and foreign missions, W. A. Bibb, J. N. Price and J. J. Nichols, said, "In this country we have a vast population of foreigners. The home mission board is trying through the preaching of the gospel to win these multitudes to God."

The executive board for the incoming year was L. F. Mackey, J. E. Thompson, J. C. Mackey, J. R. Weaver, George E. Mayhall, Geo. C. Cole, J. M. Smith, J. C. Biggs, J. J. Nichols, David Hettich, A. J. McCune, J. W. Keach, Charles A. Bibb and T. J. Smith.

Salt River Association convened with Frankford church, August 29, 1906. Elder W. A. Bibb preached the associational sermon from the Scripture: "I am the door; by me if any man enter in, he shall be saved and shall go in and out, and find pasture."

By invitation the following visiting brethren were enrolled: E. S. Graham, J. C. Armstrong, D. J Evans, M. J. Breaker, R. K. Maiden, J. W. Crouch M. S. Whiteside, W. H. Burnham, C. F. J. Tate an C. A. Mitchell. The report of the executive boar showed that Adiel, Annada, Mt. Zion, Peno and Spencerburg had been helped. Brethren M. E. Broaddus and George T. Baker are named as having done service for the board and forty-six baptisms are reported. The committee on home and foreign missions, J. D. Biggs, G. C. Cole and P. S. Waddell, said, "Papal fields in which we have missionaries are Italy, Brazil, Mexico, Spain, France, Bulgaria and Argentina. The pagan are China, Japan, Africa, India, Siam, Burma." The committee on Sunday Schools, John W. Treadway, William L. Maddox and George T. Baker, said, "We believe that where a church has preaching only one Sunday in the month that a live, progressive Sunday School is almost, if not altogether, essential to its progress. God's house should be opened for worship every Sabbath." The committee on state of churches, Luke Kirtly, J. W. Keach and Jas. Smith, said, "An increase by baptism of one hundred and thirty-five; the total contributions are $12,500." The committee on temperance, J. B. Crouch, A. J. McCune and J. C. Mackey, said, "We are told by good and competent judges of our courts that nearly nine-tenths of the crime committed throughout the length and breadth of the land is due to use of intoxicating liquors."

The committee on obituaries, T. J. Ayres, W. A. Bibb and J. N. Price, said, "Your committee reports the death of thirty-one members. Of this number, two, at least, John B. Dunbar, Esq., of Mt. Pisgah, and Sister Elizabeth McGary, of Noix Creek, were enlisted under the Master's banner for more than half a century."

September 2, 1907, we met with Eolia church. The sermon was preached by Elder J. B. Crouch from the Scripture: "God is faithful, by whom ye were called unto the fellowship of his Son Jesus Christ, our Lord," The moderator was absent. Re-organization was effected by the election of W. A. Bibb, moderator, and L. T. Patterson, clerk. The visiting brethren were G. W. Givens, —— Benson, George Steel, M. S. Whiteside, W. D. Bolton, J. C. Armstrong, S. M.

Brown and J. T. Muir. The executive board reported that they had helped Spencerburg, Adiel, Peno, Mt. Zion, Annada and Ashburn. The committee on State missions, W. J. Patrick and A. J. McCune, said, "The motive and mold for Christian evangelism find expression in the words of our Lord: 'The poor have the gospel preached unto them.' There is great destitution in Missouri, as Warrenton, Washington and Hermann in our part of the State, besides dozens of other fields in country towns and cities."

The committee on home and foreign missions, J. B. Crouch, C. C. Price and T. M. King, said, "In the general summary of the work of our two conventions we find there were $1,039,275 contributed to home missions and $4,279,448 contributed to foreign missions." The committee on Sunday Schools, G. T. Baker, E. B. Omohundro and J. C. Mackey, said, "We believe the basis of all true excellence in this work is honest, efficient, sympathetic, Christian teaching; that our schools will be effective or not in the same proportion as our teaching force is zealous and well trained." The committe on state of churches, J. H. Terrill, J. E. Griffith and G. C. Cole, said, "We are sorry to see so many of our churches not giving to missions, and we recommend they give regularly to all."

The following action was taken: "Moved and carried that Rev. W. J. Patrick be and he is requested and empowered to write a history of Salt River Association." The new board were L. F. Mackey, J. C. Mackey, Geo. E. Mayhall, J. M. Smith, L. T. Patterson, J. R. Weaver, Geo. C. Wise, J. C. Biggs, J. J. Nichols, J. N. Price, A. J. McCune, J. W. Keach, Charles A. Bibb and O. M. Fuqua.

Salt River Association met with the Curryville church, September 2, 1908. Elder W. P. Pearce preached the introductory sermon. His text was: "O Lord, revive thy work."

These brethren accepted seats as visitors: H. E. Truex, J. W. Crouch, R. K. Maiden, —— Couch, W. H. Burnham, Milford Riggs, T. L. West, Joseph

Stirmlinger, Abe C. Jones and W. J. Couch. The Association resolved: "That with intense interest in our general work and with fraternal courtesy to agents, we ask that all claims be presented in the order of our regular proceedings in Salt River Association." The executive board reported aid given to Ashburn, Annada, Peno, Mt. Zion, Spencerburg, Walnut Grove, Adiel. The brethren doing work under the board were W. A. Bibb, M. E. Broaddus, J. D. Watson, R. O. Smith, Luke Kirtley and E. L. Barkley. $450 was expended. The committee on orphan's home, Edward Biggs and R. O. Smith, gave the institution strong endorsement and urged its support. The committee on obituaries, J. H. Terrill and J. E. Griffith, said, "Sister Letitia Barnard was baptized by Elder Jeremiah Vardeman. Her life was consistent and worthy. Dr. H. P. Lewis was brought into the kingdom of God under the preaching of Rev. Smith Thomas, of Kentucky. While he ministered to the physical needs and comforts of the sick, he did not forget to do what he could for their spiritual comfort." Elder E. Jennings and others who had passed away were given fraternal mention. The executive board for the incoming year was L. F. Mackey, J. C. Mackey, Geo. E. Mayhall, J. M. Smith, L. T. Patterson, J. R. Weaver, Geo. C. Wise, J. C. Biggs, J. J. Nichols, J. N. Price, A. J. McCune, J. W. Keach, Chas. A. Bibb and O. M. Fuqua. The resident ministers in 1908, were: J. B. Crouch, A. P. Rogers, W. J. Patrick, R. D. Robertson, W. A. Bibb, Jos. N. Barbee, J. H. Terrill, W. P. Pearce, Geo. T. Baker, M. E. Broaddus, Geo. W. Wright, R. T. Campbell and R. O. Smith. The Association adjourned to meet with Spencer Creek church at 11 o'clock, a. m., Wednesday before the first Sunday in September, 1909.

WENTZVILLE CHURCH.

First minutes are dated March 7, 1901. Rev. F. M. Birkhead, moderator; also Pastor; C. E. Hutchinson, church clerk.

Bro. Birkhead resigned as Pastor, March 10, 1893.
Bro. J. P. Charles called as Pastor, April 25, 1893.
Bro. B. H. Bibb called as Pastor, March 27, 1894.
Bro. Hutchinson called as Pastor, March 12, 1898.
Bro. Reid was acting Pastor, December 12, 1900.
Bro. S. L. Palmer called as Pastor, December, 1901.
Bro. J. Reid called as Pastor, April 19, 1902.
Bro. A. R. Finley called as Pastor in June, 1905. Bro. Finley is still acting as Pastor.

REV. EDMOND JENNINGS.

Bedford county, Virginia, was the place of his nativity and September 22, 1835, was the time of his birth. In 1854 he came to Missouri and soon settled in Pike county. March 14, 1860, he married Miss Lucinda J. Hawkins, daughter of Mr. and Mrs. James Hawkins, of Pike county.

In early life Brother Jennings made a public profession of faith in Jesus Christ and was baptized by Rev. John T. Williams. In 1853 he was ordained to the ministry at old Noix Creek church. He was zealous and efficient in the ministry, giving a large part of his time to weak churches and destitutions. In 1858 he organized Mt. Zion church which he served as Pastor four years. He perhaps at no time received for his work enough to support his family, but his zeal, nothing abated, led him to earn bread with his hands, and preach on such salary as might come to him.

He was a man of good presence, cordial manner, active life, exuberent vitality. His voice was sonorous and agreeable. His manner in the pulpit was reverent and ardent. His labors were sometimes blessed by revivals and many conversions. His labors were mostly among the country churches, of which he was Pastor for various periods of time. He was in the active ministry more than a half century and spent his last few years in quiet home life.

His death occurred in his home, Louisiana, Mo., October 26, 1907, at the age of seventy-two years, one month and four days. His burial sermon was preached by his Pastor the Rev. W. P. Pearce, Rev. J. N. Barbee assisting in the service. His body was laid to rest in the Louisiana city cemetery.

CHAPTER XIII.

CONCLUSION.

The history of Salt River Association has been varied, advancing and constructive. She was strong from the beginning. Situated in the heart of the Mississippi valley, organized by men of large capacity and and of spiritual power, she stood on natural, intellectual and spiritual vantage ground from the first.

The good news of salvation, the gospel of Jesus the Christ, was the burden of their proceedings. They were strong, discerning, generous men; most of them were laymen. One of the good things in the New Testament economy of gospel advancement is that, in the service to which we are called, we are brethren, whether one is a minister or not a minister. The door is wide open to every one who has received Christ to exhort others to come and be saved. Recently, what is called the Laymen's Movement, has touched Salt River Association. This movement has in it the possibilities of large usefulness if wisely directed. The organization of Salt River Association was largely a layman's movement.

One of the problems in religious thought and life has for many years been the question of molding, teaching and training young people. Home government has been relaxed, the Sunday School holds only a part of the youths after they esteem themselves young men and the multitude of mechanical appliances has released both young women and young men from the close application to toil that was once a necessity in every home. This toil has a moral virtue. It protects from idleness and evil company. It forms industrial habits, without which one may not hope to attain the best in any of the walks of life. "A wholesome habitation of the will to objective activities" can be had only by actual performance of duty. The solution of this problem has been only in part satisfactory.

There has been a change in church architecture within the last forty years that is radical, aggressive and that may be turned to advantage in service. It makes our houses less imposing, but gives better adaptations to varied church activities. In most cases the main audience room suffers by the change, but for this there is more than a compensation to the Sunday School and, all the smaller assemblies. The Greek-Roman basilica in use as a hall of justice before the advent of Christ, was adopted by Christian worshipers as the form of their sanctuary. It underwent many modifications, but in its main feature it held its place through the centuries. We now have it in the churches of New London, Bethel, Spencerburg, Cyrene, Clarksville and Ramsey Creek. The new and composite style has been built by the churches of Bowling Green, Louisiana, Salem and Frankford. It is Gothic with American impress, subtractions and additions.

OUR MISSIONARIES ABROAD.

Five missionaries have gone from Salt River Association to the foreign field. They were Miss Emma Morton, who became Mrs. Ginsburg, Elder James L. Downing and wife, who was Miss Addie Martin, Elder Walter E. Wiatt and Mrs. Francis Wiatt Darrow.

Mrs. Ginsburg.
(By her mother.)

Mrs. Emma Morton Ginsburg, was born in Kentucky, January 16, 1865. She is the oldest daughter of the late Rev. H. T. and Mrs. Mary A. Morton. She was educated by her father. She taught in South Carolina and several other States very successfully. She also taught in McCune College in Louisiana, Mo. While there she met Mr. Bagby, of Brazil, and heard his stirring appeal in behalf of Brazilian missions. From that time she yearned for an opportunity to offer her services to the foreign mission board. When the sad news came of the death of Miss Maggie Rice, she at once expressed a desire to fill her place.

Her offer of service was accepted by the foreign mission board. She said "Good-bye," to her family and an invalid sister that she never saw again, for God took her home. She sailed June 16, 1889, from Newport News, for Rio. On the way the ship took fire and they were lowered in small boats, remained all night with waves dashing high over them, yet she was not afraid; she knew who was guiding and caring for her. By the time she reached Rio, she had yellow fever, but was kindly and tenderly cared for by Rev. and Mrs. Bagby.

At the farewell service given her at Louisiana by the church and Pastor, Elder J. F. Kemper, she sang "The Crowning Day is Coming," and the Lord has crowned the labors of her husband and herself with many a blessing. God has wrought great things among the nations in these twenty years that Sister Ginsburg has been in Brazil.

Elder Walter E. Wiatt, is a son of Dr. W. E. Wiatt and wife, who is a daughter of Prof. A. Slaughter and wife. He made a profession of faith in Christ in Cyrene, Mo., and was baptized into the fellowship of the church in that place by Elder J. E. Chambliss, the Pastor. He took a regular course of educational preparation. The following letter from him, taken from the *Central Baptist* of January 14, 1909, gives his field of labor. He sailed in 1904.

"MOULMEIN, BURMA.

"The Burma Baptist Missionary Conference, which is composed of missionaries only, met at the Baptist College, Rangoon, October 28th, 29th, and 30th, 1908, with about seventy-five missionaries in attendance. The general topic of the meetings was, "The awakening of the Church of Burma." We realize the need of a revival in Burma, and are praying for it most earnestly.

"For the past two or three years the subject has had prominent place in our discussions at the Conference and you will see from the general topic above that we yet consider it of great importance. There have been revivals among the Karens, the Musos, and now there are some signs of an awakening among the Taungthus; but, as yet, very few Burman Buddhists have accepted Christ. There has been marked progress during the past three or four years which has not been unobserved by the Buddhists themselves as their renewed activities signify.

"Realizing that the teaching of Christian doctrines was undermining their ancient faith, they have adopted the methods of propagation used by Christians, and now have a printing press in Mandalay and schools in most of the larger cities, and some of their most noted Phoongyees are those who are making tours here and there holding what we would call evangelistic meetings. This awakening interest in religious matters affords us a good opportunity for presenting the claims of Christ, and we ask the prayers of all who read this on behalf of both missionaries and the native Christians that we may not be found wanting in zeal at this time.

"'In His Name' was the theme of the first devotional service of the meetings, and as the leader spoke of 'power in the Name, power to save, power to keep,' we felt that there was no lack in the source of our supplies.

"These Conferences, where we exchange ideas as to methods of work, discuss topics of general interest, and where we have special seasons for prayer and praise, are alway helpful. They are a veritable feast to those who come from the frontier stations where a white face besides the missionary's is sometimes not seen for months.

"At the close of the Conference, the Convention, which is composed of both missionaries and native Christians, met at Vinton Memorial Hall and continued in session for three days. The chief item of interest in the report of the managing committee, which gives annually an epitome of the work done under the auspices of the Convention, during the year, was an account of what we hope will yet prove to be a general awakening among the Taungthus, or hill people, of Upper Burma. Without special effort on the part of anyone, quite a number of these people have come in to the Station at Taunggyi to Miss Payne, the missionary in charge there, asking for baptism.

"In a letter received from Miss Payne during the convention she said that about one hundred inquirers had been to see her, and of these a large number asked for baptism. Sad to relate, there was no ordained man there to baptize them. The nearest missionary was unable to get to Taunggyi on account of illness, and there were no native ordained men near. Surely this is a call for workers. The convention at once took steps to send some one up there to help for awhile at least. Miss Payne wrote that among the number of inquirers was one old man who had heard Dr. Judson preach. The seed sown in this old man's heart has been all these years germinating, and who knows but that the awakening among the others up there may be due also to some of this same sowing. 'He that goeth forth and weepeth, bearing seed for sowing, shall doubtless come again with joy, bringing his sheaves with him.' Will you not join us in prayer that there may be a real revival among these people?"

Mrs. Frances Wiatt Darrow. Sister Darrow is a daughter of Dr. W. E. Wiatt and wife, of East St. Louis. She became a Christian and united with the church in Cyrene, Mo., and was baptized by Dr. J. E. Chambliss. The following interesting article gives a good account of the service into which the hand of the Lord has led her. It was written by her husband, Elder Arthur C. Darrow.

"Moulmein, Burma, March 9, 1908.

"In 1901 my wife, Frances Wiatt Darrow, and myself were appointed as missionaries of the American

Baptist Missionary Union to take up work among the Talains in Burma. In 1902 we sailed and were stationed at Moulmein. Two years later Rev. Walter E. Wiatt, my wife's brother and my sister's husband, joined us in Moulmein to take charge of the work of the Missionary Union among the Burmans. Moulmein is one of our largest mission stations in Burma. The Missionary Union has twenty missionaries in this important station working among the Burmans, Karens, Taloins, Telugus and Tamils, English speaking peoples and Chinese. Moulmein is situated at the junction of three rivers. The scenery about Moulmein is said to be the most beautiful in all the East. It has a population of about 56,000, in which are represented nearly all the races of India. It is one of the leading seaports in the country, having a large export business in teak wood, rice and ivory. Dr. and Mrs. Judson began work in Moulmein in 1827. One or two of the converts baptized by him are still living. Mr. Wiatt enjoys the pleasure of living on the Judson Compound and of using buildings more than a half century old. In the Moulmein station considered as a whole we have about forty churches and three thousand members. During the past year about three hundred have been baptized."

Dr. James L. Downing and Wife. Brother and Sister Downing went to Brazil in 1891. Sister Downing was Miss Addie Belle Martin, a daughter of Deacon Robert J. Martin and wife, who was a daughter of Mr. Fountain Edwards and wife. She became a Christian in early life and united with Walnut Grove Church, Pike county, Mo. I have this from Dr. Downing:

"ODESSA, MISSOURI, May 22, 1909.
"Bro. Patrick,
    "Bowling Green, Missouri.
"Dear Bro.: You asked for some facts of the foreign field and I state the times we went and came back. The first time we went in July, 1891, and came back

August, 1893. The second time we went April 5, 1899, and came back October 9, 1901.
"Respectfully,
"J. L. DOWNING."

These five missionaries all went to the foreign field with the confidence, sympathy and cooperation of the churches to which they belonged and many have been the prayers offered for our Father's blessing upon them. Their lives have been preserved, their labors have been honored and their fellow-disciples in Salt River Association are grateful in their fellowship of service.

Substantial work has been done in the department of Sunday Schools. Institutes and conventions have been held to increase the efficiency of the officers and teachers. The most effective service of this kind has been institutes held by a competent man appointed by the board of missions to hold a session in each of several parts of our bounds. The most efficient service in institute work was done by Elder Bland Beauchamp, who made them veritable normal schools for equipping Sunday School workers. Able men came in and helped in Sunday School institutes. Among them were M. L. Laws, N. J. Smith, R. M. Inlow, Charles Rhodes and Harvey Beauchamp.

In the earlier days of the Association there was maintained a healthy, consistent, corrective church discipline, in which horse-racing, gambling, swearing, dancing, adultery, Sabbath-breaking, lying, drunkenness and such like sins were forbidden to be practiced by church members. We now have great reason to hear some quote and exhort, saying, "Brethren, if a man be overtaken in a fault, ye which are spiritual, restore such a one in the spirit of meekness; considering thyself, lest thou also be tempted."

Our ministry has usually been able to instruct and exhort to the edification of the disciples. The fruit has been abundant. The revival in the vicinity of Spencerburg in 1832 was intense, far-reaching, all-conquering. Esquire Luke Lewis and Col. William G. Hawkins were fruit of that triumphant work of grace and they rejoiced to tell how the gospel was the power of God unto salvation and that multitudes were saved. The preachers preached the word of God, and by the sword of the Spirit the wicked were slain and lived again through the blood of the Lamb. And there were many other gracious revivals. The finer Christian graces, faith, hope and charity, gentleness, meekness and patience were cultivated by the fathers. Surpassingly beautiful I repeat, are the words introduced in the Association in 1831: "On motion of Brother D. Biggs it is agreed that the messengers of this Association do request all the members of their respective churches to engage in solemn prayer to God for a revival of religion among us, between sunset and dark of each day."

Some excesses have disturbed the welfare of the churches. A perversion of sanctification calling itself "sanctification" brought division and loss in some cases. One of the worst features of such excesses is that some take the perversion for the real doctrine and so reject the doctrine. Now sanctification is a gracious, Scripture doctrine and must be held in its integrity, even if some abuse the holy doctrine. In like manner baptism, in the form and place God has given it must be firmly held notwithstanding blind leaders of the blind in violence to the Scriptures attach a saving virtue to baptism. The perversion of a doctrine is not an argument against the doctrine itself. "Hold fast the form of sound words." In all things we should live up to the standard we teach. The foreigner who visits the home land of the missionary should be able to see the lives of the home land Christians illustrating the truths preached by the missionary.

God has given the people of Salt River Association a goodly land. The land has milk and honey as of Carmel and Esdraelon. The stream from which our name was taken, Salt River, draws water from eleven counties and fertilizes vast stretches of farm and pasture lands. Cuivre River, rising in the vicinity of Mexico and coursing its way through regions that have at sometime been within our field, enters the Mississippi at Old Monroe, was reserved by the government for navigation. These two rivers have many contributing streams. Between and beyond these rivers, springs from the hillsides and brooks through the valleys feed a score of creeks, which holding themselves aloof from all lesser floods, deliver their treasures into the mighty Mississippi.

Reckoning our broadest limits, there are lowly habitations, beautiful homes and stately mansions; thriving villages, flourishing towns and commercial cities. Our schools provide that every child may receive a beneficent education, fitting him for any advance step he may elect. Our large products, in the hands of a busy, progressive population, enrich the markets of St. Louis, Chicago and the East. These limits have, perhaps, three hundred miles of gravel and macadam road, and rail and river transportation. Our wealthy men are generous and considerate while our laboring man is princely in his independence.

Our sun is bright, our rains refreshing, our soils are fertile, our harvests abundant; our air is salubrious, our climate bracing; our God is gracious and He calls us to a holy calling. Let us be thankful and serve Him.

There is a large place in the world for Baptists. Our distinguishing doctrines provide a way for all saved people to come to us. The doctrine of personal salvation before church membership enables us to recognize any saved man as a brother wherever he is found. In this we rejoice. Our doctrine of soul-liberty helps in this same recognition, for if a man is saved we concede to him the right under God to choose his affiliation and we will call him brother. We stand in the impregnable doctrines of grace.

Christ has made us free. We desire that our fellow-men share in this abounding grace and Christ-given freedom, "bringing into captivity every thought to the obedience of Christ."

FULLNAME INDEX

----Daniel 34 David 50 57
    Davie 32 George 84 227
    Henry 119 Jane 62 Jerry
    133 Jimimie 93 Johnnie 82
    Mary 227 Milley 62 Paul
    53 Peter 74 Queen 119
    Uncle George 304 William
    83
ABBOTT, Laura 330
ACUFF, C C 74
ADAMS, 207 Elizabeth 166
    George W 299 Nancy 166
    W S 147 153-154 Walter S
    166
ADMIRE, G 118 George 120 T
    H 277 W R 298
ALDEN, Mr 15 Noah 15
ALEXANDER, C W 284
    George 367 L T 360 S D
    299
ALLEN, 45 J O 267 John 45
    Sarah 45
ALLISON, N T 284
ALLOWAY, C S 319
ANDERSON, Bro 31 E 159
    237 J 152 James 29 31 157
    227 Jennetta 364 Mrs N R
    363 R 354
ANDRESON, E 356
ANTHERBUS, 367
ANTHROBUS, B E 366
APPLEGATE, J L 318
ARDERY, John 279
ARGIN, 121
ARMITAGE, Dr 16 Thomas 15

ARMSTRONG, Brother 153 J
    C 333 365-366 372-374
    William 75 Wm 86
ARNOLD, W 75
ARTHUR, John J 361
ATKINS, E M 297 H 297
AUTERY, E 199 202 220
    Elijah 232
AYRES, 207 Elder 153
    Elizabeth 245 J H 69 J S
    290 293 J T 207 Mary
    Winnie 247 Mollie E 287 N
    152 154 N Virginia 38
    Nathan 103-104 200 277 S
    B 69 Sue E 69 157 T J 67
    203 236-237 245 287 318
    325 349 351 354-356 358
    360 365 373-374 Thomas J
    245
BACON, 121 C 154 Charles
    198
BADEN, Priest 140
BADGER, 190 Robert 154
BAGBY, Mr 380 Mrs 381 Rev
    381
BAILEY, 59 130 Ira M 149 J E
    317 328 J M 68 John 129
BAIN, J H 154
BAINBRIDGE, 54 Absalom
    172 Darius 54 57 172 Elder
    57 Mary 172
BAKER, B 268 Barnabas 273
    G T 120 375 Geo T 77 376
    George T 78 237 327 374

BALL, B F 370 Henry 180
  Horatio 180
BALLARD, S H 358
BALLOU, 11 Mrs 11
BARBEE, 367 J N 167 J N
  358 360 368 378 Jas N 368
  Jos N 371 376 Rev 368
BARKER, Jane 277
BARKLEY, Brother 66 E 365
  E L 66 376 John 363 Susan
  363
BARNARD, Letitia 376
BARNES, Elder 55 J G 33
  James 55 57
BARNETT, Ann 45
BARRETT, James 300 T W
  267
BASKETT, Almeda 79 H N 79
  155 276 286 Horatio N 40
  42 79-80 Horatio Nelson
  321 J H 274 282 J N 79
  Mary J 180
BAXTER, 163 207 Worth 207
  357 364
BEAMER, Elizabeth 295
BEASLEY, Noah 23 Sally 23
BEATTY, Button 367 Dolly
  367 Elisha 367
BEAUCHAMP, 23 B 315 364
  Bland 120 230 291 293 305
  316-317 360 364 385 Bro
  288 Brother 234 H 328
  Harvey 317 385 John 23 25
  27 Manervil 367 S A 287-
  288 291 Sylvester Allen 87
BECKHER, Ambrose 247
BECKNER, A 271 280 283 318
  Ambrose 363 Lucretia 363
BEECHER, Henry Ward 210
BEESON, Prof 243
BEGEMAN, H C 347

BELL, Nancy 237
BENN, Corben 67 Corbin 283
BENSON, 374
BENTLEY, Lavina 62
BENTLY, Robert 354
BERRY, L M 268-269 289-290
  292 Martha 295
  Theodore 295
BIBB, B H 351 377 Benjamin
  306 Byron 71 203 357 365
  C 267 C A 331 Charles A
  308 373 375 Chas A 376 E
  T 203 Elder 224 H 366
  Jessie 331 L C 316 363 M L
  167 237 273 292 M T 166
  272-273 277 Margaret I
  307 Martha J 295 Martin T
  203 Mary 306 Mary A 307
  Rev 329 W A 36 66 70 72
  120-121 156 161 206 240
  242 283-285 298 309 311
  317 324-329 348 351 354
  365-367 370-374 376 W H
  264 268-269 271-272 295
  297 W P 121 161 356 367
  371-372 Web P 230
  William A 34 William
  Albert 306 William Henry
  308 Wm 33 Wm A 36-37
  Wm H 296
BIGGS, 52 Anna 51 53 287
  Aunt Betsey 81 Betsey 42
  Bro 35 46 53 369 Brother
  39 45 76 228 234 242 290 D
  58 386 Dalton 103 123 169
  244 364 Davis 24 39 43 45-
  48 50-51 53-56 58 70 84 88
  108 148 244 247 323 Ed
  291 Edward 371-372 376
  Eld 51 Elder 62 Elizabeth
  Mccune 81 Emma 287

Index.

BIGGS (Cont.)
  George 84 George K 52 148 Imoriah 51 J C 278 290 293 354-355 358 371-373 375-376 J D 35-36 38-40 70 72 77 97 156 160-161 204 222 225 228 237 244 246 257 267 269-270 276-278 280-282 284-285 289-290 295-296 301 307 317-318 320 325-327 332-333 345 348-349 352 354-356 358-360 364-365 368 370-372 374 J Guy 78 James D 39 76-77 81 157 242 267-268 270 281 285 316 363-364 James Duvall 39 104 323 Jas D 78 275 John 50-51 John D 200-201 223 244 281 285 John Davis 323 Johnnie 82 Lucy 244 M C 78 284 326 M R K 225-226 266-271 282 Marion 87 167 Martha 287 Milton 77 Morris 71 Mr 24 85 Peggy 84 R K 65 Robert 51 W K 294 William 41-42 47-48 56 61 81 83-84 108-110 148 150 167 323 Wm 56 58-60 Wm H 215 Wm K 287 Wm M 115
BINNIN, A M 319
BIRCH, W 200 W H 198
BIRD, A N 36
BIRKHEAD, 121 Bro 369 377 Elder 368 F M 66 121 240-241 251 272 278 280-282 284 297-299 310 316-317 325 331 355 377 W N 355
BLACK, B B 166 G L 36 316
BLACKWELL, B F 297 J M 328

BLAND, James T 238 Jesse 238 Lizzie 238 Stephen 238 W 226 Wm H 238
BLASDEL, E E 358
BLEDSOE, 130 William 129-130
BLENNERHASSETT, R S 208
BLUNT, Olive 370
BOIS, 121
BOLTON, D C 268 W D 206 371-372 374
BONDURANT, Bro 63 E 60 Edward 62-63 108 Ephraim M 286 G T 274 283 J R 278 281 James H C 361 Martha 237
BONEY, H N 358 365 R H 351 W N 354
BOULWARE, Elder 59 Mordecai 57 Theodoric 59
BOWER, 340 Bro 293 Brother 87 Capt 86 Doctor 88 Dr 85-87 Elder 147-148 G M 110 Gustavus M 75 J 108 M R 73 Mariah 72 Michael 72 Michael R 73
BOWERS, 70 Brother 109-110 117-118 Elder 117 J 179 Jacob 118
BOWLES, T R 279
BOWLING, Daniel 78 95
BOX, Prudence 18
BOXLEY, Elizabeth 20
BOYD, 207 Edna 78 H M 65 Harvey 207 Wm 78
BOYER, W L 318 324 358 364
BOZARTH, Eli 74
BRADLEY, Bettie 228 Brother 153-154 J 226 299 J J 152 198 228-229 351 J S 263 Joseph 300

BRAGG, Joseph 55
BRANDON, Ann 287 W M 270
   William 291 Wm 287 291
BRASHEARS, Clarinda 67
   Elizabeth 363 Jamima 119
   Kate 119 Martha 363
   S 117 Solomon 119
BRASHERE, Thomas 54
BREAKER, M J 360 365 372-373
BRENT, Mr 92
BRICE, Wm 59
BRIGGS, Rebecca 119 Robert 119 Robert Sr 117
BRIGHT, E C 152
BRISCO, Rosaline 120
BRISCOE, Bettie 234 J H 66
   Jack 235 James 323 John P 326-327 S 60 Sister 236
   Susan B 363
BRITTON, J H 184 John 184
   Mrs James H 183
BROADDUS, M E 77-78 120 227-228 250 256 295-296 374 376
BROADHEAD, James O 193 198 207
BROADUS, A 119 Brother 119 John A 97 Rev 96
BRONSON, O L 293
BROOKS, J D 233 Mary J 233 W P 360 370-373
BROWN, Amanda 363 Brother 236 George 67 H M 200 J J 198 332 J T 257 James 67 71 James A 304 306 John 67 John T 235 363 Levin 74 Polly 72 Rebecca B 246 S M 294 318 324 332 354 360 366 370 372-375
   Sanford M 234 372

BROWN (Cont.)
   Sister 236 Susan A 304 W 153 W W 71 305 356 360 367 371 Walter 367 Wm 67-68
BROWNING, Mrs 318
BRUNK, W 154
BRYAN, Elizabeth 144
BRYANT, 175 Jas 328
BUCHANAN, Ann 20 J W 236 Mr 25 102 Mrs 236 Mrs Lucian 363 Sister 27 236 T 32 Thomas 20 23-25 27 47 61 Thomas J 105
BUCK, William C 87
BUFORD, A 25 Abraham 119 Brother 263 James 95 Mary 119 Nancy 27
BULLOCK, Luly 144 Thomas 144
BUNYAN, 163
BURCH, Wash 354 Z T 299
BURK, C F 280
BURKHEAD, 367 F M 241
BURKHOLDER, Betty 328 R P 328
BURKS, C S 70 354 356 J C 329 331 Thomas 153
BURNHAM, W H 33 204 230 238 272-274 276 295 315 325 373 375
BURNS, Robert 20
BURRUS, Phillip 123
BUSBY, Brother 234 236 Mary 279 W C 76-78 198 225 234 267 370
BUSH, Elder 160 J Porter 94 President 360
CALDWELL, Brother 164 235 Catharine 361 J 225 J O 236 Jane 325 Patsey 159

Index.

CALDWELL (Cont.)
    R B 363 S K 306 360 Sam
    235 Tom 164
CALHOUN, 88
CALLAWAY, James W 373
    Jas W 367 W 372 William
    121 356
CALLOWAY, Brother 298 Wm
    300
CALVIN, C H 249 Mary Olive
    249
CAMPBELL, Bro 367 R T 72
    120 158-159 364-366 370
    372 376 T R 234 Thomas
    367 Thomas R 229 W T 324
    351-352 358 360
CANNON, 121 Ida G 298
    Isaac 274 276 280 283-284
    324 365 J R 298 365
CAPPS, B 272 Daniel 59
    David 185 232 Elder 148
    232 Elizabeth 185 Jacob
    147 149 185 187 231 243
    Sarah 185 Waggoner 59
CAREY, Wm 91
CARLETON, T C 295
CARMAN, Joseph 60
CARMER, H 152
CARPENTER, B B 152 Elder
    152 Zacheus 28
CARR, James 118 180 201
    Jane 181 John 42 Joseph
    W 361
CARROLL, James 273
CARSON, Alethea 90 Brother
    88-89 118 Grandfather 88
    W 118 William 46-48 56 61
    75 88 150 267 364 Wm 55-
    56 59-60 90 109
CARSTARPHEN, Brother 221
    235 C 95 Chappel 78

CARSTARPHEN (Cont.)
    Ezra 225 235 257 Mrs 234
    Sister 236
CARTER, Nancy 20
CARTMELL, J N 274
CARVER, Ada 37
CASH, A J 246 Martha J 245
    363
CATES, A 153
CATHCART, 53
CATSTARPHEN, Kittie 234
CAVE, W D 354
CAVERLY, Mrs W H 299
    William 299 Wm 300
CHAMBLISS, Dr 329-330 J E
    324 329 381 383
CHARLES, J P 377 Jno P 333
    John 351
CHASTEN, R J 267 Robert J
    296-297 Sarah A 296
CHEWING, E W 161
CHEWNING, E W 241-242
CHRISTY, Lucy 92
CLACK, Brother 73 Elizabeth
    72 Spencer 72 142
CLARE, George 117 P R 281
CLARK, 173 Christopher 172
    David 55 77 I N 316-317 J
    B 306 355 J H 342 J S 306
    John S 304 Johnson 352
    Thomas 326 William H 78
CLAY, 88 S W 300
CLEAVELAND, Wm 201-202
CLEAVER, Mary 119
CLEGGETT, Judge 101
CLEMENS, Mr 252
CLEVELAND, Brother 258
    Elder 98
COBBS, K A 306
COCKERELL, John 274
    Littleton 180

COCKREL, Loyd 121
COLDWELL, Joseph 59
COLE, Dr 317 325 Emmett 167 G C 306 374-375 Geo C 373 R S 356 360-361
COLLAND, F 231
COLLARD, F 109 Mary 233
COLLINS, Brother 202
COLVIN, Brother 234 G T 299-300
COLWELL, T M 267
CONN, Mildred A 77 Nancy 77 Thomas 77
CONNER, J S 356
CONSTANTINE, 17
CONWAY, Samuel 43-44
COOK, Brother 227 Ernest 315 317 J E 316 372 J F 160 204 227 277 281 285 309 324 355 Susan E 239 Wm 239
COPPAGE, Isaac 74
CORNELL, Martha M 239
CORNWALLIS, Lord 91
COTTER, John 354
COTTLE, Joseph 173
COUCH, 375 W J 376
COUNTS, Brother 59
COWHARD, Sarah 239
COX, B H 357 H C 357 363 Henry 371 Henry C 360 James 119 John 175 Lettitia 119 Lizzie 363 Mary 119 Milton 277 363-364 Polly 175 Sarah 119
CRAIG, Lewis 129 S O 328
CRANK, Jas 363 367 Luta 367 Robert A 229
CREHSHAW, 121
CRENSHAW, Nancy 120 W N 319

CREWS, Brother 110 Martha Jane 252
CROUCH, J B 206 374-376 J M 373 J W 327 373 375
CROWELL, William 211
CRUTCHER, S 154 Samuel 153
CULBERTSON, Brother 120 J 118 153 198 James 119 200 William 317
CURL, John B 28
CURRY, J H 75 John H 74 Matilda 74
DALE, John 28
DALTON, Rebecca 365
DAMARON, Margarett 251
DANIEL, C G 345 J T 324 John 59
DARROW, Arthur C 383 Fannie Wiatt 330 Frances Wiatt 383 Mrs Francis Wiatt 380 Sister 383
DAVENPORT, A C 153 155 182-183 J G 222 226 264 John 71
DAVID, Brother 29
DAVIES, Benjamin 88
DAVIS, Betsey A 299 C W 161 299 325 351 360 E 109 Elder 62 122 Ephraim 26 28 108-109 174-175 Francis 28 John 75 Matthew 109 Mr 123 William 109 122 Wm 113
DAWSON, F L 355 Frank L 281 J C 95 J L 273 280 283 286 317-318 360 365-366 J M 100 James L 229 355 Lewis A 268 S P 157 286 316-317 325 356 360 S P Sr 157 Samuel P 365 W L 283

Index.

DAY, 121
DE LAFAYETTE, Marquis 86
DEFOE, W 198
DENTON, Isaac H 160
DESINE, William 56
DEW, Brother 235 Evangelist 235
DICKEN, C W 292
DICKERSON, Sister 204
DIGG, 190
DIGGS, Mrs 190 Mrs J H 190
DILLARD, E B 297 327
DILLENDER, Wm 238
DINGLE, Edward 214 J S 292-293 Mary A 214 Winder C 150
DISHEA, Gov 86
DIXON, 121 Annie B 309 J J 309
DODD, 207
DOKE, J S 200
DONALDSON, Nancy 74
DORSEY, E W 122
DOUGHERTY, J E 32
DOUGLASS, S A 318
DOW, E W 243 318 324 348 Ernest 350 Ernest H 348 Grove S 348
DOWELL, Elizabeth 162 J 198 James 162 Lucy 162
DOWNING, Addie Belle 384 Brother 384 Dr 384 J L 294 318 355 358 360 385 James 241 James L 380 384 Jas L 72 Sister 384
DOYLE, Susan 42 W H 161
DRAPER, Mrs P F 363 R F 351
DRUMMOND, Mary J 252
DUCKWORTH, 356 358
DUDLEY, 162 Ambrose 144 Elder 162 Lucy 72
DULANG, Emily 166
DUNBAR, John B 374 Rev 126
DUNCAN, 11 28 42 50-51 124 Harriet 178 188 J M 228 John 149 153 155 Lewis 117 120 153 155 174 176 178-179 181-182 185-186 188-189 201-202 223 R S 153 166 171 176 183 186 189 195 198 201-202 221-223 226 263-264 268-270 273 276-277 279-280 325 364 Sarah C 188 Sarah J 189 T H 283 W E 189
DUTTON, J H 147 153 John H 182 Mary 196 Mary R 182 Mrs 196-197
DWIRE, D P 167
EAMES, J S 121 241 299 335 351 364 367
EASTIN, Polly 72
EDWARDS, 300 A M 70 371 Ann 156 Annie G 300 D C 157 E J 66 71 Eliza 156 Ernest 354 Eugene 356 Fountain 384 Guy 331 H G 225-226 Hiram G 147 149 J A 226 269 300 Jane 71 John C 169 L A 152 L V 300 Leland V 300 Lina E 300 Luther 240 329 Maducia 295 Mary J 295 N B 71 Nora Thurmond 359 R B 228 300 Rhoda J 228 S A 154 223 295 Simpson 156-157 W H 157 228 W R 157
ELESTON, G W 120

ELLEDGE, Brother 109-110 J 110
ELLEGE, Brother 154
ELLIOT, Mary Angeline 92
ELLIOTT, W F 333
ELLIS, A 153 Absolam 78 D 152 154 158 D D 306 Duncan 158 168 223 321 Elizabeth 78 Hannah 158 Hezekiah 73 Mary 72 Nancy 158 R D 37 152 R T 317 Rachel 326 Reason D 158 Resin D 359 Sarah Ann 158 Thomas 78 Thomas G 158 W S 32 William S 33 Wm S 36
ELSTON, 121 Frank 121
ELTON, Thomas T 110
ELY, Isaac 55 95 L B 273 277 279 281 317 332
ELZEA, Deacon 306 H L 306 S H 96 Sister 236 Susan 92
EMERSON, G W 358 Geo W 360 365 George W 370 J A 355
ENGLISH, J B 206 278 281 284 290 295
ERNEST, Eliza 233 Joe 233
ESTELL, W K 167
ESTES, Jenny 296
EUBANK, Alexander 253
EVANS, Christmas 163 D J 373 J S 255 James 78
FAGG, T J C 216 Thos J C 207
FARMER, Sallie B 328 Sallie F 328
FARRINGTON, Mildred 299
FAULCONER, John M 57
FELTON, C A 232
FERGUSON, David 309 Leanna 309 Mary 304

FERGUSON (Cont.) Nancy J 308 William 268 272
FERREL, G H 296 George H 296
FERRELL, E 153 Elizabeth 295 Jethro 295 John 236
FERRILL, Ezekiel 159
FIELD, Justice 224
FIELDER, Amina 298 Geo 23 32 George 22 Mrs Mack 299
FINLEY, A R 377 Bro 377 W 198 Warren 78 95 150
FISK, Stephen 199 211
FLOOD, Elder 147 152 J J 152 Noah 59 86
FLOYD, J 148 Matthew 168
FORD, Geo 301 John 236 363 John S 236 Lewis 26 29 Reuben 13 S H 201 268-269 273 281 318 358 Sam 358 Susan 27 Thomas 118
FOREMAN, Ben 95 W 109 231
FORMAN, William 46-47 55
FORTUNE, Emma 315 J 315
FOSTER, G W 160 225-226 230 264 272 278-279 Sarah 126
FOX, Ezra 60 Norman 226
FRAILE, 110
FRAZER, Geo E 327 Lizzie 326 Melly 326 Moses 327
FRAZIER, E D 42
FREEMAN, J A 315
FREYMUTH, Mr 191
FRIER, J D 204 James M 63 M F 365
FRISTOE, 99 Elder 59 Thomas 59
FRY, Sister Harrison 359

Index. 397

FULLER, Andrew 163 Brother
250 J B 157 222 227 250
FUQUA, Brother 73 109 Elder
90 Hurley 109 J M 147
John N 166 Lida 166
Nancy 166 O M 375-376
Sarah H 166 W 222 W B
324 W T 283 285
William 56 Wm 57 109
FURGERSON, David 120
Elizabeth 120 Lucinda 120
GAMMON, B G 316
GARNETT, J D 231
GARRETT, J D 232
GATES, J 200
GENNIE, C L 298 Rosie E 298
GENTRY, 91 Amanda F 92
Bro 53 97 Brother 58 91 96
99 101 109 118 C 61 68 150
Caroline M 92 Christy 57
59 67 75 78 91-93 95-96 99-
100 103 109 Christy Jr 100
Elder 59 98 153 215 Evodia
92 Evotia 96 Hattie C 92
Jane Harris 91 Joseph 92
Joshua Henry 92 Lucy 92-
94 Mary Jane 92 Mr 92 94
96 98 Mrs 92 Overton
Harris 92 Rev 96 99
Rhodes Rollins 92 Richard
91-92 Richard Tandy 92
Ruben 92 Susan 92 Tandy
100 Thomas Benton 91
William Tandy 92
GIBBS, W N 205
GIBONY, W A 157 352 354
GIBSON, Brother 202 Dulena
A 296 J J 158 J L 332 J R
320 334 James R 296-297
Jas R 296 Jesse 159 R 226
264 Robert 157 160 T J 207

GIDINGS, R 123
GILBERT, Chas 229 R N 324
351 370
GILL, Everett 370
GILLILAND, 56 Brother 237-
238 David P 225 J A 274
James R 270 P 237 R 274
S 117 Virginia 237
GILMORE, Brother 110 178
Elder 117 Mary 178 Robert
149 176 178 180-182 185
GINSBURG, Emma Morton
380 Mrs 380 Sister 381
GIPSON, Elder 224 J J 198
202 220-222 225-226 264
268 J R 155 John 155
GIVENS, Bro 247 Brother
247-248 Emma 37 G W 374
J M 37 John Green 246
Louisa 354 Louisa M 247
Mary A 247 307 Matthew
29 Mr 25 S G 71 206 226
237 240 246 264 267 272
274 278 284 291 299-300
304-305 315-317 324-325
345 354 356-357 360 Sallie
27 Sallie A 247 Samuel
Green 246 Sarah E 247
GLOVER, P 147 Philip 119
Samuel T 207
GOGGIN, Thomas C 253
GOLDSMITH, 101
GOOCH, Roland 63 65
GOODMAN, Brother 113
Garret 113 J A 354-355 M
S 20 40 115 341 Mary E
227 Prof 20-21 341 William
N 228
GOODNIGHT, Isaac 137 Mr
137
GOODRICH, A C 268

GORDON, A G 315 A J 78 O A 297 300 Pearl 161
GOSSETT, Walter 166
GRAFFORD, Henry 281 M B 328 365 Mrs 281 Roberta 331
GRAHAM, E S 120 373
GRANT, Elder 148 226 W D 70 120 153 155 176 185-186 189 199 William D 149 William Davis 179
GRAVES, Brother 194 H 95 J R 266 Mildred 182 Washington 182 192 194
GREATHOUSE, William 78 Wm 95
GREEN, Col 98 J S 200 225 364 James S 222 Mrs J S 89 Mrs James W 331
GREENE, Clem 92 J P 355
GREENHALGH, John 55
GREENLIEF, Brother 117
GREGORY, Banester 61 Bannester 47 J R S 371 J S R 297 351 355 358 360 Susan 43
GRENWELL, Prof 243
GRIFFIN, 150 Brother 278 Elder 152 J E 367 J J 166 282-285 317-318 320 324 J N 147 153 155 166 202 222 226 264 272 James N 183 Jas N 278 S M 278 Sarah 166
GRIFFITH, Almeda 79-80 J E 271 375-376 Jas E 274 276 Joel 45 47 113 Peggy 45
GRIGSBY, E L 299
GRIMMET, S S 283
GUTHERIE, Sarah 237
GUTHRIE, J H 333

GUTTERY, Brother 363 Demas 362-363 Demas E 361 Jennie 362-363 Jennie E 361 S 274-275 Samuel 78 317 Sister 363 Sister W B 361 W B 78 361
HACKER, Bro 35 J D 35 72 161 204 206 238 293 295 299 316-318 360 John D 361
HAINES, Elder 98
HALE, Brother 231 Ozeas 56 Ozias 231
HALL, A 324 Adam 296 Fanny 296 H 267 Hiram 296-297 S S 297 W T 297 Will S 366 371 William S 366
HALLEY, Bro 368 P W 299 316-318 325-326 334-335 351 355 360 371 Pascal W 229 T 202
HALLY, P H 167
HAM, Brother 109 Jabus 54
HAMMERS, Wm 67
HAMMOND, Bertha 367 Richard 367
HAMMPTON, J M 95
HAMPTON, J M 100 Jas E 101 Joseph 78
HANCOCK, D J 272
HANES, Rev 239
HANSFORD, Brother 133 Mary 178 Mr 133 Thomas 133
HANSON, Frederick 238
HARDESTY, B F 226 264 F D 120 276 285 298 320 Frank 121 Mary D 298 Mary M 298
HARDIN, C H 345 Geo 62 Gov 216 252

Index.

HARKER, J D 35
HARLOW, 121 Brother 224
HARPER, Elijah 289
HARRELSON, J F 281 Mrs 281
HARRIS, 102 Brother 102 Elder 148 G C 351 J C 354 Jane 91 Lucinda C 238 M C 351 Mr 101-102 Reuben 118 181 Robert 297 W A 101 William 181 253 Wm 238
HARRISON, R 325 Rev 329 Richard 328-329
HARRISS, Samuel 13 101
HARVEY, George 358 360
HATCH, Lucy 244
HATCHER, Brother 153 235 H 285 Harvy 255 283
HATHAWAY, Sarepta 105
HAUSER, A F 157
HAVERILL, A 273
HAWKINS, 118 Benjamin T 62 Col 124 Deacon 62-63 123 Fannie 326 G W 226 Gertie 327 H 60 Harmon 61-62 J B 226 264 272 285 317 324-326 J F 95 J W 290 293-294 360 365 James 377 Jincy 62 Lucinda J 377 Moses 95 Mrs James 377 Susan 354 Ursa 327 W G 63 102 123 224-225 266-270 William G 62 323 386 Wm G 123
HAYCRAFT, Brother 118 Elder 147 P N 103 150
HAYDEN, Deacon 259 E 153 223 266 Edw 225-226 Edward 277 H 109 Jane D 125

HAYNES, J 154 220 Josiah 157
HEADRICK, Tillitha A 238 Tillman T 238
HEDGES, Brother 280 J F 60 70-71 199 202 222 226 247 264 278 280 John F 153 155 213 Margaret 213 Sarah M 355 Thomas 42 71 Thomas B 70 Thos B 59
HELPER, J N B 291
HENDERSON, 207 R A 329 Rev 96
HENDREN, Brother 58 73 Robert 73
HENDRICKS, 196
HENDRIX, Flora 326 John 326
HENDRON, Brother 110 Rev 126
HENLEY, V 155
HENRY, 17 Bob 95 Mr 129 Patrick 216 William 144
HEPLER, E W 325 J N B 40 284 297 315
HERNDON, John C 149 151
HERRIFORD, Paul 74 Sarah 74
HESKET, Mrs 327 Sister 365
HETTICH, David 241 372-373
HICKLIN, C B 200 O B 286 361
HICKMAN, J 272-273 289 J J 309 Joshua 35 272-273
HIGBEE, J L 273 276 305 Joseph L 304
HIIXSON, B F 238
HILL, Elder 148-149 151-152 Mary 119 181 R C 152 181 183 Robert C 150 181

HINTON, I T 146
HITCH, Deacon 305 Eleven 304 Hester F 304 Jennie 304 John C 304-305 Pauline 304
HIXSON, B F 35 77-78 96 120 226 234 263 268-270 272-273 276-277 285 316 364 Brother 234
HOBBS, Brother 154 L L 285
HOBSON, Margaret Eliza 250
HOCKER, J 75 John 74
HODGEN, Isaac 141
HOGAN, N B 267
HOGUE, John 157
HOLLIS, Jesse A 196
HOLLOWAY, W 60
HOLMAN, Dr 261 R 223
HOLMES, Wm H 59
HOOSE, Elder 266
HOPKE, Alton 367
HOPKINS, Elizabeth 237 R G 316
HORNER, 225 Elder 224 J H 223
HOSTETTER, E 153 Enoch 159 Enos 365 H H 263 Henry 299
HOUSER, Evangelist 235
HOUSTON, 121
HOWELL, E K 226 Eli M 238 L D 361 Larkin D 238 Mary J 239 Permelia 239
HUBBARD, 177 Bro 177 Brother 149 177 231 244 Charles 172 D 153-154 David 55-57 59 70 78 108-109 118 146-149 151 153 172 174 176-177 185 199 231-232 243-244 Elder 55 57 59-60 117 151 232

HUBBARD (Cont.) Eli 232 J 147 231 John 231 Joseph 232 T 152
HUDSON, Eva 371 S T 305 319 358
HUGHES, 21 H 22
HUME, Mary 181
HUMPHRY, Elizabeth 239
HUNT, J M 316 Minister 138 Mr 139
HUNTER, Brother 113 Edward Dudley 247 Louisa M 247 Thos 113
HUNTINGTON, Charles 239 Charles R 239 282
HURLEY, Brother 87 109 118 199 203 Elder 64 117 147-149 151-153 171 199 211 Mr 208 211 Rev 126 195 William 64 74 103 108 120 154 171 199 203 207 211-212 256 Wm 70 86 154 179 183 195 199
HUTCHERSON, J T 325 351 354-355 358 360 363 Lee A 351
HUTCHINSON, Bro 377 C E 377 Charles 181
HUTT, Mrs Col T G 183
HYDE, G W 267 311 315-318 320 325
INGE, Eliza A 361
INGMIRE, Brother 154 Elder 232 F W 232
INGRAM, 207
INLOW, Brother 69 163-165 D V 68-69 98 153-155 157 199 Dudley V 68 Elder 162 Henry 77 162 R M 163 385 Salome 162 Samuel P 359 Sister 165 Sister Samuel P

Index.

INLOW (Cont.)
   359 Solona 78
INSLEM, Brother 110
JACKSON, Gibson 20
   Leroy 42 44 47-48 55 58 Mr
   42 Polly 42
JACOBS, Sarah A 156 W T
   263 349 354-356 358 363
JACOBY, Crysena 27
JAMES, Asa 216 Elizabeth
   132 Mr 129 Richard 132
JANES, Bro 25 James 25
JEANS, Jeptha 20
JEFFERSON, 17
JEFFRIES, 303 G C 279 315
   George 303-304 George C
   303 John 77 Joseph 118
JENKINS, Bro 25 Gibson 25
JENKS, C W 326 Mollie 327
JENNINGS, B A 226 239
   Brother 206 348 377 E 70
   202 222 226 237 247 264
   269 272-273 275 278 282
   284-285 287 300 304 315-
   317 319 325 349 356 358
   360 363-364 366 371 376
   Ed 71 206 238-240 Edmond
   238 377 James A 238 S G
   239 Tyre 110
JESSE, W F 266 W J 277 W M
   166 William M 153
JESSUR, David Hubbard 59
JETER, Jerry B 190
JETT, J P 157 S F 156-157
JEWELL, William 89 166 226
   267 273-274 278 280 321
   348 Wm 226 314
JINKS, Mrs S V 363
JOHNS, Mary A 251
JOHNSON, 207 A M 281 284
   290 Almeda 359

JOHNSON (Cont.)
   Benjamin 63 Brother 168-
   169 196 258-259 Deacon 63
   Elder 63 G J 270 Hannah
   G 159
   J B 202 J M 42 69-70 117-
   118 154-155 160 162 166
   199 202 220 222 247 J T
   202 James 207 James W
   159 Jno M 64 John M 119
   150 152-153 155 159 168
   199-200 202-204 John T
   153 Jonn M 152
   Marguerite M 62 Martha
   330 Polly Jane 119 Rev 196
   Sally 119 168 T E 228 T T
   30 68 70 109-110 148 151-
   155 158 185-186 190 198
   Thomas 11 Thomas T 62
   108 118 147 149 154
   Thornton 203 Thornton T
   159 196 Thos T 62 108 W H
   H 263
JOHNSTON, R H 152
JONES, Abe C 298 300 367
   376 Belinda Nowlin 192
   Bessie 355 Dabney 46-47
   58 61 77 161 257 G W 318
   John 113 Mr 162 Mrs
   Larue 234 R A 257 366
   Sister 236
JUDSON, 384 Adoniram 108
   Dr 383-384 Mr 108 Mrs
   384
KAYLOR, Elder 98 Robert 222
KEACH, Brother 76 83 103-
   105 Elder 77 215 274
   Father 103 257 J H 69 76
   103-104 154 202 222 226
   264 272 274 J M 286 355
   358 360 365

KEACH (Cont.)
  J W 78 354 373-376 James
  M 78 Jas M 370 John 120
  John H 78 83 150 155 199
  234 John Hawkins 274
  Sarah A 104
KEITH, 157 J R 266 S S 70
  120 237 324-326 334 351
  356-357 360 371
KELLEY, 121
KELLY, 45 Claud 320 Jane
  168 Joseph 168 Robert 121
  Sally 168 Susanna 45
  Vincent 45 47 61
KELTNER, J W 329
KEMPER, J F 157 281 283-
  284 295 317 333 371 381
KENDRICK, T J 263 318 325
  Thomas J 306
KENMAN, L 109 Levi 109
KENNEDY, Armstrong 175
  Polly 175
KENNEY, T M S 324
KERTLY, Luke 167
KESLER, James A 245
KESSLER, Sallie E 237
KEY, Davis L 300 Ella 300
KILLAM, D S 285 D T 283 286
  298 317-318 325 332-333
  Kate 298 Miss 366 W S 298
KILLUM, D T 280
KIMBALL, D M 226
KINCAID, Sister Wm 204
KING, Benj 287 289-290 292
  Benjamin 284 Brother 257
  298 C E 161 360 Charles E
  298 300 Chas E 72 Deacon
  290 H M 69 71-72 76 104
  157 160 202 222-223 234
  236-237 257-258 262 287-
  288 317

KING (Cont.)
  Henry M 201 224 237
  Joseph L 365 Rachel 287
  292 T M 286 293-294 375
KINMAN, E 199-200
KINNAIRD, Harriet 178
KIRTLEY, Elijah L 361
  Luke 67 241-242 305-306
  356 376 Mollie 371
KIRTLY, Luke 374
KNAPP, A S 110 Brother 110
KONZELMAN, Andrew 332
  Brother 332
KONZELMANN, A 320-321
LACY, J W 371
LAHR, Ida Dawson 228
LAIRD, K A 237
LAKE, B 269 Burgess 78 257
  G A 78 306 371 G S 318
  Geo A 282 363 Geo S 326
  George 257 Henry 306
  Jeptha 363 Mary 103 O W
  306 Sarah 363 William 280
  283 315
LAMB, Brother 156 E T 153
LANDRUM, A D 28 30 34 42
  71 119-120 147 149-155
  157 159-160 169 177 179
  185 198 232 Bro 29 31 42
  Brother 30 109 117 149 199
  Elder 28-29 149 Mr 29
LANSDALE, 95
LARUE, Caldwell Jones 256
LAWS, M L 273 277 385
LAYLIN, J J 306 Mrs J J 304
LAYTHEM, James 54
LEACH, Nancy 20
LEACHMAN, Brother 153-154
LEAK, A M 60
LEAR, Jas W 95
LEDFORD, G W 78 363

LEDFORD (Cont.)
  George W 78 James 77
  Nancy 77
LEE, Elder 56 James 176 John
  56-57 Nancy 176
LEFEVER, Brother 221
LEFTWICK, George W 253
LELAND, Elder 16 John 16
LEWELLEN, E L 363 367 Ida
  B 364 Samuel 59 148
LEWIS, Alice 354 Brother 286
  C B 199 201-202 232-233
  244 Elizabeth 245 F H 268
  277 281 315 H E 294 H P
  287-288 290 293 376 John
  108 Lou 287 Luke 286-287
  290-291 386 Sally 72 T H
  283
LILLARD, J M 60 James 35
  James M 103
LILLEY, Lucy 228 300
LIMERICK, Emily 295
LINCOLN, Mr 102
LINDSAY, Clem B 229 J T 317
LINDSEY, Elizabeth 181 J T
  328 John 330 Maggie 328
  Margaret I 307 Martha 328
  330 Mollie 328 Pike 157
  326 328 330 W C 328
LINEY, Lyda 166
LITER, Chris 70 J M 237
LITTREL, James 55 Joseph 55
LOCKHEART, D P 316
LONG, Brother 66 C C 366 J
  W 66 72 161 371-372
LONGMIRE, John 72 Stacy 72
LOONEY, John 57
LOWE, Caroline 361
LOWER, A E 367 373
LOWRY, W P 226
LUCAS, Mary 326

LUCK, A R 332 Brother 122
  322 Diggs 62 283 Elder 226
  Henry L 322 J W 320 334
  Lucy 62 Mary V 238-239
  Mrs Diggs 71 Thomas H 64
  W F 201-203 222 225-226
  264 267-269 272 276 Wm
  258 Wm F 121 237
LUCKETT, Catharine 365 W
  S 278
LUNDRUM, Elder 200
LUNEY, Benjamin 74 J 75
  John 74 Mary 74
LUTHER, J H 226 267
M'DONALD, Nancy 105
MACKEY, Elizabeth 326 J C
  321 325 354-355 358 360
  365 370 372-376 Jas C 36 L
  F 228 358 360 365 370-373
  375-376
MADDOX, W L 240 William L
  374 Wm 238
MADISON, 17 James 15
MAGRUDER, 121 A B 334
  Brother 322 Dennis 322 E
  320 334 E M 120-121 Elias
  334 I M 120 R C 298 S A
  298 W M 320
MAHAN, John C 74 Peter N
  74
MAIDEN, R K 371 373 375 R
  R 295
MAJOR, J 223 James 269 283
  295 Kate 295 W D 281 295
  William D 33
MANLY, W R 318
MANN, Leona 372
MANSKE, A F 357
MANZKE, A F 306
MAPLE, J C 273 277 290 342
  Mrs 342

MARBLE, S 147
MARKEY, James C 40 Lou 37
MARSHALL, William 129-130
MARSTON, S M 267 S W 267-268 270 285 295
MARTIN, A 108 Addie 380 Addie Belle 384 Charley 327 Col 78 95 J M P 283 354 J S 70 366 John S 363 R J 240 R T 71 Robert J 384 Susan 71 Wm 141
MATHENY, M P 230 278 281
MAUPIN, Brother 282 J W 306 Rev 240 W N 121-122 230 237 241 282 284 297 299-300 324-325 334 364
MAXFIELD, Dan W 241 Mattie 363
MAYES, Ada 285 298
MAYFIELD, W H 324
MAYHALL, Geo E 161 371-372 375-376 George E 373 J B 225
MCATEE, J W 77-78
MCCLAY, Girty 298 L 285 Lewis 298
MCCLELLAN, John 237 Lucy 237
MCCLURE, Samuel 109
MCCOY, Elder 122 William 42
MCCREE, Wm 59
MCCUNE, 240 280 282 307 318 348-350 380 A J 243 278 284 286 317-318 361 370-376 Brother 280 John 20-21 42 Joseph 365 Polly 21 42
MCCUTCHEN, 59
MCDANIEL, J 155
MCDANNOLD, A 155 Alex 238-239 Alex Jr 238

MCDANNOLD (Cont.) Alexander 359 Brother 280 321 Edgar 317 371 H G 371 N 153 224 271 Newton 23 220 223 280 T J 284 286 315 317-318 321 Thomas J 319 321
MCDONALD, Hiram 105 Sister 105
MCDONNOLD, 27 A 33 A L 33 Alexander 29 31 Edgar 35 Marmie 37 N 32 Newton 26 31 Ruben 27 31 T J 37 Thomas J 33 Thos J 33 William R 37
MCELFRESH, A B 202 Elder 57
MCFALL, J C 200
MCGARY, Elizabeth 374
MCGEE, A M 360 365 Gabrella 364 Stafford 54
MCGREW, Elizabeth 77 George T 77 J C 274 280 283 286 317-318 321 326 J V 306 James C 78 Jas C 276 Joseph 78
MCGUIRE, Allen 57 Elder 57 W 155 198
MCILROY, David 317 J W 317-318 325 364 John W 228 Thos 116
MCKAY, Col 140 Samuel 140
MCLEAN, J 201 233
MCLEOD, James 113 William 109 Wm 113
MCMANAWAY, A G 254 J M 157 254 355-357 360 365
MCPIKE, A 267-268 Benjamin H 65 J 198 226 James 222 Jas E 287 W B 226 242 267 273 282 285 316 Wlm B 66

Index.   405

MCQUIE, Brother 58 149
   Elder 63 68 Jas 317 Mary J
   180 R E 237 249 268 273
   316 318 371-373 W 117 153
   186 Walter 42 59 62-63 68
   70 78 118 147 149 176 180-
   181 185-186 188-189 203
MCREA, Francis 43
MEADOWS, Anna 298
MEFFORD, Tib 299
MEGOWN, Blanche 234 J S
   366 371-372
MELLECHAMP, D E 297
MERIWETHER, Dr 34
MERRILL, Brother 280 G C
   280
MIDDLETON, Charles 296
   Mrs Charles 296
MILLER, 121 A P 61 63 66
   152-153 155 169 198-202
   224-226 263 265-270 273-
   274 276 280-281 284 315
   317 Alexander 169
   Alexander P 40 Alexander
   Phillips 169 C F 120 298
   Fannie 169 Judge 169 220-
   221 223 225 284 Mariah
   248 Sarah 169
MILLERCHAMP, Fitch 367
MILLICHAMP, D E 372
MILTON, Uncle 77
MITCHELL, A G 29-31 35 65
   151-154 156 158 175 198-
   199 201-202 222 225-227
   238 243 250 263-264 269
   271-272 274 278 280-283
   295-296 306 315-316 318
   320 Albert 203 258 300
   Albert G 156 158 228 300
   Albert Gregory 308 Annie
   B 309 Bro 30 294 C

MITCHELL (Cont.)
   A 120-121 238 284-286
   294-295 298 300 305 307-
   308 315-317 319 331-332
   366 373 Charles 241
   Charles A 34 295 348
   Charles Albert 308 Chas
   241 Chas A 230 Elder 175
   Harriet 365 J H 269 J J
   152 154 200 J W 200
   James A 158 John 300
   John J 203 Lewis 229
   Martha 300 Nancy J 308
   Sarah 300 Susan 233 T N
   351 T R 40 326 W 231 W N
   300 W W 34 64 120 153-
   154 158 160 198 202 222-
   223 272 275-276 300
   William 233 William W 64
   154 Wm 258 Wm W 230
MOCK, George 59 67
MODISETT, 271 Bro 97
   Brother 154 271 Elder 65
   152-153 155 160 200 271 M
   M 65 69 71-72 76 98 103
   154 157-158 160 166 199
   203 206 221-222 225-228
   232 237 239 247 250 263-
   264 270-272 330 334 341
MOORE, Amanda F 92 B B
   166 Benjamin B 62 Brother
   202 Elisha 92 J B 315 J C
   167 200 J L 201 J R 270 L
   S 270 Levi 153-154 188 222
   Martha 72 Mrs S E 165
   Nancy 62 188 Rachel 62
   William 177
MORGAN, Brother 234 D W
   280-281 283 285 295
   Elizabeth 128
MORLEY, Nettie 327

MORRILL, D T 270
MORRIS, Anna 51 Hattie C 92
  Jesse 51 John 21 Linnie
  354
MORTON, Emma 380 H T 243
  316-317 319 372 380 Mary
  A 380 Susan 72
MOSBY, Sallie 361 W W 157 Z
  W 263
MOSELY, John E 320
MOSHER, A 232 I A 233 Lucy
  V 233
MOSLEY, J E 272
MOSS, 106 C K 100 Daniel 20
  105-106 Edward 185 Elder
  105-106 Elizabeth 188
  Peter 59 118 Sarepta 105
MOTLEY, Brother 202 D J
  268 270 D W 277 J 153 222
  J W 188 James A 188
  Jordan 188 M E 222 273
  277 315 351 363 M M 283
  M T 273
MOUNTJOY, 27 Bro 21 25 E
  25 Edmond 20-22 24-25 27
  Mary 20
MOXLEY, D J 334 J V 282 284
  324 John 297
MUIR, J F 371 J T 358 364-
  366 372 375
MURPHY, J D 273
MUSGROVE, Brother 348
  Prof 243 T J 317 325
MUSICK, 125 Brother 125
  Jane D 125 L C 42 59 78
  104 109 124-125 153 155
  160 166 185 201-202 214
  222 232 258 268 277
  Lafreniere Chauvin 124
  Lewis 124-125 M 124 Mary
  Nevel 124 N 124

MUSICK (Cont.)
  Thomas 166 Thomas R 54-
  55 124 Thomas Roy 125
  Thos H 222
NEELY, Samuel 78
NEFF, J W 305 318 326
NELSON, I T 155 Ira T 322 J
  B 285 Sarah 298 Sister 371
NEVINS, J T 296 366 372
NICHOLLS, 191 Elder 195 J
  155 Joseph 180-181 190-
  191 195 Rev 195
NICHOLS, J 263 277 299 J J
  372-373 375-376 James
  108 Mr 236 Mrs 236 Sister
  236
NICKLIN, W H 295
NICKOLDS, James 299
NOAH, Alphonzo 297
NOBLE, Andrew H 238
  Caroline 239
NOEL, E 226 Rev Mr 184 S
  264 S T 265 Samuel 206
NORTHERTON, John 28
  Margaret 28 Winfred 28
  Wm K 28
NORTON, Dr 98 100 J J 93
  James H 299 Rachel 119 T
  P 367 Thomas P 357
NOWLEN, Peyton 129
NOWLIN, D W 182-183 193
  195-196 David W 192 Rev
  193-195
NUTGRASS, Daniel 326
  Laura 326
O'BANION, J 152
OGDEN, Armstead 250
  Brother 250 Deacon 250 E
  A 365 H T 222 228 280 361
  Henry T 227 Henry Taylor
  250 Margaret Eliza 250

Index.

OGDEN (Cont.)
    Thos 229
OLIVER, A P 273 J M 267
    Joseph 56
OMOHUNDRO, E B 356 375
OVERALL, 121 Elizabeth 120
    J T 223 225 John 121
    William 120
OVERTON, Eveline 72
OWEN, Clark 326 E 154 E D
    272-273 Julia B 363
OWENS, G 147
OWING, George W 119
PACE, J C 117
PAGE, Eliza 156 S E 316 332
    Thomas 156-157 Thos 228
    W J 325
PAINTER, W R 98
PALMER, Brother 237-238
    John 59 John W M 237 S L
    377 W B 296-297
PARKER, Elizabeth 120
PARKS, Brother 119 N 119
    Rev 96
PARSONS, B 60 Lou 371 Mary
    354
PATRICK, 312 B R 292 316
    318 325 336 Bower R 293
    347 Bower Reynolds 336
    Bro 288 384 Brother 234-
    235 348 Dr 329 349
    Elizabeth Ann 336 Jane D
    336 Mrs 339 Rev 240 W J
    35 66 69-70 78 120 156 223
    236-237 240-241 255 270-
    273 278 280-281 284-285
    288 290 292-293 297-298
    307 315-320 323-329 332-
    334 351-352 354-357 360-
    361 363-365 367 370-371
    375-376

PATRICK (Cont.)
    Wiley J 65 77 158 238 246
    269-272 312 334 336 349
PATTERSON, A 75 Archibald
    74 Catherine 330 Elder 60
    L T 355 360 365 374-376
    Lem T 371 Martha 330
    Samuel M 330 Susan 354
PAXTON, Harriet 364
PAYNE, A W 355 358 360 370-
    372 Miss 383
PEAK, E 60
PEARCE, Mrs George 67 W P
    375-376 378 Wm P 157
PEARY, Robert W 157
PEAY, Fannie 169 G W 154
    157 200 202 220 Geo W 71
    169 286 George W 147 154
    198 J J 204 Matilda 71
    Robert W 157
PECK, Elder 22 60 J M 86 127
    John M 11 60
PENDLETON, G W 295 H T
    270 Susan 295
PENIX, Cynthia A 354 J J
    159-161 364 Nancy H 354
    W 153-154 William 159 199
    278 Wm 159-160 198 201
    220
PENN, Lizzie C 361
PENTUFF, J R 372
PEPPER, Brother 113 Samuel
    113
PEYTON, Henry 356
PHELPS, Gillum 207 J G 329
PHILLIPS, Sarah 169
PIERCE, T W 279-280
PIMBLY, Missouri 326
PITTMAN, Bro 294 N R 294
    356

PLACE, 225 J J W 200 221-222 J W 160
PLUNKET, 20
PLYMOUTH, 15
POGSON, M H 295
POLK, Mr 102 President 102
POOL, Amy 72 Anthony 72 Fanny 74 Otha 354
POSTON, Salome 162
POWELL, Anna 298 J R 155 363 Jack 157
PRICE, 121 C C 239 241 361 375 C Columbus 238 Drucilla 213 J N 373 J N 355 374-376 Wm H 238
PRITCHARD, Sally 72
PULIS, W D 371
RABE, Mary 72
RAFFERTY, A C 325 328 J 200
RALLS, Brother 252 Col 252 Daniel 252 J 200 268 John 119 200 252 257 282
RANDALL, A F 157 160 204 226 264
RATCLIFF, Elder 55-56 J 55-56
RAUFER, A G 240 361 366
RAY, C N 270 D B 268-269 277 281 283 315 317-318 324 355 F M 320 324 John 78
READ, Ann E 237
READING, James Lee 161
REDMAN, Evodia 92
REED, Angus 157 Beula 367 Oliver 77-78 Wesley 367
REEDS, Margaret 188
REGISTER, Monroe 89
REID, Alexander 348 Bettie A 11 318 332 Bro 377

REID (Cont.)
Brother 121 156 234 292 340-348 351 Dr 348 I W 235 J 271-272 274 276 278 280 283-284 291 315 319-320 324-325 349 351-352 356 377 James 11 35 40 72 120-121 156 159 234 239-240 272-273 283 305 307 318-319 324 340-342 344 346 355-356 364 366 372 James Albert 342 Jas 274 282 290 297 370 Mr 332-333 Mrs 342 Mrs James 340 Rev 240 S 237 Sister 342 346 348 T Lacey 342
RENEAN, Carrie 37
RENEAU, Carrie A 349
RENFRO, Elder 149
REYNOLDS, Sister 204
RHOADS, Charles 371
RHODES, Charles 366 385
RICE, A J 326 Ann 326 Geo P 327 H B 77-78 167 327 367 Isaac 326 John 326-327 Maggie 326 381 Susan 326
RICHARD, Mr 129
RICHARDS, D H 316 318
RICKS, J 118 J M 153 John M 120
RIDER, R P 38 352
RIDGELY, P R 291
RIDGEWAY, Elder 55 Vivian 55
RIED, James 348
RIGGINS, J E 296 Lillian 296
RIGGS, Barzel 203 284 Bethuel 42 54-55 172 174-176 178 Elder 54 175 J W 203 276 280 283 286 293 317-318 325 James W 287

RIGGS (Cont.)
    Jas W 273 Lucretia 287
    Milford 375 Nancy 175-176
RILEY, D L 13
RINEY, J A 327 366 370
ROBERDS, William 55 231
ROBERTS, Rebecca 365
ROBERTSON, Brother 325 R
    D 206 255 324-325 335 351
    356 360 370-371 376
ROBEY, G W 236
ROBINETT, J D 290
ROBINSON, A 357 J M 200
    John M 200 Lydia A 300
    Simeon P 203
ROBNETT, J D 166 230 272-
    274 277-280
RODGERS, 21 A P 64 66 169
    198 200 202 204 206 212
    220 222 226 237 268 270-
    273 276 278 280 283-285
    287 300 305 325-326 351
    354 356 360 371 Alex P 64
    Ann 365 Brother 351 Elder
    64-65 224 Mr 22 Timothy P
    68
RODNEY, Bettie A 342
ROGERS, 371 A P 258 317 376
    E L 305 F G 371
ROLLINS, 92 Dr 92 94 Rhodes
    92
ROSE, Brother 269 Dan L 354
    John A 269 Mason 216 269
    T M 282
ROSECRANS, Gen 65
ROSS, Mary Olive 249 S 274
ROTHWELL, W R 171
ROUTEN, Deacon 293 P H
    290 292
ROWAN, Judge 140
RUDDELL, 22-23 Elder 22

RUDDELL (Cont.)
    Mr 22 Paul 23 Rev 22 Sally
    23 Stephen 20 22-23
RUDELL, Brother 20
RUDESELL, P H 225
RUNKEL, C C 295 Mary 295
RUSH, John 43-44 47
    Margaret 43
RUSSELL, W T 267
SALING, W 75 William 75
SALLEE, Mrs Jordan 184
SALLING, H 202 Henry 207
SAMSON, J 231
SAMUEL, Martha 72
SANDERS, Richard 20
SANDERSON, Amanda B 252
    D T 328 371 Daniel T 252
    E J 36 40 70 158 206 255
    298 300 317 319 321 325
    328 354 Emmet 240
    Emmett J 252 G W 72
    Henry L 252 J A 222 J E
    204-205 James A 227
    James M 252 John E 252
    Martha Jane 252 Mary C
    252 Mary J 252 Robert 255
    Robert B 252 S M 331 370
    372 Samuel M 252 Sarah C
    252 Sister Samuel M 359 T
    N 34 40 160 204 252-255
    264 266 268 272 278 296
    315 318 325 331-332 360
    366 Thomas E 252 Thomas
    Newman 252 Vella 331
    Virginia A 252 Wm A 252
SANSON, J 109 J P 360
SAPP, Frances 233 John 233
    Matthew 20
SAWYER, E H 272
SCHULTZ, Ruth 327

SCOTT, 259 Martha 330 Miss 259 Mr 259
SCROGGINS, James 359
SEAMAN, W J 326 354
SEARS, 207
SEATON, L B 266-267
SEELY, Alethea 90
SELF, Sarah A 304 Thomas H 304
SEMPLE, 51
SENCLAIR, Robert 60
SENTER, W M 332
SERPELL, Jane D 336
SHANNON, Betsey 42 Billie 71 J E 71-72 200 220 226 267-268 276 282 318 320 325 John E 70 261 Mrs 71 Mrs J E 84 Peggy 84 W O 280 283 325
SHARP, 190 Brother 164 202 Mrs John 190 R N 163
SHAW, Anna Rodney 342 Catherine 188 James 188 Julia Ann 188 Robert 188 Williamson 355
SHELBY, Gov 85-86 J 266
SHELTON, J B 182 J C 264
SHEPHERD, John 71 Martha 365
SHIELD, 121
SHIELDS, Patsy 120 Thomas 120
SHIPP, B 225
SHIVES, 365 H M 366 M V 272 277 318 325 360 372
SHORE, F T 351
SHOUSH, F M 305 364
SHULSE, Eleanor 119 Mary 119 Susanah 119
SHULTZ, Anna 326 Peter 326 Polly A 326 Wm 326

SHY, 207
SIMMS, B M S 161 B W M 157 B W N 329 360 364 Brother 234 Rev 329-330
SIMPSON, D H 232 Elsie 331 W 202
SISSON, Henry 63 65 154 202 W T 356
SITTON, 54 121 A F 272 Elder 174 G G 200 J A 272 J C 244 J G 202 221 232 266 272 J J 201 Jesse 42 47-48 174 John G 243 Joseph 47 William 47 54 61 110
SKEGG, Mr 129
SKILLMAN, C G 158
SLAUGHTER, A 242 280 282 286 328 330 381 Brother 278 Laura 330 Mr 282 Mrs 282
SLOSS, Robert 118
SMARR, John 272
SMITH, 229 A 95 Adoniram 78 B 273 277 Bro 97 Brother 184 216 232 234 261 322 D C 329 Drucilla 213 E T 205 Ed T 348 Edward T 322 Edwin B 227 Elder 63-64 152 214 216 224 G 223 G B 71 167 226 264 277 284 Green B 282 Green Benjamin 212 Hawkins 54 Howard P 72 J F 33-34 71 76 152-153 166 199-200 203 226 238 249 264-265 269-272 274 281 318 J Frank 100 203 213 234 345 J M 370 373 375-376 J P 202 J R 33 284 J T 285 317 James F 63 103-104 150 152-155 157 166 188 198

Index.

SMITH (Cont.)
   224-225 261 273 322 364
   James Frank 214 217 232
   247 Jas 374 Jas F 222
   Jennie Drake 361 Joe 311
   Joe Ab 311 Joe H 311 John
   J 230 311 John Johnson
   311 John R 227 L P 373 L
   R 264 Luther 367 Margaret
   213 Martha W 311 Mary
   74 Mary A 214 Mattie B
   365 Mr 311 Mrs Champ 71
   N 202 N J 385 N R 207 227
   Nancy 311 Nathaniel R
   227 R O 376 Rev 214-215
   Robt 369 S F 37 S P 161
   Sarah 354 Sarah A 365
   Susan 326 T J 228 300 325
   373 Thomas 365 Troy
   James F 184 Uncle Jack
   230 311 W B 230 W E 199
   W H 365 W L 269 300
   William E 315 Wm H 328 Z
   T 230 Z Taylor 230
SNETHAN, John Sr 18
   Prudence 18
SNETHEN, John 212
SNIDER, Josh 95 Nathan 95
SNYDER, Elizabeth Ann 359
SPALDING, 95 R M 95 S P 78
SPARKS, J J 263
SPARROW, G C 229
SPAULDING, B A 92 R M 92
SPEARS, Mary 156
SPENCER, 12 27 52 J H 168
   W T 198 William 141
SPIRES, M 147
SPOTSWOOD, Dortha 119
SPRINGSTON, M 172
SPURGEON, Charles H 163
SPYRES, Brother 185 187

SPYRES (Cont.)
   M 153 Mahlon 182 185 187
   Malen 153
STALEY, David 253
STANDLEY, A 232
STANFORD, T 152 Thomas
   200
STARK, 256 Anna 256 E W
   255 Eugene W 255 J 231 J
   O 256 Maggie 359 Senator
   255-256 Thornton 247
STEADMAN, Brother 157 W
   H 157 267
STEEL, George 279 374 Nettie
   367
STENDROW, 56
STEVENS, A M 332 B 118
   125-126 B Q 125 257 Ben
   256-257 Benjamin 78 119
   125 Elder 148 215 Sarah
   126 Sarah Foster 126
STEVINS, Brother 118
STEWARD, John 239
STEWART, A W 356-357
   Annie 367 Belle 363
   Charles W 118 J C 318 325
   354-355 363-364 J P 72 298
   366 Mary 367 Sarah E 247
STIRMLINGER, 310 J 325
   Joseph 310 324 355 375-
   376
STONE, W H 158 230 295-296
   299 320
STORY, Mrs Doctor 295 Mrs J
   H 296
STOUT, 174
STURGEON, Bro 26-28
   Brother 28 Elder 26 John
   H 26-27 John Hume 27
   Margaret 28 Thomas 27
   William K 29

SUGGETT, Bro 53 Brother 119 Elder 55-56 59 148 151 James 55-56 59 119
SUMMERS, Daniel 78
SUTER, John J 89
SUTTON, J D 299 N H 274 299 Polly 23
SWAN, Dennis 120
SWEENEY, Thomas 150 William G 150
SWEENY, J G 165
SWIFT, J W 320
SWIGGERT, Wallace 78
SWITZLER, W F 88
TALBOT, 190 J H 154
TALIAFARO, J W 298
TALIAFERO, J W 285
TALIAFERRO, John 238 Lucy 238 Mary S 239
TANNER, Myra 361
TATE, Brother 235 C F J 157 371-373 F C 325
TAYLOR, Bro 48 Brother 58 73 Cora 367 Evangelist 235 J 57 Jeremiah 47-48 55 103 106 214 John 11 Laura 367 S F 324 371
TEASDALE, John 154
TERREL, J H 156
TERRELL, 121 J M 317
TERRILL, J H 67 72 298 375-376 J M 334
THOMAS, Benjamin 54 J 60 223 J A 199 277 J H 153 202 225 Jemima 62 John A 233 Lucy 72 Mrs Dr 318 R S 146 151 Smith 98 376
THOMPSON, J 155 J E 371-373 Mahala 300 S F 40 325 327 349 354-357 367 369 William 88

THROGMORTON, 235 W P 157 324-325
THURMOND, Maggie 355 Phillip 31-32
TIIPTON, W M 280 Wm M 334
TILDEN, 196
TILFORD, Elder 153
TILLER, John 319
TILLETSON, Michael 20
TINKER, Elizabeth 62 O C 71 355
TINSLEY, A M 33 278 Addison 156-157 355 Alvin 355 Casandra 156
TIPTON, Brother 206 C M 328 Lydia 120 Rev 309 W M 33-34 77-78 121 156-158 161 206 230 240 278 281 284-285 295 298 314 316-317 319 328 355-357 360 366 371 Wm 307 309 368 Wm M 240
TODD, Alex 239 Alexander 238 Emily A 239 T P 370-371
TOLIVER, A B 299 Joe 299
TRABUE, C C 141 M J 287
TRAVIS, R 60
TREADWAY, J W 37 357 John W 374
TREDWAY, J W 324
TROTTER, Joseph 42
TROWER, J W 70 206 237 356 358 360 365-366 371-373
TRUEX, H E 375
TRUITT, A C 365 S C 351 370-371
TUCKER, B S 221 Brother 356 C B 122 Preacher 335 Rev 241 S W 237 Sherman 348

Index.

TUCKER (Cont.)
  W S 72 159 305 318 325
  327 356
TURLEY, James 58 119 161
TURNBULL, Brother 299
  Morgan 299
TURNER, Anna 43 Brother 31
  58 C L 44 Catherine 330
  Charles 356 Charles L 44
  47-48 Chas L 43 E 55 75
  Edmond 58 Edward 55-57
  74 Elder 55 57 59 George
  43-44 47 L 199 Lawson 233
  Lucretia 74 Phoebe 43
  Susan 233 Terisha 31
  Thomas 56
TURPIN, Albany 156 John W
  156
TUTT, B G 325 355
TUTTLE, J H 171 266 279
TWAIN, Mark 252
TYLER, President 102
TYZZER, Dr 365 370
UNDERHILL, Hiram 94
UNSEL, H T 280 R W 271
UNSELL, Elizabeth J 284 H F
  160 H T 274 276 283 317-
  318 J 263 Lee 161 R W
  280-283 Sister 284
UTTERBACK, Brother 153
VAN HOOSE, A 266
VANCE, B M 318 326
VARDAMAN, Jeremiah 78
  William H 78
VARDEMAN, 130-135 140 A
  M 292 305 318 366
  Amasiah 130 Billy 194-195
  Bro 53 Brother 58 60 73
  109 259 Eld 181 Elder 59
  67 117 137 140 142-143
  152 162 Elizabeth 128 132

VARDEMAN (Cont.)
  144 181 J 67-68 117 J B
  315 317 Jeremiah 59 67 70
  76 86 105 108-110 118-119
  127-130 132 138 376
  Jeremiah Jr 119 Jerry 78
  86 John Jr 128 John Sr 128
  Lucinda 119 Luly 144
  Morgan 130 137 Mr 76 105
  129-130 134-137 139-141
  143 145 Mrs 144 Rev 144
  193-195 S M 278 W H 153
  155 165 181-183 193-195
  199 201 225-226 266 279
  285 315-317 325 W H H
  223 William 119 257 259
  William H 120 149 Wm H
  68-69 162 234
VERMILLION, R 222 226 264
  267 Reason 284
WADDELL, G R 161 274 318
  364 Geo R 159 George R
  159 James P 159 Lois 159
  Mildred 159 P P 315 P S
  374 Sallie A 247 W W 153
  160 202 224 W W Jr 263
  William 71 William W 154
  159 Wm W 159
WADE, Polly 184
WADELL, W 147
WALKER, J 147
WALLER, Edmond 103 274
  Edmund 214 George 28
  123 Rev 103
WALTON, F M 365 T N 364
WAMBLE, Mary A 185
  Sampson 185
WARNER, 207 J D 207 Laura
  355
WASHINGTON, 17 Gen 12 85
  George 15 President 15

WASSEN, Fannie 43
WATERS, C A 357 360 371 J
    W 285-286 298 366 John W
    365 Landy 285 298 Lela
    298 Mary 298 Mrs John W
    365 Robert 298 W M 35 37
    366
WATKINS, Jesse 182
WATSON, J D 72 159 206 230
    376
WATTS, B H 33 37 Paulus 229
WAUGH, W A 239
WAYNE, 129
WEATHERFORD, Matilda
    188 Thomas 188
WEAVER, J R 372-373 375-
    376
WEBSTER, 88
WELCH, J E 171 184 194 196
    James E 155 Rev 194 196
WELDY, 302-303 Angeline
    279 Brother 302 George
    302
WELLS, Carter 183 Carty 207
    Evangelist 235 Helen B
    183 Perry 22
WEST, T L 371-372 375
WESTOVER, J T 223
WHEELER, E M 225 Elder 70
    J M 264 272-273 J T 166
    226
WHITAKER, Caroline M 92
WHITE, 129 George W 354
    Shadrach 129 W 273
WHITESIDE, Brother 238
    258-259 348 E D 278-279
    Elder 226 George W 81 I
    325 Isaac 280 J 152 Jacob
    106 158 John F 334 365
    Lydia V 158 M S 36 106
    121 159 225-226 228-230

WHITESIDE (Cont.)
    237 240 251 264 268 270
    272-273 275-276 278 280
    282-285 297 300 304 315
    319-320 325 332 334 356
    358 360 363 373-374 M T
    310 Margarett 251 Mary A
    237 251 Mrs G W 81 Mrs
    John F 365 Pastor 238 Rev
    299 Russell 329 Russell B
    159 William 334 351 355
WHITFIELD, 127
WIATT, Mr 384 Mrs Dr 331 W
    E 324 328-330 381 383
    Walter E 329-330 380-381
    384
WICKS, F M 222 237
WIGGINGTON, W R 273
WIGGINTON, Mrs Edward
    296 W R 166 266 277
WILBURN, W S 373
WILHOIT, 99
WILKINSON, Brother 154
WILLIAMS, 207 Benjamin 207
    Brother 154 157 C M 292-
    293 354-355 C W 265 Dr 95
    242 Elder 224 Elijah 56 F
    225 George 59 Grandfather
    88 J R 200 J T 35 40 71-72
    97 157 160 196 200-201
    204 206 217 223-226 242
    249 258 263-273 275-276
    278-281 287 320 Jas 316
    Jeff 316 Jno T 64 John T
    64-65 377 John Thomas
    217 326 Mr 218 Mrs 86 218
    Mrs J T 217 Professor 242
    Rev 196 Sister 87 242 W H
    315-318 325 Wm 54
WILLIAMSON, Mattie 367
WILLIS, Mrs H S 365

WILLSON, David 232
WILSON, Brother 225 D 199
    D M 223 David 264 268
    270 Elizabeth 45 J 267
    Silas 45 47-48
WINN, Jane 361
WISE, Cordelia 120 Geo C 316
    318 375-376 George C 316
    John R 204 Malvina 120 W
    W 71 118 120 153 155 166
    224
WITHERS, Elizabeth Ann 336
WITHROW, Anna 256
WITTEN, Dove 328
WOOD, 157 172 J 118 J W 241
    Mrs 104 Sallie Keach 363
    Sarah A 104
WOODS, 173 Anderson 56 60
    86 117 Brother 59 117
    Elder 56 59-60 John 118
    Zadock 173
WOODSON, J W 263 Sue E 69
    T P 222
WOOLFOLK, Dr 183 Helen B
    183
WOOTON, James G 55 231
WORSHAM, Jane 355
WORSON, Frank 43
WORTHINGTON, Francis 237
    J J 148-149
WRIGHT, G W 327 Geo W 376
    George W 157 John 229
    Mary 172 Thomas J 173
    Thomas Jefferson 173 Thos
    J 172 Wm 59 73-74
WYLIE, G W 363 Geo W 287
    George W 270
WYMAN, E A 226
YAGER, C L 357
YATES, B F 295 Margaret 295
YEAGER, C L 367 Charles L
    367
YEAMAN, Dr 40 276-277 W
    Pope 37 40 229 275-278
    311 345
YEATER, Martha W 311
YOUNG, Lily 296
ZIMMERMAN, Brother 60
    George W 57 59
ZUMAULT, John L 238 W J
    239 William J 238-239
ZUMWALT, N H 279 T M 285
    W H 281 W J 226

www.ingramcontent.com/pod-product-compliance
Lightning Source LLC
Chambersburg PA
CBHW050426240426
43661CB00055B/2289